THE LIFE OF
JAMES MONROE

JAMES MONROE (by Vanderlyn)

THE LIFE OF
JAMES MONROE

By
GEORGE MORGAN

AMS PRESS
NEW YORK

Reprinted from the edition of 1921, Boston
First AMS EDITION published 1969
Manufactured in the United States of America

Library of Congress Catalog Card Number: 76-106979
SBN: 404-00594-2

AMS PRESS, INC.
New York, N.Y. 10003

DEDICATION

*To that sound democracy of the fathers which elevates
statesmen and exacts from them masterful
service for all the people, regardless
of race, creed or condition*

PREFACE

Readers will discern that there is an attempt here to re-create Monroe the Man, and so place him that he will stand out against the background of his own times. There are enough books about General Washington to fill an ample alcove in any library; there is an Adams literature; and there is a Jefferson literature of considerable proportions; but neither Madison nor Monroe has fared so well. Madison wrote to Lyman C. Draper that a life like his, which had been so much a public life, "must, of course, be traced in the public transactions in which it was involved." This is just as true of Monroe's life; and it explains why we have endeavored to follow the flow of coincident events — to make the text full, accurate and consecutive, covering the personal and social as well as political experiences of its subject.

Luckily for Madison, his first biographer was intimately acquainted with him, but Monroe was unfortunate in that no one who lived in, or near to, his own epoch wrote an adequate account of his career. When a man serves his country as long and as well as Monroe did, his whole story ought to be told, not only for the satisfaction of a certain inborn intellectual curiosity — but because of the example conveyed in it for succeeding generations. Especially is this true of one who, like Monroe, had the great good fortune to serve his fellows throughout the foundation period when principles were established, freedom achieved, the Constitutional cornerstone laid and the work of nation-building assured beyond peradventure. Monroe bore a part in so many undertakings during his fifty years of public life, his activities were so varied, his correspondence was so wide that he cannot but be classed as a chief participant in the vital beginnings — those blessed beginnings — of the great republic.

Nevertheless one finds few books about him. Historians and biographers, pursuing elusive truth along lines of their particular activities, are apt to realize when a thing is amiss; and we have their word for it that existing lives of Monroe, however useful, lack reach and comprehensiveness. Dr. Daniel C. Gilman's life (1883), dealing with the half-century between 1776 and 1826, is the best — a well-considered, brief, biography; but it is essentially an outline; and it is lacking alike in fullness of fact and in those Boswellian details that help to put back the breath of reality into a character of the past. While accurate and readable, it is altogether too thin a book, being amplified scarcely beyond the bounds of an article in an encyclopedia. What is there, between its covers, is good; what is not there is much missed by the student. No reflection is meant upon it, supplemented as it is by Prof. J. F. Jameson's scholarly bibliography of Monroe and the Monroe Doctrine, nor upon other careful sketches, such as Schouler's. What we would like to make clear is that in the course of a century much illuminating Monroe matter has appeared in some hundreds of letters, memoirs, journals, narratives and local histories and that here, for the first time, these unfamiliar details have been assembled in an annotative way and drawn upon to enliven, strengthen and complete the story of Monroe's career.

We have, of course, relied largely upon the documents in the possession of the United States Government, the various historical societies and the private collections mentioned in the footnotes accompanying the text. Under act of March 3, 1849, Congress bought the Monroe papers; and an alphabetically arranged Calendar of them was issued by the Bureau of Rolls, Department of State, 1893. Based upon the letters and documents thus listed are the seven volumes of the Writings of Monroe, edited by Stanislaus Murray Hamilton and issued by Putnam in a limited edition in 1898-1902. On March 9, 1903, President Roosevelt transferred the Monroe papers from the Department of State to the Library of Congress and on June 27, 1904, Worthington C. Ford, then chief of the Division of Manuscripts, and Herbert Putnam, Librarian, gave out a compilation of the papers arranged chronologically by Wilmer Ross Leech, of the Division of Manuscripts. From English, French and Spanish sources, also, thanks to Henry Adams, have come numerous supplementary or confirmatory details bearing upon Monroe's diplomatic experiences.

These, then, are a few of the many reasons for this volume; but there is a special reason, and this special reason we shall at once underscore.

It has now been close upon one hundred years since the United States promulgated the Monroe Doctrine. Actually, as well as historically, this Doctrine is a part of the nation's creed. Its own centenary will be likely to find it much more in the public mind than heretofore. People wish to define it — to study it *ab ovo* — they wish to know the circumstances under which it was adopted, and wish to stand for a moment in the shoes of the man who promulgated it — the fifth President, the last of the Revolutionary Executives, James Monroe, a patriot soldier in his youth, a diplomat who underwent bitter experiences, a statesman in the formative period of the Union and the intimate associate of its founders. Where was he bred? Where schooled? What did he do to help win the first and second wars of independence? Why was he twice chosen President and why, especially, did he enunciate the rule, applicable to the whole western hemisphere, associated with his name? This study of James Monroe and his times will help, we hope, to commemorate the centenary of his presidency and the centenary of the Monroe Doctrine.

CONTENTS

ILLUSTRATIONS

RECORD OF ACTIVITIES YEAR BY YEAR

Born, Monroe's Creek, Westmoreland County, Va., April 28, 1758. Father, Spence Monroe, Scotch stock; mother, Elizabeth Jones Monroe, Welsh stock

College, William and Mary, 1774-1776

Soldier, enlisted in Third Virginia, 1776. Lieutenant in Continental Line; battles, Harlem Heights, White Plains, Trenton (wounded), Brandywine, Germantown, 1776-1777

Aide, November, 1777, aide-de-camp to General Stirling; at Valley Forge; at Monmouth; rank Major, 1778

Military Commissioner from Virginia to Southern Army, 1780

Law student, under Jefferson, 1780

Virginia Legislator; member of the Executive Council, 1782

Virginia Member of Continental Congress, 1783-1786

Married to Eliza Kortright of New York, 1786

Law and Legislature, 1786-1787. Lived in Fredericksburg, Va.

Member of the Virginia State Constitutional Convention. In opposition, 1788

United States Senator, 1790-1794

Minister to France, 1794

Recalled, took leave December 30, 1796

Returned to America and published book vindicating himself, 1797

Governor of Virginia, 1799-1802

Appointed by Jefferson Envoy Extraordinary and Minister Plenipotentiary to act with R. R. Livingston at Paris, and Charles Pinckney at Madrid, January 12, 1803. With Livingston, signed Louisiana Purchase Treaty, April 30, 1803. Commissioned Minister to

England, April 18, 1803. Commissioned Minister to Spain October 14, 1804. Left Spanish Court for London, May 21, 1805. Commissioned with William Pinkney, to negotiate treaty with England, May 12, 1806

British Treaty signed December 31, 1806

Left England for home October 29, 1807

Virginia Legislator, third time, 1810

Reëlected Governor of Virginia, fourth time, 1811

Appointed by Madison Secretary of State (till 1817), 1811

Secretary of War, *ad interim*, September 26, 1814 to March 3, 1815

President, first term, March 4, 1817

Tour of East, June 2, September 17, 1817

Seminole War, 1818

Florida acquired, 1819

Missouri Compromise, 1820

President, second term, March 5, 1821

Message enunciating the Monroe Doctrine, 1823

Visit of La Fayette, 1824-1825

Retired to Oak Hill, Loudon County, Va., 1825

Regent of the University of Virginia, 1826

Member of the Virginia Constitutional Convention, 1829

Death of Monroe, 1831. Died in New York City, July 4, 1831

Reinterred at Richmond, Va., July 5, 1858

LIFE OF JAMES MONROE

CHAPTER I

THE MONROES AND THEIR NEIGHBORS IN THE NORTHERN NECK

Son of Spence Monroe and Elizabeth his wife, who were of the plain people, unrelated to the aristocratic Tuckahoes, James Monroe was born near the head of Monroe's Creek, in Westmoreland County, Northern Neck of Virginia, on the twenty-eighth of April, 1758. Young George Washington, who had long since buried Braddock at the foot of Laurel Mountain, was now writing an order for his wedding clothes to his own agent in London; Dinwiddie, Governor of Virginia, had gone back to that same London; and from it would soon come his gay and gambling successor, Francis Fauquier, who would give his name to one of the newer counties of the Northern Neck.

As Accomac by the ocean is the lowermost, so this celebrated Northern Neck is the uppermost of the nine peninsulas of the Old Dominion. On one side, the Northern Neck follows the flow of the Potomac, border to border with Maryland, all the way to the mountains; on the other side, it follows the flow of the Rapidan from its springheads in the Blue Ridge all the way to the spot where the wide-mouthed Rappahannock enters the Chesapeake Bay. Most readers will readily and fondly recall the romantic story of young Washington, the Fairfaxes and the Northern Neck. One remembers, off hand, how the many millions of acres contained in this territory were granted by the British Crown to

Ralph Lord Hopton and others, sold by them to John Lord Culpeper and passed on to Lord Fairfax.[1] Nowadays there are more than twenty counties in this vast region, but in Spence Monroe's time (aside from a few, such as Culpeper, newly erected) there existed only the ancient lower, mother counties — Lancaster, Northumberland, Westmoreland, Richmond, King George, Prince William and Stafford, some of which will soon celebrate their tercentennial anniversaries.

Many of the plantations were penetrated by saltwater creeks and coves, rich in foodfish and in those gustatory delicacies and delights dear to the palates of the proprietors. Choice estates fronted on the Potomac; others, just as advantageously placed, looked out upon the Rappahannock. By the latter, dwelt "King" Carter of Corotoman — Robert Carter, agent of the Fairfaxes — who, in the time of Spence Monroe's father, Andrew, "ruled the Northern Neck," though he probably did not quite succeed in ruling his family of fifteen children. It was he who was so important a person that the congregation of Old Christ Church, Lancaster, always waited outside until he had preceded them within.

To some of the Tuckahoe people, Virginia was an outlying part of England. "The Virginia planter," says Robert A. Brock,[2] than whom there is no better authority, "was essentially a transplanted Englishman in tastes and convictions and emulated the social amenities and culture of the mother country." The tidewater gentry regarded themselves as adventurers

---

[1] "The Northern Neck was granted at different times by King Charles I and II to Lord Hopton, the Earl of St. Albans and others, and subsequently by King James II to Lord Culpeper, who purchased the rights of other parties. Lord Fairfax, who married the daughter of Lord Culpeper, became the proprietor of this princely domain known as the Northern Neck."— Philip Slaughter, History of St. Mark's Parish. See also Jefferson's Notes on Virginia, where the various grants are listed. The last Fairfax grant was made in 1780. On November 15, 1786, Gov. Patrick Henry, by a grant recorded in the same book, assumed for the State the eminent domain of the Northern Neck.— William and Mary College Quarterly, Vol. VI, pp. 222-226.

[2] Narrative and Critical History of America. Edited by Justin Winsor, Vol. III, p. 153.

in a region unhappily far removed from the mother-
land, yet blessed with black men to do the necessary
work. They did not bethink them of the days on ahead
when they would have deadly trouble with the British
and still deadlier trouble with the blacks. Their peril,
as it seemed to them, was the red peril that lurked in
the wilderness; and the thought of it hardened some
of them, especially those on the border. Down by the
little havens, the oyster creeks, the rich bottoms that
had once belonged to the Indians, they were so secure
from massacre as to distress themselves less about the
dispossessed redmen than about possible pirates, such
as the well-remembered Blackbeard. Indeed, high
living, with its pleasures and trains of evil, was the
worst enemy of both gentry and clergy. "The common
Planters leading easy Lives," wrote Hugh Jones, in
"The State of Virginia," "don't much admire Labour,
or any manly Exercise, except Horse-Racing, nor
Diversion except Cock-Fighting in which some greatly
delight. This easy way of Living, and the Heat of
Summer, makes some very lazy, who are then said to
be Climate-Struck!" Climate-struck, no doubt, was
the Accomac man, neighbor of Colonel John Custis of
epitaph fame, who when rebuked for his unending
otium cum dignitate, replied: "What's the use to worry,
when all you have to do is to fall overboard to find your
dinner?" But, though lassitude might creep over one
in summer, as the bay breezes blew softly in, it was
different when frost came; then a fierce desire to hunt
the fox, the coon, the 'possum might seize a man and
carry him far afield. It was in reality a lively age — an
outdoor age, a hard riding age, an age of adventure,
of thumb-biting, of duelling, much richer in activities
than the student is apt to credit it with. It was also
a ripe age in the sense that the peculiar Virginia civilization of which we have hinted had been developing
for something like a century and a half.

Master Fithian, a Princeton divinity student, who,
as tutor, lived for a year at Nomini Hall, seat of another

Carter, known as Councillor Carter, left a diary full of illuminating pen-pictures descriptive of an aristocratic Virginia home quite as English as any to be found in cavalier England. Religion and the lack of it were equally to be noted at Nomini Hall. A dabster in theology, Councillor Carter swung first to one sect and then to another; a born musician, "his house resounded with the tinkling guitar, the silvery harmonicum (just invented by the all accomplished Benjamin Franklin), the violin, the flute, harpsichord, and organ."[1] Fithian, adds Professor Harrison, went down to Virginia a "blue" Presbyterian, "but after a year's residence at 'Nomini Hall' became almost a 'perverted' Episcopalian in point of reverence for dancing, horse-racing, cock-fighting, stepping the minuet, toasting the ladies, and other genial amusements then prevalent in the Northern Neck." There were six hundred negroes on the sixty thousand acre place; and some of them expected to be remembered with "bits" and "half-bits," rum-and-water and "pisimmon" beer. The gentry rode from plantation to plantation forming house-parties, or giving balls, ladies in gorgeous quilted skirts, bodices and brocades of the period, with creped hair, fantastically wreathed with artificial flowers and strings of pearls, "danced until dawn glistened over the rosy Potomac."[2] Professor Harrison adds that "the old baronial style of living was in this decade in its full glory; the Byrds of Westover, the Harrisons and Carters of Brandon and Shirley, the Lewises of Kenmore, the Fairfaxes of Greenway Court and Belvoir, the Masons of Gunston Hall, the Calverts over the Potomac, as it swept grandly from its cataract to the Chesapeake, the Pages and Nelsons of Rosewell, the Lees of Stratford and Chantilly — all kept up an easy-going, semi-feudal state, into which the Washingtons as easily fell by right of

---

[1] George Washington: Patriot, Soldier, Statesman, by James A. Harrison, 1906.
[2] Master Fithian, a gallant soldier, died of camp fever at Fort Washington, 1776.

lineage, as well as of wealth, and influential position in colonial circles." [1]

On the Rappahannock side, the year James Monroe was born, Colonel John Tayloe built Mt. Airy manor-house, still standing, "considered by many the hand-somest in Virginia." Not far away is the equally noted "Sabine Hall."

If in Monroe's boyhood days, the Northern Neck was still the country of the Fairfaxes, it was also that of the Balls, Beales, Brents, Brockenbroughs, Brookes, Bushrods, Conways, Corbins, Fauntleroys, Graysons, Grymes, Lees, Marshalls, Masons, Masseys, Mercers, Mountjoys, Newtons, Peacheys, Pressleys, Seldens, Steptoes, Stiths, Taliaferros, Turbervilles, Traverses and Turners of "Smith's Mount."

The old vestry-books contain these locally notable names and many besides. Some of Monroe's contemporaries figure in the county chronicles and in traditions and anecdotes well remembered between the Potomac and Rappahannock rivers. One recalls "Jemmy" Steptoe. He was born at Hominy Hall, Westmoreland, studied at William and Mary College; migrated to Bedford, where "as a slip of gentility homesick in the wilderness," he sighed for a companion; married a daughter of Colonel James Callaway, she being one of twenty-two children; and served fifty-four years as County Clerk. Such was the significant record of one of Monroe's boyhood neighbors, whose Aunt Ann married a brother of Washington, and whose Aunt Elizabeth married Philip Ludwell Lee, becoming the mother of an illustrious line of Lees.

In the days of Monroe's early manhood, the Northern Neck was less and less a Fairfax land and more and more the historic home-country of Washington, Jefferson, Madison and Marshall.

---

[1] Of Mary (Ball) Washington, at sixteen, a Williamsburg letter, October 7, 1722, addressed to "Dear Sukey," says: "Madam Ball of Lancaster and her sweet Molly have gone Hom. Mamma thinks Molly the Comliest Maiden she knows. Her hair is like unto Flax, Her eyes the color of yours and here Chekes are like May blossoms."

In Civil War times, the counties of Stafford, Prince
William, Fairfax, Loudon, Fauquier, Culpeper and
Orange were the scenes of constant manoeuvres, count-
less skirmishes and those great battles between brother
and brother so fascinatingly depicted on our historic
scroll.

But Westmoreland was the most celebrated of the
colonial counties. So noteworthy was the culture of that
south shore of the Potomac, and so numerous were the
celebrities who lived in Westmoreland itself, that it
was designated, in the classical hyperbole to which our
grandfathers were prone, "The Athens of America." [1]
Athens or no Athens, it is, indeed, a most noteworthy
matter that Westmoreland should have given us so
great a number of public characters — the Lee brothers
of the Revolutionary period and the equally able Lees
of more recent celebrity. "Within an hour's ride" are
the birthplaces of three presidents of the United States.
The man who proposed the Declaration of Independence was born here; and the man who wrote it, another
president, lived only a little way to the northwest in
the upper part of the Northern Neck. Madison[2] too,
was born in the Northern Neck — "at the house of his
maternal grandmother, Mrs. Eleanor Conway, on the
north bank of the Rappahannock, in the County of
King George."

Lightfoots, Ludwells and Fitzhughs lived their lives
in these and other parts, intermarrying with the Lees
and producing in each generation, men and women of
uncommon spirit. For one example, we have, in the
Revolutionary period, "Light Horse Harry," or

---

[1] This is a favorite phrase. Writers on the Lees dwell upon the fine life at
the Potomac and Rappahannock seats. Among R. E. Lee's biographers, John
Esten Cooke tells especially of Stratford house; Philip Alexander Bruce of Westmoreland's great men; and Dr. J. William Jones of Lee's forebears in Westmoreland. A notable book is "Westmoreland County, Virginia, 1653-1912," compiled
by Judge T. R. B. Wright, of Montross. "Manors of Virginia in Colonial Times,"
by Edith Tunis Sale, dwells upon Westmoreland and its notabilities.

[2] Son of James, son of Ambrose, son of John, son of John, first of the name in
Virginia, James Madison, Jr., President, "was born at Port Conway at twelve
o'clock (midnight) sixth of March, 1751."

"Legion Harry," or "Dragoon Harry," with whose mother, in her maidenhood, young Washington was in love, and, for another example, General R. E. Lee of the Civil War period, who, named after his uncles, Robert and Edward Carter, was related not only to the colonial celebrity, Governor Alexander Spotswood, chief of the Knights of the Golden Horseshoe, but to the world-famous Robert Bruce.

We have here noted these ancestral connections with the purpose of indicating the character and quality of the neighborhood where Monroe was brought up, and not with any purpose of stressing his own gentility. Rather do we seek to suggest a contrast. He was not an armiger. Though, like Washington, who was "bred a man of honor in the free school of Virginian society"[1] it should be kept in mind that Monroe was less blue in his blood and grew to be a much plainer, a much more democratic man, than many of his contemporaries. Moreover, "it should be remembered," declares John T. Morse, Jr., "that, by good rights, neither Washington, Jefferson, nor even Madison, before they became distinguished, would have been entitled to take rank in the exclusive coterie of the very best Virginia families."[2] When Washington applied to the aristocratic Colonel Wilson Cary for the hand of one of his daughters — though not Mary Cary, it seems — [3] he was informed, with some loftiness, that the lady sought was accustomed to ride in her coach."[4]

---

[1] George Washington, by Woodrow Wilson, 1897.

[2] Life of Thomas Jefferson, by John T. Morse, Jr.

[3] Moncure D. Conway says that the "Lowland Beauty" was Betsy Fauntleroy, afterwards the wife of the Hon. Thomas Adams. Mary Cary married Edward Ambler. Washington had at least two love affairs before he married Mrs. Martha Custis. See chapter V, *infra.*

[4] In his address at Richmond, Va., October 13, 1891, on "The Colonial Virginian," R. A. Brock said: "It is conclusively demonstrated in preserved record, printed and manuscript, the latter embracing the registry of land patents from 1620 and the records of several county courts, that the settlers were preponderantly English. There was a considerable number of Welsh and a sprinkling of French, Italians, Irish and Dutch. . . . Welsh blood has been among the motive powers of many eminent sons of Virginia, and of their descendants in the South. . . . There were refugee Huguenots who found asylum desultorily in Virginia before 1700, but the chief influx was in that year, when more than five hundred

Not only so, but Monroe finally became a Loudon man; and the pioneering people of the middle counties and the piedmont certainly had less of the Anglican tincture than the Tuckahoes. The drop of Scotch, or Scotch-Irish, blood was big; and so was the Welsh drop; and the infusion made a difference. Moreover the "blue blood," so to say, turned red in contact with the real America — its open life, its hardships, its necessity of making common cause; and, finally, its sunny, homely sociabilities connected with the log cabin, the log school and the much-loved meeting-house in the wilderness. New types were developing. The Taylors of Orange were a strong and famous family. One of them, George, a great-uncle of President Madison, had seven sons in the Revolutionary army. The celebrated Colonel John Taylor, of Caroline, whom we shall meet later in these pages, was of this stock on his father's side and of Pendleton lineage on his mother's. Zachary Taylor, too, is another President to be credited to these parts; for he was born just south of the Fairfax line — at Hare Forest, four miles from Orange Courthouse. Similarly, we take note of many families — the Dabneys, Maurys, Fontaines, all of Huguenot stock; the Winstons, Henrys, Slaughters, Strothers from the Isle of Thanet, and their multitudinous kith and kin. There was many an old farmer with a crest on his snuff-box. Scotch penetration of Anglo-Saxon Virginia was pronounced

came and settled chiefly at Manakintown. . . . Of the Scotch but few immigrants before the union of Scotland and England, in 1707, may be identified. After the union 'Scotch Parsons' so potent as educators and merchants, who quite monopolized the trade of the country, pervaded Eastern Virginia. The list of families in the colony, who in vested right used coat-armor, as attested in examples of such use on tombstones, preserved book plates, and impressions of seals, is more than one hundred and fifty. The virtue of such family investment by royal favor may appear somewhat in the fact that the Virginia rebels, Claiborne, Bacon, Washington and Lee were all armigers, and among others were the Amblers, Archers, Armisteads, Banisters, Barradalls, Beverlys, Blands, Bollings, Byrds, Carys, Carringtons, Cloptons, Claytons, Corbins, and so on throughout the alphabet in swelling numbers and comprehensive examples of ability and worth." Meade listed some 250 highly important Virginia families of the colonial period. In the matter of felon blood, Jefferson allowed it but a one-thousandth part.

from the time the tobacco traders settled at such places as Leeds, Dumfries and Falmouth. Scotch merchants grew rich. A street in Glasgow was called "Virginia Street." James Monroe and Patrick Henry were by no means the only celebrated Virginians of Scotch origin. The Barbours of Culpeper were well at the front in their days; especially is Justice Philip Pendleton Barbour, of the United States Supreme Court, to be credited with what Professor Tucker characterizes as his "severe and sustained logic." And the "Cohees" (Quoth-hes) certainly became a power in the Commonwealth.

But the Monroes! The name in Gaelic means "red bog." It is a territorial surname. In Ireland, anciently, it was simply Ro. The first man in history to bear it was Occon Ro, "whose son Donald, born in Ireland, went to Scotland in the beginning of the eleventh century to assist King Malcolm II." Malcolm gave him the Barony of Fowlis. "His descendants added to the original name the syllable Mon." At subsequent periods, "this name was spelt variously: Monro, Munro, Monroe, Munroe." Ro itself survives in such names as that of E. P. Roe. In Massachusetts[1] today, "Munroe" is the spelling ordinarily used; in Virginia, the name is "Monroe."

---

[1] See the Munroe genealogy by John G. Locke, Boston and Cambridge, 1853; also the History of the Munros of Fowlis, with genealogies of the principal families of the name, to which are added those of Lexington and New England, by the late Alexander Mackenzie, Inverness, 1898; also a sketch of the Munro Clan, by James Phinney Munroe, Boston, 1900. There is a great deal about the Massachusetts Munroes in A. B. Muzzey's "Reminiscences and Memorials of the Men of the Revolution," as well as about the Scotch Munroes. George Munro, ninth baron of Fowlis, was slain at the battle of Bannockburn, under Robert Bruce of Scotland, in 1314. Robert Munro, twenty-first baron, was killed in the service of Gustavus Adolphus of Sweden, defending the civil and religious liberties of Germany in 1633. Sir Robert, twenty-fifth baron, was a zealous Presbyterian and, being remarkable for size and corpulency — the same figure with Colonel Munro of our Revolution — he was nicknamed "the Presbyterian mortar-piece." His grandson, Sir Robert, twenty-seventh baron, who succeeded his father in 1729, was greatly distinguished for his military services. He was in the battle of Fontenoy. "He was killed in the battle of Falkirk, as was his brother, Dr. Munroe." "Up to the year 1651, there had been three generals, eight colonels, eleven majors, thirty captains, and five lieutenants of the Munroe stock. At the battle of Worcester, where Cromwell was victorious, several Munroes were made prisoners, and some of them were bound out as apprentices to farmers in

It has been asserted that the Virginia Monroes "came from a family of Scotch cavaliers, descendants of Hector Monroe, an officer of Charles I." Thus President James Monroe is given cavalier ancestry. This somewhat misleading statement is repeated in many books. While the Monroes in Scotland were of the cavalier cut and quality, they were hardly so in Virginia. Dr. Lyon G. Tyler, who has gone more painstakingly into the subject than anyone else, says that "the family in the Northern Neck of Virginia seems to be totally different from a family of the name in Southside Virginia." There were Andrew Monroes, it appears, in the Southside family, as well as in the Northern Neck family. We hear of the Rev. Andrew Monroe of the upper parish, Isle of Wight. John Blair, President of the Council under Dinwiddie, and acting governor, married Mary Monroe, daughter of the Rev. John Monroe and his wife Christian.

Whatever may have been the relationship of James Monroe with the Southside Monroes, or the Massachusetts Munroes, we do not attempt to trace.

As revised by Dr. Tyler for this book, President Monroe's pedigree, according to the records of Maryland and Westmoreland County, Va., is as follows:

"Andrew[1] Monroe, settled in Maryland in 1647. He took sides against Lord Baltimore; and, at the end of the troubles, fled across the Potomac to Mattox, where many of the Protestants sought refuge. He married Elizabeth ————, and died before 1668, when a deed from his widow Elizabeth to his children names them

---

America." Among these was William, the ancestor of the Massachusetts Munroes. There were eleven of these in the old French war, and fourteen in the Revolution. They lived around Lexington and Concord, and were descendants of the clannish William's six sons. All fourteen were in the Lexington company of Theodore Parker's grandfather, Captain John Parker. Ensign Robert was killed at Lexington; and Captain Edmund Munroe, by a cannon ball at Monmouth. Another Lexington Munroe was the stalwart Colonel William, Washington's host on the Lexington battleground, in 1789.

F. B. Sanborn, in his "Life of Thoreau," says: "The Munroes of Lexington are descended from a Scotch soldier of Charles II's army, captured by Cromwell at the battle of Worcester in 1651, and allowed to go into exile in America. His powerful kinsman, General George Monroe, who commanded for Charles at the battle of Worcester, was, at the Restoration, made Commander-in-Chief for Scotland."

as Elizabeth, who married Bunch Roe, Susan, Andrew[2], George and William.

"Andrew[2] Monroe (Andrew), born about 1664, married Elinor Spence, daughter of Captain Patrick Spence (died in 1685) and had issue Elizabeth, married Arrington, Andrew' Spence, and Susannah who married Charles Tyler. This Andrew died 1713-1714.

"Andrew[3] Monroe, (Andrew[2], Andrew[1],) died in 1735, leaving a wife Christian, and children Elinor, who married Dr. James Bankhead, Sarah, Spence[4], and Andrew.

"Spence[4] Monroe (Andrew[3], Andrew[2], Andrew[1],) married Elizabeth Jones, sister of Hon. Joseph Jones, who died in Fredericksburg in 1806, and had James[5], President of the United States, Andrew, Joseph Jones and Elizabeth who married William Buckner.

As the first Washington in Westmoreland, John, brother of Laurence, was master of a ship, so the first Monroe, Andrew, was a mariner. He commanded a pinnace under Cuthbert Fenwick, general agent for Lord Baltimore. He was with Richard Ingle in 1644, and "was evidently a Protestant." [1]   When Ingle declared for parliament, Monroe took sides against Lord Baltimore. "Like many other men in that day he could not write." He settled first on Kent Island close by the Eastern Shore, where William Claiborne started a colony, about 1630. Claiborne's quarrel with Lord Baltimore caused many of the English settlers to sail across the bay and up the Potomac. Numbers of them planted at Chickacoan, in the Northern Neck. Our sea-captain, Andrew, settled at Appomattox — not the Appomattox so celebrated in the annals of the Civil War, but what is now Mattox, Westmoreland. Charles Tyler, founder of the Tyler family of the Northern Neck, whose descendants intermarried with the Monroes and Spences, probably left Maryland at the same time and for the same reason.

The Virginia Archives show that successive grants of land were made to Andrew Monroe from 1650-1662,

---

[1] William and Mary Quarterly, Vol. IV, p. 272. Two old books that deal with early Maryland are Alsop's "Character of the Province of Maryland," by George Alsop, reprinted in 1869 and "The Day Star of American Freedom," by George Lynn-Lachlan Davis, 1855.

and to John Monroe from 1695 to 1719. James
Monroe, the President, "was born on land of which
his ancestor who first migrated to this country was
the original grantee." [1]   There are numerous references
in the Archives at Richmond to a later Andrew Monroe,
of the Virginia House of Burgesses. He sat in the
Assembly from 1742 to 1747. Quaint enough, surely,
is the old Westmoreland document in which Andrew
Monroe and others report upon the death of a man-
servant who threw himself into a creek and was
drowned. They caused him to be "buried at ye next
Cross-roads," and a stake to be "driven through the
middle of him in his grave, he having wilfully cast
himself away." Another document mentions the
"pernicious vermin wolves," which the Washingtons
and Monroes and others hunted to extermination.

Hugh Blair Grigsby speaks of James Monroe's father,
Spence, as a "carpenter"; and it is a fact, as the
records prove, that, in 1743, "Spence Monroe apprenticed himself to Robert Walker of King George,
Joiner." "But," comments Dr. Lyon G. Tyler (in
William and Mary Quarterly, Vol. IV, p. 274), "the
inference which he (Mr. Grigsby) draws that James
Monroe was of low social scale is incorrect. His fathers
and his ancestors were justices and officers in the
militia, and had respectable estates and owned many
slaves. It must be remembered that Virginia was
settled chiefly by the people of the English cities, in
which the dignity of the trades was stoutly maintained.
The gentlemen of the counties of England apprenticed
their sons to the grocers, the weavers, and the tailors,
and they did not for that reason cease to be gentlemen.
A premium was put upon the trades by inhibiting the
right of voting or of office-holding to any but a member
of one of the merchant guilds. I have found that
many of the old leading Virginians apprenticed their
sons to some tradesman, and that merchandizing was

---

[1] Virginia Calendar of State Papers.

very popular. The carpenter's trade was especially honorable.[1] No family was more honorable or more influential than the Cary family of Elizabeth City and Warwick Counties; and yet both the father and grand-father of Colonel Archibald Cary, of the Revolution, called themselves, 'carpenters' as well as 'gentlemen.' They, no doubt, served first as apprentices, as the custom required a regular probation of five years; but afterwards they performed the part of directors and contractors, leaving the manual labor to slaves. . . . These are the facts from the records, but it is also true that, however respectable, the Monroes never held the same state in society as the Lees, Washingtons, Allertons, Ashtons, and a few other great families of Westmoreland and King George counties — a fact which is shown by the absence of intermarriage and the inferiority of their estates and offices compared with these powerful neighbors."

Let it be noted here that James Monroe was not the only celebrated American statesman of the old Captain Andrew stock. Andrew, second, had a fourth child Susannah, named in his will (1713). One of Susannah's sons by her third husband, Captain Benjamin Grayson, was the celebrated Colonel William Grayson, who mar-ried General William Smallwood's sister Eleanor. He was a brother of Spence Grayson and as we have shown of blood-kin to Spence Monroe. Colonel Grayson distin-guished himself in the Revolution, especially at Monmouth where he was at the head of one of the fighting regiments; in public life prior to the adoption of the Constitution, which he opposed, and as one of the first United States Senators from Virginia. He died at Dumfries, March 12, 1790, on his way to Congress.

---

[1] As witness the Worshipful Carpenters' Company of London; and the Carpenters' Company, which built Carpenters' Hall, in Philadelphia, meeting-place of the First Continental Congress. In this connection William G. Stanard writes to the author: "Most sons of Virginia planters and farmers farmed them-selves; but occasionally one was a mechanic. Larkin Chew, of Spotsylvania County, head of a large and quite prominent family, sometimes styles himself 'gentleman' and sometimes 'carpenter' or 'builder'. One of the Carys was a builder."

He was conspicuously able in an age of brilliant men.

We come finally to Monroe's mother, who brought good Welsh blood to the blending. In the main, as we have seen, English was the stock of the Northern Neck, and both the Monroe family of Westmoreland and the Jones family of King George had intermarried with families of English lineage. Still, as was said by the biographer of the Hon. David S. Jones, of New York, common as the name is "the characteristics of the Welsh race are plainly discernible in almost every member of the family, and are very marked in almost all who have become prominent in any walk of life — almost to a man choleric, sanguine, social, hospitable, independent and honorable." Hospitable, independent and honorable, the Joneses of King George certainly were; and it may be added that no man influenced James Monroe more than did his mother's affectionate and attentive brother, Judge Joseph Jones, whose solicitude for his nephew's welfare and advancement was unending. This Virginia worthy was a judicious-minded man of high character and qualifications, who left his impress not only upon James Monroe but upon the affairs of the continent. He was twice a delegate to the Continental Congress, and for many years served as a Judge of the District Court. As one learns from R. A. Brock (who insists that "genealogy is now admitted to be one of the chief supports of history"), the King George family to which Elizabeth Monroe belonged "was the same with that of Adjutant-General Robert Jones, Commodore Catesby Jones and General Walker Jones" each of note in the history of his country.

We have little direct testimony concerning Monroe's mother; but there are numerous letters extant written by Judge Jones[1]; and, if she were like her brother, as she seems to have been, she must have possessed sterling qualities that served her well in the rearing of her son.

---

[1] The letters of Judge Joseph Jones have been published by Worthington C. Ford. Judge Jones' father, James Jones, kept an ordinary in King George, which his widow, Esther, continued to keep after his death.

Site of "Monroe Hall"

CHAPTER II

Boyhood, College Life and Early Campaigning

We know less than we would like to know about the boyhood of Monroe. He never wrote the story of his own early experiences; nor did he have any such admirer as Parson Weems to go around among the old people of Westmoreland, Richmond and King George Counties, gathering up the anecdotal matter that might now serve us in lieu of fragmentary data. No doubt our Westmoreland lad was busy enough. He sailed, he fished, he rode, he followed the hounds and bird dogs. Probably he was out and about with the black boys much of the time. It was the custom. For instance, it is on record that the youngest of Thomas Lee's six sons, Arthur, the unhappy diplomat, had a happy youth among the negroes of his own age in this same Westmoreland country. Here bob white whistled in the upland fields, and the red bird in the briers down along the branches. Westmoreland was a great place for sheltering pines and cedars; and, where cedar berries grew, there birds were sure to be found, winter as well as summer. Waterfowl fed in the creeks; or passed honking overhead, in V-shaped squadrons. To imaginative boys like "Legion Harry" Lee and other lads of the Northern Neck, the "V" was Virginia's initial on wing. And, as for the Potomac fish, whole schools of them flashed their silvery sides within sight of the watchful boys on the banks of the creeks and coves. All must have been familiar with the London ships that moored at the landings. At Hobbs' Hole in the Rappahannock, as Jefferson tells us in his "Notes on Virginia," the water was four fathoms deep; and at Nomini Bay on the Potomac, four and a half fathoms. Monroe's Creek was about the best on the shore —

navigable for vessels four miles from its mouth, and
for small boats another mile. No doubt grain was sent
down in scows. If there were no mill at the head of the
creek, then there was something lacking in the Monroe
neighborhood. If there were no mill pond in which the
Monroe sky mirrored itself, then the boy of the house
missed much indeed. Probably both mill and pond
were there. Mattox, the next creek, was three miles
long. Historic Pope's was but two. Lower Machodac
resembled Monroe's. It was healthier back from the
creeks on the high ground. As yet the alluvial bottoms
retained their fertility; and great quantities of tobacco,
as well as cargoes of wheat, passed out at the mouths of
the two rivers. It was when the soil had lost its magic
quality and the waters their bounty that the old order
perished in Westmoreland. "Chantilly, Mount Pleasant, Wakefield," sighs Bishop Meade, "are now no
more. Stratford alone remains. Where now are the
venerable churches? Pope's Creek, Round Hill, Nomini,
Leeds, where are they? Yeocomico only survives the
general wreck. Of the old men, mansions, churches,
etc., we are tempted to say *Fuit Ilium, et ingens gloria
Dardanium!*"

Leeds, or Leedstown, on the Rappahannock, must
have been well known to young Monroe. "It was
doubtless named, either by the Fairfaxes or Washingtons, after the town of Leeds, in Yorkshire, near
which both of their ancestral families lived." [1] So says
Bishop Meade, who adds: "For one thing, it deserves
to retain a lasting place in the history of the American
Revolution. As Boston was the Northern, so Leeds
may be called the Southern cradle of American Independence. This was the place where, with Richard
Henry Lee as their leader, the patriots of Westmoreland
met, before any and all others, to enter their protests
against the incipient steps of British usurpation. At

---

[1] The Virginia Historical Magazine, Vol. XXI, p. 385, says that the name of
John Monroe's house in Richmond County, "Fowlis," "showed that the Virginia
family remembered the old home in Scotland."

this place did they resolve to oppose the Stamp Act, nor allow any citizen of Westmoreland to deal in stamps."

Spence Monroe, as well as John Monroe, joined in the movement. Their signatures are among the one hundred and fifteen appended to the famous resolutions. It is a distinguished roll, comparable to any other in America. Doubtless James Monroe, now nine, heard the talk about the hated stamps, and bristled, as boys do, in defiance of the foe. It must have cost a man like Richard Henry Lee downright compunctions thus to help nullify a Crown measure. It is true, as Bishop Meade says, that "Virginia had been fighting the battles of the Revolution for 150 years before the Declaration." Her Masons, Lees and Henrys were transplanted John Hampdens. Nevertheless, Lee seems to have welcomed the repeal, in spite of the ominous declaratory act accompanying it. He led a movement to raise a fund of seventy-six pounds, eight shillings, and sent it to Edmund Jennings, Lincoln's Inn, London, with the request that the money be expended for a Reynolds portrait of Lord Camden, "as a token of admiration for his opposition to the Stamp Act." But his lordship "forgot" to sit for the portrait; and, instead, a fine one of Lord Chatham, by Benjamin West, was copied and sent to Virginia. Such were the early amenities of an age destined to develop acute and bloody differences. And, "under influences like these," says Dr. Daniel C. Gilman, "the young Monroe was trained in the love of civil liberty."

At any rate, it is clear that he breathed in Americanism with his first conscious breath. He sprang from stock that was native to American soil at least a hundred years before the War of the Revolution. Whatever was foreign in him had been bred out; he was truly a son of the western world, altogether rid of alien preconceptions, and quite ready to take on the plantation democracy of the seventeen-seventies and the new doctrines of his age.

The old Monroe house near Monroe's Creek no longer stands; luckily there is a good print of it. Unmarked even by a heap of chimney-bricks, its site is no great distance from Washington's birthplace, Wakefield, between Pope's Creek and Bridge's Creek, where, a hundred years ago, George Washington Parke Custis placed a slab of freestone, but where one now sees a plain shaft, encircled by a fence of iron pickets.

So narrow is this part of the Northern Neck that, when one looks south, he at times may see the smoke of the Rappahannock river steamers; or, when he looks north, the smoke of the boats on the Potomac. Those on board the Potomac steamers, if bound upstream, might well be in Washington within a few hours. On the left they would pass the site of Richard Henry Lee's Chantilly, as well as Stratford, ancestral home of the Lee family. Nor could they do better, perhaps, than recall what Bishop Meade says of Richard Henry Lee who, with one incapacitated hand, wrapped in a black silk bandage, worked harder for America with the other hand than any of his contemporaries:

"Was there a man in the Union who did more in his own county and State and country, by action at home and correspondence abroad, to prepare the people of the United States for opposition to English usurpation, and the assertion of American independence? Was there a man in America who toiled and endured more than he, both in body and mind, in the American cause? Was there a man in the Legislature of Virginia, and in the Congress of the Union, who had the pen of a ready writer in his hand, and to which so many papers may be so justly ascribed, and by whom so much hard work in committee rooms was performed?"

Similar thoughts occur, as one passes George Mason's Gunston Hall, farther upstream, and then again arise other like thoughts with a glow to them, and gratitude in them, as one recognizes glorified Mt. Vernon on the cliffs of the Fairfax shore.

But, away down below, broad, indeed, is the Potomac and far off are the wooded hills — dim at times and misty, quite unreachable, even with a sailor's eye.

Spyglass or no, the old halls fail to come out of the
distance; how could they, since some crumbled long
ago, and others were burned, and still others were
seized upon by the "hants," who liked to quit the
old churchyards now and then for cannier quarters?
Yet, if one but use those little reconstructing faculties
with which the mind is blessed, he may readily replace
the old seats and repeople the whole region. One might
thus ride in the same coach with the writer of the
"Journal of a Young Lady of Virginia in 1781," as she
passed from seat to seat, visiting for a while at each —
"Belleview," home of Thomas Ludwell Lee; "Selving-
ton," home of Thomas Seldon; "Chatham," home of
William Fitzhugh; and so on from house to house for
many a mile. Thus in Bishop Payne's day might a
wayfarer in Westmoreland, traveling on the ridge
between the Potomac and the Rappahanock, have
come upon the Parson's Road, leading from Pine
Forest glebe to Round Hill Church. This kinsman of
Dolly Payne Madison (also of William Payne, who
felled General Washington with his fist, during a
political dispute at Alexandria, receiving thereafter
not a challenge but an apology) declares that the
Parson's Road was one of the most pleasing he ever
saw. "It led for several miles in a direction perfectly
straight, under an avenue of beautiful oaks." It was
cut through the forest for the Rev. Archibald Campbell
— a character of particular concern to us because of
the part he played in Monroe's development.

How education was regarded in the Monroe family
is shown by the fact that, about 1750, it brought over
from Scotland, as a teacher, the Rev. William Douglas,
a truly excellent man. It was he who taught Thomas
Jefferson for four years. Good teachers were not easy
to procure in Virginia in those days. George Wythe's
own mother taught him Latin and Greek. Patrick
Henry's family sent to Scotland and engaged Thomas
Campbell, the poet, to come to Virginia, as tutor; but
he was obliged to forego his voyage hither. Archibald

Campbell was his uncle. One of the most interesting
Virginia schoolmasters of the period was Charles
O'Niel, of Orange County. He taught at the Pine Stake,
near Raccoon Ford. He played whist for silver, and
"took his julep regularly."[1] His method of flogging
bespoke the devicefulness of true genius. Let us who,
in this humane age, are too soft to use the gad, remember that Dominie O'Niel merely did as others were
accustomed to do when he thrashed his unruly pupils.
Mark Twain may be said to have died before his time
if he left this world without hearing of O'Niel's
ingenuity in the matter of enforcing discipline on
Raccoon Creek. He used to mount a culprit "on the
back of an athletic negro, who seems to have been
kept for the purpose." Thereupon, the negro, who
probably enjoyed the performance, quickly, dexterously
and unyieldingly pinioned his rider, clamping him hand
and foot; and thus held him while O'Niel laid on.

A Westmoreland worthy, well known to the Monroes,
was John Marshall's father, Colonel Thomas, "grandson of Thomas Marshall, carpenter." So said Wilson
Miles Cary, the genealogist. There was something of
a Marshall-Monroe parallel in lineage. The Marshalls
were Welsh. Thomas Marshall's wife was Mary Isham
Keith, daughter of a Scotch clergyman, but descended
on the mother's side from the Turkey Island Randolphs.
The Randolphs had seven seats on the James, Turkey
Island being the original one. Both James Monroe
and John Marshall, therefore, were of Scotch-Welsh
blood, intermingled with seventeenth century Virginian. Colonel Thomas, mathematician, astronomer,
soldier, was also a surveyor under Washington, whose
close comrade he was throughout life. He was two
years older than Washington, and is said to have been
his classmate in Westmoreland. "Washington's field-
notes at sixteen," says Justice James T. Mitchell,[2]

---

[1] Old Churches, Ministers and Families of Virginia, by Bishop Meade, 2 vols.;
vol. II, p. 90.
[2] Commemorative address by Mr. Justice James T. Mitchell, in Musical Fund
Hall, Philadelphia, Pa., on John Marshall Day, February 4, 1901.

"show his precocity; and the youthful Washington was but *primus inter pares* with his associates." Colonel Thomas moved from "the Forest," "a few hundred acres of poor land in Westmoreland," to Germantown, now Midland, south of Manassas. There, "in a little log cabin," almost within spyglass sight of the dome of the Capitol at Washington, was born John Marshall, oldest of fifteen children, September 24, 1755, year of Braddock's defeat. James Bradley Thayer[1] says: "At Midland all they can show you now, relating to Marshall, is a small, rude heap of bricks and rubbish — what is left of the house where he was born." The Marshalls moved on west to a six-thousand acre tract in the mountain region of Fauquier. Their house there, Oak Hill, "an unpretending frame building," still stands. Chief Justice Marshall used to say: "My father was a far abler man than any of his sons. To him I owe the solid foundation of all my success in life."

John Marshall was in Westmoreland a great deal when a boy. At fourteen, he attended Archibald Campbell's school, where James Monroe, two and a half years younger, was a pupil; and they were together there for one year.

Parson Campbell was a power in Washington parish, Westmoreland. His glebe was near Johnsville. He had two residences, one called Pomona, the other, Campbellton. He had been long in Virginia — since 1730; and his "scanty school" is said to have been the one attended by Washington and the elder Marshall. If so, it must have been a good school for mathematics, as well as for Latin. In any event, it is certain that Parson Campbell taught his own sons Archibald and Alexander, and at the same time prepared John Marshall and James Monroe for college. Madison also appears to have attended the school at Campbellton. There it was that both Marshall and Monroe were well-

---

[1] John Marshall, by James B. Thayer; the Life of John Marshall, by Albert J. Beveridge, 4 vols., Vol. I, p. 7.

grounded in Latin. To Marshall the frontier youth, the
skill in philology thus acquired was of the greatest use
when he became the first interpreter of the Constitution
of the United States. As for Monroe, he not only
acquired a sense of the root-meaning of words, but
obtained something more than a smattering of a tongue
he would need when he should go to live in France and
Spain

Thus, at sixteen, Monroe, tall and strong, left home
for college. He now quit one neck of land for another
— a very similar neck, this time between the York
River, six miles to the north, and the James, or "Jeems,"
as every one called it, six miles to the south. He was at
an exceedingly romantic and historically fruitful spot —
the Powhatan-Pocahontas-John Smith country. Most
likely the romance, the fascination of history, got into
his blood; and along with it that Lafayette-like love
of liberty which ever after characterized him. From
the time (1683) Bruton church 'was built of brick "on
the horse-path in Middle Plantations old-fields," and
from the time (1693) the "free school and college" was
put up near by, this spot on the high watershed of the
York-James peninsula gave promise of becoming the
most important place in Virginia. And it did so become;
for just after that, when the province-house at Jamestown was burned, Governor Francis Nicholson removed
the capital to the Middle Plantations, where there were
fewer mosquitoes and where the soil, the springs and
the air were as kindly and wholesome as could be.
Nicholson was an impulsive man, hot and peppery; and
so much in love with Martha Burwell, daughter of
Major Lewis Burwell, of King's Creek, that he swore
nobody else should have her. If her father should let
her marry, he would cut the throats of "the bridegroom,
the minister who should perform the ceremony, and
the justice who should give the license." She did
marry — Colonel Henry Armistead, being the happy
man; but not until Nicholson, a good soul really,
founder of King William School, now St. John's College,

Annapolis, had gone away, to be governor somewhere else.

To the unsophisticated and impressionable Monroe, Williamsburg seemed to be a place of very great consequence. Josiah Quincy, fresh from Boston, New York and Philadelphia, had in mind larger capitals with which to compare the Virginia city when he visited it not long before Monroe entered college; but such young men as those from Campbellton school had no colonial criterion wherewith to gauge it. Quincy found excellent farms around it, and whole fields of peach trees in bloom. The soil was sandy; the streets were unpaved and dusty; and the houses were mostly wooden. It had two ports, each a mile away — one to the south, Princess Anne's port on Archer Hope Creek, James River side; and Queen Mary's Port on Queen's Creek, York River side. Oddly enough, the road to this landing was sometimes called "Gallows Road," sometimes "Lovers' Lane," as though the man who was to marry and the man who was to hang trod the same path. What is called the Old Capitol (built in 1751, burnt in 1832) was then new — a charming structure on colonial lines, of which Independence Hall in Philadelphia is so familiar an example. It stood at the east end of Duke of Gloucester Street, which was seven-eighths of a mile long and ninety-nine feet wide; and the college stood at the west end. At the college, the street forked into encircling roads, and the grounds and group of buildings thus set off, with a statue of Norborne Berkeley, Lord Botetourt, in front, made an impressive and pleasing show. For, at the time of which we tell, the courtly and amiable Botetourt, who on state occasions rode from palace to capitol behind his six milk-white horses, was in his grave under the college chapel; and Dunmore, a coarser man, of the royal Stuart blood, was governor.

Had not the free colonial idea already possessed them, Monroe, Marshall and other matriculates of the time might have regarded William and Mary as the gateway to some higher British institution. It was the custom of certain Virginia gentlemen to import blooded horses, such as Colonel John Baylor's celebrated "Fearnought," and send their sons to schools in England or Scotland. Col. John Baylor, Sr., was himself a Cambridge University man. Ten Lees were educated in England — Arthur at Eton, Edinburgh, Lincoln's Inn and Middle Temple. Of one hundred and seventeen Virginia boys sent abroad prior to 1800, nineteen were from Monroe's county of Westmoreland.[1] William and Mary was then the richest college in America, with an annual income of $20,000. It is a piquant, if minor, fact that a tax on peddlers who peddled in Virginia, went to the college. Again one is interested to note that from 1700 to 1776, through the donation of Robert Boyle, eight or ten Indians were annually maintained and educated at the college. George and Reuben Sampson were the Indians whom Monroe knew there in 1775. Monroe also probably knew the three Murray boys, sons of the Earl of Dunmore, who, with other young royalists were students in 1774. Porto Bello, Dunmore's hunting-lodge, was but six miles away, over by the York. Almost every distinguished Virginian of the time made it a point to visit Williamsburg[2]; and many of them belonged in the college circle. Washington was appointed surveyor by William and Mary in 1749; Peyton Randolph, first president of the Continental Congress, was an alumnus of forty years standing; George Wythe was schooled there in 1740; John Tyler, Sr., Governor of Virginia, in 1754; John Tyler, Jr., President of the United States, in, 1802-07; Edmund Randolph, in 1766; Judge Spencer Roane, in 1779, and General Winfield Scott in 1804. Of the

---

[1] Virginia Historical Magazine, Vol. XXI, pp. 196,197. William G. Stanard investigated the subject. See also article by R. H. Greene, New England Historical and Genealogical Register, Vol. XLII, pp. 359-362.

[2] Lewis Hallam, of the American Company of Comedians, had made the Williamsburg playhouse, back of the capitol, quite famous as the American home of Shakespearean plays. Sarah Hallam, a cousin of Lewis, lived afterwards for many years at Williamsburg.

Committee of Thirty-One who framed the Virginia Declaration of Rights and the State Constitution, at least eleven, if not eighteen, were William and Mary men. So were four out of Virginia's seven Signers of the Declaration of Independence; and so were fifteen out of the thirty-three members of the Continental Congress. Three out of Virginia's seven Presidents of the United States — Washington, Jefferson, Madison, Monroe, William Henry Harrison, John Tyler, and Zachary Taylor — attended William and Mary.

Jefferson, a freckled, red-haired William and Mary College youth, was fifteen years older than Monroe. He had come and gone before Monroe shied away from the gay Sukeys of the Apollo room, or the girls who came in coaches to Bruton church. From the day Patrick Henry's Stamp-Act oration stirred his soul till the day on which both he and John Adams died, July 4, 1826, fiftieth anniversary of the Declaration of Independence, Jefferson was consistently and persistently a liberty man against privilege and human exploitation. When he was in the Virginia Legislature, he tried to overturn slavery. Himself the eldest of eleven children, he did overturn primogeniture. What he did for democracy is best measured by the enmity he provoked among the multitudes who opposed him. Many of his contemporaries hated him with extreme bitterness. Writers of a certain school make it a point to minimize his merits and magnify his faults, which indeed were numerous and of a piece with the pronounced qualities of his ardent nature. "Long Tom," people called him. "His shoulders were unusually square, his neck long and scrawny, the skin of his face adust, as if scorched, and of a brick-dust red, his hair foxy and bushy at the temples. Once seen, he never could be forgotten." As for his voice, it was "very peculiar, very pleasant, seldom raised to a loud tone and his words came 'trippingly off his tongue.'" "For so gaunt a man his step was light." His carriage presented "the very curious and unusual contrast of a rapid graceful movement, with a long, awkward, bony frame." [1]

Jefferson's father, Colonel Peter, a regular Samson who could up-end two one thousand pound hogsheads of tobacco at once, frequented Raleigh Tavern, "the most famous hostlery in the colonies." In fact there is a "curious deed on record in Goochland County of a sale of two hundred acres of land by William Randolph of Tuckahoe to Peter Jefferson for Henry Wetherburn's biggest bowl of arrack punch." Henry Wetherburn kept the Raleigh, in a portico over the door of which was a leaden bust of the Elizabethan hero in whose honor the tavern was named. It was an old frame building with entrances on both fronts. An owner of the Raleigh who comes, with fitness, into these pages was Anthony Hay (died, 1772), father of George Hay, who married Eliza, daughter of James Monroe. It was George Hay who prosecuted Aaron Burr in the great treason trial at Richmond. The Apollo was the main, or banqueting, room of the Raleigh. Here Jefferson, who called Williamsburg "Devilsburg," danced with his Belinda.

Monroe's accounts are still to be seen in the bursar's books. A recorded incident shows his immaturity. With other students he signed a petition to the president and masters against the extravagance, partiality and unwarrantable insolence of the Mistress of the college, Miss Maria Digges; but when up before the Board he admitted that he had never read what he signed.

In Monroe's time there were about sixty students at the college. In his own class was another Westmoreland

---

[1] Tactful, slow to anger, he nevertheless upon occasion went headlong into things untried and untested. John Randolph told A. J. Stansbury how Jefferson had urged upon his planter friends a plough with a new mould-board — "the mould-board of least resistance." When the ploughs were cast, the teams could not draw them through the soil. Again, he was carried away with a plan of his own to establish a saw-mill on a wind-swept hilltop near Monticello. The power was to be obtained out of the air by means of vertical sails. Not until the mill was almost built did his engineer say: "I have been wondering in my own mind how you are to get up your sawlogs?" Jefferson was aghast. "I never thought of that!" said he.

ful neighbors.

The following is the account against James Monroe, when a student at William and Mary College, as it stands in the Bursar's book.

		Mr. James Monroe	Dr.			
1775 March	25	To the Table for Board from 20th June, -	113*	9	18	7½
1776 March	25	To D° for d° 1 year, -	123	13	"	"
March	26	To Stock, due by him for Balce contra, -	42	6	10	—

* The figures in this column refer to the Journal; the other three columns mean pounds, shillings and pence.

		Contra To Jo Jones Esq aforesaid, -	Cr.			
1774 June	20	By Cash for Advd Board, -	103	6	10	
1775 January	19	By ditto D°	111	3	8	7½
				9	18	7½
Sept.		By Cash, -	122	6	10	
1776 March	25	By Balance, -	126	6	10	
				13		

ACCOUNT OF MONROE IN BURSAR'S BOOK

lad — John Bankhead; Carter Braxton's son, George, from King William; William Alexander, from Fairfax; Booth Armistead from Elizabeth City; Col. W. Miles Cary's son Wilson from Warwick; Henry Ashton from Caroline; Joshua Tabb, from Warwick; John Francis Mercer, afterwards Governor of Maryland — all these were classmates of Monroe, and some of them shared with him the never-to-be-forgotten experiences of the winter and spring of 1775 and the first half of 1776. The Boston Tea Party, the Port Bill, the First Continental Congress and Patrick Henry's leadership of the Virginia democracy were by this time familiar stories. King versus Congress — that was the subject of daily debate. It was now the spring of the rising tempest; of Henry's great oration in St. John's Church, Richmond; it was the spring of Concord and Lexington; and was to be the summer of Bunker Hill. What must Monroe and his classmates have seen, heard and thought at the old capitol, at the college and at the Raleigh Tavern during the various excursions and alarms of the Powder House period? It was a time of recurring excitement, of thrills; hardly a week passed but what the gooseflesh crept up and down the spines of the William and Mary boys, anxious as they were to break away from their musty books and seize the muskets they knew they must handle. "After all we must fight!" said Patrick Henry, in his electrifying speech, on Thursday the twenty-third of March; and, when the phrase was repeated at William and Mary a few hours later, the students echoed, "We must fight!" But Lord Dunmore was still at the Palace. He was the big man in Virginia — the King's man. He was in communication with General Gage at Boston, and acted in concert with that officer. On the evening of the twentieth of April, day after the battle of Lexington, Captain Henry Collins of the armed schooner "Magdalen," at Burwell's Ferry, on the James, landed a body of British marines and led them to Williamsburg where they broke into the powder magazine, a stone octagon, built by Spotswood in 1716, seized fifteen half-barrels of gunpowder, and made off with it to the vessel. In the morning there was a great gathering on the green. Probably all Williamsburg was there. We may be sure that Monroe was there. The people were more excited than ever. Their rights had been invaded. The whole big quarrel with the King had been brought home to them overnight. They threatened Dunmore. They sent off couriers to arouse the military companies, who responded at once. Patrick Henry was especially prompt. He rallied the Virginia volunteers, who had been organized by order of the convention, placed himself at their head and marched toward Williamsburg with the avowed purpose of reclaiming the raped gunpowder for the people to whom it belonged. This meant a great deal to Monroe; it was the first armed resistance to the Crown. It meant a great deal to Dunmore, too. He sent his wife and family on board the man-of-war "Fowey"; and then dispatched a messenger with £330 to Doncastle's Ordinary, where Henry had halted his troops. The money was in payment for the powder seized by the marines. On the surface it was an apologetic peace-offering; in reality it was a move made to gain time. Apparently his lordship had repented of the Powder Plot and given in; and Henry went north to sit in the Second Continental Congress, then about to meet at Philadelphia. But Dunmore did not mean to give in. News soon came that he was assembling a fleet of war boats in the Chesapeake. He was threatening Hampton. By and by he seized Norfolk. Later he burned it. All these events, of course, belong to history; but they were what Monroe fed on in his room at college when he might have been deep in "*De Bello Gallico*"; or they were the rumors he heard in the streets whose very names smacked of royalty, when he ranged them at night, playing at war with comrades no less eager than himself. But Monroe was never flighty — always a reasoner. What had he against the King? Perhaps he had not thought a great deal on the merit of the American cause. He hardly needed to think about it. It was in the air. The taxation quarrel had lasted so long as to generate an inveterate hostility. The sun rose and set upon this inveteracy; and in the watches of the night the challenge was: "Who comes?"

Most likely the silk-stockinged gentry of Williamsburg, the college boys on the campus and the ladies at the windows wanted to know who had come when one day there appeared in the streets a corps of frontiersmen so oddly arrayed as to astonish onlookers accustomed only to the sight of mild-mannered militiamen. Who were these fierce fellows "in green hunting shirts, home-spun, home-woven and home-made, with the words 'Liberty or Death' in large white letters on their bosoms"? In their hats were buck-tails. In their belts were tomahawks — yes, and scalping knives. "Their savage and war-like appearance excited the terror of the inhabitants." Who were they? Monroe knew at once; for there among them was Lieutenant John Marshall, his fellow-student at Campbellton school. They were the minutemen of Culpeper, Fauquier and Orange.

Monroe and Marshall probably had not seen each other for a year. Marshall had spent that time reading Horace and Livy with another excellent Scotch parson — the Rev. James Thompson, a member of the Marshall household at Oak Hill, in Fauquier. Now nineteen, and lieutenant in the minutemen, Marshall having learned that the captain who was to drill his company could not be present, set forth very early one morning in May 1775, walked ten miles, and appeared betimes on the musterfield[1]. Soon he was surrounded by minutemen eager to learn the news.

---

[1] The musterfield was on the property of John S. Barbour, a half-mile west of Culpeper Courthouse. An old oak marks the spot. These minutemen, raised at the instance of Patrick Henry, were the first to take arms in Virginia. There were one hundred and fifty from Culpeper, one hundred from Orange, and one hundred from Fauquier. They carried the rattlesnake flag.— Howe's Virginia Historical Collections.

He talked to them an hour about the bloody business
up Boston way. And he not only thrilled them, but
drilled them. One of the men who was on the field
that day said to Horace Binney:

"His figure I now have before me. He was about
six feet high, straight and rather slender, of dark complexion, showing little if any rosy-red, yet good health,
the outline of the face nearly in circle, and within eyes
dark to blackness [really brown], strong and penetrat-
ing, beaming with intelligence and good nature." His
hair was raven-black. Every one fell under his charm.
"Never did a man possess a temper more happy."[1]

After the drill, Marshall challenged the minutemen
to a game of quoits. Then he walked the ten miles
back to Oak Hill, reaching home before sunset. It
was said of Marshall "that he was the only man, who,
with a running-jump, could clear a stick laid on the
heads of two men as tall as himself. On one occasion
he ran a race in his stocking feet with a comrade.
His mother, in knitting his stockings, made the legs
of blue yarn and heels of white. This circumstance
combined with his uniform success in the race, led the
soldiers, who were always present at these races, to
give him the sobriquet of 'Silver Heels,' the name by
which he was generally known among them."[2]

How these woodland heroes "startled Williamsburg"
is set forth by other diarists, including Captain Philip
Slaughter, who was in Captain John Jameson's company. Lawrence Taliaferro was colonel, and Thomas
Marshall major of the regiment. "Shirt-men," Lord
Dunmore called them; and he gave them a more formidable character than did the caustic John Randolph of
Roanoke,[3] who said, in the United States Senate, that
they "were raised in a minute, armed in a minute,
marched in a minute, fought in a minute, and vanquished in a minute."

---

[1] Eulogy on John Marshall, by Horace Binney, pp. 22-24.
[2] John Marshall by James B. Thayer, 1901.
[3] John Marshall by Allan B. Magruder, 1885.

One of the William and Mary students, Richard Nowell, rode express through five States, carrying a message from Washington to Greene. So swiftly and faithfully did he execute his duty, that Washington presented him with a sword. H. B. Grigsby was wont to speak especially of "two tall and gallant youths" who made their mark as junior officers under General Washington. His reference was to Marshall, identified with the Eleventh Virginia Regiment of the Continental Line; and Monroe, who served with distinction in the Third Virginia. One comes upon a mention now and then of Monroe's early service as a cadet. It has been said that he marched to Boston and took part in the siege. Hardly. Maybe he rode express, and returned in time to train. That he was a cadet, there is no doubt whatever; for it was as such that he joined Colonel Hugh Mercer's Third Virginia. Mercer was appointed colonel February 13, 1776. There was an Andrew Monroe in the second company.[1] According to the Orderly Book[2] of General Andrew Lewis, who succeeded Patrick Henry as Commander-in-Chief of the Virginia forces, and who made his headquarters at Williamsburg, "cadets were young men serving in the ranks with a hope of obtaining a commission." A notice reads: "All Gentlemen cadets are desired to attend the parade constantly." The Virginia troops were encamped either at College Camp — just back of William and Mary — or at Springfield, sometimes called Deep Spring. Multitudes of soldiers and civilians enlivened the city throughout the spring and summer of 1776. General Charles Lee was one of those who were lionized. Not a few notable Virginia officers, soon to leave for the battlefields, were enjoying the last days home they would ever see — Major Andrew Leitch, mortally wounded at Harlem Heights; Major Edmund Dickinson, killed at Monmouth; Colonel

---

[1] W. T. R. Saffel's Records of the Revolution, 1858.

[2] Orderly Book of that portion of the American Army stationed at or near Williamsburg, Va., under the command of General Andrew Lewis, from March 18, 1776 to August 28, 1777, with notes by Charles Campbell, Esq., 1860.

Richard Campbell, killed at Eutaw Springs; Captain
Richard Parker, died in front of Charleston; Captain
Charles Porterfield, killed in Camden fight; Cap-
tain John Blair, also killed at Camden, and Captain
John Fleming, killed, like Mercer, at Princeton. Colonel
William Taliaferro and Colonel Isaac Read were to lose
their lives in the cause.

These were all much older men than Marshall and
Monroe, as were the members of the Virginia Convention which met on the fifteenth of May — for
instance, Colonel Meriwether Smith "who wore a
cocked hat and took much snuff when earnestly engaged
in conversation." [1] This was the Independence Convention. It proposed that Congress should "declare
the United Colonies free and independent States."
It ordered the organization of seven new regiments.
On the twenty-ninth of June, Virginia became an independent State, with Patrick Henry as the first republican governor.

When did Monroe join the Third Virginia? Mercer,[2]
made Brigadier, was succeeded by his friend George
Weedon, keeper of the "Sentry Box" inn at Fredericksburg, an ardent Whig and thorough soldier, who
became Colonel, June 19, 1776. On this same day
many cadets were promoted; but not Monroe. Nor
is he mentioned anywhere in General Lewis' Orderly
Book. In the entry at Springfield Camp, for July 15,
we have this: "A List of the Gentlemen Cadets' names
to be given in this afternoon, now with the regiment;
likewise those that are absent, and the reason for their

---

[1] Colonel Meriwether Smith (1730-1794) of Bathurst, Essex County, Va.,
was a member of the old Congress and the Virginia Conventions of '75, '76, and
'88. Monroe once said to Dr. Edward Bathurst Smith, of St. Louis: "Your
grandfather was one of the earliest and most ardent patriots of the Revolution.
He, from the beginning, struck out boldly and confidently for independence and
nothing else." — William and Mary College Quarterly, Vol. VI, p. 52.

[2] Mercer had been a surgeon at the Battle of Culloden. He was a captain
under Washington in the Indian War. Once he was shot down. His comrades
had gone and the Indians were upon him. He hid in a hollow tree; and then
struck out a hundred miles through the wilderness, living on roots and rattle-
snakes. His great service in the American army and heroic death at Princeton
are known to all. Mercer seemed much like Washington himself.

being absent." However, we are "getting warm," as
the children say in their game. Richard Henry Lee,
standing with two other Burgesses on the Capitol
portico wrote on a pillar the Macbethian passage:
"When shall we three meet again?" That was on the
seventeenth of June — Bunker Hill Day. Bunker Hill
news came; and, on June 24, Monroe was one of six
men who removed the arms from the palace to the
powder house. It is on record that the First Virginia
marched north August 16. At any rate, some of the
Virginians who were not in the battle of Long Island
participated, a little later, in the affair at Harlem
Heights, including Lieutenant James Monroe and the
gallant Major Andrew Leitch.

There were at that time ten companies in the Third
and Monroe was in the 7th Company, under Captain
William Washington (born February 28, 1752) a kinsman of the Commander-in-Chief. He was the eldest
son of Baily Washington, of Stafford. Six feet tall,
broad, strong and corpulent, William Washington,[1]
soon demonstrated his excellence as a soldier. He was
upright, amiable and generous, with agreeable manners.
Monroe grew to be fond of him; and, as we shall see,
Captain Washington relied upon Monroe. For a long
while, indeed, Monroe was his chief dependance.

We now hear of Weedon, Washington and Monroe
at Williamsburg; and next we hear of them at New
York. Theirs was a long summer march. The
Third Virginia arrived the day before the battle

---

[1] William Washington was Monroe's captain at Harlem Heights and Trenton.
He left the infantry to help recruit a regiment of dragoons. It was Colonel George
Baylor's regiment; and Washington was its major. This was the regiment that
suffered massacre at the hands of a detachment of British under General Grey at
Tappan, September 2, 1780. Baylor lost 67 men out of 104, all massacred while
asleep. Seventy horses were butchered. Washington escaped the massacre, and
was detailed with the survivors of Bland, Baylor and Moylan to the South. Washington and his horse won great glory in the Carolinas — at Cowpens, Guilford
Courthouse, Hobkirk's Hill and Eutaw Springs. While a prisoner in Charleston,
he fell in love with Miss Eliot, married her and settled in South Carolina, where
he was called "General." He died March 6, 1810. Hard service used up Baylor;
and he died, when still a young man, in the Barbadoes, whither he had sailed in
search of health.

of Harlem Heights. Having withdrawn from Brooklyn, the American commander fortified two lines across Manhattan. He was deeply chagrined because of an adverse affair at Kipp's Bay on September the fourteenth. Not unlike the carcass of an undressed deer, Manhattan may be said to hang by its hind hoofs at Fort Washington, and dip its nozzle in the brine at Castle Garden. In the very small of the back, east side, was Kipp's Bay, where, at what is now Thirty-Fourth Street Ferry, East River, was posted a brigade of half-raw, half-seasoned troops. Putnam was farther down the island with four thousand men. Washington himself was near at hand, in the house of Robert Murray, a rich Quaker, on Murray Hill. Lindley Murray, the grammarian, was a son. On Saturday, the fourteenth, Washington heard cannonading from British ships in East River; and saw, crossing it, "open flat-boats filled with soldiers, standing erect; their arms glittering in the sun." Sir William Howe was landing a strong detachment at Kipp's Bay, with the view to trap Putnam before he could march up by the road on the Hudson River side. Washington galloped to Kipp's Bay, only to find his troops there in a panic. "With drawn sword, he dashed impetuously in." So headlong was he that he got among the enemy; in fact, a little more and he himself would have been taken. Anger had hold of him, as when at Monmouth, long after, he felt himself betrayed. But there was no betrayal here. All were loyal enough; the trouble was that many of the men were of the militia, unused to big-thunder guns such as were awakening the echoes of Hell Gate. The sight of so many red-coats, too, made their courage ooze out; and these contemporaries of *Bob Acres* fled in spite of all that Washington could do. "Are these the men with whom I am to defend America!" he asked, with bitterness. Their conduct, he cried, was "disgraceful," "dastardly." He abandoned Murray Hill; and sent riders on the run to warn Putnam of the imminent springing of the deadly trap. Washington could not save Putnam; but a woman could — and did. Mrs. Murray spun a Penelope-like device. She welcomed the British officers at Murray Hill, set out cakes and cooling drinks and entertained them so successfully as to cause a long delay in their operations. Meanwhile, Putnam escaped up the island; and all was well. Clinton occupied the Murray house. At the Beekman house, near by, September 22, Nathan Hale entered into perpetual fame. Lossing says: "Hale was hanged upon an apple-tree in Rutger's orchard, near the present intersection of East Broadway and Market Streets."

Such was the humiliating news that greeted the Virginia troops when they joined the main army on Manhattan. General Lord Stirling, captured at Long Island but exchanged, now commanded the brigade, which consisted of the First and Third Virginia, Haslet's Delaware men and the remnant of Atlee's much cut-up Pennsylvania rifles.

Two days after the affair at Kipp's Bay, Washington, whose headquarters were at the Colonel Robert Morris, or Jumel, house, heard that the British were moving up the island. He rode towards them. Sure enough, some light infantry, Royal Highlanders and Hessian riflemen, under General Leslie, were pushing hard upon Putnam's favorite officer, General Thomas Knowlton of Bunker Hill fame. Adjutant-General Joseph Reed, of Philadelphia, who had galloped on ahead of Washington, came back in a hurry, with a cry for troops to support Knowlton. Just then, as Reed tells us, "the enemy appeared in full view and sounded their bugles in the most insulting manner, as usual after a foxchase. I never felt such a sensation before; it seemed to crown our disgrace." "Washington, too," adds Irving, "was stung by the taunting note of derision; it recalled the easy triumph of the enemy at Kipp's Bay. Resolved that something should be done to wipe out that disgrace, and rouse the spirits of the army, he ordered out three companies from Weedon's regiment, just arrived from

Virginia, and sent them under Major Leitch to join
Knowlton's Rangers. The troops thus united were to
get in the rear of the enemy while a feigned attack was
made upon the front. But, as it happened, the enemy
changed their position and the Americans came upon
them on the flank instead of in the rear."[1] They were
sharply received. Leitch was shot in the side three
times; Knowlton in the head with a musket ball.
Reed took Knowlton on his horse and bore him from
the field; but he soon died. "The men, undismayed
by the fall of their leaders, fought with unflinching
resolution under the command of their Captain. Other
troops were sent to help them, and they began to drive
the British; but by and by Washington withdrew his
whole force. He praised Knowlton and thanked the
troops under Leitch "for being the first to advance
upon the enemy." The word "Leitch" was given for
the next day's parole. The American loss was sixty;
the British, three hundred.

This was Monroe's maiden battle — fought in what
is now the heart of New York City. A few nights after
the bloody affair, he must have seen the skies just to
the south lit as with a conflagration. And, sure enough,
it was — for much of the city was destroyed.

To get in the American rear, after the battle of
Harlem Heights, Howe moved on Throg's Neck; but
Washington withdrew northward to what seemed a
safer spot, half way between Long Island Sound and
the Tappan Sea. This was White Plains. When
Monroe came up with his regiment on the night of the
twenty-third of October, the defenses were well under
way. Battle held off until the twenty-eighth. The
Delaware troops, which were in the same brigade with
Monroe's regiment, suffered some losses, and the
Maryland troops quite heavily. A twenty-hour storm
of rain and wind put an end to the battle, in which the
Americans lost one hundred and forty and the British

---

[1] Irving's Life of Washington, Vol. II, p. 35

two hundred and twenty-nine. Monroe had started in with a battle a month.

Washington now crossed to the Jersey shore. He was on the point of evacuating Forts Washington and Lee; but Congress intervened, so that further disaster followed. Howe stormed Fort Washington, November 16, and America lost three thousand good troops. Greene barely got out of Fort Lee with two thousand. Meantime General Stirling, who had crossed the Hudson south of Stony Point, "threw out a scouting party of a hundred men to take possession of the gap through which a road passed into the Jerseys." His lordship used Captain Washington's Company as scouts; and most likely Monroe was in this advance party. He was about to learn what it meant to retreat.

CHAPTER III

THE TIMES THAT TRIED MEN'S SOULS

We now come to the most notable adventure in Monroe's soldier life. This adventure was by no means a detached episode; in fact, to put it in its proper setting, we must tell of the retreat of the Continental Army from the Hudson, the Hackensack and the Passaic, all the way across Jersey to the Delaware ferries; we must tell of that memorable December of darkness and disaster — of desperation, indeed; and, finally, we must tell of Washington's spirited and skilful Hessian stroke — with the resultant passing of the crisis for him and for America. We are all the more free in these pages to speak of the Trenton crisis because Monroe bore a highly creditable, if not heroic part, in it. What happened to him at this critical Christmas helped to make of him the man he grew to be.

Monroe was not quite nineteen when, in the winter campaign of 1776-77, he saw American affairs sink to their lowest depth. Colonel Weedon wrote home to Fredericksburg: "General Howe has had a mortgage on the rebel army for some time, but has not yet foreclosed it." In a letter to his brother Augustine, Washington was equally frank: "If every nerve is not strained to recruit the army with all possible expedition, I think the game is nearly up." Again he wrote: "Could anything but the Delaware River have saved Philadelphia?" Then, too, "unluckily for himself, but luckily for the United States," Charles Lee had just been taken by the enemy. Disasters, mixed with a few blessings that looked like disasters, multiplied.

Keen was the bite of oncoming winter; ragged were the regimentals of the Virginians, Delawareans and Pennsylvania riflemen with whom Monroe marched;

38

and shoeless the feet of many among them as they trod the frozen roads or forded the icy streams. "With a handful of men," wrote Thomas Paine, "we sustained an orderly retreat of nearly a hundred miles, brought off our ammunition, all our field pieces, the greatest part of our stores and had four rivers to pass. None can say that our retreat was precipitate, for we were three weeks in performing it, that the country might have time to come." Many recruits did come to the rescue, such as the gallant and efficient Philadelphia Associators, under Cadwalader, and the Pennsylvania Flying Camp, under Ewing; but many faint-hearts also fell out, for the militia was not to be depended on in such cutting cold weather, with a confident enemy close at their heels. Then, too, Congress had retired from Philadelphia to Baltimore. That retirement, that flight, "struck a damp on ye spirits of many."

Washington, for his part, had no thought of giving in, but if forced to abandon Philadelphia, his imagination pictured for him an ever-lengthening line of retreat along the Blue Ridge as far south as old Massanutton Mountain on the Shenandoah. "My neck does not feel as though it was made for a halter," said he; "we must retire to Augusta County in Virginia." "Great Augusta" it was well called; for it stretched through its wildernesses as far as the Mississippi River. At times he faced about, and turned back, as if inviting a fight. He had lost nearly half his troops; five thousand were gone; hardly more than five thousand remained.

As for the enemy, Howe could muster thirty thousand all told, though but twelve thousand were in pursuit. Cornwallis asked Howe's permission to attack and annihilate the rebels; but Howe wished to be up to take part in the annihilation. His brother, Lord Howe, and he were issuing placatory proclamations. Sir William joined Cornwallis on December 6. With him was Major-General James Grant, in whose brigade was a formidable contingent of Hessian mercenaries —

the Grenadier Regiment Rall, the Fusilier Regiment von Lossberg and the Fusilier Regiment von Knyphausen. Such was the army that followed confidently, if tardily, on Washington's trail, rebuilding broken bridges as it came.

One soldier of the American rear-guard was Captain Alexander Hamilton, of the New York Provincial Artillery. "Erect and steady in gait," he had," a small, lithe figure instinct with life . . . a bright ruddy complexion; light-colored hair; a mouth infinite in expression, its sweet smile being most observable and most spoken of; eyes lustrous with deep meaning and reflection, or glancing with quick canny pleasantry." [1] The mouths of his cannon may not have had "infinite expression," but they barked effectively at the British van when it failed to keep its distance. Hamilton's battery, indeed, "was a model of discipline, its captain a mere boy with small, slender and delicate frame, who with cocked hat pulled down over his eyes, and apparently lost in thought, marched beside a cannon, patting it every now and then as if it were a favorite horse or a pet plaything." That is as clear and cleancut as a photograph; would we had as good a one of Monroe! We know that Hamilton was little; Monroe big and bony. We know that Hamilton had an intent look and brilliant smile; and we have reason to believe that Monroe's expression was much the same in youth as in later life — intent, like Hamilton's, yet less quizzical, less humorous, though quite as serious. Monroe must have met Hamilton on many occasions; but there seems to be no early record as to the relations of these two, who, by and by, would become rivals and political adversaries.

Trevelyan says ("The American Revolution"; Part II, Vol. II, p. 77): "The junior officer in William Washington's company was a lad even younger than Hamilton, and not his equal (as indeed very few were),

---

[1] Extract from an account by Mrs. Catherine V. R. Cochrane, youngest daughter of General Philip Schuyler.

in intellectual endowments or in personal charm. And
yet, if in the course of ages both their memories were
to perish, that of Lieutenant Monroe would in all
likelihood be the last forgotten of the two; for he was
the James Monroe who in December, 1823, as fifth
President of the United States, enunciated the policy
which defeated the machinations of the Holy Alliance,
and which deprived Spain of her American colonies.
The famous doctrine, wherewith his name is indis-
solubly associated, has been frequently revived and
reasserted with marked effects upon the history of the
world; and a very great deal more will have to be
written about it before that history attains the closing
chapter. As time proceeds, and the giant republic
grows increasingly conscious of its strength, fresh occasions will arise or be made, for the use, or misuse,
of the most formidable and far-reaching of all diplomatic weapons; and during generations and even
centuries to come the name of Captain Washington's
subaltern in the Third Virginia Continental Infantry
may still be a word of disagreeable import among the
Chancelleries of Europe."

Washington took his time in getting out of Jersey.
He knew what he was about, thanks to the young
Monroes of Weedon's excellent scouting company; and
also to his spies, who were numerous and indefatigable.
He left Princeton less than an hour ahead of the British
van; and when this van entered Trenton, at four
o'clock in the afternoon of Sunday, December 8, his
last boatload of troops was just pushing off from the
wharf. The Americans cocked their ears, too; for at
the head of about a thousand Waldeckers and Hessians
a brass band was playing — novel music for those who
marched to the sound of the fife and drum.

Counting all commands, Colonel Johann Gottlieb
Rall, who had stormed "Cock Hill Fort," an outwork
of Fort Washington, on Spuyten Devil Creek, brought
into Trenton fifteen hundred and fifty men — the
three regiments we have named, fifty chasseurs,

twenty light dragoons and six pieces of artillery. Down
stream at Burlington, fifteen hundred more mercenaries
simultaneously went into winter quarters, these being
under Colonel Carl von Donop. At Princeton was
another post; at New Brunswick, headquarters of
General Grant, was another. Altogether there were
ten such posts. Grant was to command them. He was
to persuade the population to turn Tory (which many
of the weaklings did) and to acclaim King George.
In the spring, Philadelphia was to be taken; and, with
that, the war was to end. All hail his Majesty! Such
were the sanguine expectations and plans of Sir William
Howe, who, solicitous as to his own ease, wished to
drink his Christmas punch in the city of New York.
Let us hasten to add that, though Cornwallis was
bound for a still more gladsome town — London
itself — he had a finer motive. His lordship wanted
to see his lady who pined for him, it seems; and who
died in his absence, if not because of it, two years later.
But, at New York, favored quartermasters and com-
missaries, with scandalous effrontery, were enriching
themselves. They, too, would soon be sailing for England, where they meant to set up lordly establishments.
As Christmas approached, all seemed to be going well
for King George; and for the Howes, Cornwallis, Grant
and the hireling Hessians, snugly ensconced on the
shores of a rapid river with a few rebels, all a-shiver in
their rags and wretchedness, scattered along in detached
order at the numerous ferries.

As soon as Washington had secured these passes of
the river and all the boats, he set about the task of
strengthening his army, and making the most of his
strategical position. It was something to be behind a
river, but not everything. Should thick ice form,[1] his
foes might cross at an unguarded reach of the stream,
and fall upon him. Colonel Rall gave out that he was
"waiting for a bridge of ice:" he would soon "run bare-

---

[1] As it did three weeks later, in January. "January 15th, the hearse with
General Mercer's body was conveyed over the river on the Ice."— Stryker.

foot over the ice," he said, "and take Philadelphia."
Even should the spring find Washington, unstrength-
ened, where he was, he could hardly hope to oppose
successfully the advance of an army ten times stronger
than his own. Worse than these things — even worse!
What if his Continentals should see bluer and bluer,
and finally go home? His deepest distress was due to
the most singular, the most unlooked-for, of adverse
concatenations. Unlooked for it was, because in winter
as a rule, with both armies at rest, men could go and
others come without incurring undue danger. By their
terms of enlistment, many of Washington's veterans
would be free to quit him at New Year's. Yes, it was
written in the bond that they might go. And who
could blame a shoeless, coatless, bedless man, broken
maybe, sore to his very soul, with wounds and buffet-
ings and manifold adversities, if, in his desperation,
he should turn his back upon comrades equally heart-
sick?

But dark as the outlook was, Washington did not
despair. He was the Stout Heart. He never worked
harder. He rode, he wrote, he planned. His orders and
appeals went far and wide. For one thing, he brought
to his aid two considerable bodies of Continental
troops — that of the capable and spirited Sullivan,
with the remnants of Lee's division, and that of Gates,
with four New England regiments, though the intriguing Gates himself soon passed on down country to visit
Congress at Baltimore. Not the least important of
Washington's achievements, a little later, was his compromise with certain regiments whereby they agreed
to remain on duty six weeks longer.

Other men than Washington were active too —
General Philemon Dickinson of Trenton, for instance;
and especially General Joseph Reed (who, however, for
lack of full faith and fealty, compromised himself);
General Thomas Mifflin, General John Cadwalader,
and Robert Morris, with their followers. This present
menace was peculiarly a Philadelphia menace, and

this period became the particular period, celebrated in
local story, when that city sent out the choicest of its
youth as sacrifices in a desperate cause.

Washington's main rendezvous was in the riverside
townships of Bucks. Here were Quaker farmsteads,
Quaker mills, a few log cabins in stretches of forest
and some lingering reminders of the days of the Lenni
Lenape. Here was the grave of Tamanend — St.
Tammany, a pile of stone. Here started the Walking
Purchase, of bitter memory. Here were noble hills,
ravines and sheltered spots for the troops — "swells,
dells and stretches." Springs abounded. One of them
fed four mills. Grist could be had, and much else that
seemed good in the sight of the underfed soldiers. But
there were drawbacks. Tories were numerous and
troublesome. It was the region of the outlawed Doanes.
Only that fall, a defiant sheriff at Newtown, the army
depot, had called the court of Bucks County in the
King's name.

Along with General Lord Stirling's three regiments,
Captain Washington and Lieutenant Monroe reached
"Beaumont's" in Solebury, near McKonkey's Ferry;
and their men were under cover, in wooden sheds, by
the twelfth of December. "Blue mounts," the soldiers
called "Beaumonts"; and truly the high hills in the
clear, winey air of winter must have seemed like outlying parts of the great Blue Ridge. But Beaumont
was a farmer, who gave his name to the place. It was
not far from Jericho Hill, a high outlook, "from the
top of which signals could be seen a long way up and
down the river." Monroe, with his captain and Dr.
Ryker, found quarters at William Neely's, at Neely's
mill, in Upper Makefield. Monroe made friends with
young John Davis of the neighborhood, who lived at
Neely's, and who apparently became so fond of Monroe
as to follow him into the next fight and look after him
when he was hit. Davis and Monroe campaigned
together on other occasions. Davis served under
Colonel Richard Butler, in the famous Third Pennsyl-

vania; and was a gallant soldier in General La Fayette's equally famous light-infantry corps. He was among the soldiers who helped to carry La Fayette from the field at the Battle of the Brandywine. All around Jericho Hill (so named from "Lying Jerry" or "Praying Jerry" Cooper of olden days), in cosy little valleys, were excellent farms, with roomy mansions. Stirling had one; Sullivan, one; Knox another — Chapman's. In a back room at Chapman's was Alexander Hamilton, sick of camp fever. His Captain-Lieutenant, James Moore, was sick in another house, Robert Thompson's; in fact, Moore died on the day of the Battle of Trenton. Greene was at Samuel Merrick's. He and his aides ate all the Merrick turkeys — a flock of them; as well as "the calf of the only fresh cow." They drank up the same cow's milk, and ate her butter. Lord Cornwallis said that Greene, next to Washington, was "the most dangerous man in the American army;" and Farmer Merrick must have thought him so, too. Most likely, Monroe and his messmates played similar havoc at Neely's.

On the sunny south side of Jericho Hill, was William Keith's. Here Washington and his aides were quartered; and here the chief, in secret conferences, heard the stories of his spies. One of these, a youth, who, in Trenton, had made believe that he was a simpleton, sent his report through General de Fermoy, commanding the brigade at Coryell's Ferry. Another, John Honeyman, of Griggstown, in Jersey, who had served in General Wolfe's bodyguard at the Heights of Abraham, was known as the "Tory traitor." Thus reputed and thus posing, he was permitted to drive cattle into Trenton. He learned all that was afoot there, went out ostensibly after more cattle, cracked his cart-whip to summon hidden American scouts, whom he knew to be within hearing, and permitted himself to be taken, though simulating resistance to capture.[1] Honeyman it was who helped Washington

---

[1] This famous Jersey spy lived to be ninety-three years old.

to gain a clear idea of affairs at the Hessian post.
Thanks to Honeyman, Washington could see Trenton
more clearly with his eyes shut, in the dark of his bed-
chamber, than if he had gone in the sunglare to the
top of Jericho Hill and turned his powerful spyglasses
toward that distant town. Washington learned from
Honeyman that the Hessians and British were by no
means on the best of terms. As a concrete instance of
unbrotherliness, an English officer had thrown a
punch-bowl at a Hessian's head. Through Honeyman
Washington acquainted himself with Rall's good and
bad points.

To the British, Rall, a veteran of the Seven Years'
War, was "the Hessian lion"; as a rule, "Americans
dreaded him. He, in turn, despised Americans." He
was "brave, active, lively;" he took his time in his
bath while his subordinates cooled their heels in headquarters hall. He was "a good soldier but a bad
general." Trevelyan says: "he was a brave, proud,
stupid man." The fact that he was supercilious towards
his "barbarous enemies" must have amused Washington. It certainly pleased him to have his pouncing
power underestimated at this time. We do not mean
that Honeyman told Washington all these things
about Rall; we do not know the secrets of the Keith
house. But Honeyman had kept a soldier's eyes open;
and ears, too; and either from him or others, Washington gathered all essential information as to the
pickets and as to the disposition of the Hessian troops.
He learned that, for their coming Christmas cheer, the
Hessians had provided themselves with trees, holly,
eggnogg, punch, rumbo, hams and poultry.[1] All this
was as Washington wanted it to be; but if Monroe had
happened to visit Keith's house at the very moment
when Honeyman emerged, what might he have seen?

---

[1] But according to Washington Irving ("Life of Washington," Vol. II, p. 476)
the Christmas feast had little to do with the American plans; "in truth, Washington
would have chosen another day had it been in his power." He wrote to Reed:
"We could not ripen matters for the attack before the time mentioned, so much
out of sorts and so much in want of everything are the troops under Sullivan."

— a smiling general, dismissing a countryman with
thanks? Not at all. On the contrary, Washington
appeared to be displeased with Honeyman — out of
patience, indignant. Here, truly, was a traitor. Indeed, yes, a Tory and a traitor. Washington dissembled. He sent Honeyman to the log guard-house
near by, whence the spy "escaped" that same night,
returning by roundabout ways to Trenton. He told
Rall not to be concerned about the rebel army. It had
gone to pieces. He need not fear attack.

With the British off guard, Washington felt that he
could hazard a stroke. Let the Tories toast the King.
Let Rall drink deep.

In this manner did Washington modestly take a leaf
from the book of the great Ulysses.

Being thus reassured, Washington planned his
"hardy design" against Rall. Three bodies of troops
were to cross at three places — General John Cadwalader's eighteen hundred at Bristol; General James
Ewing's men of the Flying Camp at Trenton; and
Washington, with the main body at McKonkey's.
On the twenty-third, Washington wrote to Cadwalader:

"Christmas day at night, one hour before day, is the time fixed
upon for our attempt on Trenton. For Heaven's sake keep this
to yourself, as the discovery of it may prove fatal to us."

But Cadwalader was not able to cross; nor was
Ewing. Why they failed becomes clear to us after
reading the contemporary account of Captain David
Dexter of Colonel Christopher Lippitt's Rhode Island
Regiment.[1] Dexter's company was at Bristol on
Christmas Eve. The camp was a tented camp in the
woods, with dry leaves for beds. Fires blazed in front
of the tents. "In the evening a violent, cold, snow-
storm began and continued throughout the night and
the next day." Nevertheless, when darkness fell, the
troops marched to the river bank. "Here we waited
with shouldered arms several hours for the floating ice
to open a passage for boats, in which we were to cross,

---

[1] Life and Recollections of John Howland, by Edwin M. Stone, 1857.

but the vast sheets of ice which came down so fully
obstructed the passage that General Cadwalader, our
commander, ordered his division back to their tents.
We suffered more this night from cold in the snow-
storm, than on any we had yet experienced and when
we reached the camp and shook off the snow as much
as possible, and crept into our tents without fire or
light, comfort or repose was out of the question.
Cold — cold — cold; and that continually." This was
on the tidewater; McKonkey's Ferry was above it.
Captain Dexter, referring to McKonkey's, adds: "The
current of the river there, being stronger, swept the
floating ice so as not greatly to obstruct the passage
of the boats."

Let us see what happened at McKonkey's Ferry:
On the day Washington wrote his appeal to Cadwalader,
he picked out the watchword for use in the night
attack. It was Patrick Henry's "Victory or Death."
"Tom Paine's Crisis" was read aloud to the troops:

"These are the times that try men's souls. The summer soldier
and the sunshine patriot will, in this crisis, shrink from the service
of his country; but he that stands it now, deserves the love and
the thanks of man and woman."

On Christmas Eve, the Chief supped with Greene
at Merrick's. One does not read in the Jericho Hill
traditions that there was a single turkey-bone left to
pick, but no doubt the hickory-logs glowed, and Greene,
Sullivan, Mercer, Stirling, Knox and other trusted
officers who were to participate in the *coup de main,*
conferred with the Chief. That there might be no
listeners, the whole family was sent away. When the
council dispersed, each officer understood that Washington meant to drive through, come what might.

Carrington says: "There were young volunteers
from Philadelphia in that command, going forth for
the first time to study war. There were nearly ragged
and shoeless veterans who had passed such storms
and the storms of war before. Stark of Breed's Hill
was there, Glover, the man of Marblehead, a hero of

the Long Island retreat, and Webb and Scott, and William Washington and James Monroe were there. Brain and courage, nerve and faith were there." [1]

Monroe was one of the first, if not the very first, to cross into Jersey. General W. W. H. Davis, of Doylestown, talked with many old-timers of the river townships, some of whom like Coryell of Coryell's Ferry" [2] had known Monroe in their youth. General Davis says: "Lieutenant Monroe, with a piece of artillery, was sent across the river to the Pennington road, but joined the army in the march to Trenton the next morning."

The main body of twenty-four hundred men, with eighteen guns, assembled a mile inland from McKonkey's, as soon as the day began to darken, and marched to the rendezvous of the Ferry.

Every man in the ranks carried three days' rations and forty rounds of ammunition. Each brigade had two guides. Each officer's watch was set by Washington's. Profound silence was enjoined. "No man," ran the orders, "is to quit his ranks on pain of death." There was a trail of blood on the frozen ground, so poorly were some of the soldiers shod. The riflemen of the First Pennsylvania were barefooted. They were brigaded with the regiment to which Monroe was attached. Mention is made by General James Wilkinson, in his Memoirs, of this bloody trail. In fact, he gives a realistic account of the whole scene prior to the crossing.[3] He had accompanied Gates to Philadelphia. That city was in gloom; Gates was in gloom; Wilkinson was sent by Gates with a gloomy letter to Washington. Wilkinson says:

"I was on horseback early that next morning, and reached Newtown about two o'clock. On my arrival there I discovered, to my surprise, that General Washington had moved his headquarters to that place and marched with the troops in that neigh-

---

[1] Battles of the American Revolution, by H. B. Carrington, 1876.
[2] Long years after, Lewis S. Coryell was a welcome visitor at the White House.
[3] Memoirs of My Own Times, by General James Wilkinson; 3 vols., Vol I, pp. 127-28.

borhood. From Colonel Harrison, the General's Secretary, who had been left in charge of his papers, I received the necessary directions, and proceeded in quest of the troops, whose route was easily traced, as there was little snow on the ground, which was tinged here and there with blood from the feet of the men who wore broken shoes. I got up with my brigade near McKonkey's Ferry about dusk, and, inquiring for the Commander-in-Chief, was directed to his quarters, where I found him alone, with his whip in his hand, preparing to mount his horse, which I perceived as I entered.

"When I presented the letter to him, before receiving it, he exclaimed with solemnity: 'What a time is this to hand me letters!' I answered that I had been charged with it by General Gates. 'By General Gates! Where is he?' 'I left him this morning in Philadelphia.' 'What was he doing there?' 'I understood him that he was on his way to Congress.' He earnestly repeated, 'On his way to Congress!' then broke the seal, and I made my bow and joined General St. Clair on the bank of the river.

"Boats were in readiness, and the troops began to cross about sunset, but the force of the current, the sharpness of the frost, the darkness of the night, the ice which made during the operation, and a high wind, rendered the passage of the river extremely difficult; and but for the stentorian lungs, and extraordinary exertions of Colonel Knox, it could not have been effected in season for the enterprise."

It was a never-to-be-forgotten scene — this action-picture by the ferry, with its ice-laden breadth of dark and menacing water a thousand feet across, its fleet of boats, its multitudes of men, its anxious officers and those suggestions of dramatic possibility in the way of rising storm and bloody battle.

The boats had just come down on the swift current from their tree-screened hiding-place at Malta Island, in Knowles' Cove, two miles above. They were of the build known as the Durham — freight boats, between thirty and forty feet long, used to fetch iron ore from upstream and to carry merchandise. Pointed, bow and stern, these black, canoe-like craft were manned by crews of five; and were steered at either end with adjustable oars. Not only did numerous local watermen lend a hand in managing the boats, but there was a regular pontoon-corps. This was made up of Captain Joseph Moulder's Philadelphia longshoremen — eighty-

two young riggers and shipmasters, strong lads and
willing; but, chiefly of Colonel John Glover's well-
disciplined Marblehead regiment of hardy sea-bred
fellows, clad in blue round short jackets and loose
short trousers. Small of stature, brisk, Glover was
full of spirit.

Washington called for a good steersman. Captain
John Blount of Portsmouth, N. H., responded[1] and
was told to take the helm of the first boat. Then
other boats followed, bearing the men of Stephen's
brigade. Once across, these formed in a semi-circle
to protect the landing-place. Washington dismounted,
and stood with intent look, watching the struggle
with the floating ice and with the dark, swift, menacing
flood. Luck seemed against him; yet conditions in his
reach of the river were better than either above or
below. Many have since said that Providence parted
the ice for him.[2]

Washington himself boarded a boat, and followed
the men of Stephen's brigade. His aides were with
him. Having reached the Jersey shore, he stood at the
landing and watched the slow disembarkation of the
other troops. More than once he said to them as they
stepped ashore: "I hope you will fight like men."
He had chosen twelve alert Jerseymen to march with
the army as guides; and wished to engage twelve more
to scout on ahead, on horseback, but only three volunteered — David Lanning, John Guild and John
Muirhead. Washington showed no impatience. Wrapt
in his cloak, he took his seat on an unused beehive,
and sat there in silence. "The ground was covered
with sleet and snow, which was falling; although before
that day there was no snow, only a sprinkling on the
ground." "It was as severe a night as I ever saw,"

---

[1] Rambles of Portsmouth, N. H., p. 262.
[2] Upstream much ice had formed five nights before, and now the current bore
it down in clogging cakes — far less hummocky and formidable, however, than
those shown in the celebrated and much-loved painting, "Washington Crossing
the Delaware," by Emanuel Leutze, who was at Dusseldorf, looking out upon
the drifting ice-blocks of the Rhine when he put upon canvas his idealized scene.

wrote Captain Thomas Rodney of the Delaware (Kent) militia; "the frost was sharp, the current difficult to stem, the ice increasing, the wind high, and at eleven it began to snow. It was only with the greatest care and labor that the horses could be ferried over the river." Hail fell. It beat upon the evergreens and weighed down the branches. It beat in the faces of the men in the earliest stage of the march, but when they turned south it beat upon their backs. At midnight the troops were still crossing; at one o'clock; at two; but, by three, the whole army, guns and horses as well as men, was over.

Then Washington said: "Soldiers, now or never! This is our last chance — march on!" Other officers repeated his words, trumpeting them: "Now or never! March on!" It was slippery work marching, especially on upgrade stretches of the road; nevertheless the troops passed "with a quick step in a body from the river up the cross-roads to the Bear Tavern." From the ferry to this point was a mile and a quarter. Three miles and·a quarter beyond were the hickory woods of Birmingham. It was four o'clock, with six miles to go; and the troops were due to strike at five. They would be hours late. Fortunately the nights were at their longest. Daylight would creep but slowly over the hills. Stark led Sullivan's van. Presently Sullivan sent word to Washington, who was riding with Greene, that the arms were already wet. "Tell your General," said Washington, to the aide, "to use the bayonet and penetrate into the town. The town must be taken. I am resolved to take it."

At Birmingham the troops halted to rest and eat. Here, too, they were divided. Half kept on along the lower, or river, road. This was the right division, under Sullivan. The other half was to take the old Scotch road into the Pennington or upper road; and thus "move circuitously to the north of Trenton." This was the left division, under Greene; and with it rode Washington, Stephen, Mercer and Stirling.

Trenton was to be taken as with a pair of giant fire-tongs; and the arms of the tongs were now opening on the pivot at the parting of the roads.

Captain Washington who, with Lieutenant Monroe, had scouted all night on the Scotch road, rejoined the main body about this time — just before day. They had been on the watch for the enemy's patrol, for spies and for stray horsemen who might give the alarm before the impending stroke could be delivered. Monroe had been on duty many hours, and must have been exceedingly fatigued. But with Captain Washington and his comrades of the Seventh Company he now found himself on the right of Stirling's brigade. As the brigades in the lead were to dash past the junction of King and Queen Streets, and leave it to Stirling to encounter the enemy there, Monroe would be among the very first in the real fight, as he had been the first to cross the river.

It was now light enough to see on ahead; with two miles yet to march. "There, my brave fellows," said Washington, "are the enemies of your country. Remember what you are about to fight for. . . . Press on!" He had caught sight of Trenton. It was now a quarter of eight.

By the roadside, in a woodyard, stood a man with an axe. It was evident from his attitude that he meant to mind his own business.

Washington hailed him. "Which way to the Hessian picket?" he asked.

"I don't know," said the woodchopper.

Captain Forrest of the artillery spoke up. "You may tell," said he; "for that is General Washington."

The woodchopper exclaimed: "God bless and prosper your excellency!" Then, pointing to what the Hessians called an "alarm house," (house of Howell, the cooper) he quickly added: "The picket is in that house, and the sentry stands near that tree."

Orders were given to dislodge the picket. One of the Hessian outguard at that instant cried: " Who is

there?" David Lanning, the miller-guide, who was in
the very van, replied: "A friend." "A friend to
whom?" "A friend to General Washington."

The whole picket ran from the alarm-house into the
road crying: "*Der Feind! Der Feind! heraus! heraus!*"
("The enemy! The enemy! Turn out! Turn out!")

They fired, and ran; and then fired again, as soon as
they had reloaded. At this moment, when Washington,
with his sword raised, was giving his orders, a musket-
ball passed between his fingers, slightly grazing them.
"That has passed by!" said he.

Captain Samuel Morris of the Philadelphia light-
horse saw the lieutenant of the picket-guard by the
roadside, weltering in his blood. He wanted to aid
him, but could not halt. His Quaker conscience smote
him. "Poor devil!" said the more hardened ones,
hurrying on. There was a forward rush. Far back
along the road the American column quickened its
pace. As the soldiers of the left division thus broke
into a run, there came across the fields a welcome
cannon crack. In this way the right division proclaimed
its presence on the river road. Sullivan had taken
the yager picket-post. The Trenton tongs were closing
on Rall's mercenaries, and would soon so clamp them
that escape would be impossible.

But let us revert for a moment to these "Brass
Caps," as the Americans called them.

We have said that the Hessians were expected to
carouse on Christmas day; and so they did. As for
Colonel Rall, says C. C. Haven,[1] "he was a brave,
jovial officer, fond of music, parade, wine, hot whisky-
punch, and of card-playing. Stacy Potts, a Quaker,
who was his host, was no card-player and no Tory,
but a non-combatant, of course, yet good for a game
of chequers or fox-and-geese with an enemy." Rall
was over-confident, not to say reckless. He underestimated the enterprise of the "Yankee ragamuffins."
"We want no trenches; we'll at them with the bayonet."

[1] In An Historic Manual, Trenton, N. J., 1871.

Again he cut short the speech of some one who sought
to warn him: "This is all idle! it is old woman's talk."
"Fudge," said he to Major von Dechow, "these
country clowns can't whip us." True, he sent out
patrols; yet what he did was done not vigilantly but
in a lax way. He drank and played cards all Christmas
night. This was not at the Quaker's, but at the house
of Abraham Hunt, the rich merchant. There was a
particularly jolly party in the parlor, so that when a
Tory spy from Bucks, Wall or Mahl, appeared at the
street door, the negro porter refused to let him step
into the room. The intruder might stand there in the
entry, if he pleased, and write what he wished to
communicate. He did so. It was, in fact, a notification
that the rebels had crossed the river — a most timely
warning. Rall, at that moment, was dealing the cards.
He was having too good a time to permit himself to
be disturbed. He thrust the note in his pocket. He
said afterwards that if he had only read it the terrible
thing would not have happened. But we cannot feel
sure of that. Even if he had read the Tory's warning,
it is doubtful whether he would have given himself
any particular concern about it. Acting on a rumor
that had reached Princeton, General Grant had warned
him of an impending attack. Yes; and sure enough
it had occurred on Christmas Eve. An American
scouting party, out without Washington's knowledge,
had foolishly fired on one of the picket posts. Many
writers speak of Captain William Washington as the
leader of the scouts in question. Statements such as
this have caused some confusion and misapprehension.
General William S. Stryker, whom Trevelyan calls
"a skilled examiner of records," puts the mooted
point under his spotlight, and we may well accept his
conclusion. It is a good thing for us to thus get a
"last word" on this; because if, "Captain Washington,
with seventy men," knocked at the gates of Trenton
on Christmas Eve, it might be assumed that Monroe
was with him. Burr, for political reasons, sought to

minimize the value of Monroe's military services; and it is desirable, therefore, to make those services stand out exactly for what they are worth. Innuendo is harmless when the simple truth is told. Stryker's conclusive passage ("The Battles of Trenton and Princeton," p. 121) is as follows:

"The attacking party consisted of about twenty men of Stephen's brigade. History differs as to who had command of this little force. In some cases it is given to William Washington, but he was not in Stephen's brigade. There is more reason to believe that it was the company commanded by Captain Richard Clough Anderson of Colonel Charles Scott's regiment, Fifth Virginia Continental line. The subaltern officers of this company were John Anderson, first lieutenant; William Bentley, second lieutenant; Robert Tompkins, ensign. It seems that the party was scouting through Hunterdon County, without Washington's permission, and as a mere adventure drove in the picket, wounded six men, seized their firelocks and ammunition, and hastened away to join the regiment, which to their surprise was then crossing the river into the Jerseys."

Stryker re-enforces his statement with an extract from the letter-book of General Robert Anderson, hero of Fort Sumter, who was a son of Captain Richard Clough Anderson of the Fifth Virginia Continentals. In his memorandum, General Anderson tells of the brush at the outpost and of the rebuke administered by General Washington as soon as he learned what had happened. "I have frequently heard my father remark," says General Anderson, "that he never saw General Washington exhibit so much anger as he did when he told him where he had been and what he had done. He turned to General S(tephen) and asked how he dared to send a patrol from camp without his authority, remarking: 'You, sir, may have ruined all my plans, by having put them on their guard.'"[1]

At any rate the infatuated Rall regarded this as the attack of which he had been advised. Accordingly, his mellow mind dismissed all thought of winter thun-

---

[1] The Battles of Trenton and Princeton, W. S. Stryker, p. 373. See also C. C. Haven's Historic Manual, p. 30. Captain R. C. Anderson, though in a Virginia regiment, lived in Kentucky. Lars Anderson of Cincinnati was another son.

derbolts forged in the smithy of the pitiable **Mr.**
Washington at his camp of ragged rebels over by Jericho Hill. At six, in the morning, Rall was "sleeping
heavily." At eight, his brigade-adjutant knocked
frantically at his door. Rall rolled out of bed. In his
night-clothes, he appeared at an upper window. "What
is the matter? I will be out in a minute." Soon thereafter he was heard to say "My God, Lieutenant Engel-
hardt, the picket is already coming in! Push your
cannon ahead!"

Now again we go back to the column with which
Monroe was marching. King and Queen Streets con-
verge in the shape of a sharp V, pointing north. The
Pennington road brought Washington and Knox to
the very point of the V. Knox at once posted Captain
Thomas Forrest's six-gun battery and the battery
under Captain Alexander Hamilton. Forrest fired
down King Street; Hamilton down Queen. Things
were soon in a roar. Smoke clouds arose. The spirit
of the men gave great zest to the fight. Washington
watched them. "His Excellency was pleased at their
undaunted courage. Not a soul was found skulking,
but all were fierce for battle." [1] Escorted by the First
Philadelphia City Troop, he then rode to high ground
near by, took post there, and directed the whole affair.
The town was more than ever in an uproar. Fearing
to trust their wet firelocks, many of the Americans
were using their "pikes, spontoons and bayonets."
"There were a few cannon shots by the Germans, and
a little musketry."

---

[1] An officer on Washington's staff says that the General's face lighted
up as soon as he heard the boom of Sullivan's cannon on the river road. "We
could see a great commotion down toward the meetinghouse, men running here
and there, officers swinging their swords, artillerymen harnessing their horses.
Captain Forrest unlimbered his guns, Washington gave the order to advance, and
we rushed to the junction of King and Queen Streets. The riflemen under Colonel
Hand and Scott's and Lawson's battalions went upon the run through the fields
on the left to gain possession of the Princeton road. The Hessians were just ready
to open fire with two of their cannon when Captain Washington and Lieutenant
Monroe with their men rushed forward and captured them. We saw Rall come
riding up the street from his headquarters which were at Stacy Potts' house.
We could hear him shouting in Dutch: "My brave soldiers, advance!"

Knox says that the Continentals "entered the town pell mell." He adds: "The hurry, fright and confusion of the enemy was not unlike that which it will be when the last trumpet shall sound. They endeavored to form in the streets, the heads of which we had previously the possession of with cannon and howitzers; these, however, in the twinkling of an eye, cleared the streets. The backs of the houses were resorted to for shelter. These proved ineffectual; the musketry soon dislodged them. Finally they were driven through the town into an open plain beyond." Here they formed an instant. During the contest in the streets, measures were taken for putting an entire stop to their retreat by posting troops and cannon in such passes and roads as it was possible for them to get away by." It is General Stryker who now tells of Monroe's part in the most brilliant episode of the battle — the dash for the Hessian brass pieces in King Street:

"Lord Stirling's brigade, heretofore the reserve, was now about at the head of King Street,[1] and the demoralizing effect of the guns of the American batteries being noticed, an instant charge was ordered. Colonel Weedon's regiment of Stirling's brigade was in the advance, and Captain William Washington of the regiment, with his lieutenant, James Monroe, leading their men, made a quick dash down the street and took two brass three-pounder guns of the Rall regiment. Both officers were wounded in this exploit, the Captain being injured in both hands, and Monroe hit in the shoulder by a ball, which cut an artery."

It was the left shoulder, and the ball remained in it as long as Monroe lived. It is probably in his coffin today. Unless speedily succored, a man thus hit would bleed to death in a few minutes. "If surgical aid had not been promptly forthcoming," comments Trevelyan, "he might have died then and there; and his doctrine, which in any case would hardly fail to have been invented, would have borne some different title."

These Hessian guns stood in the street near Rall's headquarters. Carrington says: "They had been partly manned and were ready to deliver fire," when

---

[1] King Street is now Warren; Queen Street is now Greene.

Washington and Monroe rushed upon the gunners and brought away the pieces. Though a bullet had gone through one hand and another shot had torn the other hand, Captain Washington ran into the house in pursuit of the Hessian gunners and captured them."

Joseph White[1] helped to take the three-pounders. He wrote about it quaintly, thus:

"Our advanced guard opened from right to left; we gave them four or five cannisters of shot, following then to their main body, and displayed our columns. The third shot we fired broke the axletree of the piece — we stood there some time idle, they firing upon us. Colonel Knox rode up and said: 'My brave lads, go up and take those two field-pieces sword in hand. There is a party going, you must go and join them.' Captain A said: 'Sergeant White, you heard what the Colonel said — you must take the whole of those that belonged to that piece, and join them.' This party was commanded by Captain Washington and Lieutenant Monroe, our late President of the United States, both of which were wounded.

"The party inclined to the right. I hollowed as loud as I could scream to the men to run for their lives right up to the pieces. I was the first that reached them. They had all left it, except one man holding vent. 'Run, you dog,' cried I, holding my sword over his head. He looked up and saw it, and ran. We put in a cannister of shot (they had put in the cartridge before they left it) and fired. The battle ceased. I took a walk over the field of battle, and my blood chilled to see such horror and distress."

Can it be claimed that this quick action was in any way vital? Not at all. The surprise was itself so complete, so demoralizing to the enemy, so overwhelming, that the result would not have been very different even if Rall should have got his guns at work, full blast, in King Street; and held on there a long time. "All the outposts were struck at once." Never was a well-organized stand established by the bewildered enemy. But the hottest spot was here in King Street; and it was William Washington and James Monroe who smothered the only fire that threatened great loss of

---

[1] A Narrative of Events in the Revolutionary War, with an account of the Battles of Trenton, Trenton Bridge and Princeton, by Joseph White.

life. Their dash in the nick of time hastened the victory.

At this juncture, General Washington ordered a discharge of cannister. "Sir," said Captain Morgan, "they have struck." "Struck!" said Washington. "Yes," said Morgan, "their colors are down." "So they are!" said Washington; and at once spurred his chestnut-sorrel into a gallop, riding towards them.

Wilkinson says:[1] "I had been despatched to General Washington for orders and rode up to him at the moment Colonel Rall, supported by a file of sergeants, was presenting his sword. On my approach, the Commander-in-Chief took me by the hand and observed: 'Major Wilkinson, this is a glorious day for our country,' his countenance beaming with complacency."

He promoted Knox to be Major-General. Other officers were promoted on the field, including Monroe, who was made Captain for "bravery under fire."

John Habberton[2] speaks of Monroe as "an eighteen-year old Virginia boy who grew a great deal that morning."

Some of the Hessians got away because Ewing was unable to cross the river and block the Burlington road; but close upon a thousand of the mercenaries, with all their arms and plunder, remained in Washington's hands. The effect of the victory was a hundredfold greater than the physical results might indicate. Beaten America was back in battle quite unbeaten — never to be beaten, in fact.

Lord George Germain wrote: "All our hopes were blasted by the unhappy affair at Trenton."

The Princeton story is just as thrilling as the Trenton story. One was the other's sequel, and each was equally brilliant. But we are only licensed to follow Monroe, who was under a surgeon's care — probably Dr. Ryker's. Let it be enough to say of Princeton, that Washington outdid himself in that stroke. Lord

[1] In his Memoirs, Vol. I, p. 131.
[2] In his George Washington, p. 133.

Cornwallis thought he had "the old fox"; but
Washington eluded him. At midnight, January 3,
after the battle of Assunpink Creek, he brightened his
fires and slipped away towards Princeton by the
southerly road. He was not missed till morning.
When, at an early hour, he began his cannon-fire,
it sounded like "winter thunder in the British rear" —
startling, ominous! Lord Cornwallis cried out: "Where
can that firing be?" "My Lord," said Sir William
Erskine, "it is Washington at Princeton."

"When the army recrossed the Delaware into
Bucks," says General W. W. H. Davis[1], "Lieutenant
Monroe was taken to the residence of William Neely,
the home of young Davis. He spent some time there,
to recover from his wound, and was then removed to
the house of Judge Wynkoop near Newtown." He
could not have fallen into more friendly hands. The
Holland Dutch Wynkoops, or Winekoops, were noted
patriots — no better in all Bucks. Judge Henry
Wynkoop, "the personal friend of Washington and
Hamilton," was "a remarkably handsome man," and
an important one, serving in the Continental Congress
and in the First Congress of the United States. It
was he who gave Washington his "Bucks county
plough." His wife was Ann Knipers Wynkoop. Their
daughter won Monroe's heart. She was Christine
Wynkoop, but she was already pledged and so was
obliged to reject the young Virginian when, after the
war, he asked her to be his wife[2].

Captain Washington may have been with Monroe
at this time; but, if so, it is not noted in the Bucks
chronicles. We can imagine what a deal of talk there

[1] Life of John Davis, by W. W. H. Davis, A.M., 1886, p. 16.   Miller Neely,
Irish-born and a good American, lived to see Monroe President of the United
States. Davis and Monroe kept up their acquaintance. Similarly his son,
Major-General John Davis, Jr., a Congressman, commander of La Fayette's
escort and defender of Andrew Jackson, was Monroe's personal friend.

[2] This love affair is touched upon in "Vredens-Hof," a monograph, privately
printed, 1909, by Dr. Julian T. Hammond, Jr., of Philadelphia. "Vredens-Hof,"
built by Nicholas Wynkoop in 1739, is owned by one of Judge Wynkoop's descendants, Mrs. E. R. Stitt, wife of Admiral E. R. Stitt, Surgeon-General, U.S.N.

was in the Jericho Hill neighborhood about the battles
of Trenton and Princeton. Before he left Keith's
house, where he had been quartered, General Hugh
Mercer, mortally wounded at Princeton, told Mrs.
Keith of a curious premonitory dream of his the night
before. He dreamt that a huge bear had attacked
and overpowered him. This dream, with its seeming
sequel, was on the superstitious Jericho Hill tongue
for many a day.

As soon as he had recovered from his wound, if not
from his love affair, Monroe rejoined the army, which
remained in winter-quarters at Morristown until the
twenty-eighth of May. He was appointed "additional
aid" to General Lord Stirling. Thereafter he participated in the marches and manoeuvres of Washington's
troops during the long period preceding the battle of
Brandywine.

In that bloody clinch, General Stirling was on the
extreme American right, well up stream, with only
Bland's horse beyond. He it was whom the red-coated
flankers first struck. He was rolled back over hill
and hollow, and, along with Stephen's division, was
obliged to give ground mile on mile. It was about four
o'clock on the hot afternoon of the eleventh of September when the right wing, composed of these two divisions under Sullivan, was broken by the heavy pressure
of Lord Cornwallis bearing down with the better part
of the British army. The Third Virginia held on till
both flanks were turned. Half of the officers and a
third of the men were killed or wounded. Colonel
Marshall's horse was twice shot.

It was Trenton reversed. One may imagine the
surprise, the deep chagrin, the humiliating predicament
of Monroe and his comrades, outflanked and hard
driven, as they vainly sought to retire in order upon
Birmingham hill, with the hope and purpose of making
a stand at the Quaker meeting-house there. But,
before they could form in their new position they were
again beaten back, and it was only the arrival of

Washington, La Fayette and, finally, Greene, with
fresh troops, that saved the day.

As it is on record that he offered aid to the wounded
La Fayette, Monroe most likely took part in the
Birmingham meeting-house melee in which the Marquis
was shot. Monroe's old regiment, the Third, suffered
fewer casualties than some of the other Virginia
commands; such, for example, as the Seventh, which
was badly cut up. It was, indeed, a bitter, if heroic
day.

Not quite so bloody, and, certainly not so bitter in
the estimation of the young Virginia officers, was the
battle of Germantown, nearly a month later, on the
foggy morning of the fourth of October. Yet, even in
this fight, there was great chagrin among them because
of General Stephen's blunder and the costly *contretemps*
at the Chew House, which deprived them of the victory
they expected and really deserved. Stirling's reserve
division it was that made the fight for the Chew House;
and that, too, with the greatest gallantry, under the
eye of the Chief. Here fell Lieutenant Matthew Smith,
of "Hackwood Hall," a brave young Virginian, who
volunteered to carry a flag of truce across the fire-swept
lawn. Others equally brave led their men against the
murderous musketry of the Fortieth British regiment,
under Colonel Thomas Musgrave, who had seized the
fortress-like, many-windowed stone mansion, holding
it thereafter against all assaults. Though some of
Monroe's friends reached Philadelphia that day, it
was not as victors but as prisoners.

Monroe now became a full-fledged aide-de-camp.
He seems to have profited by the acquaintance and
condescension of Stirling, who was a most likeable
character. He was William Alexander, heir to a British
title, claimant of millions of acres of Nova Scotia land,
and lord by courtesy. He lived at Baskingridge, N. J.,
his wife being a sister of the distinguished Governor
Livingston. Stirling was eight years older than
Washington, and had been Governor Shirley's secretary

in French and Indian times. He was tall, portly, dignified — a man of polish and of courteous manners. Small wonder the young Virginian was attracted by the prospect of serving as an aide to such an officer. In General Orders, issued at Whitemarsh, November 20, 1777, a month before the establishment of the cantonment at Valley Forge, Washington appointed him a full-fledged aide-de-camp to Lord Stirling, with the rank of major. In the Valley Forge Orderly Book of General George Weedon, page 134, we read: "Lieut. John Marshall is by the Judge Advocate appointed Deputy Judge Advocate in the Army of the United States, and is to be respected as such. James Monroe Esquire formerly appointed an additional Aide de Camp to Major General Lord Stirling is now appointed Aide de Camp to his Lordship in the room of Major [William] Wilcox resigned, and is to be respected as such."

Monroe was a member of Stirling's family until midsummer of the following year. He saw the inside of things at division headquarters; and also grasped the significance of what was going on at the Potts house during the Valley Forge encampment. It was Stirling who told Washington the raw, unflattering truth as to the Conway machinations, and thus, as Saffel puts it, "upset" the Cabal. What a lesson in intrigue, in plot-hatching, was here for a youth who, by and by, would be obliged to use his wits against even such a one as Talleyrand! Later, Monroe realized that he had made a mistake when he took service with Stirling, but as a junior, at his headquarters, he certainly was in a fine school for the study of men. Stirling himself administered the oath of allegiance to the officers who had served under Conway. The oath was on a printed slip of paper, with blank spaces for name, rank and the like. The originals of these oaths are preserved today in the Government Archives at Washington, and constitute a precious set of Revolutionary autographs.

Monroe had many friends in camp, Marshall among

them. It was Attorney General Wayne MacVeagh who said of them:

"As two Virginian youths lay sleeping in their huts that winter at Valley Forge, I wonder if any such forecast of their country's future, or any forecast of their own, came to them in their dreams. Of these youths one was John Marshall, who was destined to lay broad and deep the foundation of his country's greatness, and thereby assist to secure the glory and the blessings of free institutions to untold generations of men; and the other was James Monroe, who was destined to proclaim the truth that this whole American continent, from end to end, and from sea to sea, must be regarded by all other nations as dedicated to liberty and to bequeath to us the duty of giving practical and complete effect to the noble and inspiring doctrine which bears his name."[1]

Another young Virginian at Valley Forge was Lieutenant Philip Slaughter:

"His messmates were the two Portersfields, Johnson and Lieutenant John (Chief Justice) Marshall. They were reduced sometimes to a single shirt, having to wrap themselves in a blanket when it was washed; not one soldier in five had a blanket. The snow was knee-deep all the winter, and stained with blood from the naked feet of the soldiers. From the body of their shirts, the officers had collars and wristbands made to appear on parade."[2]

But all was well when winter ended. Steuben had made the Continental Army over into an excellent fighting machine, so that, in spite of Charles Lee's extraordinary recreancy on the twenty-eighth of June, it did very well indeed at Monmouth.

Monroe's part at Monmouth is indicated in a letter addressed by him to General Washington, at four p.m., June twenty-eighth. Stirling at that time "commanded the left wing of the army, as reformed by Washington after he had checked the retreat of Lee." "Monroe with his command," notes S. M. Hamilton, "had been charged with the important duty of following the enemy's movements and of reporting them to Lord

---

[1] Address of Wayne MacVeagh, in the Hall of the House of Representatives, at Washington, February 4, 1901.— John Marshall, by John Dillon, 3 vols., Vol. I, pp. 17, 18.

[2] History of St. Mark's Parish, Culpeper County, Virginia, by the Rev. Philip Slaughter, D.D., 1887.

Stirling and also directly to the Commander-in-Chief."
Monroe says:

"Upon not receiving any answer to my first information and
observing the enemy inclining toward your right, I thought it
advisable to hang as close upon them as possible — I am at present
within four hundred yards of their right — I have only about
seventy men who are now fatigued much. I have taken three
prisoners. If I had six horsemen I think if I co'd serve you in no
other way I sho'd in the course of the night procure good intelligence w'h I wo'd as soon as possible convey to you."

Thus Monroe, barely out of his teens, had already
participated in battles at Harlem Heights, White
Plains, Trenton, Brandywine, Germantown, and Monmouth; and had borne a useful part in each.

CHAPTER IV

TRANSITION TIME

The cannon of Monmouth soon cooled; but not so its passions. Some of the heat of that exceedingly hot day — a day of dust, of fire, of long-continued fury — got into the hearts of the American officers, who ever after were embittered against Lee[1] because of his extraordinary, if not treasonable, tergiversation.

Lee's trial by court-martial began at New Brunswick on July 4, and lasted until August 12. The court moved with the army, convening successively at Paramus, Peekskill and North Castle. Did young Monroe dance attendance upon it? Its president was General Stirling, who, commanding the left wing at Monmouth, had added to his laurels by posting Carrington's Battery in the very nick of time and at the very spot where its fire took a costlier toll than even a brave and determined enemy could afford to pay. Unless Stirling released his aide immediately after the battle — a thing he would not be likely to think of at such a time, much less do — then it follows that Monroe may have become a handy helper in executing the numerous duties connected with the procedure of the court-martial. We are by no means sure of this. It is only in the concurrent data of the hour that we find warrant for the suggestion that Monroe witnessed the disciplining of this notorious and enigmatic character. But, when the Court found him guilty and when

---

[1] This eccentric man provoked more profanity than any other officer of the Revolution. How he made Washington swear at the crisis of the fight is well known. Alexander Macaulay, the traveler, met a "character" at Hanover Town, Va., whom he asked "where he had been" of recent years. "Been, sir? Why, I have been all over the world; I have been in the American army, sir; I saw the British die with heat and fatigue at Monmouth; I saw that Dammed Rascal General Lee's retrograde manœuvre; and have seen many strange things."— William and Mary Quarterly, Vol. XI, p. 182.

Congress broke him, why was Monroe unconvinced as to Lee's turpitude? On the surface, is it not rather remarkable that Monroe should have retained his faith in Lee while so many other officers, old and young alike, lost theirs? He had come under Lee's influence at Williamsburg; possibly on the Hudson; and certainly at Valley Forge. It would not have been out of character with the older man if he had flattered the obscure youth — obscure, at least, prior to the capture of the brass pieces at Trenton. While the court was taking testimony, Colonel Walter Stewart wrote of the defendant: "His complaisance to the officers is excessive, and he does everything in his power to gain their affections."

To speculate further, it may be that certain Virginians, who were under the influence of Richard Henry Lee, defended the accused officer merely because of his name. Who but had the greatest respect for the Lees? True enough, General Charles, a soldier of fortune, an eighteenth century cosmopolite, as brilliantly bookish as he was caustic of speech, was of British blood and quite un-Virginian; but Monroe may have been too mindful of Stratford and Chantilly and may have permitted his natural Potomac pride to influence his judgment. For a young man brought up as Monroe was, "Lee" was a name to conjure with, from whatever part of the world its owner came.

But to many of the American officers Charles Lee was a double-dealer — a dastard, indeed. Why did he act so capriciously? Why did he dally? He would sell out America for a dukedom — this recreant ally, this false friend who made his vows to Liberty only that he might betray her. No, they had no patience with the man — not the least. Others were silent. They could not understand such misconduct. Still others spoke up for him — Knox, Greene and "Legion Harry" Lee. "Some of the best patriot officers," says Sydney George Fisher[1] "remained friendly with him

---

[1] The Struggle for American Independence, by Sydney George Fisher, 2 vols., Vol. II, p. 196.

I [James Monroe] do acknowledge the UNITED STATES of AME-
RICA to be Free, Independent and Sovereign States, and
declare, that the people thereof owe no allegiance or obedience to George the Third, King of Great-Britain; and I
renounce, refuse and abjure any allegiance or obedience to
him; and I do [swear] that I will, to the utmost of my power, support, maintain and defend the said
United States against the said King George the Third, his
heirs and succeffors, and his or their abettors, affiftants and
adherents, and will ferve the faid United States in the office of
which I now hold, with
fidelity, according to the beft of my fkill and underftanding.

lxxv

OATH OF ALLEGIANCE, VALLEY FORGE, MAY 16, 1778

(From "Writings of Monroe," by Stanislaus Murray Hamilton)

to the last." Speaking of Monroe's Westmoreland schoolmate who was made Captain for his soldierly services on Monmouth field, Senator Beveridge[1] says: "Marshall felt that more was made of Lee's misconduct than the original offense deserved. Writing as the chosen biographer of Washington, Marshall gives both sides of this controversy." "Girardin," adds Beveridge, in a note, "follows Marshall in his fair treatment of Lee."

Moreover, there was another classmate in the case and, here it is that we find the most plausible explanation of Monroe's trust in Lee. This other classmate was John Francis Mercer.[2] Mercer was a year younger than Monroe. Like Monroe, a lieutenant in the Third Virginia, wounded at Brandywine, promoted to a captaincy rank from June 27, 1777, he had left the line to serve as aide-de-camp to Lee. He resigned in disgust on account of the finding of the court, to wit, guilty on all three charges of disobeying orders, unnecessary retreat, and disrespect to the Commander-in-Chief. Like Monroe, Mercer returned to Virginia, remained awhile inactive, studied law with Jefferson, imbibed democratic-republican doctrines, re-entered the military service and, after the war, became distinguished as a statesman. In fact, as we outline Mercer's career, we seem also to be outlining that of Monroe. It is when we come to fill in the sketch that we realize how different they grew to be. Especially if we accept Jefferson's opinion of Mercer, as given in a letter addressed to

---

[1] The Life of John Marshall, by Albert Beveridge, Vol. I, pp. 137, 138.

[2] John Francis Mercer (born May 17, 1759; died August 30, 1821) was a son of John Mercer of Stafford, author of "Laws of Virginia," who had ten children by his first wife, George Mason's aunt Catherine; and nine by his second wife, Ann, daughter of Col. Mungo Roy of Essex. John Francis served under Lawson at Guilford Courthouse; and, after the disbandment of Lawson's brigade, joined Lafayette whom he followed to Yorktown. He studied law with Jefferson, and was in the Continental Congress of 1782-85. In the latter year, he married Sophia Sprigg of "Cedar Park," West River, Md., whither he moved. He was a delegate to the Federal Constitutional Convention. He refused to sign the Constitution because of its consolidating tendencies. He was in Congress, 1792-1794, and Governor of Maryland in 1801. His daughter, Margaret Mercer, freed the slaves of "Cedar Park," and established a school for girls. She was known as "the Hannah More of America."

Madison from Annapolis.[1] But just now, so close were
the ex-aides-de-camp that it would have been strange
indeed if Mercer and Monroe had not talked themselves into accord on the subject in question.

But we know a little more of Lee than they did.[2]
Since the time of Girardin[3] who, as a guest at Monticello took his cues from Jefferson, and since Chief
Justice Marshall's day, additional evidence as to the
mainspring of Lee's action has developed. In 1857
there was discovered among the private papers of
General Sir William Howe's private secretary a plan
of campaign for the British army. The plan was dated
March 29, 1777. It proposed a scheme for the conquest
of the colonies. It was written by General Charles
Lee then in British custody in New York City; and
that, too, at a moment when Washington, in order to
save Lee from deportation as a British deserter, was
notifying Howe of his purpose to hold five Hessian
officers as hostages for Lee. That Marshall, Mercer,
Monroe and Washington himself were unaware of the
existence of Lee's plan goes without saying.

Lee was dismissed by Congress. He retired to his
"Prato Rio" estate in Berkeley County, Virginia,
where, with General Adam Stephen as a neighbor, he
lived like a hermit in "a barn-like house that was a
little more than a shell." There was a kitchen in one
corner, a bed in another, books in a third and saddles
and harness in a fourth. Chalk marks indicated par-
titions. He was well supplied with dogs. He said that
when men got to be as good as dogs he would be "as
warm a philanthropist as Mr. Adams himself."

[1] Dated April 25, 1784. Jefferson disliked Mercer's ambitions and intriguing.
The letter is partly in cypher.— Writings of Thomas Jefferson (Ford), Vol. III,
p. 427.
[2] See the Lee papers, 4 vols., New York Historical Society Collections. These
papers contain "The Treason of Charles Lee," by Dr. G. H. Moore, Librarian
of the Society, 1858. H. C. Lodge, "The Story of the Revolution," Vol. I, p. 320,
finds "a strong suspicion of treason clinging to him." Trevelyan, in "The American Revolution," p. 402, speaks of his "treason."
[3] Louis Girardin finished Burk's History of Virginia after Burk had been killed
in a duel. Girardin wrote the fourth volume.

It is apparent that Monroe was brought up in no milk-and-water school. The controversies over the battles were not quite so bloody as the battles themselves; but they were lively affairs, and left various preconceptions and prejudices which, as one fancies, influenced him during his political career. He had an excellent opportunity to see with his own eyes almost all the great characters of the Revolution. Lee was not the only celebrity with a seamy side. Much as we dislike to say it, candor compels us to confess that many a worthy had his unworthy habits — or to speak euphemistically, his weaknesses. One weakness was for the bottle. Stirling was no exception. At any rate he had his critics on that score. But, then, Stirling was maligned after he had helped to expose Conway. Even Lafayette, whom the plotters played upon, mistakenly thought Stirling actuated by sinister ambition.

As for Monroe, who was a serious-minded youth — he was twenty-one April 28, 1779 — he must have seen a great deal in army life in no way to his liking. If he had been gifted with a strong sense of humor, he might have enjoyed himself more. But he was not of that type. We have a few of his letters that date from this time; and they show that he was apt to think things over rather slowly and soberly. He seems to have had no trouble whatever with General Lord Stirling. Ardent as was his desire to remain at the front long enough to see the Revolution through, his good sense admonished him that as an aide[1] he was in the wrong branch of the service. As for getting back into the Continental line, which he had left at one of the regimental rearrangements,[2] that was out of the question.

---

[1] Hamilton was an aide and got along well for a while; but, by and by, even he was rebuked by his chief (whom on one occasion he had kept waiting) and resigned rather petulantly. Hamilton, however, was of the stuff of which heroes are made, and again covered himself with glory at Yorktown.

[2] Officers were "retired," when at the various "rearrangements" there were found to be more officers in the service than vacancies of their grade. For example, if there were only eight regiments, and ten officers bore the commission of major, two would of necessity be retired. In case the eight holding the oldest commissions desired to remain in service, the two youngest would be retired for juniority.— Virginia Magazine of History and Biography, Vol. XX, p. 279.

Thus convinced, he tried to become an officer in the
State line; but here again he made a miscalculation —
he had failed to foresee the difficulties that would trip
him. He had the best of credentials. General Washington wrote, May 30, 1779, to Archibald Cary:

"I very sincerely lament that the situation of our service will
not permit us to do justice to the merits of Major Monroe, who will
deliver you this, by placing him in the army upon some satisfactory
footing. But as he is on the point of leaving us and expresses an
intention of going southward, where a new scene has opened, it is
with pleasure I take occasion to express to you the high opinion
I have of his worth. The zeal he discovered by entering the service
at an early period, the character he supported in his regiment,
and the manner in which he distinguished himself at Trenton,
where he received a wound, induces me to appoint him to a
captaincy in one of the additional regiments. This regiment failing
from the difficulty of recruiting, he entered into Lord Stirling's
family, and has served two campaigns as a volunteer aide to his
Lordship. He has, in every instance, maintained the reputation
of a brave, active and sensible officer. As we cannot introduce
him into the Continental line, it were to be wished that the State
could do something for him, to enable him to follow the bent of
his military inclination, and render service to his country. If an
event of this kind could take place, it would give me particular
pleasure; as the esteem I have for him, and a regard for his merit,
conspire to make me earnestly wish to see him provided for in
some handsome way."

Colonel Cary,[1] of course, could do little or nothing
for Monroe. He did not get his field commission. The
Legislature was not over-eager to authorize the raising
of a regiment in which he was to be Lieutenant-Colonel;
but, it was mainly owing to the exhausted state of
Virginia's finances that he could make no progress.
Had he been a Lafayette perhaps he could have drawn
enough troops together at his own expense to re-enter
the service; but he had no considerable funds of his
own. Marshall was a supernumerary; so was he.
Marshall was back in the land of his lady-love; but
Monroe had left a sweetheart behind him. He was

---

[1] Known as "Old Iron," because he owned iron works — a small-bodied,
fiery man, who, as Speaker of the Senate, took a leading part in the Revolution.
He was the hero of Jefferson's dictator-and-dagger story. He sided with Pendleton, as against Patrick Henry.

unhappy — out of luck, despondent. In one particular — loss of place in the line, which he could not regain — his friend Mercer was in the same predicament. The best they could do was to enter the Governor's office as aides. There was one advantage in the arrangement — they could while away the time in the study of law. Jefferson had not practiced since 1774, but he welcomed the young officers, both as students and as aides.

Monroe found many changes at Williamsburg. The times were out of joint. Charles Campbell, the Virginia historian, calls attention to the fact that in the early part of 1779, "the demoralizing influences of war were making themselves manifest." It was a period of money-making, stock-jobbing and selfish speculation. Washington noted the phenomenon with some alarm. April 22, 1779, he wrote from the camp at Middlebrook, Conn., "Alas, what is virtue come to — what a miserable change has four years produced in the temper and dispositions of the sons of America! It really shocks me to think of it!"

But even if distemper had seized people and public finances were low, Jefferson was in full activity. He was busy not only with state affairs but was remodelling the curriculum of William and Mary College. Both Jefferson and Washington disliked the idea of sending American youth over the sea. Monroe wanted to leave Williamsburg and make his way to France. Jefferson gave him letters; but at the same time he felt that it was better to study at home than abroad.[1] However, William and Mary was not to profit then by Jefferson's plans. The York-James peninsula was exposed to invasion; so the State Capital was transferred from Williamsburg to Richmond, which seemed

---

[1] Washington wrote to Governor Brooke of Virginia: "It is with indescribable regret that I have seen the youth of the United States migrating to foreign countries." Washington, like Jefferson, wanted a national university. With Washington, too, originated West Point Academy. See an excellent monograph by Herbert B. Adams on William and Mary College in Circulars of Information of the Bureau of Education, No. 1 (1887) pp. 11-89.

a safer place than events soon proved it to be. The change hurt the college. At the same time it left Monroe in a quandary. Should he stay and study law under the celebrated George Wythe, or should he follow Jefferson to Richmond? He wrote to his uncle, Joseph Jones[1] on the subject; and here, dated March 7, 1780 is the reply:

"This post will bring you a letter from me, accounting for your not hearing sooner what had been done in your affairs. If your overseer sends up before next post-day you shall hear the particulars. Charles Lewis, going down to the college, gives me an opportunity of answering, by him, your inquiry respecting your removal with the Governor, or attending Mr. Wythe's lectures. If Mr. Wythe means to pursue Mr. Blackstone's method, I should think you ought to attend him from the commencement of his course, if at all, and to judge of this, for want of proper information is difficult; indeed I incline to think Mr. Wythe, under the present state of our laws, will be much embarrassed to deliver lectures with that perspicuity and precision which might be expected from him under a more established and settled state of them. The undertaking is arduous and the subject intricate at the best, but is rendered much more so from the circumstances of the country and the imperfect system now in use, inconsistent in some instances with the principles of the Constitution of the national government. Should the revision be passed the next session, it would, I think, lighten his labors and render them more useful to the student; otherwise he might be obliged to pursue the science under the old form, pointing out in his course the inconsistency with the present established government and the proposed alterations. Whichever method he may like, or whatever plan he may lay down to govern him, I doubt not it will be executed with credit to himself and benefit to his auditors. The Governor need not fear the favor of the community as to his future appointment, while he continues to make the common good his study. I have no intimate acquaintance with Mr. Jefferson, but from the knowledge I have of him, he is in my opinion as proper a man as

---

[1] At this time Joseph Jones (born, 1727; died, in King George County, October 28, 1805) was in the Continental Congress, where he served from 1778 to 1783. He had been in the House of Burgesses, on the Committee of Safety and a member of the Convention of 1776 so lauded by Hugh Blair Grigsby. He was in the Convention of 1788. A Judge of the General Court, 1778-79, he again served in that Court in 1789-90. He was a Major-General in the Virginia Militia. Two of Washington's letters were addressed to him. Judge Jones had endeavored to bring about the restoration of Weedon to the Continental line, Weedon having resigned because of a dispute with Woodford. See Writings of George Washington, W. C. Ford, Vol. VIII, pp. 304, 356.

can be put into the office, having the requisites of ability, firmness and diligence. You will do well to cultivate his friendship, and cannot fail to entertain a grateful sense of the favors he has conferred upon you, and while you continue to deserve his esteem he will not withdraw his countenance. If, therefore, upon conferring with him upon the subject, he wishes or shows a desire that you go with him, I would gratify him. Should you remain to attend Mr. Wythe, I would do it with his approbation, and under the expectation that when you come to Richmond you shall hope for the continuance of his friendship and assistance. There is likelihood the campaign will this year be to the South, and in the course of it events may require the exertions of the militia of this State; in which case, should a considerable body be called for, I hope Mr. Jefferson will head them himself; and you no doubt will be ready cheerfully to give him your company and assistance, as well as to make some return of civility to him as to satisfy your own feelings of the common good."

What better advice could Monroe have had? It was his crucial time — many young men go through just such a period of uncertainty, of hesitation. The past closes in behind them; on ahead, nothing beckons. And, just here, another letter carries on our narrative for us. Hearing from a Berkeley man (Mr. White) that General Charles Lee was in that neighborhood, Monroe wrote to him under date of Aylett's Warehouse, June 15, 1780:

"When I left you in Philadelphia, my wish and expectation was immediately to go to Europe; on my coming to Virginia, being under age, I found it difficult to make such disposition of my property as wo'd admit of it. I meant however to go this fall, and as I wish'd to go in the character of an officer, for that purpose I went up to HdQs, by Philadelphia (where I wish'd much to have seen you) to require from His Excellency and Ld Stirling a certificate of my good conduct. This I meant to present to the Virginia Assembly and from them procure an appointment. His excellency gave me the letter I co'd have wish'd and Lord Stirling also treated me with gentlemanly politeness. What I have to expect from this Assembly is incertain, but as they have no interest in the appointment I desire, I believe I have no probable grounds to found my hopes on. I am retiring from them to my uncle's, Mr. Jones, near Fredericksburg (the Chief Justice of this State) where I propose staying perhaps this year. If it was my house, my dr General, you sho'd make it yours, but at present I only

live in expectation of it. I may however take the liberty with my
uncle to press you if you come that way to call and see me."

To Lee, Monroe must have seemed an unsophisticated, well-meaning young man whom he could not
help substantially, but whom he could flatter and
thus encourage. He replied, July 18:

"The good figure you make flatters my vanity, as I have always
asserted that you wou'd appear one of the first characters of the
country if your shyness did not prevent the display of the knowledge and talents you possess. Mr. White tells me you have got
rid of this *mauvaise honte*, and only retain a certain degree of
recommendatory modesty. I rejoice in it with all my soul, as I
really love and esteem you most sincerely and affectionately."

Monroe wrote to Lord Stirling, September 6, 1782:

"Believe me, I have always been happy to hear from you. For
my part, till very lately, I have been a recluse. Chagrined at my
disappointment with your State in not attaining the rank and
command I ought, and chagrined at some disappointment in a
private line, I retired from society with almost a resolution not to
enter it again. Being fond of study I submitted the direction of
my time and plan to my friend, Mr. Jefferson, one of our wisest
and most virtuous republicans, and under his direction and indeed
by his advice, I have hitherto till of late lived. Lately I have taken
part in the civil line of the State and have been elected into the
Legislature, and afterwards by the Legislature into the Executive
Council of the State, which latter office I at present fill. I am happy
to make my acknowledgments to your Lordship and to General
Washington for your and his friendly letters to this State in favor
of my conduct while in your family, and without which I could not
have expected among so many competitors, at my age, to attain
in this degree the confidence of my country."[1]

Is it too much to say that, but for his disciplinary
adversities in the unlucky and unhappy times when
he lacked employment, Monroe could hardly have
withstood the defeats and gratuitous knocks of his
subsequent career? Though he did not get what he
wanted, he secured something ever so much more
important — the complete confidence and constant
friendship of Thomas Jefferson. We have failed to

---

[1] For the Lee-Monroe correspondence, see New York Historical Society Collections, Vol. III, pp. 428, 429; there is another letter, long and rambling, from
Lee to Monroe, pp. 430-432. See also Writings of Monroe, by Hamilton, I.

find any ~~ ~~~ of the first meeting of these two men whose names are so often bracketed; perhaps they had met at Williamsburg long before; but it was at this time that Monroe began to look to Jefferson for guidance. One was still untalked of; the other already quite a notable man not only in Virginia affairs but throughout the colonies. To some of us it seems singular that Jefferson should have quit the larger continental theatre of action for the smaller Virginia stage. But he knew what he was about. He was essentially a theorist, a reformer and an American into whose head had come the idea of democratizing certain outworn English constitutional customs. His liberalism was apparent in his effort to bring about the repeal of the laws of entail, to humanize the criminal code, to lessen the evils and menace of black bondage and in other ways to relieve mankind of its curses and burdens, so that happiness might be pursued. Possibly he felt that in some cases, happiness might be caught; for as Tucker[1] says, Jefferson possessed "a bold, sanguine, uncompromising temper," in contrast with that of Edmund Pendleton, who was "cautious, temporizing and conciliating." Between them, with the aid of other legislative committeemen including George Wythe, quite old, and James Madison, quite young, they had begun a revision of the laws of the state, improving them along lines of a freer, better humanity and adapting them to the republican form of government. Chancellor Wythe, be it noted, played the part of constitutional Nestor in this governmental reconstruction. He was at the head of the first law school established in America — that of William and Mary College. Not only were Jefferson and Madison his pupils, but John Marshall sat at the old man's feet. At a later period Henry Clay did likewise. It is worth while, in passing, to emphasize this present conjunction of Wythe, Jefferson and Madison, who was well called the "Father of the Constitution of the United States":

---

[1] The Life of Thomas Jefferson, by George Tucker, 1831, 2 vols., Vol. I, p. 107.

and the significant upcoming of Monroe, who, still a student, and tarrying in Jericho, was destined to be greatly influenced by all three of the men we have named and to be associated in extraordinary degree with both Jefferson and Madison. Modest as Madison was, he already had developed the power that accompanies intellectual persistence; and, finally, it was by his unwearied exertions, "in opposition to the endless quibbles, chicaneries, perversions, vexations and delays of lawyers and demi-lawyers," that the early Jeffersonian reforms were achieved. "For Jefferson," says Dr. H. J. Eckenrode, "the Revolution only began with the Declaration of Independence. That was necessary that other things might follow — abolition of entail, reform of the criminal code and disestablishment of the Episcopal Church."[1]

As yet, Monroe was not even in the ante-chamber of the Jeffersonian-Madisonian legislative forum. Before his entrance into public life he was to go on one more tour of military duty — not northward, this time, but southward. Jefferson kept an anxious eye on the South. Trouble was brewing for him — dire trouble and humiliation. He had made it clear that he was skilled in the difficult science of imparting humanity to legislative acts; but could he govern? Was he really an executive capable of holding the wild horses he must drive? One good year of his governorship was gone; another had come, and this was to be his year of humiliation. June 1, 1780, began this second year — this unhappy year; and in that month of June Monroe found himself in the Carolinas.

Bancroft says, Vol. V, p. 384: "North Carolina made a requisition for arms on Virginia and received them. With a magnanimity which knew nothing of fear, Virginia laid herself bare for the protection of the Carolinas." Patrick Henry had made frequent draughts upon the resources of the State in order that he might feed, clothe and arm the Continental troops. In spite

---

[1] The Revolution in Virginia, by H. J. Eckenrode, 1916.

of what Jefferson's enemies say on this score, he, too,
left few stones unturned except such as were beyond
his financial strength. But finances were particularly
bad.[1] Jefferson tried to raise and equip troops for the
south; establish a gun factory, and arrange with the
governors of North and South Carolina to hold back
the Cherokees. There were many Continental super-
numeraries, like Monroe and Marshall, who would
have gone South with alacrity if their services could
have been put to use. But Governor Jefferson was
able to raise only about half a battalion of infantry to
guard the prisoners taken at Saratoga and now quartered near Charlottesville. "Confusion reigned in the
Government," declares Eckenrode. Lax Colonial methods had not been improved by the war. Patrick Henry
had done what he could and Jefferson was doing all
he could; nevertheless affairs were in disorder. Enlist-
ments were for short terms. General Peter Muhlenberg
was sent down by General Washington. He suggested
a conscription law. Jefferson wrote encouragingly to
Gates, but did not act with decision. So says Eckenrode,
who adds:

"Right here it is just to acquit Jefferson of neglect of duty.
Few more conscientious and industrious executives ever lived;
he was always engrossed in the details of his office, and if he erred,
as it clearly seems he did, he erred from want of judgment and
driving power rather than from any lack of zeal or labor. His
failure to arrange an adequate defense of the State was apparently
due in a large part to two causes. Foremost came Jefferson's
penchant for strict constitutionalism, for strict construction ideas
did not originate with the Federal Constitution, but descended
from the Colonial period. The Revolutionary War was mainly a
war of strict construction patriots against broad construction
imperialists. It was this exaggerated respect for the Virginia
Constitution which prevented Jefferson from using strong means
of doubtful legality at times when it was more expedient to go
than to reflect upon the exact order of the going. The other reason

---

[1] Colonel William Grayson wrote, May 29, 1781: "No money in Virginia to
buy anything with and no credit." Daniel St. Jenifer of St. Thomas wrote from
Philadelphia to Weedon, June 5, 1781, that Grayson was indefatigable in pro-
curing arms.— Weedon Papers, in the Library of the American Philosophical
Society, Philadelphia.

for his failure to do his full duty lay in his inability to grasp the principles on which military operations are successfully conducted; to the last Jefferson was a man quite without military understanding, a deficiency even more unfortunate when he became President of the United States than it had been when he was Governor of Virginia. Both these failings arose from the fact that he was a doctrinaire and not a man of action. . . . But as it happens Moses frequently occupies the place of Joshua."[1]

It is good to make a mental mark on the margin of this paragraph. We have in it a handy little key that unlocks page after page of history for us. We shall need it by and by, in this very book, when we come to tell of troubles that threatened to overwhelm the party of Jefferson, Madison and Monroe.

But, for the moment, we must check ourselves. We should hasten to remind our readers that this present period is long prior to the Jeffersonian era of which so much has been written. Monroe was still a junior — still inconspicuous. No doubt his neighbors at times asked him how his Trenton shoulder was; but some of them must have regarded his affair of the captured cannon as a trifle, since they themselves had lost fathers, brothers, sons, and, unhappily, were in a way to feel the bloody sword whistle in savage swirl above their own heads. The war was still on.

It was Jefferson who made a Military Commissioner out of Monroe and sent him "to collect information regarding the condition and aspects of the army in the South." Twenty-two years old, a law-student under Jefferson, with means enough to live without pay from the state, he bore his new rank of lieutenant-colonel as lightly as though still scouting in the Jerseys.

Let us see what was on foot. The British plan to cut the continent in two on the line of the Hudson — a plan probably based on an older one devised by De Callier for the French Government — had failed with the bagging of Burgoyne and the balking of both Sir William Howe and Sir Henry Clinton. What had the King gained? Hardly a thing. What did he hold? A

---

[1] The Revolution in Virginia, by H. J. Eckenrode, Ph.D., 1916, pp. 196-200.

town or two — no more. What now? What would
the British do now? Shift the war to the South.
Sweep the Carolinas as with a bloody broom. Sweep
Virginia, also. *Sic Semper*, indeed! Let Madame Virginia feel at her throat the iron weight of the dragoon's
boot! Such was the new scheme devised by the King's
ministers for the reduction of rebellious America.

In May, Clinton took Charleston; and along with it
Lincoln's whole army, except Buford's command which
escaped northward only to be hacked to pieces at
Waxhaws, near the North Carolina boundary. It was
a bitter time for the Carolinas and a bitter time for
Virginia. Her best regiments were in British hands;
her militia was dispersed; the blood of many of her
youth stained the sword of the ravaging Ban Tarleton
as yet untamed by Dan Morgan; and there was now a
constant black cloud in the south threatening death.

According to Kapp, General Kalb, who was passing
southward with the Delaware and Maryland troops,
did not find in Virginia as many things to facilitate
his progress as he had expected. But, then, he was
accustomed to European roads and distances and to a
cooler climate. About the time Monroe reached Cross
Creek, Kalb at the Virginia-North Carolina boundary
wrote to his wife: "Here I am at last, considerably
South, suffering from intolerable heat, the worst of
quarters, and the most voracious of insects of every
hue and form." Flies bit him. Ticks beset him.
Chiggers buried themselves under his skin. "My whole
body is covered with these things," said he. But a
little later, under Gates in Camden battle, the stings
of British bullets[1] were much worse for this brave and
worthy old campaigner, who, unhorsed but undis-

---

[1] "As he advanced, he was struck by several balls and the blood poured from
him in streams; but he still had strength to cut down a British soldier, who had
actually set a bayonet in his breast. Yet his hour had come. He was recognized
by his epaulets. 'The rebel general! the rebel general!' was heard in the English
ranks. Mortally struck and bleeding from eleven wounds, he sank exhausted to
the earth."— Life of Kalb, by Friederich Kapp, 1884. The Baron died at Camden, three days later, August 19.

mayed, tried in vain to beat back the victorious troops of the British Legion.

Monroe, of course, was not a participant in this, or any other, Carolina fight. He was an observer merely; and that only for a short time. He wrote to Jefferson from Cross Creek, June 26, 1780, telling of arrangements he had made for a line of communication between that point and Richmond. This line had been found highly desirable — necessary, indeed — because of the want of intelligence concerning the Southern movements of the enemy, and the anxieties felt on that account. "Congress," adds S. M. Hamilton,[1] "expressed its appreciation by continuing this important line, established by Jefferson and Monroe, from Philadelphia to Washington's headquarters." Monroe wrote that Cross Creek was the place from which Governor Nash at Newberry and Baron de Kalb at Hillsborough got their intelligence. He had met Nash as well as General Caswell but had not as yet obtained the particular information required. At the same time he had gathered and verified news from the south concerning Clinton, Cornwallis, Tarleton, the troops under Kalb, the militia under Caswell, and Rutherford and much else highly desirable to know. His long and important letter shows that, at twenty-two Monroe was sagacious in his outlook, orderly and accurate in his statements and frank in his admissions as to what he had failed to accomplish. While there is nothing facile or fine or impressive in the letter, it clearly indicates his trustworthy and solid character. His Carolina reconnaisance was in every way creditable to him.

Monroe's mission took him into war territory at a critical and romantic period. All South Carolina was being Toryized and terrorized except the sections in which now arose Francis Marion, Jethro Sumter and their fellow-partisans. Marion began to play "Swamp Fox" in the Peedee country that same summer; and, coincidently, there assembled those fearless frontiers-

[1] Writings of Monroe.

men, scornful of kings, who, when October came, struck like lightning at King's Mountain.

Moreover, Greene was on his way down from the North. It was Congress that had appointed Lincoln and it was Congress that had backed Gates; twice had Congress burnt its fingers; so now Congress kept hands off. Washington sent Greene, who, with his aides Barnet and Morris, passed south in company with Steuben and his aide Duponceau. They "talked books" as they journeyed along the forest roads — a congenial company; and no worse as soldiers for being bookish. Cowpens was fought January 17, 1781; Guilford Court-House, March 15, 1781; Hobkirk's Hill, April 28, 1781; Eutaw Springs, September 8, 1781. Monroe's old captain, William Washington, with the First and Third Dragoons; "Legion Harry" Lee, General Dan Morgan; Col. Isaac Shelby, Col. Ben Cleveland; the Seviers; the Campbells; Major "Hal" Dixon; General Griffith Rutherford, General Joseph Graham and General Joseph McDowell (called "Quaker Meadows Joe" to distinguish him from his cousin "Pleasant Meadows" Joe); Colonel Willie R. Davieson, fresh from his law books, tall, handsome, a knightly figure, "happiest when leading a charge" — these were some of the regulars and partisans who helped to save the Carolinas and the American cause.[1]

Cornwallis claimed that he had vanquished Greene; nevertheless he drew off towards the coast. He assumed that, if he should cut loose from his base and march into Virginia, Greene would follow him. But Greene's move was diametrically opposite — he struck out for the south, as Cornwallis struck out for the north. Bold indeed was Greene's strategy; but it had

[1] North Carolina, 1780-81, being a History of the Invasion of the Carolinas, by David Schenck, LL.D., 1889. Schenck defends the militia. Life of W. R. Davieson, by Fordyce Hubbard. Tarleton's Campaigns, 1780-1781. Judge J. B. O'Neall's Annals of Newberry District. Lyman C. Draper's King's Mountain. The local books are laudatory of their own heroes as a rule; but they must be read to gain a true idea of the characters of the time.

this drawback — it left Virginia open to bloody rapine and slaughter.

Already four successive British waves had rolled in between the Virginia Capes — that of Mathews; Leslie's, 2500 men; Arnold's, 1600; and Phillips', 2600. Each had done great damage. If Arnold were not the worst of the invaders, he was the most hated. Traitor that he was, he burnt a warehouse of tobacco at every smoke. But Washington sent, first, General Peter Muhlenberg; then, Baron Steuben; then the Marquis de La Fayette with 1200 Continentals, supported by Wayne with 1000.

It is hard to indicate just what Monroe did in the way of soldiering after his return from North Carolina. Once he is reported "absent in the field." His old commander, Weedon, at Fredericksburg, was one of the busiest of the State's defenders. Another and still better defender was General Thomas Nelson, Jr., who was quartered at Williamsburg. Though Richard Henry Lee complained, in a letter to Weedon, of a "terrible want of all things — arms, cavalry, ammunition," Jefferson was still true to the Continent, sending half the lead from the lead-mines for use in the Carolinas. He was doing the best he could for Virginia and for her neighbors. The Weedon Papers [1] show clearly how anxious the average planter was to play a man's part, whatever the cost. R. H. Lee, writing from Westmoreland, recommended "the bearer, Mr. John Monroe" to Weedon's kind attention and asked for him "a position in the army more worthy of his past services."

In fine, these letters to and from Weedon show that

---

[1] Calendar of the Correspondence relating to the American Revolution of Brigadier-General George Weedon, Hon. Richard Henry Lee, Hon. Arthur Lee and Major-General Nathanael Greene, in the Library of the American Philosophical Society, 1900. There are letters from Muhlenberg, Steuben, Thomas Nelson, Jr., and John A. Washington, Judge Bushrod's father.

General Weedon's letters, mostly in his own hand, were presented through Dr. James Mease, to the American Philosophical Society, by Colonel Hugh Mercer, of Fredericksburg, son of General Hugh Mercer and a nephew of General Weedon's wife.

there was going on in Monroe's country at that time
a great deal more than one gathers from reading the
general histories. Not only was "the Marquis in want
of vinegar, bacon and shoes," but Weedon begged for
him "a quarter cask of wine."

If in his Virginia campaign, Lafayette met Monroe
there seems to be no record of it. Together at Brandywine, and good friends years after, they now appear to
have ridden on roads apart. Campbell, in telling of
Col. John Bannister of Battersea, near Petersburg,
(son of the botanist), lieutenant-colonel under General
Robert Lawson says: "The two other Colonels in the
brigade were John Mercer, afterwards Governor of
Maryland, and James Monroe, subsequently President
of the United States. But Lawson's corps was dissolved
when Leslie retired from Virginia, and thus the horse
commanded by Colonel Bannister was lost to the state
when cavalry was pressingly required."

But in spite of all that could be done either by the
Virginia authorities or by the resourceful and elusive
La Fayette (who was but a year older than Monroe)
the Cornwallis-Tarleton tornado, sweeping up from
the south, cut a wide swath. La Fayette adroitly kept
out of the way, biding his time till Wayne should join
him with a thousand seasoned troops. The storm, he
knew, would spend itself.

It was Jefferson who was out of luck. He was in the
saddle day and night, seeking to save the State's stores
as well as his family. But Simcoe drove Steuben from
Point of Forks, confluence of the Fluvana and Riviana,
and burnt the stores, while Tarleton spurred off on a
raid of some eighty-odd miles into Albemarle in search
of Jefferson and the Legislature. Indeed, the British
dragoons chased through Virginia as on a grand hunt.
Jefferson, at Monticello, with ten minutes warning,
got away by virtue of a crosspath, a swift horse and a
shielding woods on the mountain side. The honorable
legislature likewise escaped, passing with more haste
than dignity from Charlottesville to Staunton beyond

the Blue Ridge. Corn and cattle were taken; plate and precious things; and as many as 30,000 blacks were lost to their masters. Tucker tells us that 27,000 of them died of smallpox and camp-fever.

To Jefferson this *contretemps* was tragic in the extreme. Tragic it was, sure enough; but there was no reason why he should have felt so excessively humiliated as to go into retirement at "Poplar Forest" — his lesser Monticello, an octagonal brick dwelling by the Blue Ridge. His term as Governor had ended two days before Tarleton tried to seize him; and now Gen. Thomas Nelson, Jr., was in the executive chair. Jefferson, it seems, was hurt by a fall from his horse. Moreover he had plunged into the writing of his "Notes on Virginia" that he might oblige M. de Marbois, who had asked him all sorts of questions about the State. These were his excuses for making a hermit of himself in the forest depths of Bedford. His real reason was a bruised heart — a deep disgust, the revulsion of a sanguine man, who, leading his fellows in pursuit of statutory happiness, had come upon a situation undreamt of in his philosophy. Even the news from Yorktown, which reached him before the leaves grew red, did not purge him of his gall. Along with Adams, Franklin, Jay and Laurens, he was named as a Minister Plenipotentiary to negotiate a treaty with Great Britain; but there were charges against him before the Legislature, so he declined to leave Virginia while they were pending. It is true George Nicholas, who had acted impulsively in bringing the charges, apologized to Jefferson; nevertheless our Achilles sulked in his octagon.

Monroe — who had written Jefferson a long letter dated Richmond, September 9, 1780, in which he thanked him for various kindnesses, expressed his desire to serve the State, "like many worthy Republicans," without compensation; and declared that, though he did not wish to go out of the State with Lawson, he would join his command should it remain

in Virginia — now again addressed him. We begin to
make note of a certain steadiness and fidelity in Monroe.
With him, talk against a man like Jefferson went in
one ear and out at the other. But he was not afraid to
speak his mind — even to rebuke so great a one as
Jefferson, who promptly responded.

Of Jefferson's letters to Monroe more than a hundred
are in print, as against many more than two hundred
to Madison. In this first Monroe letter, dated Monticello, May 20, 1782, Jefferson warms up to the young
friend and follower who was not afraid to be frank.
Monroe's rebuke .and admonition were couched in
terms of excusable eulogy. The people, he wrote, have
"frequently elected you . . . to please you, but now
they have called you forth into public office to serve
themselves." That phrase challenged the attention of
the philosopher who used it as a sort of text when he
sent his reply. His letter is at least a thousand words
long. He is extremely dubious as to "the right of the
State to make a man serve it whether he wish to do so
or no." "If we are made in some degree for others, yet
in a greater are we made for ourselves." "It were contrary to feeling and indeed ridiculous to suppose that
a man had less right in himself than one of his neighbors
or indeed all of them put together." One smiles.
What a far cry from that unsophisticated yesterday to
this ribald and unphilosophical today! But Jefferson
was writing to a young man of whom he thought a
great deal — a disciple capable of subtleties. He could
not pocket his pride. He was still sore, still nursing his
grand grudge; but Monroe's mixed bolus of bitter-
sweet was the very restorative he needed. His re-
entrance into public life was retarded by Mrs. Jefferson's
death, and by other untoward events, but he would
have gone abroad as a peace commissioner if Congress
had not withdrawn the appointment. For one thing,
as far as Monroe was concerned, his friendship was
fixed. We are assured that Jefferson "invited Monroe
to join him in France and become a member of his

household there." And another matter that was fairly well settled by this time was Monroe's future calling. His own bent, his uncle's encouragement, his preceptor's infectious zeal for governmental betterment caused him to look upon himself as destined for a political career.

CHAPTER V

"No Hoop for the Barrel"

Monroe began his political career in 1782. He was twenty-four years old. He was elected in King George County to the Virginia Assembly, thanks to Washington's letter about him to Colonel Archibald Cary. Monroe acknowledged his indebtedness to Washington in a letter dated Richmond, August 15, 1782: "The introduction you gave me some time since . . . although it failed me in that instance, has availed me in another line." It did not help him to a seat in the saddle but it helped him to a seat in the House of Burgesses. He promised to so conduct himself as to give Washington no cause for regret in having done him such a good turn.

Shortly after his arrival in Richmond, Monroe was chosen by the Assembly to serve as a member of the Executive Council. Madison, now in Congress, had so served. Benjamin Harrison, a conservative, who had succeeded Thomas Nelson, Jr., also a conservative, was then Governor. It was a time of reaction, of a return to conservatism. Even R. H. Lee and Patrick Henry, who were rivals for political leadership, became less liberal. According to Albert J. Beveridge[1], the Virginia Legislature, during these years, "was not a body to inspire respect." Madison was disgusted with "the temper of the Legislature, and the wayward course of its proceedings." There was confusion in the revenue department. The method of drawing bills was bad. Marshall was surprised that "gentlemen cannot dismiss their private animosities, but will bring them in the Assembly." "Our Assembly," wrote

---

[1] In his Life of John Marshall, Vol. I, pp. 205-212. Senator Beveridge has numerous references to Monroe in the four volumes of his illuminating work.

Washington, "has been employed chiefly in rectifying the mistakes of the last and committing new ones for emendation at the next." He wrote to La Fayette that Virginia "was about to pass some of the most extravagant and preposterous edicts . . . that ever stained the leaves of a legislative code." These lapses on the part of the public men of Virginia, reminding one, as they do, of similar lapses in the Continental Congress which had deteriorated in marked degree, are to be explained by that demoralization, due to eight years of war, already referred to in the citation from Campbell.

The Virginia Assembly met in "a small wooden building." Of the two rooms occupied by it, the smaller anteroom was "a scene of conversational tumult." A burly door-keeper stood guard at the entrance to the larger room where the lawmakers sat. Johann David Schoepf, a traveler, who visited Richmond in 1783, looked in upon the "legislative majesty of Virginia" with some wonder. There was too much "movement, laughter, talk"; "these Solons were not quiet five minutes at a time." In Beveridge we find also an unaddressed letter from Marshall to Monroe[1], in which the leading members and their work are touched upon. "Legion" Harry is to displace R. H. Lee; and Marshall "does not know 'whether the public will be injured by the change.'" In telling of a tilt between the honorable speaker and Patrick Henry, Marshall says: "The Speaker replied with some degree of acrimony and Henry retorted with a good deal of temper; 'tis his peculiar excellence when he altercates to appear to be drawn unwillingly into the contest and to throw in the eyes of others the whole blame on his adversary. His influence is immense."

As for the duties of the Privy Council or Council of State, Beveridge says: "The Council consisted of

[1] Marshall to Monroe, December 12, 1783; Ms. Draper Collection, Wisconsin Historical Society; also American Historical Review, Vol. III, p. 673. Of this letter, Senator Beveridge says: "It has been assumed that it was written to Thomas Jefferson. This is incorrect. It was written to James Monroe."

eight members elected by the Legislature either from
the delegates or from the people at large. It was the
Governor's official cabinet, and a constitutional part
of the executive power. The Governor consulted the
Council on all important matters coming before him,
and he appointed various important officers only upon
its advice." While members of this Council, both
Monroe (in 1782) and Marshall (in 1782-83) saw the
workings of the new political machine "first run by
Patrick Henry, perfected by Thomas Jefferson, and
finally developed to its ultimate efficiency by Spencer
Roane and Thomas Ritchie." Marshall, as Beveridge
tells us, profited by his knowledge of this machine when
in after life it became his "great antagonist." Monroe,
too, profited by the political knowledge gained during
his brief period as a Councillor. Surprise was expressed
that one so young as Marshall should be given so
important an office. He "took part in the appointment
of surveyors, justices of the peace, tobacco inspectors
and other officers." But Monroe, as we recall, was
even younger than Marshall. Each had stood up under
hard knocks in the great school of the Continental
army and both were men well-equipped for public
service whatever their age[1].

Beveridge brings out the friendly association of
Marshall and Monroe in the early eighties. They were
even closer comrades then than during the war.
Marshall as a young man was of a particularly winning
disposition. His liveliness was pronounced. It was
the time of his courtship of Mary Willis Ambler,
daughter of Jacquelin Ambler, who lived first at York
then at Richmond. And here now is something curious
involving the love affairs of certain celebrities: Jacquelin
Ambler's brother Edward married Mary Cary, who
was "very beautiful, heiress of a moderate fortune
and much sought after." Tradition long declared that
one of the young Virginians who "sought after" her

---

[1] Marshall quit the Council and, though he lived in Henrico County was re-
elected to the Legislature from Fauquier.

was George Washington. But this story, it seems, has been exploded. Or rather, it has been amended for it was another of Colonel Wilson Miles Cary's daughters, sister of Mary Cary, who captivated the young Colonel. Erring tradition merely mixed those equal beauties up. Mary Ambler's mother was none other than Jefferson's sweetheart Rebecca Burwell[1]. The war had reduced the Amblers in fortune and they lived not in a mansion but in a small frame house. When they moved to Richmond, they were glad to get any sort of dwelling, since the town was small and primitive. "Where we are to lay our heads, Heaven knows!" wrote Eliza, Mary Ambler's sister. Eliza had heard so much of John Marshall that she expected to see in him a young knight, a paragon; but instead of that he was a "tall, loose-jointed young man thin to gauntness," in ungainly dress, slouch hat and with rustic bearing. Nevertheless, Mary Ambler fell in love with him at first sight, as he did with her. She saw in the young captain that nobility of character and exceedingly happy and sunny and lovable nature upon which Monroe and his other comrades had long remarked. Marshall made love as he made war. He "fascinated the entire Ambler family." "Thus began a lifelong romance, which," says Beveridge[2], "in tenderness, exaltation, and constancy is unsurpassed in the chronicles of historic affections."

When Marshall married, he needed money. Monroe was in like straits. Marshall's father sold some of his land; and Monroe wanted to sell his. Marshall wrote to Monroe: "I do not know what to say to your scheme of selling out. If you can execute it, you will have made a very capital sum, if you can retain your lands

---

[1] In the Green Bag, Vol. VIII, p. 481, is an account by Susan Randolph of Jefferson's love affair with Rebecca Burwell: "He is a boy and is indisputably in love in this good year 1763, and he courts and sighs to capture his pretty, little sweetheart, but like his friend, George Washington, fails. The young lady will not be captured!"

[2] See Beveridge's Marshall, Vol. I, p. 152. Also "An Old Virginia Correspondence," letters of Betsy Ambler Carrington to her sister Nancy; Atlantic Monthly, Vol. 84, pp. 535-549. Also, Historical Magazine, Vol. III, p. 165.

you will be poor during life unless you remove to the
Western Country, but you have secured for posterity
an immense fortune." [1] Probably the two had talked
of going west. Colonel Thomas Marshall journeyed
to Kentucky in 1780; and about the time of which we
are telling, moved there for good, becoming Surveyor
of Revenue for the District of Ohio. John Marshall
reminded Monroe that he could learn what he wished
as to the value of Kentucky lands from the folks who
had gone on ahead. Marshall, says Beveridge, "mixed
fun with his business and politics." On February 24,
1784, he writes to James Monroe that public money
due the latter could not be secured. "The exertions
of the Treasurer and of your other friends have been
ineffectual. There is not one shilling in the Treasury
and the keeper of it could not borrow one on the faith
of the government." Marshall confides to Monroe
that he himself is "pressed for money," and adds that
Monroe's "old Landlady, Mrs. Shera, begins now to
be a little clamorous. . . . I shall be obliged, I apprehend, to negotiate your warrants at last at a discount.
I have kept them up this long in hopes of drawing
money for them from the Treasury." Beveridge adds:[2]
"Very few of Marshall's letters during this period are
extant. This one to Monroe is conspicuously noticeable
for unrestraint and joyousness. As unreserved as he
always was in verbal conversation, Marshall's correspondence soon began to show great caution, unlike
that of Jefferson which increased, with time, in spontaneity. Thus Marshall's letters became more guarded
and less engaging; while Jefferson's pen used ever more
highly colored ink and progressively wrote more entertaining if less trustworthy matter." In the gossipy
Marshall-Monroe letter referred to, Marshall tells
Monroe all about the youth of Richmond who "are all
treading the broad road to matrimony. Little Steward

---

[1] Marshall to Monroe, December 12, 1783, Draper Collection, Wis. Historical
Society; and December 28, 1784, Monroe Mss., VII, p. 832.
[2] Beveridge's Marshall, Vol. I, pp. 182, 183.

(could you believe it?) will be married on Thursday
to Kitty Haie and Mr. Dunn will bear off your old
acquaintance, Miss Shera. Tabby Eppes has grown
quite fat and buxom, her charms are renovated and to
see her and to love her are now synonymous terms.
She has within these six weeks seen in her train at least
a score of Military and Civil characters. . . . Farewell,
I am your J. Marshall."

Thus did the mind that was to do so much toward
moulding the nation disport itself exuberantly; and
no doubt Monroe entered as fully into the spirit of the
lively letter. Interesting, too, was a Marshall letter of
April 17, 1784, in which the political news is given.[1]
"I have been maneuvering amazingly," writes Marshall,
"to turn your warrants into cash; if I succeed I shall
think myself a first rate speculator." Monroe is mentioned in an entry in Marshall's Account Book, June 26,
1784, "Col°. Monroe and self at the Play 1-10." A
week later are these entries: "to the play 13" and
"Pd for Col°. Monroe 16-16." Marshall won and
lost at whist, and very likely Monroe did too. Monroe,
it may be here said, was interested in lotteries; and
there are references in his correspondence to invest-
ments in them made in behalf of his friends.

Monroe now left the local for the Continental legislature. It is well to note that his fitness to represent
the State should so soon have been recognized. On
June 6, 1783, he was elected a member of the Fourth
Continental Congress for the one-year term that began
on the first Monday in November. Twice re-elected,
he served also in the Fifth and Sixth Congresses —
three years altogether. Then by the rule of rotation
he was automatically retired. Similarly, Madison, in
Congress, 1780-1783, for the three-year period preceding Monroe's, went out to re-enter after a three-
year interval in 1786-1788. No State had more than

---

[1] Marshall to Monroe, Ms. New York Public Library. A facsimile of the
first page of this letter is given by Beveridge, Vol. I, p. 212.

seven, nor less than two, delegates; and it was the rule that a State vote should count as one.

John Quincy Adams said of Monroe[1]: "Had he been born ten years before, it can scarcely be doubted that he would have been one of the members of the first Congress, and that his name would have gone down to posterity among those of the signers of the Declaration of Independence. Among the blessings conferred by a beneficent Providence upon this country in the series of events which composed that Revolution was its influence in the formation of individual and national character. The controversy which preceded the Revolutionary War necessarily formed by a practical education the race of statesmen by whom it was conducted to its close. The nature of the controversy itself, turning upon the elementary principles of civil society, upon the natural rights of man, and the foundations of government, pointed the attention of men to the investigation of those principles; exercised all the intellectual faculties of the most ardent and meditative souls, and led to discoveries in the theory of government which have changed the face of the world." Monroe had been obliged to give up his Latin and Greek at William and Mary, but he had gone to an infinitely better school than the honored institution in which he had matriculated — the great school of debate and armed conflict between crown and continent.

One thing certain: the thirteen independent republics of the Atlantic seaboard more than ever needed men who could use their heads. Even while the war was on, Congress found itself impotent in certain vital matters. There was lack of unanimity among the States; they were like an untrained team each of which pulled as it pleased. They were proud, as well as obstinate. Let it be remembered that they were ununited by the scores of ligaments and nerves that string the States together in this age of rails and wires

---

[1] In his Eulogy of James Monroe, delivered at the request of the Corporation of Boston, August 25, 1831

and macadam. Let us bear in mind also that the passion for the American Union per se, now a second nature with most of us, was as yet undeveloped —in some quarters, indeed, unfelt.

Off and on for ten years public men had urged a closer and stronger union. Washington had made pleas for it. Jefferson called for "young statesmen" with broad views. Paine had said in "Common Sense": "Nothing but a continental form of government can keep the peace of the continent." He wanted a continental conference to frame a continental charter; "our strength and happiness is continental, not provincial." He saw clearly; if others — some others — did not. "We have every opportunity to form the noblest and purest constitution on the face of the globe," said he, as if glimpsing far into the future. But the Articles of Confederation, as drawn up by so strong a conservative as John Dickinson, a member of the committee appointed by Congress June 11, 1776, were modified and weakened before their acceptance by Congress, November 15, 1777. Even then some of the States withheld their assent. The main drawback was their unwillingness to surrender their claims to vast stretches of western lands. Golden were the sunsets in that direction; and each State was loath to lop off the undeveloped riches it might in time secure. Finally, February 19, 1780, New York ceded her rights to western lands; and, on January 2, 1781, Virginia surrendered to Congress all claims in the great region northwest of the Ohio River. Maryland then accepted the Articles; and, on July 9, Congress ratified them.

Already, however, the Articles had been tried and found wanting. There was no Executive; no Supreme Court; no real power in Congress itself. What, then, could Congress do? It could make peace, coin money and establish courts for various purposes, such as the trial of piracy cases. Provided it did not trench upon the powers of the State, it could do other useful things. It was a sort of budget committee, too; it could make estimates. But while it could vote a tax it could not collect it. Here was a fatal weakness; for how could it raise a revenue to pay soldiers, or the interest on the eight millions borrowed from France and Holland? And there was another fatal weakness. It was powerless to regulate commerce. Both that right and the right of taxation belonged exclusively to the States. Another thing — the citizen, the individual, was amenable to the State, not to the Confederation. "Congress," says Andrews,[1] "could not touch individuals; it must act through the State Governments, and in these it had to enforce the payment of taxes." As Andrews puts it, "the States complied or not as they chose. In October, 1781, Congress asked for $8,000,000; in January, 1783, it had received less than a half a million." Elson [2] says: "Eighteen months were required to collect one-fifth of the taxes laid by Congress in 1783." The Treasury was empty, the States were unresponsive with their quotas of money, and credit abroad was about gone. Strange to say, specie was not so scarce as it had been earlier in the war. Robert Morris paid the soldiers with hard money at Head of Elk. "The heads of the kegs were knocked out for effect, and the specie rolled out, to the great joy and astonishment of the soldiers. So excited were they that one of them shouted at the top of his voice, "Look! look! Jonathan by jingo! it is hard money."[3]

Was Morris, then, a magician? Morris was a great patriot, a great financier; he had little to do with the hard-money phenomenon. The money was in the country, but not in the hands of Congress, which was financially debilitated. Here, indeed, was a paradox;

---

[1] History of the United States, by E. Benjamin Andrews, 1894, 2 vols., Vol. I, p. 224.

[2] Elson's History of the United States. Albert Bushnell Hart says: "The total sum required from 1781 to 1788 was about $16,000,000. Of this there had actually been paid during the seven years $3,500,000 in specie and $2,500,000 in certificates of national indebtedness. The annual cash income was therefore about a half a million, which was entirely absorbed by the running expenses of the government, leaving nothing for the payment of interest."— Formation of the Union, 1775-1829.

[3] American Review, Vol. VI, p. 76.

yet not the only paradoxical matter associated with this period. Why were so many unhesitating advocates of free America weakly hesitant when it came to the question of binding the States together in an unbreakable bond? They had risked their necks against the British King; they would risk nothing against King Misrule, whose real name was Anarchy.

Abroad the defects of government under the Articles were apparent. In Great Britain it was regretted that peace had not been made with each State instead of with the States conjointly. What an opening that would have been for future conquest! The English disbelieved in the reality of American union. The King thought that stable government here was out of the question. As Bancroft notes,[1] there was at Boston, in August, 1780, a convention of five States which declared for a "more solid and permanent union with one supreme head" and a competent Congress to manage such affairs as are not entrusted to the States. Albany approved of this. Hamilton urged that a Convention be held to set up a "vigorous" General Confederacy; and he wished it to be done at once, without further consultation with that many-headed party of which he was none too fond. "Call a Convention of the States," advised General Greene, and establish a Congress upon a Constitutional footing. Knox said the army wanted "a hoop for the barrel." A Convention at Hartford warned Congress that "the States in attempting to retain too much of their independence might finally lose the whole." The staves of the barrel would fall apart. In the opinion of the New Jersey Legislative Council and Assembly, "Congress represented the Federal Republic." After the final ratification, James Duane wrote to Washington that "by the accomplishment of our Federal Union we are become a nation." But Washington had no illusions on that score. He said: "There must be something more than

---

[1] History of the Formation of the Constitution of the United States, by George Bancroft, 1882, 2 vols., Vol I, p. 12, *et seq.*

a recommendatory power in Congress." In February
he appealed to Jefferson, Pendleton and Wythe to favor
the enlargement of the powers of Congress. "I declare
to God," said he, "my only aim is the general good."
It was necessary for him to say this because his enemies
accused him of seeking to strengthen the nation imperi-
ally so that he might set up as its monarch. In reality,
he abhorred the thought. To Monroe's uncle, Joseph
Jones, "whom," says Bancroft, "he regarded with
sincere affection and perfect trust," Washington wrote
that unless Congress should be strengthened "the
States would be annihilated in a general crash."
"The fable of the bunch of sticks," he added, "may
well be applied to us." In a letter to Duane, Hamilton[1]
portrayed in a masterly way the defects of the Confederation. "Madison wrote vigorously on the vices
and evil practices of the system."

By this time, too, the Continental Congress had
become a peripatetic body. Its proper meeting place
was Philadelphia, but it had permitted itself to be
driven away from Independence Hall by a few money-
less and mutinous troops — eighty only, who had come
clamoring down from Lancaster. There were other
troops at the barracks in Philadelphia and these too
had lost patience with Congress, which was not as
much to blame for unhappy conditions affecting the
soldiers as were the various States.[2] The demoralization of Congress was of a piece with the demoralization
and general laxity of the country.[3] "It was less a
Government than an exigency committee." When it
left Philadelphia it re-assembled in College Hall at
Princeton; and the new Congress, to which Jefferson
and Monroe belonged, met there on Monday, November
3, with seven States represented. After it had chosen

---

[1] Justin Winsor, Narrative and Critical History, Vol. VII, p. 215, et seq.

[2] In quick succession had occurred "the Mutiny of 1781, the Newburgh episode, and the Mutiny of 1783 — menaces of an army driven in desperation to
turn against its creators." "The fault lay in the neglect of the States to make
payment possible, a neglect far less excusable than the mutiny itself."— The
Continental Congress at Princeton, by Varnum Lansing Collins, 1908.

[3] E. B. Andrews, History of the United States, 2 vols., Vol. I, p. 273.

General Thomas Mifflin president, it adjourned, on the
fourth, to meet at Annapolis, Md., on the twenty-sixth.
But, at Annapolis, as there were not enough members
in attendance,[1] it was necessary to adjourn and re-
adjourn. This was continued from day to day until
on Saturday, December 13, it was found that twenty
delegates were present — enough to proceed to business.
Monroe's Virginia colleagues were Thomas Jefferson,[2]
Samuel Hardy, John F. Mercer and Arthur Lee.

The State House at Annapolis where Congress sat
(in what is now the Maryland Senate chamber) is a
fine colonial hall seated upon a rounded hill-top, from
which one may look down upon the beautiful estuary
of the Severn and the broader distant waters of the
Chesapeake Bay. Had Monroe sailed due east across
the bay, he would have come close to the spot on Kent
Island where his first American ancestor settled more
than a hundred years before. It was almost within
sight of Bay Ridge bluff at Severn mouth. But it is
doubtful if Monroe gave thought either to old Captain
Andrew or to the winter sun-sparkle on the Chesapeake.
He was too much interested in what was going on
around him. The place itself must have caught his
fancy. From Capitol Hill, as a hub, the streets of the
town radiated like the spokes of a wheel. Probably
Annapolis was alive with visitors, in anticipation of the
coming of Washington. Peace, it will be remembered,
had been agreed upon provisionally, November 30,
1782; proclaimed to the British Army, April 19, 1783 —
Lexington Day — and definitely arranged September
30, 1783. So Washington was to sheathe his shining

[1] Justin Winsor says: "There was so little interest to secure the attendance of
members of Congress that there was no time between October, 1783, and June,
1784, when nine States were in attendance — the necessary quorum — to act
on the treaty of peace."— Narrative and Critical History of America, Vol. VII,
p. 217.

[2] For a lively account of the election of the five delegates, and Virginia political
manoeuvring at this period, see a long letter by Thomson Mason to J. F. Mercer,
in "George Mason" by Kate Mason Rowland, Vol. II, pp. 55-65. See also
"Letters of Joseph Jones," Monroe's uncle. "Joseph Jones," says Mrs. Rowland, "hurried from his seat in Congress to attend the Assembly, and he wrote
regularly to Madison while in Richmond to report the progress of affairs."

sword. First, though, he said good-bye to his comrades.
This initial farewell was at noon on December 4 at
Fraunces' Tavern in New York. "With a heart full of
love and gratitude I take leave of you," said he. Then
there were affectionate hand-claspings, embraces. "In
every eye," wrote Marshall,[1] "was the tear of dignified
sensibility; and not a word was articulated to interrupt
the majestic silence and tenderness of the scene." He
left the room, passed through the corps of light infantry and walked to Whitehall Ferry, where he boarded
his barge for the Jerseys and the South. At Philadelphia
he settled his accounts with the Treasury. He had
served eight years without pay. On the evening of the
nineteenth he arrived at Annapolis. That night the
State House was illuminated. Washington's purpose
was to deliver his commission to Congress, which body
he notified next day.[2]

Congress arranged for a dinner in his honor on Monday, the twenty-second; and, at noon on Tuesday gave
him a public audience in the legislative chamber. In
one of the galleries, which was "bright with a beautiful
group of elegant ladies," sat Mrs. Martha Washington
and her two grandchildren, Nelly and Parke Custis.
Staff officers accompanied Washington as he entered
the hall. In his right hand he held his commission and
a copy of his address; and in his left hand his sheathed
sword. Charles Thomson, the faithful secretary, met
and led him to his seat by the President's chair. All
delegates stood uncovered — an unusual honor. When
President Mifflin signified the readiness of Congress to
receive the commission, Washington, in a short farewell, gave up his command. Having handed over the
commission and a copy of his address, he resumed his
seat; but, when Mifflin replied, he arose and stood until
the President had ceased to speak. Great the solemnity;

---

[1] The Life of George Washington, by John Marshall, Vol. IV, p. 620.

[2] "The General had been so reserved with regard to the time of his intended
resignation, that Congress had not the least apprehension of its being either so
soon or so sudden." — William Gordon, History of the United States, Vol. IV,
pp. 386-389.

deep the feeling; indeed, it is doubtful whether Monroe, or any other patriotic witness of the ceremony, ever allowed the scene to fade out of his recollection.

John Trumbull painted it, and William Makepeace Thackeray put it into his "Four Georges," [1] contrasting the opening feast of Prince George in London and the resignation of Washington. "Which," he asked, "is the most noble character for after ages to admire — yon fribble dancing in laces and spangles or yonder hero who sheathes his sword after a life of spotless honor, a purity unapproached, a courage indomitable, and a consummate victory?"

Next morning Washington hastened to Mt. Vernon, arriving there the same day, Christmas Eve. He had been home but once — and that only for a hurried visit — in eight long years. "The scene has closed at last," he wrote to Governor Clinton. "I feel myself eased of a load of public care."

[1] Thackeray's Four Georges, p. 114; Lodge's Washington, Vol. I, p. 339; Harrison's Washington, pp. 383, 384.

CHAPTER VI

IN THE CONGRESS OF THE CONFEDERATION

"In December, 1783, when Mr. Monroe took his seat in Congress," said John Quincy Adams in his Boston address to which we have referred, "the first act of that body should have been to ratify the definite treaty of peace with Great Britain, which had been signed at Paris on the preceding third of September. That treaty was the transaction which closed the Revolutionary war and settled forever the question of American independence. It was stipulated that its ratifications should be exchanged within six months from the day of its signature; and we can now scarcely believe it possible, that, but for a mere accident, the faith of the nation would have been violated and the treaty itself cancelled for want of a power in Congress to pass it through the mere formalities of ratification. By the Articles of Confederation no treaty could be concluded without the assent of nine States; but only seven States were assembled in Congress. Then came a captious debate, whether the act of ratification was a mere formality for which seven States were as competent as nine, or whether it was the very medullary substance of a treaty, which unless assented to by nine States, would be null and void — a monstrous and tyrannical usurpation!"[1] The eulogist continued:

"Among the mischievous consequences of the inability of Congress to administer the affairs of the Union was the waste of time and talents of the most eminent patriots of the country in captious, irritating and fruitless debates. The commerce, the public debt, the fiscal concerns, the foreign relations, the public

---

[1] Eulogy of James Monroe (reprinted with the Madison Eulogy as Lives of James Madison and James Monroe by J. Q. Adams). Madison spoke of John Quincy Adams' Boston Address, August 25, 1831, "as a just and happy tribute" to Monroe.

lands, the obligations to the Revolutionary veterans, the inter-course of war and peace with the Indian tribes, were all subjects upon which the beneficent action of Congress was necessary; while at every step, and upon every subject, they were met by the same insurmountable barriers of interdicted or undelegated powers. These observations may be deemed not inappropriate to the apology for Mr. Monroe, and for all the distinguished patriots associated with him during his three years of the service in the Congress of the Confederation, in contemplating the slender results of benefit to the public in all the service which was possible for them, thus cramped and crippled, to render."

On January 14, 1784, with twenty-three delegates present from nine States, the definitive treaty was ratified. The Journal of Congress shows that much routine work was done by Monroe.[1] Early in the session of the Fourth Congress he evinced an aptitude for parliamentary business. When he took hold of a thing he kept hold, as a rule, until the matter was disposed of. From the Journal and original "Papers of the Continental Congress," we see just how he voted on numerous questions and note the various committees on which he served. His name frequently appears in the records and always honorably.[2]

There were three matters of moment in which Monroe figured — one involving many questions connected with the great back country; another having to do with the Federal regulation of commerce; and still another, equally important, bearing upon the Mississippi outlet to the Gulf of Mexico.

What should be done with the vast domain beyond the Alleghenies?

Had Congress power to regulate the commerce of the country, or should it be left to the whims and vagaries of thirteen Congresses, each antagonistic to the other?

---

[1] "He was tall and well-formed, quiet and dignified in manner and simple in dress. He had little talent as an orator or writer, but his sensible views upon public questions, his spotless integrity and rare devotion to duty made him an influential man in Congress and elsewhere."— Moore's American Congress, p. 85.

[2] It would obstruct the narrative unduly should we attempt to summarize from S. M. Hamilton's Writings of Monroe, Vol. I, pp. XXVIII-LVII, Monroe's routine and Committee work in the old Congress. He examined many claims and reported upon many subjects.

Should Spain control the Gulf, and plug up the Mississippi, or did it of right belong to the inheritors of the Allegheny watershed of the vast valley of that river?

In each of the three subjects we are endeavoring to stress, danger lurked — danger of downright disruption; on the contrary, in the statesmanlike solution of the various problems involved were to be found the future security, prosperity and happiness of the United States.

Thanks to the foresight of Franklin, Adams and Jay, the Treaty of Peace stipulated that the territory should include the wilderness "Crown lands" from the mountains to the Mississippi.

In 1779, Virginia opened a land office with the purpose of selling her wild lands. Congress protested. There was a long and dangerous dispute over the unappropriated lands, threatening to disrupt the Confederation. Maryland refused to sign the articles unless Virginia should relinquish her pretensions. Then New York set the example of ceding her wild lands to the General Government. Connecticut followed her. Next came Virginia, December 20, 1783.[1] No doubt Monroe deemed it a great privilege, when, on March 1, 1784, with his colleagues he signed the parchment deed transferring the rights of Virginia in the Northwest Territory to the United States. Jefferson's seal on this deed is gone; the seals of Hardy and Lee are broken; but that of Monroe remains intact. Not all of the Virginians were of the mind of these delegates. At Richmond it was proposed to revoke the release, but under the leadership of Monroe's uncle, Joseph Jones, the cession of March 1, 1784, was confirmed.

Already our pioneers were occupying vantage points in the great region. Especially numerous were the settlers in what is now Ohio, whither General Rufus Putnam had gone with the definite purpose of organizing a new Commonwealth. In view of the heroic campaign

---

[1] Journal of Congress, Vol. I, p. 383.

of General George Rogers Clark, Virginia, with its
original charter-claims, had more than a common
interest in the disposition of the vast and fertile region
destined, as it seemed, to be the very heart and hope
of the republic.

Jefferson was concerned about it for more reasons
than one. Slavery was a sore subject with him, as it
was with most of the advanced thinkers, even then,
whether South or North. His "*post nati*" scheme,
first advanced in 1779, provided for gradual removal
of the blacks beyond the limits of the United States.
The colonization idea was referred to as his in his Notes
on Virginia, issued about the time of which we are
telling. He wished to keep slavery out of the whole
region. So did his followers. Their impulses and
deliberate conclusions on this theme were alike creditable to them in the very highest degree. "The design
of Jefferson," says Bancroft, "marks an era in the history of the universal freedom." Jefferson bore witness
against slavery "all his life long." He and Chancellor
Wythe, in codifying the laws of Virginia, sought to
provide for gradual emancipation.

Four days after the Virginia cession an ordinance
was reported in Congress for locating and regulating
the sale of public lands. On April 23, the Jefferson
Ordinance of 1784 was reported. It contained this
clause: "That after the year 1800 of the Christian era
there shall be neither slavery nor involuntary servitude
in any of the said States (to be carved out of the Western territory) otherwise than in punishment of crimes,
whereof the party shall have been convicted to have
been personally guilty."

Bancroft dwells with emphasis upon Virginia's con-
tribution toward a better union. "In the Fourth
Congress," says he, "Jefferson carried forward the
work of Madison with alacrity." They were a power.
They were indefatigable. Not only did they work for
an extension of Federal authority, but each had a
vision with respect to the opening of the west. "At

that time slavery prevailed throughout much more
than half the lands of Europe." Jefferson "following
an impulse of his own mind," not only proposed to
check the extension of slavery at the north and south
line, but "slavery was to be rung out with the depart-
ing century," so that in all the Western territory,
whether held in 1784 by Georgia, North Carolina,
Virginia, or the United States, "the sun of the new
century might dawn on no slave."

But there was a sad set-back. When a vote was
taken, April 19, 1784, on the motion of Richard Dobbs
Spaight, of North Carolina, to strike out the anti-
slavery provision, the chairman put the question
"Shall the words moved to be struck out stand?"
Seven affirmative votes would have been enough.
Jefferson, who mentions Spaight as a "young fool,"
writes to Madison (April 25): "The clause was lost by
an individual vote only. Ten States were present.
The four Eastern States, New York and Pennsylvania
were for the clause; Jersey would have been for it, but
there were but two members, one of whom was sick in
his chambers. South Carolina, Maryland and Virginia
voted against it. North Carolina was divided, as would
have been Virginia, had not one of its delegates been
sick in bed." Bancroft adds: "The absent Virginian
was Monroe, who for himself has left no evidence of
such an intention, and who was again absent when in
the following year the question was revived. For
North Carolina the vote of Spaight was neutralized by
Williamson."

Let it be noted that the Jefferson Ordinance of 1784,
minus the no-slavery provision, was enacted April 23;
and provided a temporary government for the Northwest Territory.

Jefferson's disappointment was shared by many dis-
cerning men. With such as Timothy Pickering, it
amounted to disgust. In his letters to Rufus King,
Pickering harps on the necessity of restoring the clause.
King was a rising young statesman. While volunteer

aide to Glover in Bull Hill fight, that General ordered
him post haste from the breakfast table to report on
an outbreak of cannon fire. As King left his chair,
Colonel Trumbull's friend, H. Sherburne, took it.
When King returned a little while after Sherburne was
being borne away on a litter, his leg shattered by a
cannon-ball. New to Congress, King was already a
man of note. Prompted by his own feeling, as well
as by Pickering, he tried to restore the lost clause. In
his Life of Rufus King, Dr. Charles R. King[1], following
the notes of Prof. Charles King, says: "When, then,
on March 16, 1785, the consideration of the proper
disposition of the public lands was resumed, Mr. King,
seconded by Mr. Ellery, of Rhode Island, moved the
proposition that there shall be neither slavery nor
involuntary servitude in any of the States described in
the resolve of Congress of the twenty-third of April,
1784, otherwise than in punishment of crimes, whereof
the party shall have been guilty, and that this regulation shall be an article of compact and remain a fundamental principle of the Constitution between the thirteen original States described in the said resolve of the
twenty-third of April, 1784."

This was referred to a committee of which King was
chairman. He reported it, April 6, with a proviso that
slavery be allowed "until the first day of the year
1801, but no longer." Thereafter it gathered dust in
the secretary's docket.

Now in the preliminaries, Congress had proposed to
carve ten new States out of these Western lands.[2]
This was as early as 1780. Somewhat later, Theodorick
Bland introduced a pioneering ordinance for colonizing
the territory northwest of the Ohio. The stipulation
as to ten States, in the resolve of 1780, which was

[1] The Life and Correspondence of Rufus King, 6 vols., Vol. I, p. 33 et seq. Charles
King, President of Columbia College, was Rufus King's son; Charles R. King, M.D.,
of Andalusia, Philadelphia, his grandson.

[2] Bancroft's Formation of the Constitution, Vol. I, p. 106; Laws relating to
Public Lands, p. 338; Journal of Congress, Vol. III, p. 535; Pickering "formed
a complete plan for settling lands in Ohio." Pickering's idea was to exclude
slavery. Pickering's Pickering, Vol. I, p. 510.

embodied in Virginia's act of cession and in the Ordinance of 1784, caused trouble. In 1786 Nathan Dane moved the appointment of a committee to remedy it. Monroe was chairman of this important committee. Having purposely dwelt upon the facts relating to the no-slavery clause, we now revert to Bancroft's reference to "the absent Virginian" who was sick in bed when wanted in Congress. In this matter, the excellent Bancroft leaves Monroe in a less enviable light than we should like. We do not think his inference warranted. We are obliged to take exception not so much to what Bancroft actually says as to his way of saying it. The thing that reflects upon Monroe is the juxtaposition in the sentence dealing with his absences or alleged absences; one explained; the other not explained. When a man is sick in bed, he is too sick to go to Congress. There have been heroic instances in which legislators have risked their lives in order to cast their emergent votes; but they belie the rule. As to why Monroe was absent the following year, if he were absent, we have insufficient knowledge. He was one of the active men in Congress and had much to manage. Like other delegates he was absent at many roll-calls. The Journal of Congress shows this. But at times members were away as commissioners, or busy in the performance of other public duties.

Bancroft[1] indulges in other strictures. Speaking of Monroe's committee to report on a form of temporary government for the Western States, the historian of the Constitution says:

"On the tenth of May this committee read their report. It asked the consent of Virginia to a division of the territory into not less than two or more than five States; presented a plan for their temporary colonial government, and promised them admission into the confederacy on the principle of the ordinance of Jefferson. Not one word was said of a restriction of slavery. No man liked better than Monroe to lean for support on the minds and thoughts of others. He loved to spread his sails to a favoring

---

[1] Bancroft's Formation of the Constitution, Vol. I, pp. 98-118. Papers of Old Congress, Vol. XXX, p. 79.

breeze, but in threatening weather preferred quiet under the shelter of his friends. When Jefferson, in 1784, moved a restriction on slavery in the western country from Florida to the Lake of the Woods, Monroe was ill enough to be out of the way at the division. When King in the following year revived the question, he was again absent at the vote; now when the same subject challenged his attention he was equally silent. At first Monroe flattered himself that his report was generally approved; but no step was taken toward its adoption. All that was done lastingly for the West by this Congress was the fruit of independent movements. On the twelfth of May, at the motion of Grayson seconded by King, the navigable waters leading into the Mississippi and the St. Lawrence, and the carrying places between them, were declared to be common highways, forever free to all citizens of the United States, without any tax, import or duty."

Grayson had joined the Virginia delegation in Congress on March 11, 1785. He at once began to work with Rufus King and William Ellery in their effort to restore Jefferson's no-slavery clause to the ordinance affecting the new territory. As to the number of States to be set up, that subject was transferred from Monroe's committee to a grand committee, which reported on July 7. Grayson proposed to create five States in the region now covered by Ohio, Indiana, Illinois, Michigan and Wisconsin. The South voted yea on this — Maryland, Virginia, North Carolina and Georgia. South Carolina was divided; "the north did not give one vote in its favor; and the motion was lost." It was then agreed that there should be at least three States in that region. We quote Bancroft again:

"The cause which arrested the progress of the ordinance of Monroe was a jealousy of the political power of the Western States, and a preventing desire to impede their admission into the Union. For himself he (Monroe) remained on this point true to the principles of Jefferson; to whom he explained with accurate foresight the policy toward which Congress was drifting." "When the inhabitants of Kaskaskias presented a petition for the organization of the government over their district, Monroe took part in the answer, that Congress had under consideration a plan of temporary government for their district, in which it would manifest a due regard to their interest."[1]

---

[1] Journals of Congress, Vol. IV, p. 688, 689.

In view of Monroe's fidelity as a zealous disciple of
Jefferson; of his wish that slavery might in time be
relegated to the limbo of outworn customs, and
especially of his actual concert with his kinsman and
colleague, William Grayson, it is unfortunate that
Bancroft should make him out to be altogether too
politic, too non-committal, too ready to count the
odds.

There is no proper warrant for the assumption that
Monroe purposely stayed away from Congress on the
day Spaight made his motion. It would be just as fair
to assert that Spaight, knowing Jefferson's friend
Monroe to be too ill to be present, seized upon the
occasion to call for a vote. Neither assumption is allowable. There is no evidence worthy of acceptance in
the court of history. But we may draw one conclusion
— make one conjecture: if Jefferson, who was so angry
with Spaight as to call him a fool, had thought Monroe
censurable, he would have said so. But Jefferson had
not the slightest grudge against him, trusted him constantly and gave repeated proof of the warmth of his
friendship. Monroe was so much younger than Jefferson, Grayson and Madison as to defer to them. He had
left college to go to fight, and felt his deficiency in comparison with old graduates. Moreover what Jefferson
and Madison thought of Monroe may be best understood by reading a passage from the "Life and Times of
Madison" by W. C. Rives.[1] Referring to the "close and
confidential correspondence" between Madison and
Monroe "which continued, with rare interruption for
near half a century," Rives sketches Monroe's career;
and adds:

"A friendship of a most intimate character grew up between
them, which, like that between Jefferson and Madison, though
not without one or two transient intermissions, attended them to
the close of their lives, and was warmly and affectionately cherished
by each. It is a rare and noble spectacle in the history of humanity
to see three men of such eventful lives, coming from the same State

---

[1] Rives' Madison, Vol. I, pp. 19-21.

and neighborhood, united for so long a time by bonds of the closest
friendship, and attaining in succession, one after another in the
order of their ages, the supreme magistracy of their country —
a station, in their day at least, as exalted as any among men."

"Mr. Monroe was less distinguished by original genius and
philosophical breadth of views than either of the three friends,
but he had a basis of good sense and sound judgment, fortified by
untiring application and indomitable perseverance, which made
him equal to every exigency of public affairs. His patriotism was
of a noble cast, and his integrity, often tried, was recognized as a
proverb; so that Mr. Jefferson, writing to Mr. Madison a year
or two after the time we are now treating, and wishing to convey
a vivid conception of the rectitude of another whose character
he was describing, says: 'For honesty, he is like our friend Monroe:
turn his soul wrong side outwards and there is not a speck on it.'
(Writings Jefferson, Vol. II, p. 90.) His sentiments always bore
the impression of his military training; and if his temper sometimes threw off a hasty spark, it was ever a scintillation of honor,
and was soon extinguished in the current of those generous affections which nature had given him in large and overflowing
measure."

Grayson framed and pushed an ordinance for the
disposal of western lands. "The land ordinance of
Jefferson, as amended from 1784 to 1788," says Bancroft, "definitely settled the character of the national
land laws." Then, on July 13, 1787, a new ordinance
— the Ordinance of 1787, designated by Daniel Webster
as the "great Charter of Rights," became a law of the
land.

The Northwest Territory was to have a governor —
General Arthur St. Clair became the first — a secretary
and three judges. When there were 5000 male inhabitants a General Assembly could be instituted. Mc-
Laughlin says: "The Ordinance was a great State
paper." No one man put it together. It grew.

In telling of this empire-making ordinance we have
been obliged to follow its development from year to
year. Now we go back, and give some account of
Monroe's field work in connection with the big back
country beyond the Alleghenies. While in Richmond
with Marshall, as we already have indicated, Monroe
had become deeply interested in the West. He had

long shared Washington's faith in the development of the trans-Appalachian country; and his work in committee had brought him in touch with various phases of the subject. Probably no one had a more intimate and sympathetic knowledge of some of these phases. Few public men thought more, or wrote more, about them. On June 3, 1784, he was associated with Sherman, Read, McHenry and Dick on a committee, to which was referred "the question of raising troops for the defence of the northwestern frontiers." Why were the British so tardy? What was their purpose in holding fast to posts in territory no longer theirs? It could not but be sinister. Monroe took much to heart this suspicious tardiness on the part of an ex-enemy which would strip off the "ex" and go at it again if the chance should offer.

Next month (July 22) he started on an extended tour of the territory. It was the summer recess. Congress had adjourned (June 3) and was to meet no more at Annapolis, but was to convene at Trenton on October 30. This was the summer of La Fayette's first post-Revolutionary visit. It was the summer, too, of Jefferson's visit to Dr. Franklin at Passy. Monroe had helped to select the site of the new capital by the Potomac; and then had gone down into King George County and thence to Richmond. He wrote a long letter to Jefferson from King George, July 20, in the course of which he said:

"The day after to-morrow I sit out [sic] upon the route through the Western Country. I have changed the direction and shall commence for the westward upon the North River, by Albany, etc. I shall pass through the lakes, visit the posts and come down to the Ohio and thence home. This route will necessarily take me all the time during the recess of Congress."

Evidently our young statesman who preferred "sit out" to set out was of the mind to see things with his own eyes. Here is another reference to his tour of observation, this likewise being an extract from a letter to Jefferson, under date of New York, August 9:

"I am so far on my way in performance of my trip thro' the Lakes, rivers, etc. You will observe by this time that I have changed my route to commence for the Westward here up the No. river, thence to the Lakes, to Detroit and thence to the Ohio — from the Ohio home. Upon the Ohio I purchase horses. Perhaps I may visit Montreal. Had I a month more to spare, I wo'd go to Boston, up the Kennebeck River to Quebec and thence on. I will certainly see all that my time will admit of. It is possible I may lose my scalp from the temper of the Indians, but if either a little fighting or a great deal of running will save it I shall escape safe. I sit out up the No. river in very agreeable company. Mr. Vaughn and family are of the party."

Such was the quaint phraseology and such were the confidences of this epistolary time. Pray take note also of the touch of humor — a rare thing in Monroe's correspondence. Indeed there are but few humorous anecdotes or incidents that relate to Monroe. One of the best is connected with just such a tour as this we are describing. With his negro valet, he had lodged in a wayside house. They were to set out before daybreak; and it was still dark in the room in which they had slept when Monroe called his servant. "Get up, Sam," said he, "and take a look out doors to see what kind a morning we have for our journey." Sam stumbled about awhile, opened a door and reported: "Hit er powerful dark mornin', Marse Jeems; and it smell o' cheese." Sam had opened a cupboard door, instead of the door of the house.

Monroe wrote that he hoped "to acquire a better knowledge of the posts which we should occupy, the cause of the delay of the evacuation of the British troops, the temper of the Indians towards us — as well as the soil, waters and in general the natural view of the country."

At Schenectady he was told by men lately from Oswego that a British officer there would challenge him. One of his informants, McFarlin, said that the officer had instructions from his commander-in-chief. Monroe at once wrote to Governor George Clinton at Albany. He was unable to understand, he said, why the British

continued to hold military posts in New York State.
Sir Guy Carleton had sailed away from New York in
the preceding December. "It is surprising to me,"
wrote Monroe, "that General Haldimand[1] hath not
evacuted these posts long since."

Ezra L' Hommedieu, a former member of Congress
from New York, had informed Clinton at an earlier
date that Haldimand had refused to permit Baron
Steuben even to visit the posts. In the same letter
L'Hommedieu[2] had declared that in his belief the
State of Virginia intended to seize Niagara. Such were
the alarms of a time when the thirteen Commonwealths
hardly knew the pleasures of peace even after peace
had come.[3]   Clinton replied next day, censuring the
unjustifiable conduct of Haldimand in continuing to
hold the posts. Monroe likewise wrote to Governor
Harrison of Virginia in regard to Canada and to his
friend Madison "on the importance of garrisoning the
Western forts about to be given up by the British."[4]

As for General Haldimand, he was quite capable of
playing a deep game. First, he had tried to restore
Vermont "to the King's obedience." When he found
that he could not do that, he began to manœuvre in
order to postpone evacuation. What if the States
should disunite? It looked that way. He manœuvred,
too, in behalf of the loyalists. It had been stipulated
in the peace treaty that the British should help to
apprehend and restore runaway slaves; and that in
turn the Americans should facilitate the payment of
British debts. What they did was just the opposite.
In Virginia Patrick Henry and his party prevented the
repeal of the State laws rendering such debts uncol-
lectable. Henry claimed that the British had not carried
out their agreement in the matter of the runaway, or
kidnapped, blacks; and that, therefore, they themselves

---

[1] Public Papers of George Clinton, First Governor of New York, Vol. VIII,
p. 339.
[2] Frederick Haldimand was Governor-General of Canada.
[3] Hommedieu to Clinton, September 3, 1783.
[4] Calendar of the Correspondence of James Monroe, pp. 52, 53.

were not bound to be concerned about the payment of old debts. But the supposed stand-off was no stand-off at all; for the British decided to be mulish in a third matter — they hung on to the frontier posts. Haldimand gave as his excuse for the continued British occupation of the western territory that he had received no orders to evacuate. This was the matter that puzzled and irritated Monroe.

In a Richmond letter, dated December 2, John Marshall congratulated Monroe on "a safe return to the Atlantic part of the world." John Tyler wrote from Richmond, November 28: "I am happy to find you have escaped the Indians and the British in your late route through Canada."

Once again, next year, Monroe journeyed westward. This was the year known as "*L'année des grandes eaux.*" In April the Mississippi rose thirty feet above any previous mark. There was to be a talk with the Shawnees at the mouth of the Great Miami and Monroe had the opportunity to go with the Indian Commissioners. He had private, as well as public, reasons for making the trip. For a long while it was in his mind to go grow up with the West. The lure of the wild land was on him, and he liked, too, to be on horseback and out in the open. He invited Madison to go with him. He wrote his itinerary for Jefferson,[1] "I intend to take within my view," said he, "the country lying between Lake Erie and the Ohio and the Potommack or Ja⁸ River, as it may suit me to return by the northern or southern part of the State. I pass thro' Lancaster and Carlisle at the latter of which posts I join General Butler."

The other Indian Commissioners were George Rogers Clark, Philip Schuyler, Samuel Holden Parsons and Robert Howe. Monroe left New York, August 24, and spent the fall months with the Commissioners. "But the danger from the Indians," he wrote in his next letter to Jefferson, January 16, 1786, "made it impru-

---

[1] Monroe to Jefferson, New York, August 25, 1785.

dent for me to pass the river, and the delay at Fort
Pitt, and upon the Ohio, the water being low, [in contrast with the spring floods], consum'd so much of the
time allotted for this excursion, that I was forced to
leave the Commiss^{rs} at Limestone and take my course
directly through the Kentucky settlements and the
wilderness to Richmond." He journeyed by Daniel
Boone's route from Limestone, or Maysville, to the
Lower Blue Licks, thence to Lexington, and reached
Richmond November 14. He was doubly disappointed:
he had not been present at the making of the Shawnee
treaty — a picturesque event, well worth traveling
through the wilderness to see; nor had he viewed as
much of the new country as he had hoped to traverse.

In a report to Congress based on his observations
during this journey, Monroe said that the West contained a great deal of uninviting land. Winsor says:
"He saw and heard enough about the country to
believe that the stories about the inordinate fertility
of the soil were the work of the land speculators."
But the grand attraction of the West had by this time
seized upon the imagination of the people. One company bought 5,000,000 acres of western land for
$5,000,000. All through the East the talk was of the
wonderful West.

When Congress reassembled, late that fall of 1784,
it was at Trenton. Writing to Madison[1] from that
town, John F. Mercer expresses regret at the "relaxation and inattention of the members of Congress."
He added that "nothing was more ardently desired by
the British nation than a renewal of the war with us.
Such was the opinion of Colonel Monroe after a visit
to Canada." In the same letter Mercer said: "The
contributions of Virginia to the General Government
alone keep the wheels in motion."

Monroe must have found his old fighting ground of
eight years before an interesting place to revisit; but

---

[1] Calendar of Correspondence of James Madison, Bureau of Rolls, Vol. IV,
p. 520.

it is hardly likely that he had time to go over into
Bucks. Jericho Hill was still there; and so were the
friends he had made; but Congress soon transferred
itself to New York. It met January 11, 1785, in the
old City Hall, which stood on the site of the Treasury
Building, at Wall and Nassau Streets; and ended its
days there March 2, 1789.

Monroe's capacity for congressional service of the
first importance was put to proof at New York as it
had been at Annapolis. The Fifth Congress missed
Madison. The Madison-Monroe correspondence in
1784-85 contains frequent reference to the difficulties
of the trade situation. How should commerce be
regulated? State tariff and tonnage laws were doing
more harm than good. Then, too, America was lax in
carrying out some of the provisions of the Peace
Treaty; and this shortcoming had brought on British
retaliation. One State wanted one thing; another,
another. British goods were coming in too fast to suit
New England, which, with Pennsylvania, demanded
protection. Two of America's three famous Websters —
Pelatiah and Noah — issued tracts in advocacy of
better government. The vigorous-minded and patriotic
unionist, James Bowdoin, Governor of Massachusetts,
insisted that Congress should be vested with necessary
powers to regulate the trade of the United States,
"manage its general concerns, and promote the common interest." Bancroft declares that "the nation
looked to Congress for relief." Speaking especially of
Monroe, Bancroft adds:

"When Jefferson embarked for France, he (Monroe), remained
not the ablest, but the most conspicuous representative of Virginia
on the floor of Congress. He sought the friendship of nearly every
leading Statesman of his Commonwealth; and every one seemed
glad to call him a friend. It was hard to say whether he was
addressed with most affection by Jefferson or by John Marshall.
His ambition made him jealous of (Edmund) Randolph; the
precedence of Madison he acknowledged, yet not so but that he
might consent to become his rival. To Richard Henry Lee he

turned as one from whose zeal for liberty he might seek the confirmation of his own.

"Everybody in Virginia resented the restrictive policy of England. Monroe, elected to the Fifth Congress, embarked on the tide of the rising popular feeling. He was willing to invest the Confederation with a perpetual grant of power to regulate commerce; but on condition that it should not be exercised without the consent of the nine States. He favored a revenue to be derived from imports, provided that the revenue should be collected under the authority and pass into the treasury of the State in which it should accrue.

"He from the first applauded the good temper and propriety of the new Congress, the comprehensiveness of mind with which they attended to the public interests, and their inclination to the most general and liberal principles, which seemed to him 'really to promise good for the Union.' They showed the like goodwill for him. On bringing forward the all-important motion on commerce, they readily referred it to himself as the chief of the committee, with four associates, of whom Spaight from North Carolina, and Houston from Georgia, represented the South; King of Massachusetts, and Johnson of Connecticut, the North.

"The complaisant committee lent their names to the proposal of Monroe, whose report was read in Congress on the twenty-eighth of March. It was accompanied by a letter to be addressed to the Legislatures of the several States explaining and recommending it; and the fifth day of April was assigned for its consideration.

"But it was no part of Monroe's plan to press the matter for decision. 'It will be best,' so he wrote Jefferson 'to postpone this for the present; its adoption must depend on the several Legislatures. It has been brought so far without prejudice against it. If carried farther here, I fear prejudices will take place. It proposes a radical change in our whole system of government. It can be carried only through investigation and a conviction of every citizen that it is his right. The slower it moves, therefore, in my opinion, the better.'"[1]

Jefferson gave Monroe's "compromise proposal for revenue" the stamp of his approval.

"Months passed away," adds Bancroft: "but still the subject was not called up in Congress; and the mind of Monroe as a Southern statesman, became shaken. The Confederation seemed to him at present but little

---

[1] Bancroft's History of the Formation of the Constitution of the United States, Vol I, pp. 191-197. The corrections in the Ms. committee report are in Monroe's handwriting. The letters that passed between Monroe and Jefferson, Monroe and Madison, and Jefferson and Madison, June 1784-August, 1785, contain numerous references to Monroe's measure.

more than an offensive and defensive alliance, and if the
right to raise troops at pleasure was denied, merely a
defensive one. His report would put the commercial
economy of every State entirely and permanently into
the hands of the Union; which might protect the carrying trade, and encourage domestic industry by a tax
on foreign industry. He asked himself if the carrying
trade would increase the wealth of the South and he
cited 'a Mr. [Adam] Smith on the Wealth of Nations'
as having written 'that the doctrine of the balance of
trade is a chimera.'"

We have quoted freely on this subject because it
helps us along with our study of Monroe. Only recently
he was a neglected supernumerary of the Continental
Line; now, as we see, he was deep in statecraft —
studious, hardworking, sagacious; as circumspect and
as full of foresight, indeed, as any of his elders. One
of these it was to whom was now committed the cause
of the opposition[1] — Richard Henry Lee. This veteran
lover of Virginia urged that to give Congress such
power as Monroe proposed "would expose the five
staple States, from their want of ships and seamen, to a
most pernicious and destructive monopoly."

Monroe's measure was never pushed. Monroe himself deferred to the judgment of his elders. Nevertheless the idea, widely discussed, helped to educate the
public for what was bound to come. Other things were
tending to enlighten and broaden people. Preachers
became teachers in that they helped to efface exaggerated State lines. It made no difference to a zealous
revivalist whether he were in Connecticut or Carolina.

---

[1] Monroe wrote to Jefferson, New York, July 15, 1785: "The report proposing
a change in the first paragraph of the 9th and 10th Articles of Confederation
hath been before Congress in a committee of the whole for two days past. The
house was to take it up again in the same manner. It hath been fully discussed
and in my opinion the reasons in favor of it are conclusive. The opposition however is respectable in point of numbers, as well as talents, in one or two instances.
. . . Some gentlemen have inveterate prejudices against all attempts of Congress
to increase the powers of Congress, others see the necessity but fear the consequences." In this letter Monroe mentions two foreigners who subsequently
figured in American political affairs — Mazzei, and Don Diego de Gardoqui.
The Don had just been presented to Congress.

This was a practical force, kneading in the mass, like other forces of democracy; and helping to convert our colonial population into true Americans.

But, at the same time, there were contrary forces at work — forces that pulled apart, that tended to create chasms rather than to cement. Let us illustrate: It was in the power of Congress to select commissioners from its own membership for the settlement of disputes between any two of the thirteen States. Thus, when boundary trouble arose between Massachusetts and New York, nine judges were named to constitute a Federal Court which was to sit in the case. Monroe was appointed to the court and on March 21, 1785, accepted the judgeship. But there was a curious hitch. Three of the nine declined to serve. Agents of the States involved named three other men and requested that a commission be issued for a meeting of the court at Williamsburg, Va., on the third Tuesday of November. On November 2, the agents complained of difficulties and delays on the part of the appointees and asked that the hearing be remitted "to such a day as the parties should agree upon." On May 15, 1786, Monroe informed Congress that "some circumstances would put it out of his power to act as a Judge for the decision of this controversy." Accordingly he resigned. September 27 next, the agents notified Congress that they had agreed upon a person to serve in lieu of Monroe. But the court never met. The case was settled at Hartford, Conn., by agreement, December 16, 1786. However, Congress refused to take cognizance of so irregular a proceeding.

Now what was the hugger-mugger in this mysterious boundary matter? John Quincy Adams breaks into poetry about it. In his Boston address is this passage:[1]

"Mr. Monroe did not assign, in his letter to Congress, his reasons for resigning the trust which he had previously consented to assume. They were probably, motives of delicacy, highly creditable to his character; motives flowing from a source

[1] Monroe Eulogy, by John Quincy Adams, August 25, 1831, pp. 225-232.

'Beyond the fixed and settled rules
Of vice and virtue in the schools.'
motives emanating from a deep and conscientious morality, of
which men of coarser minds are denied the perception, and which,
while exerting unresisted sway over the conduct actuated by them,
retire into the self-conviction of their own purity."

Here we have more mystery; but, in his next utterance, the eloquent eulogist turns on for us a matter-of-
fact spot light.

"Between the period when Mr. Monroe had accepted and that
when he withdrew from the office of a Judge between the States
of Massachusetts and New York, discussions had arisen in Congress relating to a negotiation with Spain, in the progress of which
varying views of public policy were sharpened and stimulated,
by sectional interests, to a point of painful collision. . . . It was in
the heat of the temper kindled by this cause of discord in the
Federal Councils that Mr. Monroe resigned his commission."

Notwithstanding his heat of temper over the Spanish
menace, Monroe continued his efforts to lessen the
governmental evils of the hour. But for the menace
to the South, he probably would have followed Madison.
As it was, according to Bancroft:[1]

"Monroe still loyally retained his desire that the regulation of
commerce should be in the hands of the United States, and his
opinion that without that power the union would infallibly tumble
to pieces; but now he looked about him for means to strengthen
the position of his own section of the country; and to Madison he
wrote [September 3, 1786], 'I earnestly wish the admission of a
few additional States into the confederacy in the Southern scale.' "

The Spanish menace, plus another menace that grew
out of it, provoked sectional feeling in Monroe. He
had been inclined to it by reason of State pride as early
as 1783, when, October 19, he wrote to George Rogers
Clark, "urging that a new State should be set up with
the tradition of Virginia, so that the Commonwealth,
now becoming aware of her isolation among her sisters,
might have an efficient ally in the Federal Councils."[2]

Monroe and Rufus King were appointed, August 14,

---

[1] Bancroft's Constitution, Vol. II, p. 297.
[2] The Westward Movement, by Justin Winsor, 1897, p. 247.

to go to Philadelphia for the purpose of acquainting the Legislature of Pennsylvania with the embarrassed state of the public finances and urging co-operation. King was accustomed to speak extemporaneously. His biographer adds:

"In this Pennsylvania mission, however, he essayed to deliver a written speech, and as he was the junior[1] of the two commissioners, it fell to him to open the business. The scene was imposing. The Legislature of Pennsylvania sat in Carpenters' Hall, where oft and again the Continental Congress in the darkest moments of the war of Independence had deliberated and resolved. Many distinguished men sat in the Legislature, and the procedure was a novel one, and on that account attracted much interest. Mr. King had already earned a high reputation for eloquence. He began in all due form, but soon, trammeled by the form of words he had prepared and learned, he became embarrassed, and after vainly struggling for a while to proceed, he turned to his colleague, Mr. Monroe, and begging him to take up the argument, sat down overwhelmed with confusion. Mr. Monroe, of more cool and equable temperament, and without any pretension as a speaker, made a calm, sensible, logical address. During this Mr. King was collecting himself. Rallying his powers and being, as he always was when he undertook to speak, master of his subject, he determined to dismiss from his mind all thought of the written speech and proceed in his accustomed manner."

So when Monroe sat down King[2] got up, gracefully excused himself for being disconcerted by the "august presence" of such distinguished auditors, and proceeded to deliver a long remembered address.

This mission was Monroe's last important work in the Congress of the Confederation, from which, by the rotation rule, he retired on the first Monday in November, 1786.

---

[1] This is a mistake. Rufus King was born in Scarborough, Maine, March 24, 1755 — nearly three years before Monroe.
[2] Rufus King gives an account of this incident in his Ms. notes. It is also noted in a "Sketch of Rufus King" by William Coleman in *Delaplaine's Repository*.

CHAPTER VII

Monroe and the Federal Constitution

We have spoken of the specie in circulation at the close of the war. But hard money soon grew less plentiful; and, as for the paper currency of Congress and the States, it was of varying value — often worthless. Now, it stands to reason that contracts made on paper money basis should not have been settled by obligatory process in specie; yet in some sections such settlement was demanded. Moreover, the troubled world grew harsher — stern laws were passed providing for imprisonment for debt. Many a good husband and father went to prison, while wives and daughters wept at the bars. Jails, too, were outrageously unsanitary. Beggars were told to move on, from township to township, from State to State. Speculators were out and about; and wicked enough, to be sure. "Times such as existed," says Justin Winsor[1] "were ripe for the machinations of demagogues and malcontents. . . . It was almost inevitable that the Courts should be resisted. The mob found a leader in one who had been an officer in the army and had some military experience — Daniel Shays." Fortunately for New England and the whole country, James Bowdoin, Governor of Massachusetts, was a strong man. He put down the Shays insurrection, and order was restored. Incidentally, great good came out of this evil — this warning. It was a warning to the people of America to drop the old government under the articles for "perpetual Union," and adopt the kind of union that would indeed be perpetual. Schouler concludes that the two events decisive of the coming effort to reform the Federal Government were the Shays Rebellion and

[1] Narrative and Critical History of America, Vol. VII, p. 229.

the failure of the proposed amendment for a five per
cent import duty, for twenty-five years, so earnestly
urged by Hamilton and Madison. Both of these
statesmen were now out of Congress — Madison because
of the rotation rule, and Hamilton because of a reaction
in New York toward States' right. Clinton, who
subsequently opposed the Constitution, was in power.
Schouler declares that the rising commerce of her
metropolis made New York selfish. When the import
amendment came before her Legislature, sitting in
the same city with the feeble and expiring Congress of
the Confederation, she rejected it. "One State among
the whole thirteen blocked the wheels"; but by-and-by
those wheels would turn again; for Madison and
Hamilton were both young, both intellectual to a high
degree, both filled with zeal — one for a centralized
government of the better classes; the other for a strong
government of the whole people. For, though they
were now working for the same object — stability
and efficiency of government, they differed as to the
form of that government, as well as to its spirit.
Madison did not distrust the ploughman, the woodchopper, the man-before-the-mast. Hamilton did.
Men of brains should manage public affairs; clod-
hoppers should take back seats. Madison and Monroe
shared with Jefferson certain beliefs and hopes in the
mass of the people, upon whom Hamilton, for his part,
looked with condescension if not distrust. It was
Hamilton's well-meant remonstrance to Rhode Island's
rejection of the import plan of 1782 that caused the
democratic-republicans to take alarm. Rives[1] contrasts
that paper with Madison's Address to the States,
April 18, 1783. In one was "enlightened caution";
in the other, "we meet with high-toned and uncompromising notions of Federal power — broad and
startling doctrines of implication from powers expressly
granted and a fond and constant recurrence to the

---

[1] Life and Times of James Madison, by William C. Rives, 1859; 3 vols., Vol. I,
p. 433.

necessity of a single directing will." That phrase "a single directing will" angered many a man. Whose will? It angered many, and it pained others — men like Monroe's uncle, Joseph Jones, "Washington's confidential friend," who knew how deeply hurt Washington himself was at such lack of discretion, such lack of delicacy. Madison was different. Schouler paints him: "Tentative and cautious by nature, and bearing, moreover, an important responsibility in the administration of affairs, Madison took care to commit himself in public only to what was presently feasible." Fortunately for America these two young statesmen, so unlike in character, were pulling together for a government worthy of the people who had won the Revolution.

On March 28, 1785, joint commissioners of Maryland and Virginia, acting upon a suggestion made by Madison, met at Mount Vernon to arrange a compact in commercial matters. Washington was their host. They agreed to recommend uniformity in duties on imports, uniformity in commercial regulations and uniformity in currency. Washington thought they might go further; so did Mason; whereupon the whole matter was reported to the Virginia Assembly. The upshot of the Mt. Vernon meeting was a call, issued by Virginia, for a gathering at Annapolis of commissioners from the thirteen States to adopt a body of commercial regulations.

Madison and Monroe were both at the Annapolis conference which, with John Dickinson as chairman, was held in September, 1786. Five central States were represented — not enough for conclusive action; but a great beginning was made, because it was then and there determined that a Federal Constitutional Convention was a necessity of the age. The Commissioners agreed that Philadelphia was the place where the deputies could most conveniently assemble; and they fixed upon the second Monday in the ensuing May as the appropriate time for the opening session.

At Annapolis, it was really a putting-together-of-heads; and two of the heads that bent towards each other over the council table were those of Madison and Hamilton. These two great Constitutionalists were acting in concert with a third — none other than Washington.

No one could have been more plain-spoken about the need of better government than Washington. To him the existing one was "a half-starved, limping government always moving upon crutches and tottering at every step." "It is as clear as A B C," said he, "that an extension of Federal powers would make us one of the most happy, wealthy, respectable and powerful nations that ever inhabited the terrestrial globe. Without this we shall soon be everything which is the direct reverse."

The "legacy" left by Washington upon the disbandment of the army was a circular letter issued in June, 1783, to the Governor of each State. No presidential message was ever read with keener interest than this eloquent address "to the citizens of America, the sole lords and proprietors of a vast tract of continent." He said: "The honor, power and true interest of the country must be measured by a continental scale. To form a new Constitution that will give consistency, stability and dignity to the union and sufficient powers to the great council of the nation for general purposes, is a duty incumbent on every man who wishes well to his country."

On February 16 of the same year had appeared the well-reasoned proposition of Pelatiah Webster to remodel the government; but it required the vastly stronger and resounding trumpet-call of the chief himself to fix attention upon the theme. Yet something else than eloquent argument was needed. It was well enough for Hamilton to talk about the "epidemic phrenzy" of State sovereignty; or for John Jay to cry out that "our distresses are accumulating like compound interest"; or for Washington to assert that "a nominal head, which at present is but another name for Congress will no longer do"; — these trenchant expressions were a need of the time, but practical work was also demanded and so was a practical man.

As it happened, the man of the hour was Madison. From its state of despair, as Bancroft expresses it, "the country was lifted by Madison and Virginia." He adds, with excusable warmth, "We now come upon the week glorious for Virginia beyond any event in its annals, or in the history of any republic that had ever before existed." Acting upon the suggestion of the commissioners to Annapolis, Virginia invited deputies of the several Legislatures to meet for the purpose of laying the foundations of a solid and permanent government. And now, at last, we are on the eve of the Federal Constitutional Convention, presided over by Washington, whom Franklin named for the chair.

The fifty-five delegates, journeying, in the main, on horseback, arrived from time to time; and Philadelphia again felt itself to be the host of the picked men of the continent. Bells rang for Washington, as the City Troop escorted him into the city. When, on the fourteenth of May, the Convention met, it was found necessary to adjourn from day to day to await other arrivals. Madison, who had his heart in this greatest work of his life, profited by the situation. With his colleagues, he concerted the Virginia plan, so called; and arranged a tactical method of procedure. Monroe's rival, Edmund Randolph, then nearly thirty-four, of brilliant parts, but with what Bancroft calls "a strain of weakness in his character," was put forward as spokesman. In "the race for public honors," adds Bancroft, he had taken "the lead of Monroe." Paraphrasing somewhat and speaking with typically American unrestraint, the historian of the Constitution[1] declares that altogether the delegates formed "the

---

[1] Bancroft's History of the Formation of the Constitution of the United States, Vol. II, p. 6, *et seq.*

goodliest fellowship of lawgivers whereof this world holds record." Several were signers — Clymer, Gerry, Morris, Read, Sherman, Wilson, Wythe; John Rutledge dated from the time of the Stamp Act Congress and eighteen of the delegates had sat in the Continental Congress. Gouverneur Morris had removed to Philadelphia and was a member from Pennsylvania. But Pennsylvania's most helpful worker was James Wilson. Bancroft speaks of him as "one of the wisest men in the Convention, if not the clearest headed constitution-maker." Mason, Dickinson, the Pinckneys and others of equal note took part in the great task. The small States fought for and secured equality in the Senate. The slave-holding States insisted upon a clause reckoning three-fifths of the slaves in the apportionment of members of the House of Representatives. The commercial States secured a third compromise "which forbade the Federal prohibition of the slave-trade until 1808, in consideration of new commercial facilities."[1]

Since Monroe was not a member of the Convention, we are confining ourselves to the barest outline concerning its compromises and its splendid handiwork. No doubt it was one of the regrets of his life that he was not present in Independence Hall when the Constitution was framed.

As against Madison's Virginia plan, Charles Cotesworth Pinckney presented the South Carolina plan. These two plans were considered in committee of the whole till June 13, when nineteen resolutions, based on Madison's scheme, were favorably reported. On June 15 another scheme known as the New Jersey plan was brought forward. This was, in substance, the old scheme of the Confederacy. It was thrown out. Four resolutions were added to the nineteen; and then the twenty-three were referred to a committee of five which was to report them in the form of a Constitution. On July 26 the Convention adjourned to meet on the sixth of August.

[1] Schouler's History of the United States, Vol. I, p. 41.

Monroe knew what was going on. On July 27 he wrote to Jefferson: " If what the Convention recommended should be rejected, they will complete our ruin. But I trust that the presence of General Washington will overawe and keep under the demon of party, and that the signature of his name to the result of their deliberations will secure its passage through the Union." He must have written something like that to his kinsman, William Grayson; for that worthy, less complaisant, wrote to Monroe, May 29: "The weight of General Washington is very great in America, but I hardly think it sufficient to induce the people to pay money or part with power."

On account of the rotation rule, Monroe was no longer in Congress, but had returned to the Virginia Assembly, sitting as a member for Spottsylvania County. In the letter to Jefferson just quoted there is another passage of importance. Speaking of Governor Edmund Randolph, he says:

"The Governor, I have reason to believe, is unfriendly to me and hath shown (if I am well inform'd) a disposition to thwart me; Madison, upon whose friendship I have calculated, whose views I have favor'd, and with whom I have held the most confidential correspondence since you left the continent, is in strict league with him and hath I have reason to believe, concurr'd in arrangements unfavorable to me; a suspicion supported by some strong circumstances that this is the case hath given me great uneasiness — however in this I may be disappointed and I wish I may be so. I shall, I think, be strongly impressed in favor of and inclined to vote for whatever they recommend."

From this we are not to infer that Monroe felt himself very much out of favor. Nor did his Madison grievance last long. Both Randolph and Mason refused to sign the Constitution, when the Federal Convention had finally framed it and referred it to the various Legislatures. After the adjournment, September 17, 1787, Monroe wrote to Madison about the feeling in Virginia: "It is said that Mr. Henry, General Nelson, Harrison and others are against it. This insures it a powerful opposition, more especially when associated with that of the two dissenting deputies."

Certainly there would be a great struggle in Virginia over the Constitution. The Convention that was to ratify or reject was called to meet at Richmond on June 2, 1788. Monroe was elected as a delegate from Spottsylvania County. A few days before his departure from Fredericksburg, he addressed a letter to his constituents telling them of his proposed course, and giving them his reasons; but a delay in printing the letter,[1] and its inadequacy when it got into print, caused him to withhold it.

Bright was the weather and gay the birdsong around the old Capitol when the pick of the Virginians of a famous generation came together to discuss Mr. Madison's work. The place was packed; and so, next day, the Convention met in the New Academy on Shockoe Hill, with Edmund Pendleton presiding. Much of the time Chancellor Wythe was in the chair.

Madison led his own fight. With him were Randolph, Marshall, Pendleton, Wythe, Wilson Nicholas, George Nicholas, Corbin, Innes and Harry Lee. Opposed were Henry, Mason, Tyler, Grayson, Dawson, Harrison — and Monroe. Monroe made his first speech on the tenth of June; his second on the thirteenth.

In explaining why Monroe resigned as a commissioner of Congress in the Massachusetts-New York boundary case, we reproduced some pertinent passages from the red-letter Boston address in which John Quincy Adams reviewed the life and character of his subject. The explanation was that Monroe had become disgusted with the sectionalism developed during the New York

---

[1] A unique copy of this letter in the form of a small, twenty-four-page pamphlet was found by John P. Weissenhagen of the Bureau of Rolls and Library, Department of State. Someone had written on it "Honble James Monroe, Oak Hill, Loudon County, Va." Someone else had written "Mr. Monroe's pamphlet Convention, 1788." In Monroe's own handwriting are the words "erasures made in some instances improperly." It is a long essay on democracy and the Constitution. Hard work was put on it. This is reprinted as Appendix I, in Vol. I of Hamilton's Writings of Monroe. Appendix I is a reprint of the pamphlet, by Monroe, "Observations on the Federal Government," sent by Monroe to General Washington, February 15, 1789.

sessions of Congress, and in the heat of temper had cut loose from the court.

By the same token, this was one reason why Monroe now found himself, much against his will, on the side of those who, at the outset, demanded amendments to the Federal Constitution.

What was this old matter that made the blood boil and caused so many true-hearted men to fight a Constitution they had really longed for?

And this brings us to the point where we may as well admit that one is apt to feel apologetically inclined in reviewing the personnel of the opposition. Why do we feel that way? When telling of Henry or Mason or Monroe, why do we regret that they questioned our great system of fundamentals in government? Armed cap-a-pie with all the destructive implements of hindsight criticism, not a few historians assail the anti-Constitutionalists of 1788. But, though they are merciless, we do not mind them. The thing we mind is that admirers of Henry, Mason and Monroe should likewise regret the participation of those worthies in the fight against what has proved to be one of the most pronounced successes in the history of human experiment. It is plain to us now that, generally speaking, those who favored the Federal Constitution were right and those who opposed it were wrong; therefore, we wonder what possessed Richard Henry Lee, George Mason, Patrick Henry and James Monroe when they challenged it. Why did Lee fight it from the very beginning? Mason weighed it in his mind; and then demanded something better. No one questions his pure patriotism, his depth of learning in that most difficult of sciences — government. Why, then, his recusancy? Patrick Henry was long silent about the new Federal Government, wishing it well. Monroe's uncle, Joseph Jones, heard Henry say in the coffee-house at Richmond that his only reason for returning to the Legislature in 1784 was that he might "strengthen the Federal arm." He was a unionist; yet he and

Monroe, also a unionist of the first water, now put up a poor mouth on the subject of a strong union. Many another able and honest man who sat in the hall thought as Monroe did. It is the easiest matter in the world to glorify the urgers and proponents of the Constitution, with its proven excellences, and to damnify those who saw fit to challenge it at the outset. Henry was a Missourian before Missouri was set up. Monroe, too, wanted to be shown.

The simple truth is that in Virginia there was almost an even division of sentiment. The influence that bore Monroe toward the Constitution came out of himself and out of his loyalty to the doctrines and desires of Jefferson; the influence that bore him away — aside from the spirit of party, powerful then as now — was bred by certain fears within him on account of the threatened occlusion of the Mississippi River; the great sectional spectre even then looming up and the negations of liberty involved in too rigid a consolidation. The mind of a man like Monroe is not incapable of projecting imaginary pictures upon the screen of the future. He must have drawn back in alarm from some of the sombre mind-pictures of clashing sectionalism visualized in his midnight ponderings.[1]

The debates lasted three weeks. Bancroft[2] speaks of the onslaughts of Henry, Mason and Grayson "feebly supported by Monroe," and "greatly aided" by Harrison and Tyler. Bancroft could not forgive Monroe for dropping out of step with Madison. "Day by day they were triumphantly encountered by Madison, on whom the defense of the Constitution mainly rested." Pendleton, George Nicholas, John Marshall, James Innes, Henry Lee and Francis Corbin all helped him to hold the line of battle. Everything bearing upon

---

[1] In a long letter to Andrew Jackson, December, 1816, Monroe said that he served three years in the old Congress and in the new rather longer. In each he saw aristocratic tendencies dangerous to democracy. Firm opposition defeated the marplots.

[2] "Monroe, leaving his inconsistency unexplained, was drawn toward the adversaries of Madison."— Bancroft's Constitution, Vol II, p. 300.

the subject was fought out,[1] as the Constitution was considered clause by clause. Henry cried: "The Constitution is a severance of the Confederacy." Randolph said: "The question is now between union and no union, and I would sooner lop off my right arm than consent to a dissolution of the union." Monroe, with Henry, called for checks and balances to guard the liberties of the people. Marshall defended the plan for a judiciary. And so it went — Mason strong; Henry vehement; Madison, the embodiment of patience, alertness and practical good sense. As he very well knew, his strength was in his theme.

"Mason was right in the main," admits Bancroft, "but somehow he lacked the broad-mindedness of his Mt. Vernon neighbor." "Mason," [2] says Fitzhugh Lee, "desired to erect a republic whose strength at the centre was only great enough to carry out the object for which it was created; while the creator — the States themselves — should be left undisturbed in the exercise of all power not specified as having been relinquished. He had a full appreciation that the safety of the State was the safety of the union. He was the champion of the State and of the people." He wanted a one-term, seven-year President; no property-qualification and no counting of slaves alongside freemen as a basis of representation. He advocated the "emancipation of slaves, or power to prevent slavery's increase." Limitations should be put upon the power of Congress as well as upon that of the executive.

Henry excelled himself in the closeness, cogency and force of his reasoning if not his eloquence, which was indeed of that same magical quality characteristic of one of the greatest of orators. He was bound to put this new thing through fire; and if the gods had given it down, as its sponsors said they had, it would stand the fire — yes, it would be all the better for it. He

---

[1] Jonathan Elliot's Debates, Vol III, p. 23, et seq. For Monroe's two speeches see Debates of the Convention of Virginia by David Robertson, p. 154.
[2] Rowland's Mason, Vol. I, p. viii.

wanted purification by fire; he wanted amendments —
he demanded amendments. The "awful squinting of
the new government" alarmed him — this government
with consolidating tendencies. "It squints toward
monarchy," he cried. In thus harping upon the danger
of a return to kingcraft, he played a tune very sweet
in the ears of Jefferson, Grayson, Monroe, Richard
Henry Lee and others of the democratic-republican
movement.[1]

Monroe agreed with Henry[2] as to the dangers of
consolidation. He thought he could foresee the time
when the country might fall under the yoke. He
dreaded the idea of a king. A President once elected
might secure his own re-election for life. He dreaded
the idea of conflict between the State and national
authorities. "He loved the Union," says Howison,
"and believed that the States loved the Union; but
he thought their government ought to be strictly a
union of the States and not a melting together of the
people. He believed democratic independencies might
safely confederate. The great leagues of the world
passed in review before him; the Amphictyonic, the
Achaean, the Germanic, the Swiss Cantons. . . . He
compared the Confederation and the Constitution:

---

[1] Living generations after the monarchical danger is past, men of today wonder
at those who suffered from king-on-the-brain. Yet it was, and is, an actual
obsession. Old John Tyler, of Virginia, was as much a king-hater as Wat. To
Lee, Monroe and Tyler, history seemed a long record of misery wrought by kings
and their tools. America must go kingless and be happy. R. H. Lee, in a letter
to Monroe, Chantilly, January 5, 1784 "fears our country will lose those blessings
of liberty so arduously labored to secure." Why a standing army? Let the
people protect the frontiers. Grayson's home was in Dumfries, and on his untimely
death in 1790, he was buried in the family vault of "Belle Air," the seat of his
brother, the Rev. Spence Grayson, rector of Dettingen parish, Prince William
County. When Grayson's house at Dumfries was burned, valuable papers were
lost.

[2] Wythe, Virginia Debates, 1788, p. 446; Wirt's Life of Henry, p. 210; Howison's Virginia, p. 327. "James Monroe argued against the system of election
which was destined twice to make him President."— Formation of the Union,
by Albert Bushnell Hart. In "The Era of Good Feeling," Harper's Magazine,
Vol. LXVIII, pp. 936-956, Thomas Wentworth Higginson compares what Monroe
said in the Virginia Convention with what he said when he was President, on
internal improvements. In 1788 he thought the country between the Atlantic
and Pacific "too extensive to be governed but by a despotic monarchy;" in 1822,
he thought "the American system capable of expansion over a vast territory."

add to the first absolute power over commerce and he would approve it; take away from the last the power of direct taxes and he would approve it. This right to tax the people was the point he dreaded[1]: how could a few representatives from a country covering nearly a million square miles tell what would be most suitable subjects for taxation; what would least oppress and what would be best endured?

Suddenly, on the thirteenth of June, Patrick Henry played his best card: he called on Monroe, as a member of the Sixth Congress familiar with its secret proceedings to tell the people of Virginia a strange tale that was bound to startle them.

There is no doubt that Henry himself had been shocked, as well as startled, by this same matter when Monroe had revealed it to him in a letter [2] dated New York, August 12, 1786. Up to the moment of the receipt of the letter, Henry had favored constitutional reform; thereafter he watched its progress with suspicion.[3]

The strange matter was this: Don Diego de Gardoqui, diplomatic representative from Spain, arrived in New York in the early summer of 1785. "We take his stile," wrote Monroe to Madison, July 12, "from his letter of credence (from the King of Spain) and call him *Encargado de Negocios.* He is a polite and sensible man." In numerous letters to Jefferson, Monroe refers to Gardoqui. John Adams had met him in Spain. So had Jay. John Quincy Adams wrote of him July 20, 1785: "At tea this afternoon, at Mr. Ramsay's,[4] I met Mr. Gardoqui. His complexion and looks show sufficiently from what country he is. How happens it that revenge stares through the eyes of every Spaniard? Mr.

---

[1] Wythe, Virginia Debates, 153-158-159; 208.

[2] The original of this letter, presented by Henry's grandson, William Wirt Henry, is now in the National Archives.

[3] Henry "exerted himself to defeat the proposed treaty in so far as it provided for the relinquishment of the Mississippi."— Life, Correspondence and Speeches of Patrick Henry by William Wirt Henry, 3 vols., Vol. II, p. 291.

[4] Griswold's Republican Court, p. 76. Ramsay, the historian was a member of Congress from South Carolina.

Gardoqui was very polite and enquired much after my father."

Gardoqui and John Jay, Secretary of Foreign Affairs, soon put their heads together with the purpose of arranging a treaty. Jay was skilled in the art of treaty-making — Congress knew that. "But in Gardoqui," says A. C. McLaughlin, "Jay found a foeman worthy of his steel."[1] "The wily Spaniard, proving the feeble-ness of Congress, probably aware of the intrigues on the frontier, and conscious that no harm could come to the Spanish cause by delay, so long as Spain actually held the country in dispute, was unyielding to the last degree. . . . Jay was instructed to insist on the recognition of the thirty-first parallel and the free navigation of the Mississippi to its mouth, rights guaranteed by the treaty with England. Over this question he and Gardoqui debated and puzzled until Jay was weary."[2] Worse still! Some of the Eastern leaders, in so far from considering the interests of the Southwest, threatened to secede unless given what they sought. According to Monroe,[3] there was a party who advocated a dissolution of the Confederation on other grounds. Its object was to break up the settlements on the western waters; "to throw the weight of population eastward and keep it there"; in short, to hold on to the government in the East.

"In conversations at which I have been present," wrote Monroe, "the eastern people talk of a dismemberment so as to include Penna. (in favor of wh. I believe the present delegation, Petit and Bayard, who

---

[1] The Confederation and the Constitution (The American Nation, Vol. X, p. 94). See Jay, Correspondence and Public Papers, Vol. III. Secret Journals of Congress, III, p. 569-586, IV, 87-110; also (paper) VIII, for 1785, 86 and 87; Bancroft's Constitution, II, p. 293, et seq.; Eulogy of John Quincy Adams, pp. 225-232.

[2] For the Motion of the Delegates of Virginia, drawn by Monroe, on the subject of Spain and the Mississippi, see Writings of James Monroe, by S. M. Hamilton, Vol. I, pp. lviii and liv.

[3] "Monroe was uneasy at this time concerning the projects of Jay and his party. He saw in them an attempt to break up the Union, and he wrote to the prominent men in Virginia to ascertain and influence their views on the subject." — George Mason, Rowland, Vol. II, p. 25. His letters were to Mason, Henry and Madison.

are under the influence of Eastern politics, would be)
and sometimes all the States south of the Potomac."[1]

Jay, a patriot, a statesman, was under heavy pressure. Finally he agreed to the occlusion of the Mississippi for twenty-five years, in consideration of certain
trade advantages. He was uninformed as to the great
growth of the Southwest. As it happened, the advantages would accrue to the northern and eastern States;
the disadvantage would be felt by the Southwest, and
by the Kentucky district of Virginia. That State under
its charter reached westward as far as the Father of
the Waters. Monroe regarded the Mississippi as a
Virginia river; or at least, as half Virginian, since it
washed the back-country boundary. We do not mean
that Monroe went into all these details. He general-
ized; and that, too, in his accustomed manner —
guardedly, and without offense. Nor did he tell the
Convention how he and his fellow-workers in the five
southern States had attempted to overreach Gardoqui.
As a matter of fact[2] they had arranged quite a little
counterplot. They approached the French *Chargé
d'Affaires*, who was in correspondence with the French
Ministry. This was Louis Guillaume Otto,[3] who wrote
to the Comte de Vergennes: "In the midst of this (Jay-
Gardoqui) fermentation the leaders of this party came
to me to explain to me the necessity of having recourse
to your good offices, and of putting this negotiation
wholly into the hands of his Majesty" — Louis XVI.
They wished Vergennes and Jefferson to take up the
subject. France could bring pressure to bear on Spain.
France was reminded that there was danger lest
England should get a grip in the great back country to
everybody's detriment. They wanted an open Mis-

---

[1] All this was "proposed by a set of men so flagitious, unprincipled, and determined in their pursuits" as to satisfy Monroe that they had extended their views
to the dismemberment of the government. W. W. Henry's Patrick Henry,
Vol. II, p. 297.

[2] Otto to Vergennes, New York, August 23, and September 10, 1786; Monroe
to Madison, New York, August 30 and September 3.

[3] Later Comte de Mosloy. He married a New York belle, Miss Livingston,
a relative of Mrs. John Jay.

sissippi for flatboats to New Orleans, which should
be an entrepôt for exports only, dutiable at two and one-
half per cent ad valorem and to be shipped thence in
French, Spanish or American bottoms. Let Jefferson
negotiate at Madrid. Go over Gardoqui's head. There
was more than one way of skinning a cat. "It is possible," concluded Otto in his letter to Vergennes, "that
the passion of the delegates who spoke with me may
have led them to exaggerate some details." We may
imagine this scene — in lower Manhattan, late in
summer; eager-faced delegates, closeted with the cool
and collected diplomat, to whom they revealed their
plan for circumventing the wily Spaniard. There were
occurrences, no doubt, that Monroe had no wish to
speak of. The leading facts were all he need bring out.
These surely were significant enough — these would do.

Congress had voted, June 3, 1784, that the free
navigation of the Mississippi was a *sine qua non* to a
reciprocity treaty. In May, 1786, Congress had
appointed a committee of three to confer with Jay,
King, Pettit and Monroe. In August of that year Jay,
backed by King and Pettit and opposed by Monroe,
reported in favor of the occlusion of the Mississippi
for twenty-five years. This was what Gardoqui wanted.
Washington said he could not understand why. It
would be better, he said, to make New Orleans "a free
mart." Madison was equally displeased. "Monroe,"
says Justin Winsor,[1] "fancied he saw in the opposition
of New York a purpose to profit by the closing of the
river so as to gain time to develop the western communication by the Hudson." Then, in 1786, Congress,
in secret session, repealed its instructions to Jay. The
repeal was not published. Congress was ashamed to
publish it. This, then, was Monroe's tale as told before
the Convention at Henry's behest. To an inflamed mind
here was dramatic material by no means comic; a
villain, a very Mephisto of a Don; a plot — a sinister
Spanish plot; a barter, a most piratical barter; betrayal

[1] The Westward Movement, p. 348.

in the house of one's friends; with secession — ugly
word — as the sequel; and, finally, the fiery Henry in
the rôle of chorus, if not avenger!

As a matter of fact, there was no unseemliness in the
presentation of the matter to the Virginia Convention.
Let Grigsby[1] tell of the scene:

"The speech of Monroe was well received. It made upon the
House a strong impression, which was heightened by the modesty
of his demeanor, by the sincerity which was reflected from every
feature of his honest face, and by the minute knowledge which he
exhibited of a historical transaction of surpassing interest to the
South. But if the impression was felt by the members generally
it was felt most keenly by those who were anxious about the sales
of their crops and for the prosperity of their families. The members from the West were furious. They had just learned for the
first time the imminent hazard to which their most valued privilege had been exposed, and they did not conceal their indignation."

Grayson followed Monroe and endorsed what he had
said. But Madison had one advantage over them — he
had been in Congress later than either. He could give
reassuring news. Congress had put an end to the talk
about the occlusion of the Mississippi. It had resolved
"That the free navigation of the river Mississippi is a
clear and essential right of the United States."[2] Not
only so, but it had put an end to the Jay-Gardoqui
negotiations and referred the whole matter to the new
government under the Federal Constitution. Eastern
opinion had changed — was now friendly. Thus did
Madison meet the issue upon which Henry and Monroe
had relied to win the day.[3]

And so the debates proceeded. Once Henry arose
to catastrophic and spectacular heights. It was in the
old Capitol, in June, at the close of a hot day, suddenly
and ominously darkened by a thundercloud about to
burst. Henry surpassing himself, a master-tragedian,
enacting the downfall of his country, put upon his

---

[1] History of the Virginia Convention of 1788, by Hugh Blair Grigsby, p. 240;
Writings of James Monroe, S. M. Hamilton, Vol. I, pp. 189-192.

[2] Secret Journal of Congress, September 16, 1788.

[3] It did win the members from the Kentucky district. Ten of fourteen voted
against ratification.

audience a spell too tense to bear. Speech and storm reached their climax together. "The effect could not be borne; the members arose in confusion, and the meeting was dissolved."

Virginia finally ratified, but by a close vote — a majority of ten in a total of one hundred and sixty-eight. The honors went to Madison, though everyone felt that Washington's influence had been a powerful help to him. But deeper than personal influence and deeper than anything in the debates was the genuine union sentiment throughout the State. The people ratified the Constitution because they wanted it.

However, Henry and his helpers made a powerful impression. They were responsible for certain of the amendments made at the very outstart of the Federal Government.

Many, like Monroe, who had opposed the Federal Constitution at once accepted it. Indeed, it was not long before Monroe was in the new Congress. Others required more time to become reconciled to the change in government. A great force to this end were the papers that appeared in the *Independent Gazetteer*, a New York daily, under the title of "*The Federalist.*" They were all signed "Publius," but Hamilton wrote fifty-one of them; Madison, twenty-nine; and Jay, five. Issued in book form, they were read everywhere and with excellent effect.

CHAPTER VIII

MARRIAGE — MAKING HIS WAY

"You will be surpris'd to hear," wrote Monroe to Jefferson (under date of New York, May 11, 1786) "that I have form'd the most interesting connection in human life, with a young lady in this town. As you know my plan was to visit you before I settled myself. But having form'd an attachment to this young Lady (a Miss Kortright, the daughter of a gent^n of respectable character and connections in this State, tho' injured in his fortunes by the late war) I have found that I must relinquish all other objects not connected with her. We were married ab^t three months since. I remain here untill the fall at w^h. time we remove to Fredericksbg^g in Virg^a. where I shall settle for the present in a house prepared for me by Mr. Jones, to enter into the practice of the law."[1]

New York society had strong attractions for young men in the government service. "More than one member of Congress from other States," says the Memorial History of that city, (Vol. III. p. 20) "found their future partners within the charmed circle. James Monroe, the future President, married the daughter of Laurence Kortright; Rufus King, of Boston, the daughter of John Alsop;[2] and Elbridge Gerry, the

---

[1] Monroe had notified his uncle of his engagement to Miss Elizabeth Kortright, and had received from Judge Jones a long letter, filled with avuncular advice and kindness. He hinted that, should his nephew need accommodation, it would be his. The postscript of a letter from Monroe to Madison, New York, February 11, 1786, runs: "If you visit this place shortly I will present you to a young lady who will be adopted a citizen of Virg^a. in the course of this week." Madison, then a bachelor, wrote to Monroe from Orange, March 19, congratulating him on his marriage.

[2] She was Maria Alsop. Mrs. Mary A. Patrick, a great-niece of John Alsop, in a letter to Charles King (Life of Rufus King, I, p. 130) says: "The ceremony was performed by Bishop Provoost and Congress being in session in New York and the bridegroom belonging to it, many of its members attended it; among

Mrs. James Monroe

Sené, the celebrated miniaturist, painted this on ivory, while the Monroes were in Paris in 1794
Mr. Monroe thought the world of it—a true likeness, with all the charm of Sené's exquisite coloring

Eliza Kortright Monroe (Mrs. Hay)

She was the elder of the two daughters of James Monroe and his wife. She married Judge
George Hay of Richmond, Va., and, when widowed, returned to Paris, where she died and where she
still rests. The portrait, painted by Caruson, is on ivory. The photograph is from the original.

daughter of James Thompson, who is so flatteringly
referred to as 'the most beautiful woman in the United
States.' A visitor at Colonel William Duer's house
states that he lived in the style of a nobleman, and had
fifteen different sorts of wine at dinner. His wife,
Lady Kitty, daughter of General Lord Stirling, late
of the Continental Army, and a person of most accomplished manners, was observed to wait upon the table
from her end of it, with two servants in livery at her
back. But it has been estimated that less than three
hundred families affected society life at this time, and
these were of different grades." In fact, while many
lived well, they were usually at pains not to ape either
nobles or nabobs. Philip Livingston, the Signer, was
a merchant. Barrett, searching an old advertisement,
discovered that Philip Livingston sold needles, tea,
kettles and cheese.

The Kortrights and Gouverneurs had long been
known as substantial Manhattan families. Cornelius
Jansen Kortright, born in Beest, Gelderland, 1645,
came over in 1663.[1] Cornelius Kortright, merchant,
married Hester Cannon, sister of another equally
successful merchant, John Cannon. Up bright and
early on Easter Monday morning, 1743, Cornelius,
walked down to Kortright's wharf, on the East River
to look after one of his vessels. It was a holiday, and
the crew had deserted. "The wind," says Walter

---

others James Monroe and Elbridge Gerry. The youth, beauty and fortune of
the bride had made her a great belle, and her marriage was a serious disappointment to many aspirants. The wedding was very splendid. Six bridesmaids
attended on the bride of whom my mother was one, and at the supper was produced for the first time wine which had been purchased and put aside at the birth
of the bride for this very occasion." The pipe containing it, being bricked up,
had escaped the British soldiers who occupied this William Street house; but they
made booty of an iron chest in which were plate and Mrs. Alsop's diamonds. Aware
that a pair of pistols would explode if the chest were pried open the British took it
to London to have it opened there.

[1] According to Walter Barrett's "Old Merchants," p. 25, "the Kortrights
came to New York in a different way from the old Dutch settlers." The Kortright and "other Dutch families, such as the Romaines, went to Rio Janeiro,
in Brazil, with Prince Maurice. They expected to remain and hold that country.
They built forts, but finally they swapped off with the Portuguese for Surinam
and Curacoa. Some of the Dutch would not remain, but came to New York."

Barrett,[1] "was blowing very fresh. He found the cabin windows in danger of being stove to pieces. While endeavoring to secure them, his head and body being out of the window, the brig was driven so violently against the wharf as to dash his brains out. He was taken home a lifeless corpse — in less than one hour's absence from perfect health to a silent, mangled, lifeless corpse!"

Hester Cannon Kortright, thus widowed with six young children, a beautiful woman much courted,[2] went into business for herself, raised her family and, having survived the burning of the house over her head by the British, died in 1784 — two years before Monroe married her granddaughter, Elizabeth.

Of the famous widow's two sons, Cornelius married Miss Hendricks, owner of the "Golden Rock Plantation" in the island of Santa Cruz, celebrated for its scenic charms; and one of their granddaughters, a daughter of Thomas Willing of Philadelphia, married Baring (later Lord Ashburton) of Baring Brothers, London.

The other son of the widow Kortright was Lawrence, "one of the executors of the rich John Schermerhorn"; and closely associated with two other money-making merchants — Luke Van Ranst and Isaac Sears. Lawrence fitted out many privateers in the French and Indian war and became a commercial magnate. He was "a part owner" of the ships, all of which belonged to joint-stock companies. He was one of the founders of the New York Chamber of Commerce in 1770.

Kortright, N. Y. was named for him. It was built on ground originally bought with the purpose of establishing Kortright Manor, after the custom set by some of

---

[1] In the Old Merchants of New York City, by Walter Barrett, Clerk, Fourth Series, 1866, p. 19.

[2] Hester Cannon Kortright was a daughter of "Old Jan Cannon, merchant, who married Maria, daughter of Peter Le Grand. John, second, a sea-going captain, owned a dock and had a store facing it." "The eldest son," says Barrett in "Old Merchants" "was the celebrated Le Grand Cannon."

the neighbors, such as the Livingstons,[1] Van Cortlandts and Van Renssaelers.

Lawrence Kortright married Hannah Aspinwall. They had one son, Captain John, and four daughters: Mrs. James Monroe, Mrs. Nicholas Gouverneur, Mrs. Thomas Knox[2] and Mrs. Captain Heyleger.

The Gouverneurs, so closely associated with the Kortrights and Monroes through more than a hundred years of history, were in New York as early as 1700. Abraham Gouverneur married a daughter of Jacob Leisler, hanged for treason. Nicholas, husband of Mrs. Monroe's sister, was the most celebrated of the Gouverneurs. He was head of the house of Gouverneur, Kemble & Co. Gouverneur Street was named after him, and so was Gouverneur's Lane. Of his three sons, Isaac was killed in a duel with William H. Maxwell; Nicholas, the youngest, lived a bachelor till 1854; and Samuel L. married his cousin, Maria, second daughter of President Monroe.

Aside from his high standing as a delegate in Congress, Monroe had various recommendations to the good graces of the hospitable New Yorkers. He was well known, it seems, to the popular Miss Catherine Van Zandt, a refugee at Morristown, and greatly esteemed by the Continental officers, some of whom danced at her wedding. She married James Homer Maxwell, in 1788; and long treasured a compliment paid to her as a bride by Washington himself.

Altogether it was a delightful winter for Monroe. It was a broadening winter also, since he was much in

---

[1] Judge Henry Brockholst Livingston (died 1823), married Captain John Kortright's widow, who as a maiden was Catherine Seamen. She had two sets of children. Captain John, Mrs. Monroe's brother, who died May 23, 1810, left six children — John of Staten Island; Edmond, who married Miss Shaw; Dr. Robert, a bachelor and Gouverneur Kortright who married Miss Allaire, of Winchester, Va.

[2] Thomas Knox was a noted merchant. Of the two children, Gouverneur Knox died in 1812; the daughter, Mrs. Alexander Hamilton, lived long. Barrett wrote in 1866: "Alexander Hamilton is still alive. Had he been the son of a John Smith he would have been one of the most eminent men of the day. A great father is a heavy load for a son to carry. The sons of Clay, Webster, Calhoun, Van Buren "were really above mediocrity but the public placed them below it."

the company of men with a wide horizon. Spanish matters were up; and he heard a great deal about Spanish America and the West Indies from the Kortrights and Gouverneurs and others. Indeed it may be here set down that his New York connections and associations helped him along the course he was destined to take.

It so happened that Benjamin Franklin was in New York on business. Monroe made friends with the great doctor. "He was so kind as to favor me frequently with his company," wrote the younger man, much gratified that chance had given him an opportunity he had longed for.[1]

About this time Monroe and Madison tried to concert a plan to invest in lands on the Mohawk. "Both of us have visited that district and were equally charmed with it," wrote Madison to Jefferson, August 12, 1786. "In talking of this country sometime ago with General Washington he considered it in the same light with Monroe and myself, intimating that if he had the money to spare and was disposed to deal in land, this is the very spot which his fancy had selected out of all the U. S."

Though, in the main, his private affairs were as he would wish them, Monroe was dissatisfied with the progress of public events. It was his Gardoqui summer. He wrote to Jefferson, October 12: "I sit out [sic] tomorrow for Virginia with Mrs. Monroe[2] by land —

[1] October 5, 1781, Jefferson gave Monroe a letter of introduction to Franklin, then at Passy. Monroe, he said, had distinguished himself in the American army. He was "a man of abilities, merit and fortune" and his own "particular friend." Monroe "having resumed his studies comes to Europe to complete them." Monroe abandoned this European plan.

[2] According to *Lippincott's Magazine*, Vol. IX, p. 359, Monroe and his bride were entertained at the house of an eccentric Richmond lady. Small tables were distributed about the parlor. In came a fat negro cook, "holding before her an immense tray of batter, while behind her came a negro boy with two or three pairs of long-handled waffle-irons. Nothing abashed by that goodly company, the old cook walked straight up to the fireplace where a wood fire was burning and then and there proceeded to make her waffles with a dexterity, quickness and perfection which some other Virginia cooks might have equalled but which none could surpass. They were served 'pot and hot' with superb butter and other accompaniments, and enjoyed intensely by all present, but by

my residence will be for the present in Fredericksburg
— my attention is turned to Albemarle for my ultimate
abode — the sooner I fix there the more agreeable it
will be to me. I sho'd be happy to keep clear of
the bar if possible and at present I am wearied with
the business in w'h I have been engaged. It has been
a year of excessive labor and fatigue and unprofitably
so."

From Fredericksburg he wrote to Jefferson of his
admission that fall to the bar of the Courts of Appeal
and Chancery. In April he was admitted to practice
in the General Court. His uncle had accommodated
him with a house in Fredericksburg.[1] "Mrs. Monroe,"
he wrote to Jefferson, July 27, 1787, "hath added a
daughter[2] to our society who tho' noisy, contributes
greatly to its amus'ment. She is very sensibly impressed
with your kind attention to her and wishes an opportunity of showing how highly she respects and esteems
you."

Both Jefferson and Madison went out of their way
to befriend the Monroes. Madison, in New York,
advanced the money necessary to ship the Monroe
furniture from that city to Fredericksburg. Subsequently, in apologizing to Madison for not having
remitted, Monroe said that his money was locked up
in debts not readily collectible.

It was Jefferson's oft-repeated wish that Monroe
might move close to Monticello. Monroe himself was
equally desirous of becoming Jefferson's neighbor. So
in the fall of 1788, he exchanged some Western lands,
valued at £2500, for a farm that had been improved by
Colonel George Nicholas, on the Rockfish Gap road,

---

none more than Mr. Monroe. The lady of the house confessed that the proceeding was rather odd. 'But,' said she, 'I knew Mr. Monroe — poor man! — hadn't
had any waffles fit to eat since he left Virginia; and I was determined he should
have some. And what account are waffles if they're not hot? and what's the
use of eating if you can't sit down and eat comfortably like a Christian?' "

[1] Twenty-two letters written by Joseph Jones to his nephew, during 1786 and
1787, are preserved in the Monroe collection at Washington. They relate to
money matters and private business affairs.

[2] Eliza Monroe, who became the wife of Judge George Hay of Virginia.

near Charlottesville. He wrote to Jefferson about it, and to Madison also.[1]

In the frosty weather of that same fall he and Madison engaged in a lively political set-to for a seat in the First United States Congress. Monroe wrote to Jefferson, February 15, 1789:

"This Commonwealth was divided into districts from each of which a member was to be plac'd in the House of Representatives. A Competition took place in many, and in this, consisting of Albemarle, Amherst, Goochland, Louisa, Spotsylva, Orange and Culpeper, between Mr. Madison and myself."

There have been hundreds of exciting congressional elections, but was there ever another quite as curious as this? In the first place, Patrick Henry, a power in politics, had thrown Madison down. His philippic against him was the talk of the State, or would have been so if the State had not preferred to talk of the way Henry had elevated Richard Henry Lee and William Grayson to be the first United States Senators over the heads of all champions of the Constitution, Madison included. In the next place, Henry was accused of having gerrymandered against Madison, in favor of Monroe; and this, too, before he had heard of Mr. Gerry's manipulation in Massachusetts. French Strother, an Assemblyman for nearly thirty years, a member of the Convention of 1776 and of the Convention of 1788, an opponent of the Federal Constitution, "was solicited to oppose Mr. Madison for Congress, but Mr. Monroe became the candidate instead." The candidates rode from courthouse to courthouse making speeches to great crowds. As for the picturesque electorate: "These people," says Dr. Slaughter "seem to have had a gay time — dining parties of

---

[1] Jefferson wrote to Madison, February 20, 1784: "I hope you have found access to my library. I beg you to make free use of it. The steward is living there now, and of course will always be in the way. Monroe is buying land almost adjoining me. Short will do the same. What would I not give could you fall in the circle. With such society, I could once more venture home, and lay myself up for the residue of life,— quitting all its contentions, which grow daily more and more insupportable."

twenty-five to thirty from house to house; quilting parties, winding up with a dance; balls at Sanford's, Bell's and Alcocke's hotels in the winter varied with hare, fox, and wolf-hunting, especially when Major Willis and Hay Taliaferro came up with twenty hounds. In the summer they had fish-fires and barbecues. . . . Colonel (Frank) Taylor seems never to have missed an election; he always records the names of the candidates for office and the number of votes for each. He brings before us Mr. Madison as candidate for Congress, Assembly and Convention, addressing the people in defence of the Constitution, to which the ignorant were opposed. He is said to have spoken from the steps of the old Lutheran Church, now in Madison, with the people standing in the snow, and the cold so intense that the orator's ears were frost-bitten."[1]

It would have been slight consolation to Madison even if he could have foreseen that his ears would be warm enough later on from the thousand and one derogatory, not to say spiteful, things said of him, both by word of mouth and with partisan pens dipped in nutgall. Monroe was badly beaten. In his own words, Madison "prevail'd by a large majority of about 300." He adds: "It would have given me concern to have excluded him."

Madison's fear had been lest the Constitution should be ruined with nugatory amendments. Hence his eagerness to go to Congress; and very great joy, despite frostbitten ears, that he had overthrown Monroe.

The old Congress circulated broadsides naming the first Wednesday in January, 1789, as the day upon which presidential electors should be chosen; the first Wednesday in February for their meeting and the first

---

[1] A History of St. Mark's Parish, Culpeper County, Va., by Rev. Philip Slaughter, D.D., 1877. Another Virginia chronicle tells us that in order to get out the votes Madison's friends sent wagons around. At one polling place a very old man, brought from a long ways off, stood listening to the talk in favor of Madison. He pricked up his ears at mention of Monroe. "Is he," asked the old fellow, "a son of Spence Monroe who lived in Westmoreland years back?" "Yes." "Then I'll vote for Monroe. His grandfather befriended me — fed me, sheltered me, clothed me. I do not know James Madison; I vote for James Monroe."

Wednesday in March as the beginning of the new government.

As for the head of it, who should be chieftain but the chief himself? But he did not take hold on time. Though John Adams, the choice for Vice-President, qualified April 20, Washington, the unanimous choice for President, was not inaugurated until April 30.

It soon became plain to such close observers as Monroe that Washington's aim would be to conciliate. Jefferson was made Secretary of State, and his political opposite, Hamilton, Secretary of the Treasury. Knox was Secretary of War; Edmund Randolph, Monroe's old rival, Attorney General; and Jay, Monroe's old antagonist of the Spanish treaty, became first Chief Justice.

As for Madison, he was leader of the new House of Representatives. Altogether the various States had suggested seventy-eight amendments. Of these, Madison brought forward seventeen, embodying the ideas hammered out in the fierce contests; these were reduced to ten by the action of the Senate, and the ten became a part of the basic law of the land. They went into effect November 3, 1791. Eight were practically a reiteration of the bill of rights that had been insisted upon by those who thought as Monroe did. So with Jefferson in the Cabinet, and an amended Constitution, Monroe could well afford to rest easy.

Washington had a deep purpose in organizing a nonpartisan administration. All must be committed to the new government; all must go along together for a time, even if by-and-by they should split apart on party lines. He conciliated Patrick Henry — they were friends again; and died as such. The man who had defeated the machinations and broken the cabals of political generals in war time could be trusted to know politics. But now he hoped for less politics; or, at least, for a surcease until the government should be established. And really there was such a truce. It lasted for a long while. Many besides Washington wished it and

prayed for it. Nor should there be any stint of praise
for those who lent themselves to this patriotic purpose.
Hamilton was proud; yet he could sit cooped up with
Jefferson, whose complaisance certainly was praise-
worthy. Soon enough would oil refuse to mix with
water, and water spurn oil. The antagonisms of the
time were held under by the powerful moral influence
of the first President.

Accompanied by his wife and child, Monroe rode
with the judges that spring as far as Staunton and
Charlottesville on the circuit. There was no civil business and little criminal; but then the scenery was
delightful. Mrs. Monroe especially enjoyed it. The
Blue Ridge, with its beauties, was new to her. What
could be lovelier than a view, from the heights, of the
far Shenandoah like silver in the sun? Mrs. Monroe
was with her husband on many of his professional
excursions — to Richmond, on chancery business; and
elsewhere. Monroe's brother-in-law, John Dawson,
who had been his colleague from Spottsylvania in the
ratification convention, was now a member of the
Executive Council. John Marshall had become a leading member of the bar. In fact, there was no lack of
friends and acquaintances wherever the Monroes went.
In mid-August, 1789, they moved to their new home in
Albemarle. Here Monroe, happy in his domestic life,
watched the progress of events.

Hamilton's measure looking to the assumption of
the State debts interested him greatly. Like most
Virginians, he thought it unfair to their own State, since
Virginia already had paid a large part of her indebtedness. He had taken a hand in the location of the Federal
City and was interested greatly in the final resolve that
the temporary ten-year seat of government should be
at Philadelphia and the permanent seat by the Potomac.
In their frequent letters, Madison and Jefferson kept
him informed of Federal aggression and republican
perils, and at the same time, gave him the news of
Philadelphia and New York. Monroe wrote to Madison,

Charlottesville, July 25, 1790: "We feel ourselves particularly oblig'd to you for y'r kindness in giving us intelligence from our friends — we never hear from them, except when you extract a line from them. It revives Mrs. M's spirits, w'h from her long absence are often depress'd." He mentions the cost and hardships of a journey north — else Mrs. Monroe would visit the cities. As for news of interest in Virginia, there was dearth of it — little to interest those whose minds were occupied with larger affairs.

This Albemarle interlude was less appreciated by the Monroes than it would have been had they foreseen how rare were to be such releases from the public service. March 12, 1790, United States Senator Grayson died, leaving a vacancy which Governor Harrison filled by the appointment of John Walker until the Virginia Legislature should elect. Monroe, urged for the Senatorship instead of Walker, wrote to Jefferson, October 20, that after mature reflection he had decided to suffer his name to be used in the contest. "It will contribute greatly to my own and the gratification of Mrs. M." he wrote, "as it will place us both with and nearer our friends." Ten days later, in a letter written at Richmond, he declared: "I have determined in great measure in case of my election to abandon my profession." As he was ready to burn his bridges, he evidently had gone into the contest with some vim. He was chosen; and began at once to prepare for his residence in Philadelphia. He was to be accompanied by his wife. They planned to go by way of Annapolis and the Eastern Shore; and perhaps stop a while in Philadelphia with Mrs. Monroe's uncle by marriage, Mr. Willing, while they looked about them for a place to live during the coming session of Congress.

Thus at the age of thirty-two, Monroe resumed his activity in the political world. He produced his credentials in the Senate Chamber of the old Courthouse at the southeast corner of Sixth and Chestnut Streets, on Monday, December 6, 1790, and took the oath of

office as United States Senator from Virginia. It was
the third session of the First Congress and on the day
Monroe took his seat all thirteen of the States were
represented for the first time. It so happened, also,
that thirteen Senators responded to the roll. Monroe
was listed as in the two-year class. But he was re-elected
by the Virginia Legislature, qualified on March 4, 1793,
and on that occasion duly listed in the four-year class.[1]

There is little in the Monroe correspondence relating
to the social affairs of the new Capitol. Mr. and Mrs.
Monroe went to Virginia as often as possible; but he
complained that he was obliged to sacrifice his law
business in order to attend conscientiously to his duties
in the Senate. He made it a rule, ever obligatory upon
himself, not to neglect his public work. He kept a
carriage in Philadelphia; and he and his wife traveled
to Richmond and Albemarle in a phaeton, as Jefferson
did. Later he had a post-chariot built for this purpose.
It was stronger. The roads were abominable. Jefferson
was the socially conspicuous Republican of the time.
He dwelt in a large four-story house on Market Street
near Eighth, opposite the office of the Secretary of
State, and but two blocks west of the President's house
on Market at Sixth. Philosopher that he was, Jefferson
amused the town by trying to live in winter in a sun-
heated room. Hamilton was at the southeast corner of
Third and Walnut, quite a walk away; and Vice-President Adams occupied Bush Hill Mansion.

Dinners, receptions and balls were frequent. Washington's dinners were elegant and solemn — plate,
wine, food, all of choice quality. Maclay, who sat in
the Senate as a Republican, attended one of these
formal affairs and was impressed with its solemnity.

---

[1] His committee work in the first and second United States Congresses was
varied. He was on a committee to report on the memorial of the Kentucky
Convention; to consider the report of the Secretary of the State on coins, weights
and measures, on bounty lands; on a mint; on the admission of Vermont; on
land offices; on rates of foreign coins; on a Revolutionary land warrant; on the
protection of the frontiers; on the settlement of loan office accounts; on national
defense.— See Annals of Congress, Journals of Congress, Hamilton's Writings of
Monroe.

"Some dirty democrat did that," said Mrs. Washington one day, as she entered the newly papered hall and saw a thumb-mark where a hand had been. Her Friday evening receptions were pleasant parties. Washington was sure to drop in. He was a close observer of the proprieties. His own levee was on Tuesdays at mid-afternoon. In black velvet coat and breeches, white waistcoat, yellow gloves, silver buckles, his sword at his side, his cocked hat in his hand, he looked what he was — a goodly man and chief. A guest approached him as he stood thus; was introduced; bowed, and retired to a place in the line forming around the room. At a set time the doors were shut. Then Washington passed along the line from guest to guest, showing his civility to each. That was all.[1]

Rich merchants lived on a fine scale; and the Capital was gay, save when the yellow fever came, as it did in the successive summers, driving officials to Germantown, and causing congressional families to dread a return for the session. With frost, the scourge ceased, and the city resumed its life.

Yellow fever and the great French furore were by no means unrelated. West India vessels brought the scourge and they also brought great numbers of French refugees. Thrown off by the French Revolution, or driven from San Domingo by the fear of massacre, they walked the streets of Philadelphia in great numbers. Many were cared for by the French Patriotic Society. It is well to remember these and other facts, such as that there was a powerful republican element in Philadelphia, when we come, as we now have, to the Genet quarrel. Though Monroe kept out of the quarrel in its early stages, he was involved in a later imbroglio, destined to give him not a few heartaches and humiliations.

Friendship for La Fayette and other French comrades of our Revolution would have caused Monroe to follow affairs in France with keen interest; but, aside from that, there was a considerable party in America

[1] William Maclay, Journal, 1789-1791.

which sustained the contention that only by eruptive
violence could the twenty-five million French under the
ancient Capet regime be freed from despotic government. They had sided with La Fayette in his effort to
give France a constitutional government; and, with
the rise of the republican party in France in 1789 had
hoped for the overthrow of monarchy. Lately, with
La Fayette in a dungeon, and the furies let loose, they
joined numerous Americans of all parties in deploring
a situation that had grown profoundly tragic.

But many lacked knowledge of the actual devasta-
tion wrought by the human hurricane and bethought
them of the good that might come to the masses when
the bloody days were over. Again, those with a strong
sense of the indispensability of law and order, admiring
a government of the British type, were horrified
beyond measure. The men in power were largely of
this description. Not a few had their vain heads full
of monarchical ideas, thinking of themselves as privileged gentlemen, destined, if not predestined, to look
after the less favored citizenry. In their view, humanity
was divided into two branches — those who made silk
stockings and silver buckles and those who wore
them.

On the contrary, Jefferson and Madison and Monroe
belonged to a distinct school of advanced Americans.
Wythe had drilled it into them just how constitutional
liberty, born in the British Isles, had fled to these
shores. Old farmers had given them to understand
that they would be held accountable for all they said
and did. The same electorate had helped them to lop
off bad laws. But Jefferson, a philosophical republican,
went further than his backers. Crowns had failed,
aristocracies had failed; let the homespun people have
the say. Somehow it seemed that Jehovah had put
it into the heads of men to come to America and begin
again. Why, then, trifle? Since the Nazarene had said
men were brothers and had enunciated democracy,
and since Jehovah had opened a new world for its

practice, why not begin, why not be free, why not dig prosperity out of the God-given ground, why not be happy? Always in the republicanism of Monroe and Madison was there some such feeling as this.

But though Jefferson and Madison at first coöperated with the administration they soon found themselves at odds with it on party matters. They were not merely perverse. They had to differ with the Federalist leaders or suffer rebuke at home.

The new parties were Federalist and Republican. But since Federalism was an accomplished fact, "Federalist" now meant something different. To be a Federalist was to be the supporter of a body of doctrines looking to strong government and the rule of the big men of the country. Let the *hoi polloi* stand down. Hamilton's superior statesmanship invigorated his party. Until factions developed, this forceful man was Federalism incarnate. Washington deferred to him. Adams profited by his secret influence. King, McHenry, Pickering were among the followers who did his bidding. His editor was John Fenno, of the *United States Gazette*. Jefferson, too, had an editor — Philip Freneau, poet, of the *National Gazette*. Freneau was vituperative. Hamilton himself wrote. Jefferson wrote. John Adams was "Davila." John Quincy Adams was "Publicola." There was plenty to write about. Monroe must have resented the continued occupation of the British posts. Sir Guy Carleton, now Lord Dorchester, Governor of Canada, was pushing British interests on the border. St. Clair's defeat was a great blow though more than offset by Wayne's victory. To the southward, Spanish agents were active. In Pennsylvania Scotch-Irish borderers resented Hamilton's whiskey tax. Fries rebelled against the window tax. But the articles in the newspapers were often merely quarrelsome, without other significance. Washington, in fact, found it necessary to make peace between Hamilton and Jefferson and stop their newspaper controversy.

Decidedly more difficult to stop was the French furore

we have spoken of as a calamitous phenomenon coincident with the yellow fever visitation.

Edmund Charles Genet, aged twenty-eight, having annexed Geneva to Republican France and having been decorated by Empress Catharine of Russia with the phrase "a rabid demagogue," landed April 8, 1793, at Charleston, S. C., and proceeded to involve the United States in a war with England. He was Girondist Minister from France, in succession to Ternant. Now when the news had come of the outbreak of war, Washington had hurried to Philadelphia and on April 23 had issued a proclamation of neutrality. But this was nothing to "Le Citoyen" Genet. He made a great deal of the clause in the treaty of 1778 by which France and America were to be allies in the event of war. No one was ever more enthusiastic in a cause, or more brazen. He acted as though America were his. As Napoleonic as Napoleon, without that hero's sense or ability, Genet nevertheless won a big following and by the time he reached Philadelphia, May 16, had become an object of the gravest concern. Some ten thousand Sons of Liberty, aroused by signal guns, rallied to the standard. Tri-colored cockades were worn. *Ca Ira* was the song of the hour. People walked past the President's house calling for war with England. Washington, for his part, kept his peace. When he received Genet, May 18, the Girondist found him unimpressed. He called Washington "that old man" — said he was disappointed in him. But Washington, conscious of an outpouring of abuse against himself, remained undisturbed until July. Then when Genet converted a prize vessel "the little Sarah" into "La Petite Democrate," armed her and sent her to close the mouth of the Mississippi, Washington took steps to suppress his activities. Genet insulted Washington and threatened to appeal from him to the people. However, the affair was over. Genet never returned to France but married into the Clinton family and settled in New York. As the chief actor in a drama played before the eyes of Monroe, then going

about his duties in the Senate, he was long remembered
by our republican who, by-and-by, would himself enact
a part in another Anglo-French drama, with the scene
in Paris. Incidentally, Genet became involved in the
still unsettled matter of the Mississippi.[1] Jefferson was
endeavoring to negotiate a treaty with Gardoqui who,
however, "took a blustering tone," as he had done with
Jay ten years before. As France and Spain were now
at war, Genet planned to seize East Florida and Louisiana. "Jefferson," says Bassett, "reminded Genet that
we were then conducting negotiations with Spain, and
he caused the Frenchman to understand that a little
explosion on the Mississippi might be welcomed by the
Americans as tending to convince Spain that it would
be wise to make a Treaty."[2] Genet's successor reversed
his policy, and fortunately Thomas Pinckney, passing
from London to Madrid, arranged a treaty with
Godoy, "the Prince of Peace" of whom we shall hear
a great deal somewhat later. This treaty settled the
boundaries and opened the Mississippi to our people
in the West.

George Hammond was British Minister to the United
States, and Gouverneur Morris, American Minister to
France. In the Senate Monroe was one of eleven to vote
against the confirmation of Morris, who had sixteen
supporters, including King, Ellsworth and the Hamiltonian standbys. Here are Monroe's reasons for voting
against Morris:[3]

"His manners not conciliatory — his character well known and
considered as indiscreet — upon the grounds of character he was
twice refused as a Member of the Treasury board, once at Trenton
and afterwards at New York — Besides he is a monarchy man and
not suitable to be employed by this country, nor in France. He
went to Europe to sell lands and Certificates."

This seems a harsh estimate of a man who did a
great deal of good in his day. Monroe, of course,

---

[1] The Federalist System (American Nation) by J. S. Bassett, Vol. XI, p. 79.
[2] The Federalist System, p. 81; Roosevelt's Winning of the West, IV, 178-183;
Ogg's Opening the Mississippi, 421-459.
[3] Rufus King, Life and Correspondence, Vol I, p. 421.

meant it for a confidential purpose; but Rufus King passed it on, with other personalia of the Senate, in Federalistic times. King quotes the memorandum of Monroe and Madison sent to Jefferson when they heard his resignation rumored:[1] "In a word, we think you ought to make the most of the value we perceive to be placed in your participation in the Executive Councils." Already the fortunes of the three Virginians led them along the same road. When Jefferson resigned, Edmund Randolph came in, as Secretary of State. King thus itemizes, April 17, when John Jay's appointment was under discussion in the Senate:[2]

"Mr. Monroe declared his opinion that he was not a suitable character since he held opinions (as appears by his reports while Secretary of Foreign Affairs) against the interest and just claims of the Country. That, in the first place, in respect to the inexecution of the Treaty of Peace, Mr. Jay had avowed an opinion in favor of interest upon British Debts, and secondly had acknowledged we were the first aggressors against the Treaty; and therefore that the Detention of Posts, etc, was justifiable on the part of G. B. Further that a secret treaty existed between Spain and England, which probably had reference to the territorial rights of the former in America and consequently affected our Boundary and right to navigate the Mississippi; that Mr. Jay might be sounded on these points and it was well known that his opinions were unfriendly to our Rights and too complaisant to those of Sp: this was proved by his negotiations with Gardoqui, with whom he would have signed a treaty, stipulating to forebear the use of the river for 25 or 30 years, and to refer the question of Boundary to Commissioners.[3]

Next day Monroe moved for the production of Jay's report, while Secretary for Foreign Affairs, on British complaints of violations of the treaty. Evi-

---

[1] Rufus King, Life and Correspondence, Vol. I, p. 514.

[2] Rufus King, Life and Correspondence, Vol. I, p. 521, *et seq*. King says: "Gunn informed me that Randolph had proposed the [British] Envoyship to Madison — that the party also desired the appointment of Jefferson, and that, with a view of governing Butler, Monroe had intimated to him that it would be agreeable to the Party that he sh'd be appointed, and that thus Butler had entertained the hope if not the serious expectation that he should be nominated; and that his absence for ten days or a Fortnight from the Senate were days of suspense and foolish intrigue in relation to this appointment."

[3] Monroe supported Gallatin when the Federalists put Hamilton's rising financial rival out of the Senate. See King, Vol. I, p. 532; Coleman's Sketch of King, *Delaplaine's Repository* 1, 184.

dently Monroe viewed Jay with an altogether different
eye from those in the heads of the Federalist leaders.
One day soon he would realize this; not with reminis-
cent but with fresh pangs.

Monroe's letters to Jefferson, in March, April and
May, 1794[1] leave no doubts as to how he stood on questions connected with what he calls the "exigency of
the times." Genet's successor, Fauchet, he said, was
being received with "profound attention" by the
Federalists; but the newcomer, who was "reserved
and prudent" would soon discern the true friends of
France. These friends, in their zeal for the cause, had
tolerated Genet as long as they could in spite of his
errors. As for the aggressions of Great Britain, they
were as bad as ever. She regards no kind of form in
the pursuit of our property, seizing whatever she can
lay hands on. Urgent as the crisis was, its embarrassment was increased in the minds of Republicans by
the fact that war would place military power in the
hands of "the enemy of the publick liberty." Monroe
was suspicious of a measure introduced by Sedgewick
providing for a provisional army of fifteen thousand
men. He was suspicious of the Society of the Cincinnati.
But the "fiscal party" had a remedy. It proposed to
send an envoy to England. Hamilton was talked of
as the envoy; why not Dickinson? Jay and King were
mentioned too. "Either will answer to bind the
aristocracy of this country stronger and closer to that
of the other."

Monroe felt so strongly on the subject of Hamilton
as envoy that he wrote to General Washington about
it, offering to call and give his reasons why Hamilton
should not be sent.

Here was a new point. Had a Senator the right to
question the qualifications of an officer until his
nomination had come before the Senate? Washington
consulted Secretary Randolph who gave an opinion
to wit: "that the Secretary of State inform Col. Monroe

---

[1] Writings of Monroe, Vol. I, pp. 284-299.

verbally that his station entitles his communications
to attention; that it is presumed that he has considered
and made up his mind to the kind of interference which
a Senator ought to make in a nomination beforehand;
that upon this idea the President will be ready to
afford an interview at a given time."

Here was an occasion when a precedent was about
to be set. Washington of his own accord saw the
inadvisability of such directness as that proposed by
Monroe and endorsed by Randolph. It would be well
for Senators to express themselves in the Senate.
Washington politely acknowledged Monroe's note, but
ignored the request for an interview. If Monroe were
possessed of any facts or information which would
disqualify Colonel Hamilton for the mission, "let him
communicate them in writing." Others were doing so.
For instance, John Nicholas wrote to Washington that
he was astounded to hear Hamilton mentioned as
envoy "when perhaps more than half America have
determined it to be unsafe to trust power in the hands
of this person however remotely it is connected with
many of the odious traits in his character."

So bold a man as Hamilton could not but make
enemies and bitter ones at that, even in his own party.
Throughout the long period during which the Federalist
system prevailed, Hamilton was the strong man of
the strong-men regime. That Washington needed him,
recognized his sure genius for organizing adequate
government, was greatly in his favor, but that Washington trusted him in the midst of much distrust
remains the outstanding explanation of his success.
Washington was unquestionably the wise man of that
hour, as he had been the wise man of wartime and of
the critical period of rational consolidation. His sound
sense probably would not have served him so well if
he had not been broadened by the circumstances of
his unusual career. In the French war, as in the long
War of Independence, he had served the continent —
not Virginia. Always America was in mind, not his

native State. Hence his breadth of view, in contrast
with the patriotic prepossession, amounting to myopia,
of some of his contemporaries. As for Hamilton, he
was intellectually broad; moreover he had this advantage — there was in his heart no great prepossession
for any particular State since he was born outside the
continental bounds. This accident helped him to be
a nationalist, just as love of State made it hard for
men like Monroe to rid themselves of partiality for
their own particular part of the country.

Washington named Jay as envoy. What Washington
wanted was to prevent war. But Monroe, like other
Republicans, did not relish this seeming obeisance to
a proud power. He wrote to Jefferson: "The circumstances of sending an envoy to negotiate with Engl'd
at the time that the Minister of France, on the ground
and clothed with similar powers, is only amused with
acts of civility, shews that a connection with the former
power is the real object of the executive." [1]   Why
should we court England's favor and "degrade our
character?" Jay, too — "this person" who "had well
nigh bartered away the Mississippi."

Then in the same letter comes this passage: "The
present French Minister (Fauchet) expressed lately
the wish of his country that G. Morris sho'd be recalled
and in consequence arrangm^{ts} are making for the
purpose. Being forced to send a Republican character
the adm^n was reduced to the dilemna of selecting from
among its enemies, or rather those of opposite principles, a person who wo'd be acceptable to that nation.
The offer of the station has been presented to Ch'lr.
Livingston, as I hear, in a letter written by the President.
'Tis tho't he will accept it. Burr's name was mentioned to Randolph, but with the success that was
previously expected; indeed, it was not urged in preference to the other, but only noted for consideration." [2]
May 26 he added: "I believe I intimated to you in

[1] Monroe to Jefferson, May 4, 1794.
[2] Monroe to Jefferson, May 26, 1794.

my last that the President had offered Mr. L., after the refusal of Mr. Madison, the legation in France in place of Gv. Morris, who would be recalled; that Burr had been a competitor. Since that time he has declined and Burr has continued under auspices very favorable to his success, sole candidate. Present appearances authorize the belief that he will be appointed."

Monroe's ink had hardly dried on these words when he sent a note to Madison asking him to see Randolph "and settle the matter with him," *i.e.*, as to whether he, Monroe, should go to France.

In a letter to Jefferson[1] next day, Monroe gave all the details of the proposal and the arrangements. He said: "Early yesterday morning, and immediately after my last was written, I was called on by Mr. R. to answer the question 'whether I wo'd accept the legation to France.' The proposition as you will readily conceive surprised me, for I really thought I was among the last men to whom it wo'd be made." He told Randolph that he had espoused Burr. Was there a chance for Burr? If so, he would have none of it. He would not even think of accepting until Burr and his friends should be satisfied. Randolph reassured him on that head. To whom would the mission be offered, if he, Monroe, should refuse it? Probably Governor Paca of Maryland. "The point of delicacy being removed," continued Monroe, "I then desired Mr. Madison in conference with a few of our friends to determine what answer sho'd be given to the proposition. The result was that I sho'd accept upon the necessity of cultivating France and the uncertainty of the person to whom it might otherwise fall."

May 27, Monroe's nomination was sent to the Senate, which next day confirmed it without cavil. June 1, just before the adjournment of Congress, Secretary Randolph presented him with his commission as Minister Plenipotentiary to the French Republic;

[1] Monroe to Jefferson, May 27, 1794.

and, on the same day, Monroe wrote to Washington announcing his readiness to embark in the discharge of his duties. He thanked the President for the particular obligation conferred. It was a distinguished mark of confidence — a high trust. He would be zealous to execute it with honor and credit to the country and the administration. He wrote to Jefferson that he expected to leave Philadelphia June 10 for Baltimore where a vessel was reported to be in readiness to sail for France. He wanted Jefferson to send him a better cypher. Stirring times were ahead. "Danton has been executed — the charge, the plunder of public money — the King of Prussia withdrawn — and the British driven from Corsica."

QUEEN HORTENSE (In Girlhood)

Hortense Eugenia Beauharnais, Napoleon's step-daughter, presented this ivory miniature of herself to her schoolmate, Eliza Monroe. With it, in the enameled gold frame, was a lock of the donor's hair. The artist was Louis François Aubry. The photograph is from the original.

CHAPTER IX

Monroe in Paris — Diplomacy under Difficulties

Madison journeyed with Monroe from Philadelphia to Baltimore. The first session of the Third Congress had just come to an end and Madison was on his way to Montpelier. Monroe gave him power-of-attorney for use in the settlement of various business affairs, including those connected with the estate of Mrs. Monroe's father; handed him a letter to deliver to Jefferson, and said farewell.

To Jefferson, he wrote that, upon their return some three or four years hence, he and Mrs. Monroe hoped to settle down in their Albemarle home and enjoy the society of their Monticello neighbors. "We expect to embark to-morrow" (June 18) he added: "and to fall down the bay immediately." [1]

It was the first long sea voyage of the Monroes. Their daughter Eliza was a little girl of seven. As they sailed past Annapolis, Monroe might well have seen the top of the State House, where he had sat as a member of the Continental Congress; and might profitably have reflected upon the great changes that had occurred since that time.

But Monroe's mind was on France, most likely; and it would have been on England too, if it had been a less honest and less trustful mind. For Jay had sailed by mid-May, and perhaps was already in London, with the power to call up all sorts of trouble, if not malign spirits, out of the vasty deep, breeding high seas for his countryman who followed.

We may be sure Monroe, on the long passage over, studied his general instructions, in a document of

---

[1] Monroe to Jefferson, June 17, 1794.

nearly three thousand words,[1] as handed him by Edmund Randolph, Secretary of State. These instructions, in sixteen numbered paragraphs, may thus be summarized:

"You have been nominated as the successor of Mr. Gouverneur Morris, in the office of Minister Plenipotentiary of the United States of America to the Republic of France from a confidence that, while you keep steadily in view the necessity of rendering yourself acceptable to that government, you will maintain the self-respect due to your own. In doing the one and other of these things, your own prudence and understanding must be the guides; after first possessing yourself of the real sentiments of the Executive, relative to the French nation. The President has been an early and decided friend of the French Revolution, and whatever reason there may have been under our ignorance of facts and policy, to suspend an opinion upon some of its important transactions; yet he is immutable in his wishes for its accomplishment; incapable of assenting to the right of any foreign prince to meddle with its interior arrangements; persuaded that success will attend its efforts; and particularly, that union among themselves is an impregnable barrier against external assaults. . . . The gradation of public opinion from the beginning of the new order of things to this day and the fluctuations and mutual destruction of parties, forbid a minister of a foreign country to attach himself to any as such, and dictate to him not to incline to any set of men, further than they appear to go with the sense of the nation. . . . We. . . have pursued neutrality with faithfulness; we have paid more of our debt to France than was absolutely due. . . . We mean to continue the same line of conduct in future; and to remove all jealousy with respect to Mr. Jay's mission to London, you may say that he is positively forbidden to weaken the engagements between this country and France. *It is not impossible that you will be obliged to encounter, on this head, suspicions of various kinds. But you may declare the motives of that mission to be, to obtain immediate compensation for our plundered property, and restitution of the posts.* You may intimate by way of argument, but without ascribing it to the government, *that, if war should be necessary the affections of the people of the United States towards it, would be better secured by a manifestation, that every step had been taken to avoid it, and that the British nation would be divided, when they found that we had been forced into it.*[2] This may be briefly touched upon as the path of prudence with respect to ourselves; and also with respect

---

[1] Writings of James Monroe by S. M. Hamilton, Vol. II, pp. 1-9.

[2] Monroe, in his "View of the Conduct of the Executive," emphazies, by italics this part and other portions of the "Instructions." Hamilton, II, p. 3.

to France, since we are unable to give her aids of men or money. To this matter you cannot be too attentive, and you will be amply justified in repelling with firmness any imputation of the most distant intention to sacrifice our connection with France to any connection with England." If America be an asylum for French patriots, if persons attainted in France come hither let their reception be "not misinterpreted into any estrangement from the French cause. You will explain this whensoever it shall be necessary." Our laws have never yet made a distinction of persons. Notwithstanding the obligations of the United States to La Fayette and Washington's warm friendship for him, the President kept hands off in his case. "If we may judge from what has been at different times uttered by Mr. Fauchet, he will represent the existence of two parties here, irreconcilable to each other. One republican, and friendly to the French Revolution; the other monarchical, aristocratic, Britannic, and anti-Gallican; that a majority of the House of Representatives, the people and the President are in the first class; and a majority of the Senate in the second. "If this intelligence should be used in order to inspire a distrust of our good will to France, you will industriously obviate such an effect." Let France make plain and candid application to the United States Government and not attempt "those insidious operations on the people," such as Genet essayed.[1] Sixteen questions were asked to be answered by Monroe as to the status of affairs, such as: "Is Robespierre's party firmly fixed?" If Monroe were asked by the French as to the treaty of commerce he might say that Fauchet had never proposed it — he himself was uninstructed. So with a treaty of alliance, and other matters. If the embargo were brought up, say it was levelled against Great Britain; as for the embargo of Bordeaux, "remonstrate against it." Insist upon "compensation for captures and spoliations of our property." There should be a settlement by France of money advanced by Congress in aid of St. Domingo refugees. "*Although the President will avoid, as much as possible to appoint any obnoxious person Consul, it may happen otherwise, and must be considered as accidental.*" "To conclude — you go, sir, to France to strengthen our Friendship with that country; and you are well acquainted with the line of freedom and ease to which you may advance without betraying the dignity of the United States. You will show our confidence in the French Republic, without betraying the most remote remark of undue complaisance. *You will let it be seen, that in case of war with any nation on earth, we shall consider France as our first and natural ally.* You may dwell *upon the sense*

---

[1] Genet had been ordered home (though he never went) to be tried for malversation in office. J. A. J. Fauchet succeeded him, and was in Philadelphia as French minister at this time. Later P. A. Adet was minister.

which we entertain of past services, and for the more recent interposition in our behalf with the Dey of Algiers. Among the great
events with which the world is now teeming, there may be an
opening for France to become instrumental in securing to us the
free navigation of the Mississippi. Spain may, perhaps, *negotiate
a peace, separate from Great Britain with France.* If she does, *the
Mississippi, may be acquired through this channel,* especially if you
contrive to have our mediation in any manner solicitated."

Such, in substance, were the instructions — such
Monroe's specific admonition to conciliate France.
Monroe had with him another document — the official
reply of the Senate and House of Representatives to
the French Committee of Public Safety. This, too,
he had received at the hands of Randolph and this,
too, was filled with amicable, benevolent and laudatory
passages. Yes, Congress, ever grateful, was devoted
to France.[1]

Thus the official literature upon which Monroe fed during his sea voyage had little of a disconcerting character
about it. Conciliate France! — he would have nothing
to weep over when it came to that. As the waves
lapped the sides of his ship, he did not realize, perhaps,
how uninformed he was as to the dangers that lurked
in anything approaching an excess of conciliation. He
was a republican, heart and soul; so the wish was
father to his thought — he was altogether pleased to
feel that he could help along France, liberty, and the
substitution of parliamentary for despotic government.
He did not know that Robespierre and Saint Just, in
their effort to establish "an ideal state," had caused
fourteen hundred heads to be chopped off since June 10;
he did not know of the new *coup d'état* whereby those
Jacobins had themselves gone to their death; nor did
he know of his own great good fortune in approaching
the shores of France just as the enormous black cloud
of Jacobinism lifted to let in a little of the sun. Robespierre, Saint Just, and the drunken Henriot with nearly
a score of terrorists were executed on July 28, a day of
heat and horror, only a short time before Monroe's

[1] Writings of James Monroe, Vol. II, p. 15.

disembarkation. He was to find Billaud Varennes and
Collot d' Herbois in power, though not for long, since
a lasting reaction against violence had now set in.
By and by there would be an end to the Democratic
Republic; then would come the Bourgeois Republic;
after that, in due course, those Napoleonic times so
celebrated in the world's annals.

"Between Baltimore and Paris," wrote Monroe to
Madison, "we were 45 days. The passage was free from
storms and between the soundings of each coast short,
being only 29 days. We enjoyed our health; none were
sick except Joseph a few days and myself an hour or
two. Mrs. M. and the child escaped it altogether.
We landed at Havre and left it for this the day after.
. . . We are yet at lodgings but expect to be fixed
in Mr. M's house, which I took, in less than a week.
I found Mr. Morris from town but he came in, in two
or three days after my arrival " — which was at Havre
July 31, and at Paris August 2.

Gouverneur Morris was the very opposite of Monroe
in so many characteristics that we owe it to the reader
to sketch him as accurately as possible. He was born
at Morrisania in the Bronx, now a part of greater
New York, January 31, 1752, and died in the same
room, November 6, 1816. His father was a colonial
Judge, and so was his grandfather, who himself was
the son of a Cromwellian soldier. Gouverneur's mother
was of Huguenot stock — Miss Gouverneur. His
half-brother, Lewis, was a Signer of the Declaration of
Independence. He was a friend but not a relative —
at least not a near one — of Robert Morris, the financier
of the Revolution. He was close to Jay and Hamilton
and, as a young lawyer of brilliant parts kept well to
the front in a period of big men. Some thought him
one of the biggest. Theodore Roosevelt who in his
younger days, wrote a Life of Morris, in which that
worthy is lauded, Paine villified and Monroe whistled
rather cavalierly down the wind, regarded him as a
great man, yet not quite in the first rank of statesmen.

The Morrises of Morrisania were erratic and whimsical.
They thought themselves leaders in an aristocratic
republic. Gouverneur's elder brother, General Staats
Long Morris, was a King's man, married a duchess
and lived in London. Gouverneur was a stiff Federalist
— stiffer than John Adams. Roosevelt says of him:
"His keen masterful mind, his far-sightedness and the
force and subtlety of his reasoning were all marred by
his incurable cynicism and deep-rooted distrust of
mankind. He throughout appears as an *advocatus
diaboli;* he puts the lowest interpretation upon every
act, and frankly avows his disbelief in all generous
and unselfish motives."[1] Nevertheless he was a useful
member of the Continental Congress and one of the
makers of the Constitution. Morris was fond of
aristocratic society — of women, of intrigue, of playing
upon the weaknesses of mortals less acute than himself.
Handsome and stalwart, punctilious as to dress and
deportment, he had suffered somewhat in an accident
at Philadelphia in May, 1781. A pair of spirited horses
which he drove to a phaeton, scorning the aid of a
groom to stand at their head, ran away with him and
shattered a leg so badly that it had to be cut off. It
was replaced with a wooden one. But it is an ill wind
that blows no good; and most likely his lost leg saved
his neck on numerous occasions, for when Morris, on
private business bent, reached Paris, February 3,
1789, the French Revolution was already approaching;
and a little later the critical Parisian populace looking
at his peg leg saw in it something heroic. "That man
lost his leg in the great American Revolution — the
war for freedom." And mistaking him for "a cripple
of the American war for freedom," a maimed soldier
of Washington's army, Paris also at first mistook his
character[2]. Only later did the aristocrats complain
that Morris was too aristocratic to suit them. Here,

---

[1] Gouverneur Morris, by Theodore Roosevelt, 1888; p. 140.
[2] Footprints of Famous Americans in Paris, by John Joseph Conway, 1912, pp. 25-33.

indeed, was an anomaly; an American, with nothing
to lose by it, does not permit himself to urge a freer
government for the French; on the other hand, Frenchmen of the blood, obviously destined to terrible sacrifices, are filled with zeal for just that thing. Morris
and La Fayette thus disagreed. La Fayette warned
Washington that Morris[1] was hardly the man to
represent America in France in the time of constitutional
reform; nevertheless, in 1791, he was made confidential
agent of the United States and next year was made
Minister. At this point it should be said that, whatever
Morris's maltreatment of Thomas Paine, or however
censurable his secret hostility to Monroe, he deserves
very great credit for his frankness toward La Fayette
and his more than handsome conduct in advancing
Madame de La Fayette one hundred thousand livres
when that good woman was in dire distress. Washington
knew of his serviceable qualities, as well as of his
diplomatic depth and sagaciousness; nor is it likely
that he would have been recalled in 1794 had not
France demanded it on the heels of Genet's dismissal.

"I could be popular," wrote Morris to Washington
(February 14, 1793) "but that would be wrong.
The different parties pass away like the shadows of a
magic lantern, and to be well with any one of them
would, in a short period, become cause of unquenchable
hatred with the other." Again he wrote to Washington: "You may rely, sir, that I shall be cautious to
commit the United States as little as possible to future
contingencies."[2]

In fact, though astonishingly wrong-headed in such
matters as the future of our western country, as well

---

[1] "Permit me, my dear General, to make an observation for yourself alone.
Personally I am a friend of Gouverneur Morris, and have always been, in private,
quite content with him, but the aristocratic and really contra-revolutionary
principles which he has avowed render him little fit to represent the only government resembling ours. . . . I cannot repress the desire that American and French
principles should be in the heart and on the lips of the Ambassador of the United
States in France."— La Fayette to Washington, Paris, March 15, 1792. *Mémoires
du Général de La Fayette, Bruxelles,* 1837, Vol. II, pp. 484-5.

[2] Gouverneur Morris to President Washington, June 25, 1793.

as the future of democracy, he was long-headed to a
fine degree in certain diplomatic matters of that stormy
time. His friends were anxious about him. His brother
urged him to leave Paris. "You are right in your idea
that Paris is a dangerous residence," he replied . . . ;
"but we must take the world as it goes." His enemies
would enquire why he went away; he preferred that
his friends should continue to wonder why he remained.
"The first of all enjoyments is that which results in
doing our duty." Morris's "Diary," written by a
man who knew how to write, is filled with pithy reflec-
tions and illuminating entries. Until the Revolution
began to jar the nerves of the self-confident Morris,
he evidently enjoyed his experiences in the salons and
boudoirs of Paris and lost little flesh bemoaning the
woes of those whom La Fayette was seeking to rescue
from the thrall of despotism. Madame de Stael looked
with flirtatious sympathy upon his peg leg, and the
aristocrats whose blood was as yet unlet partook of
his wine and appreciated his witty cynicism.

Morris's house, later occupied by Monroe was at
488 Rue de la Planche, Faubourg St. Germain. Ann
Cary Morris, editor of the "Diary," says: "To judge
from the allusions he makes to furniture, porcelain
and hangings, to his garden and the general arrangement of the house, it must have been eminently fitted
for the entertaining and lavish hospitality which
characterized it. "There was a tun of sauturne in
the cellar and a tun of claret," to say nothing of pipes
of Madeira and port. Morris was a busy man.
Admiral Paul Jones lay dying. Morris went to see him.
Poor Jones, stuttering and in the death-fight, begged
Morris to look after his affairs. A will was drawn.
Morris went to his house for dinner; and then back
to the lodgings where the hero lay — he was "dead,
not yet cold."

Morris had a country place "Sainport, a modest
pied-à-terre on the Seine" not far from Paris. He
wrote of it to Robert Morris: "I have about twenty

acres of land about twenty miles from the barrier of
Paris in summer (by means of cross-roads); I have
about twenty-seven miles to Paris, and from hence to
Fontainebleau about fifteen." . . . His neat little
house had " a pretty little garden and some green
trees." The Seine was about as broad as the Schuyl-
kill at Swedesford, but deeper. That was a protection.
There was another protection — a strong stone wall.
That bloody spring — the Robespierre spring — when
Paris reeked, Morris was among his flowers at Sainport.
He was there in midsummer, and it was from Sainport
that he came to greet his successor.

Morris and Monroe are bracketed in the history of
this particular period: and so are Morris and Paine,
as well as Monroe and Paine. Thomas Paine, "Doubt-
ing Thomas," (born a Quaker at Thetford, England,
January 29, 1736-7; died in New York, June 8, 1809)
sailed in a privateer, Captain Death, when a boy;
learned to be a staymaker; became an excise man;
reached America in the fall of 1774; participated in
the Revolution as a soldier, secretary, and controversial-
ist and earned great celebrity by reason of his pamphlets. His "Common Sense" oiled the ways and made
possible the launching of the Declaration. He was
sui generis; his activities were innumerable. He drank
much at times, but not more than his contemporaries.
Notwithstanding his love of mankind and his vast
labors unrewarded, he was accused of irreligion, and
so fell under the ban of the orthodox. He himself was
certainly unorthodox; there is no doubt of that; but
Moncure D. Conway who exploded many fallacies
concerning him, makes him out a good deal of a Quaker.
There is a Paine cult; and a Paine claim, for that
matter; it is insisted that his nature was in reality
profoundly religious. But Paine[1] made enemies foolishly, as well as friends despite his folly, because he
tried hard to help mankind — not merely in America

---

[1] The Life of Thomas Paine, by Moncure D. Conway, 1892, 2 vols.
Writings of Thomas Paine, by Moncure D. Conway, 1908, 4 vols.

and France, but in England, where he was outlawed, and in other countries. That his creed was "Liberty and Humanity" makes his failure in France all the more tragic. In defending Paine, Conway is perhaps too critical of Morris. Certainly, he is remorseless. Neither Morris nor Paine appeared to care a great deal whether they had enemies or not. Each was a hard-hitter. Jefferson, La Fayette and Paine got along better. La Fayette sent the key of the Bastille to Washington by the hand of Paine. "The principles of America opened the Bastille," said Paine. "Morris," declares Conway, "was entrusted by the President with a financial mission which, being secret, swelled him to importance in the imagination of the courtiers. At Jefferson's request, Gouverneur Morris posed to Houdon for the bust of Washington; and when, to Morris's joy, Jefferson departed, he posed politically as Washington to the eyes of Europe. He was scandalized that Jefferson should retain recollections of the Declaration of Independence strong enough to desire for France 'a downright republican form of government'; and how it happened that under Jefferson's Secretaryship of State, this man whom even Hamilton pronounced an 'exotic' in a republic, was appointed Minister to France is a mystery remaining to be solved. Morris had a 'high old time' in Europe. Intimacy with Washington secured him influence with La Fayette, and the fine ladies of Paris, seeking official favors for relatives and lovers, welcomed him to boudoirs, baths and bedrooms to which his diary now introduces the public." [1] It was natural, adds Conway that such a man should try to brush Paine aside. Paine wrote to Jefferson that Morris's appointment was a "most unfortunate one," and that he should tell him so when he

---

[1] Conway, Life of Paine, Vol. I, pp. 269-270. For instance, Morris was a frequent visitor at the bedside of Madame de Falhaut. "She is still ill in bed," runs an entry in his Diary, February 24, 1791, "play sixpenny whist with her." Together they devised a Constitution for France. Morris wrote to Alexander Hamilton, October 24, 1792, "That the late Constitution of this country has overset — a natural accident to a thing which was all sail and no ballast."

saw him. A few days later, Morris wrote in his "Diary,"
"He [Paine] seems to become every hour more drunk
with self-conceit." Burke's book was good; Paine's
"Rights of Man" all wrong. Morris, the antithesis
of Paine, laughed at Paine's idea of founding a European
Republic. They could hardly agree on anything,
though there is one thing they had in common — the
wish to preserve the life of Louis XVI. That Morris
wanted to prevent Paine from returning to America
lest Paine should expose him was one of Paine's obses-
sions and that Robespierre was similarly averse to an
advertisement abroad of his various wickednesses was
another fancy of a troubled brain. Morris's mind was
reflected in his thought that if the King and Queen
should go under the axe, horrified Europe would raise
great armies wherewith to assail France. Paine's mind
was reflected in his epigram: "Kill the King but not
the man." Again he stressed his grand creed "Liberty
and Humanity." Yes, the "and" meant much. Conway
cites the words of Dumas' hero, Dr. Gilbert (in "*Ange
Pitou*") as illustrating the peculiar problem of liberty
in France. Though liberty is his passion, Dr. Gilbert
would save the King. "It is not the liberty of France
alone that I dream of; it is the liberty of the whole
world." Paine would save the life of Louis, and send
him to America. Be humane. Let him live. Let him
begin again. Paine[1] put something of a curse upon
himself when he took the stand. He was a member of
the National Convention from the Puy de Dome, in
La Fayette's part of France. Abominating monarchy,
as he did, he nevertheless was bold enough, with so
much blood about him, to cry out in behalf of humanity.
Marat browbeat him before the assembly of deputies.
Paine was unable to use the French tongue; so Deputy
Bancal translated his speech. Marat put up the plea
that Bancal was misinterpreting Paine. Thuriot cried:
"This is not the language of Thomas Paine," Marat's

---

[1] Writings of Paine, Conway, Vol. III, pp. 119-124, Reasons for preserving the
Life of Louis Capet, as delivered in the National Convention, January 15, 1793.

voice was heard above the hubbub: "I denounce the
interpreter!" Paine, still standing in the tribune,
declared the sentiments to be his. "Ah, citizens"
he said, "give not the tyrant of England the triumph
of seeing the man perish on the scaffold who had aided
my much-loved America to break his chains!" A
dramatic scene followed. All was in a ferment — an
uproar. The implacable Marat, ravening for the King's
blood, launched himself in the middle of the hall.
"Paine," he cried, "voted against the punishment of
death because he is a Quaker." "I voted against it
from both moral motives and motives of public policy"
said Paine.[1] According to Louis Blanc, there was
method in Marat's madness on this occasion. He
interrupted in order to destroy the effect of Paine's
appeal.[2] But Paine lost by seventy votes in six hundred
and ninety; and the Mountain won. Louis was guillo-
tined. Marie Antoinette likewise perished. There
was an intensification of horrors. Marat denounced
Paine, and his numerous enemies were soon clamoring
for his death.

Conway constantly finds much amiss in Morris.
Paine did not intrigue against him. Yet Paine wrote,
September 5, 1793, to Barrère — "a sensualist, a crafty
orator, a sort of eel which in danger turned into a sort
of snake," then at the head of the all-powerful Committee of Public Safety: "Gouverneur Morris, who is
here now, is badly disposed toward you. . . . Morris is
not popular in America." Morris wrote to Robert
Morris, June 25, "I suspected that Paine was intriguing
against me, although he put on a face of attachment.

---

[1] "The course of Paine in the Convention was very creditable to him," says
Elihu B. Washburne (Recollections of a Minister, II, pp. 335-336). His speech
was read for him. It created a tremendous sensation among the Montagnards
many of whom declared that it was not properly translated; and it was only when
Garon de Coulon, a member of the Convention of Paris, who understood English
perfectly, declared that the translation was correct, that the Convention was
satisfied. From that moment Paine was lost; and Robespierre and others of his
ilk became his deadly enemies.

[2] *Hist. de La Revolution*, Vol. VII, p. 396; Guizot, Hist of France, Vol. VI,
p. 136. Conway's Writings of Paine, Vol. III, pp. 125-127: "Shall Louis XVI
have respite?" Speech in the Convention, January 19, 1793.

. . . I am confirmed in the idea for he came to my
house with Col. Oswald, and being a little more drunk
than usual, behaved extremely ill, and through his
insolence I discovered clearly his vain ambition."
For one thing, Paine was not as abusive of Morris as
Morris was of Paine. Of the period under consideration,
Paine subsequently wrote:

"The internal scene here from the 31 of May, 1793, to the fall
of Robespierre has been terrible. I was shut up in the prison of
the Luxembourg eleven months, and I find by the papers of
Robespierre that have been published by the Convention since
his death that I was designed for a worse fate. The following
memorandum is in his own handwriting: '*Démander que Thomas
Paine soit décrété d'accusation pour les interêts de l'Amerique autant
que de la France.*' "

"Propose that Thomas Paine be put on trial, in the
interests of America as much as of France." Such is
the entry in Robespierre's notebook in which he
scrawled his "ideas and intentions" for the last three
months of 1793. Robespierre suspected Morris; nevertheless dissembled, because it was his business to look
after diplomatic matters and he wished to conciliate
America — a republic, the only ally of France. Morris
played on the fact that America's treaty was with the
dead king, not with the French Republic. It was well
understood that Washington relied upon Morris; and
there was a certain awe of this Republican-Aristocrat
with the peg-leg. Especially did the power of Morris
win the obeisance of citizens who thumbed their necks
hopefully at night after horrid dreams of the bloody
axe. "The terrors and schemes of Deforgues and Otto
brought them to the feet of Morris." Some sea-captains
had gone over Morris's head, when he had hectored
them, and had appealed to Paine. What had Paine
to do with it? Morris notified Minister Deforgues that
in the future the Convention must deal with him.
The Girondins including Paine, were denounced in the
Convention. As with La Fayette, Brissot, Roland,
Condorcet, the Revolution had rolled past Paine.

Deforgues spoke of the punishable conduct of Genet in America. Paine and Genet were out of it together. Conway scents a conspiracy, and who should be at the bottom of it but Morris? As a deputy, Paine was not subject to a new law for the imprisonment of foreigners; but if he could be got out of the Convention the law could be applied to him.

"Such was the course pursued. Christmas day was celebrated by the terrorist Bourdon de l'Oise with a denunciation of Paine; 'They have toasted the patriotism of Thomas Paine. EH BIEN! Since the Brissotins disappeared from the bosom of the Convention he has not set foot in it. And I know that he intrigued with the former agent of the bureau of Foreign Affairs.'"

The Assembly so decreed. Paine was arrested next day and thrust into Luxembourg.

Conway makes a powerful indictment of Morris. Party animosities in America were being repeated in France. It was Hamilton against Jefferson; Morris against Paine; as for Washington, he took his cues from the man who knew how to play a deep game subtly. Meantime Jay in England helped on the drama of the three nations.

There is a very thrilling story that runs like this:

"A chalk-mark used to be put on the dungeon door of each prisoner who was picked out for execution. The door of Paine's cell swung open, so that when the marker passed along in the performance of his gruesome task he chalked the back of the door. Shortly after, Paine closed the door, so that the mark was inside and could not be seen. When the headsmen came in search of their victims, they saw no such mark on Paine's door and so he escaped the guillotine."[1]

Moncure D. Conway refers to this providential escape of his hero; Carlyle gives a version of it, along with other erroneous incidents, in his "French Revolution"; and, strange to say, Paine himself seems to have accepted it as an actual occurrence. But John Golds-

---

[1] Footprints of Famous Americans in Paris, J. J. Conway, p. 45. This account is a variant of a tale told by Sampson Perry, a journalist who was in prison with Paine. It was copied from a newspaper into the Annual Biography, British.

worthy Alger,[1] who has put a thousand and one
Parisian details of the time under the microscope, says
that there was no door-chalking in the Luxembourg
prison, where Paine was thrust on New Year's morning,
1794, and where he was kept until October of the same
year. Benoit, the keeper, was not unkind to him.
Eighteen Americans went in a body to the Convention
and solicited his release. Among these was Joel Barlow[2]
who made two efforts to rescue Paine. Morris, on the
contrary, was not impelled to exert himself in Paine's
behalf, though he must have known that the prisoner
was in a desperately low state. He wrote of him in
his "Diary":

"I incline to think that if he is quiet in prison he may have the
good luck to be forgotten whereas, should he be brought much
into notice, the long-suspended axe might fall on him. I believe
he thinks that I ought to claim him as an American citizen; but
considering his birth, his naturalization in this country, and the
place he filled, I doubt much the right, and I am sure that the
claim would be, for the present at least, inexpedient and
ineffectual."

While yet Monroe was in America, Paine was seized
with fever, which "in its progress had every symptom
of becoming mortal." So Paine himself said, adding:
"I was then with three chamber comrades, Joseph
Vanhuele, of Bruges, Charles Bastini and Michael
Robyns of Louvain. . . . I have some reason to

---

[1] In Glimpses of the French Revolution. Myths, Ideals and Realities, pp. 33-36.

[2] If princes and nobles were driven from France there were some who were
attracted thither even in the early stages of the Revolution, while Napoleon
later on drew around him a galaxy of foreign satellites. To begin with the cen-
trifugal action, history furnishes no parallel to such an overturn of thrones, and
flight of monarchs [Written prior to the World War]. . . . As for the immi-
gration, though far less important in numbers and quality, it was not inconsiderable.
Men of all nationalities hurried to Paris between 1789 and 1792 to see or serve
the Revolution. There were English men and women like Paine (or shall we
reckon him an American?) George Grieve, General Money, Thomas Christie,
John Oswald, Helen Williams and Mary Wollstonecraft. There were Americans
like Barlow, Eustace, Paul Jones, and Joshua Barney; Germans like Cloots,
Trenck and George Foster; Belgians and Dutchmen like de Kock, father of the
novelist, and Proly, a natural son of the Austrian statesman Kaunitz; Poles, like
Wittinghoff; Russians like Strogonoff; Italians like Rotondo, Cerutti and Buon-
arotti; Spaniards, like Olavide and Miranda."— Napoleon's British Visitors, by
John Goldsworthy Alger. Many of the men named were enthusiasts; some died
by the guillotine or in dungeon depths.

believe, because I cannot discover any other, that this illness preserved my own existence. . . . From what cause it was that the intention [of Robespierre] was not put into execution I know not, and cannot inform myself, and therefore I ascribe it to impossibility on account of that illness." Robespierre meant that Paine should go under the axe. Alger says that "the Luxembourg prisoners were carried off to the Conciergerie on July 6, and were condemned, not in one batch of 168 [as the chalk-mark story had it] but in three batches of 60, 48 and 36, 144 in all, on the 7th, 9th and 10th. Robespierre was overturned three weeks later, 9th Thermidor, year II." Not a miracle, but the fall of the terrorist and the arrival of Monroe, who would be as eager as Morris was cold, saved Paine from sharing the fate of the uncrowned king he had tried to snatch from the scaffold.

While on shipboard, Monroe seems to have been in doubt as to whether Gouverneur Morris would be a help or a hindrance in getting acquainted with the important officials of France. As we have seen, even the legend of a peg-leg in course of time becomes outworn; and Morris was now looked upon with both awe and disfavor in Paris. In fact, it is asserted by Conway that Morris[1] was now manoeuvring to get out of France by way of Switzerland, with as little friction and as much impedimenta as possible. We have seen what Monroe thought of Morris when his name was before the Senate; and we have indicated his present estimate of the value, or lack of value, involved in his introductions. Foreseeing this situation, Monroe had arranged with a fellow-passenger to make him acquainted in the circle of power when lo! upon their arrival, the bloody circle had vanished as completely as the circle of Danton, and all the preceding circles, which seemed indeed but agitations made by some magic stone cast into the dark pool of destiny.

---

[1] In his Life of Thomas Paine, 2 vols., where there are many references to Morris and Monroe.

At any rate the "fellow-passenger" ceased to be of use. In a letter to Madison (September 2) Monroe wrote:

"It was not prudent to avail myself of his aid in presenting or even making known my arrival to the Committee of Public Safety, and I was averse to taking the introduction of my predecessor for as good a reason. I did not know the ground upon which the Americans stood here, but suspected, as the acquisition of wealth had been their object in coming, they must have attached themselves to some preceding party and worn out their reputations. Upon mature reflection, therefore, I resolved to await the arrival of my predecessor and present myself as a thing of course with him. I concluded it would do me no detriment as it was the official mode and more especially as he would have to file off at the moment I took my ground. This was done. He accompanied me to the Office of Foreign Affairs, notified his recall and my succession.[1] I left with the Commissary a copy of my credentials and requested my recognition from the competent department as soon as possible which was promised. But my difficulties did not end here. Eight or ten days elapsed[2] and I was not accepted, nor had I heard a syllable from the Committee or seen a member. And upon inquiry I was informed that a minister from Geneva had been here six weeks before me and was not yet received. Still further to increase my embarrassments I likewise heard that the Commissary to whom I was presented being of Robespierre's party was out of favor, and that probably his letter covering my credentials had not been read by the Committee. I could no longer bear with delay. I foresaw that the impression to be expected from the arrival of a new minister might be lost, and that by the trammel of forms and collision of parties I might while away my time here forever without effect. I was therefore resolved to place myself if possible above these difficulties, by addressing myself immediately to the Convention. I knew this would attract the public attention and if my country had any weight here produce a proportional effect not only upon that body, but upon every subordinate department."

---

[1] Morris wrote to Robert Morris, August 14: "Presenting my successor, which I did yesterday, to the Commissioners, has given me more pleasure than any event for many months." Anne Cary Morris says that he intended to return to America and found a ship but "events in Europe were so interesting" that he remained for four years. In October, 1794, he sent his household goods by the ship "Superba" to New York. Included was a large quantity of Marie Antoinette's Imperial Tokay, which Morris, during the Terror bought for twenty-five cents a bottle. The last bottle of this Tokay was opened at a wedding party in New York in 1848. Monroe had trouble with Morris's passports. Morris left France by way of Switzerland.

[2] In "Paris in 1789-94," J. G. Alger tells of the lectures or services that took place on the Jacobin Sabbath, Décadi. He adds: "On the 9th of August, the

Monroe's letter was read in the Convention which, though puzzled at first soon referred it to the Committee of Public Safety. This body made a report within two hours. Just as Monroe had anticipated, it was agreed that he should be received by the Convention, "but," says Alger, "without any of the absurd ceremonial of the monarchy, and that the President should give him the *accolade fraternelle*, in token of the friendship of the two nations." That same day a decree was issued granting James Monroe the privilege of appearing on the morrow, August 15, before the National Convention.

Here, then, we have come to one of the important events in Monroe's life — an episode of historic picturesqueness and significance.

There was at least one embarrassment in the preliminaries. An hour or two before the time set for the function, the President of the Convention sent to Monroe for a copy of his address. This President was Antoine Phillipe Merlin of Douai, a lawyer and deputy from the Department of the Nord. Elihu B. Washburne says: "He was always called and known in public life as Merlin (de Douai), to distinguish him from Antoine Merlin, another deputy from the Department of the Moselle, a lawyer at Thionville, who was known as Merlin (de Thionville)."[1] With reference to the address, Monroe says: "I thought it expedient to make the occasion as useful as possible in drawing the two republics more closely together by ties of affection by showing them the interest which every department of our government took in their success and prosperity. With this view I laid before the Convention, with suitable solemnity, the declarations of the Senate and House of Representatives, and added a similar one

---

Décadi after Robespierre's fall, the perils of idolizing public men in a republic were appropriately dwelt upon. The American Ambassador and his wife were present. They had just arrived in Paris and were probably staying close by at White's hotel"— *Hotel Philadelphie, passage des Petits Pères.*

[1] Recollections of a Minister to France, by E. B. Washburne, 2 vols., Vol. II, p. 336.

for the President. The effect surpassed my expectations. My reception occupied an hour and a half of
not merely interesting but distressing sensibility for all
who beheld it. It was with difficulty that I extricated
myself from the House and Committee of Public Safety
and indeed the crowd which surrounded it after business was over. The cordial declaration of America in
favor of France and the French Revolution . . . in
view of all Europe, and at a time when they were torn
asunder by parties was a gratification which overpowered them."

Elihu B. Washburne was American Minister to
France, 1869-1877, during the Commune. In Vol. II
pp. 330-336 of his Recollections, he. tells of his visits
to the National Archives where he looked into the
dossier of Thomas Paine and that of James Monroe.
He copied this extract from the *proces verbal* (journal)
of the National Convention of August 15, 1794:
"Citizen Monroe, Minister Plenipotentiary of the
United States of America near the French Republic
is admitted to the hall at the sitting of the National
Convention. He takes his place in the midst of the
representatives of the people, and remits to the President of the Convention a translation of his discourse
addressed to the National Convention. It is read by
one of the secretaries. The expressions of fraternity
and union between the two peoples, and the interest
which the United States takes in the French Republic,
are heard with a lively sensibility and with applause.
The letter of credence of Citizen Monroe is also read,
as well as those written by the American Congress and
addressed to the President of the National Convention
and to the Committee of Public Safety. In witness of
the fraternity which unites the two peoples, French
and American, the President gives the *accolade* (the
fraternal embrace) to Citizen Monroe."

The best contemporary account is in the *Moniteur*
(XXI, 496-500) which says: "The Minister entered
the hall amidst cries of '*Vive la Republique*'; and the

President, having announced that Mr. Monroe spoke only the English language, one of the Secretaries was ordered to read the discourse the Minister had prepared. The Minister was conducted to the President, who gave the kiss and the embrace in the midst of universal acclamations of joy, delight and admiration."

Then the Convention passed a decree containing three articles. In the first Monroe was recognized as minister — the first accredited American Minister to the French Republic. In the second article, letters of credence, his address, the addresses remitted by him, and the response of Merlin of Douai, were ordered to be printed in two languages — French and American — and inserted in the Bulletin of Correspondence.

"The frantic hatred existing and felt by the French toward the English," comments Washburne, "would not permit the Convention to recognize our mother tongue as the English language, hence they called it 'the American language.'" In the third article of the decree it was provided that "the flag of the United States of America shall be joined to that of France and displayed in the Hall of the Convention as a sign of the union and eternal fraternity of the two peoples."

While at the Hague as Resident Minister of the United States, John Quincy Adams paid his respects to the French Commissioners then, January, 1795, at that Capital. He calls them the "*Citoyens Representans du Peuple Francais.*" They spoke of Mr. Monroe's reception by the National Convention. "*Parbleu,*" said one, "it was a *scène attendrissante.*" It was "*une des plus fameuses séances*" of the Convention. There were more than ten thousand persons present. "He shed tears, he was so much affected. I saw him cry.' 'Ah!' said another, '*c'était aussi bien de quoi faire pleurer.*' Then they said one of the flags had been sent to America. In short the national character appeared in nothing more conspicuous than in the manner in which they spoke of this occurrence. They inquired if Mr. Morris was in Switzerland. I

answered them, I did not know; that I had no personal
acquaintance with Mr. Morris. 'Ah!' said the Citoyen
who appeared to be at the head of the deputation,
'La France sait parfaitment qu'il est en Suisse.' He
spoke with peculiar emphasis, but I did not think
proper to make any further enquiry of him on the
subject."[1]

Morris' adherents at once raised a cry against
Monroe. Roosevelt[2] says: "Washington wrote him
[Morris] a letter warmly approving of his past conduct.
Nevertheless, Morris was not over-pleased at being
recalled. He thought that, as things were in France,
any minister who gave satisfaction to his government
would prove forgetful of the interests of America. He
was probably right; at any rate, what he feared was
just what happened under his successor, Monroe ––
a very amiable gentleman, but distinctly one who
comes in the category of those whose greatness is
thrust upon them." Roosevelt saturated with his
subject, the aristocratic, Federalistic, anti-Gallican
Gouverneur Morris, looks with the eyes of a partisan
upon poor Monroe, who is unaristocratic, anti-Fed-
eralistic and pro-Gallican. Roosevelt says: "Monroe,
as Morris' successor, entered upon his new duties with
an immense flourish, and rapidly gave a succession of
startling proofs that he was a minister altogether too
much to the taste of the frenzied Jacobinical republicans to whom he was accredited.[3] Indeed his capers

---

[1] Memoirs of John Quincy Adams, Vol. I, p. 62.

[2] Gouverneur Morris, by Theodore Roosevelt, pp. 293-304.

[3] Rufus King said in a letter to H. Le Roy, New York, November 9, 1794: "And
as for the Mountain Mr. Monroe appears seated upon, I sincerely hope it may
prove to be formed of snow, and for the good of Mankind dissolve with the approaching summer."— Beveridge's Marshall, Vol. II, p. 222 says: "Monroe, a partisan
of the Revolutionists, had begun his mission with theatrical blunders; and these
he continued until his recall, when he climaxed his imprudent conduct by his
attack on Washington. During most of his mission Monroe was under the influence of Thos. Paine, who had become the venomous enemy of Washington.
. . . But Monroe though shallow, was well-meaning, and he had a good excuse
for over-enthusiasm; for his instructions were 'Let it be seen that in case of war
with any nation on earth, we shall consider France as our first and natural ally.'"
See American State Papers, For. Rel., Class II, 669; Ticknor, II, 113, Paine and
Monroe; Paine's Writings, Conway, III, 368-69. For Washington on Monroe's
View, see Ford, XIII, 452; see McMaster, II, 257-259, 319-370.

were almost as extraordinary as their own, and seem rather like the antics of some of the early French commanders in Canada, in their efforts to ingratiate themselves with their Indian allies, than like the performance we should expect from a sober Virginia gentleman on a mission to a civilized nation. He stayed long enough to get our affairs into a snarl, and was then recalled by Washington, receiving from the latter more than one scathing rebuke."

"However the fault was less with him than with his party and with those who sent him. Monroe was an honorable man with a very unoriginal mind, and he simply reflected the wild, foolish views held by all his fellows of the Jeffersonian democratic-republican school concerning France — for our politics were still French and English, but not yet American. His appointment was an excellent example of the folly of trying to carry on a government on a 'non-partisan' basis. Washington was only gradually weaned from this theory by bitter experience; both Jefferson and Monroe helped to teach him the lesson. . . . To appoint Monroe, an extreme democrat, to France, while at the same time appointing Jay, a strong Federalist to England, was not only an absurdity, which did nothing toward reconciling the Federalist and Democrats, but, having in mind how these parties stood respectively towards England and France, it was also an actual wrong, for it made our foreign policy seem double-faced and deceitful. While one minister was formally embracing such of the Parisian statesmen as had hitherto escaped the guillotine, and was going through various other theatrical performances that do not appeal to any but a Gallic mind, his fellow was engaged in negotiating a treaty in England that was so obnoxious to France as almost to bring us to a rupture with her. . . . If we intended to enter into such engagements with Great Britain, it was rank injustice to both Monroe and France to send such a man as the former to such a country as the latter."

This Morrisian and partisan view of Monroe's character and conduct is open to dissent. The best thing for one to do in seeking to form a just opinion is to re-read Monroe's instructions. Did he go beyond them? But for the *accolade fraternelle* it cannot be urged that the reception in the hall of the Convention was so dreadfully Gallic, or unseemly. Monroe himself must have felt that it was unusual and likely to arouse feeling on the part of those who, having lost sight of the original purpose of the Revolutionists, which was to rid France of age-long despotism, now saw only the bloody excesses of the terrorists. Referring to his presentation of the official reply of the United States Senate and House of Representatives to the French Committee of Public Safety, Monroe wrote to Madison: "I doubt not this measure will be scanned with unfriendly eyes by many in America. They will say that it was intended that these things should have been smuggled in secretly and as secretly deposited afterwards. But they are deceived if they suppose me capable of being the instrument of such purposes. On the contrary, I have endeavored to take the opposite ground, with a view of producing the best effect here as well as there. And I am well satisfied that it has produced here a good effect. It is certain that we had lost in a great measure the confidence of the nation."

But Monroe had run a greater risk than he had supposed. Secretary Randolph heard of Robespierre's downfall October 9, and wrote to Washington that he "felt himself happy that Colonel Monroe's instructions forbid him to attach himself to the uncertain fate of any individuals." Then came news of Monroe's friendly affair with Robespierre's successors. Randolph wrote a rebuke. He could see why, in the confusion of things, the hall of the National Convention had become the "theatre of diplomatic civilities."

But —

"We should have supposed that an introduction there would have brought to mind these ideas: 'The

United States are neutral; the allied Powers jealous;
with England we are now in treaty; by England we
have been impeached for breaches of faith in favor
of France; our citizens are notoriously Gallican in
their hearts; and therefore in the disclosure of
feelings something is due to the possibility of fostering
new suspicions.' Under the influence of these sentiments, we should have hoped that your address to the
National Convention would have been so framed as to
leave heart-burning nowhere. . . . We do not perceive
that your instructions have imposed upon you the
extreme glow of some parts of your address. . . . You
have it still in charge to cultivate the French Republic
with zeal, but without any unnecessary eclat; because
the dictates of sincerity do not demand that we should
render notorious all our feelings in favor of that
nation."

Randolph eased his censure with a private note;
and, December 5, said: "We are fully sensible of the
importance of the friendship of the French Republic.
Cultivate it with zeal, proportioned to the value we
set upon it. Remember to remove every suspicion
of our preferring a connection with Great Britain,
or in any manner weakening our old attachment to
France."

As a matter of fact, it was not Randolph and the
Administration who were aggrieved; it was Monroe
who soon began to feel exceedingly uncomfortable on
account of Jay. It dawned upon him that he might
be compromised in the eyes of his French friends if
Jay should negotiate a treaty inimical to French
interests. He was sincere in his deep desire to reës-
tablish the most amicable relations with France; could
he look Frenchmen in the eye if it should turn out that
he was merely making a diversion until Jay could clinch
his British treaty? He wrote to Madison, December 18:

"After all there is but one kind of policy which is safe, which
is the honest policy. If it was intended to cultivate France by
sending me here Jay sho'd not have been sent to Engl'd, but if

indeed it was intended to cultivate Engl'd it was wise to send
some such person as myself here, for it was obvious that in pro-
portion as we stood well with France sho'd we be respected by
Engl'd."

In a letter of the same date to Randolph, he reminded
the Secretary of Jay's shortcomings in the Gardoqui
negotiations, and warned him that England would
offer to give America certain things already ours.
England would agree to give up this and that — the
western posts, for instance; when she should have
surrendered them on the terms of the peace treaty long
ago.

Sure enough the Committee of Public Safety soon
suspected that something was afoot agreeable to
England and disagreeable to France. Monroe was
quizzed. What was Citizen Jay's purpose? Did he
mean to tolerate an infraction of the French-American
treaty? Did Monroe himself propose to permit such a
thing? Monroe exerted himself to soothe this dis-
quietude and, in part, succeeded. But he was unable
to reassure himself, much less the suspicious Committee
on Public Safety. Jay was secretive. He sent Colonel
Trumbull from London to Paris, who was to talk with
Monroe but in "strict confidence."[1] To have invited
Trumbull's communication[2] would have put Monroe
in a peculiar dilemma — a false position. He saw
through the artifice, and refused to enter into a secret
confab with Colonel Trumbull. When Trumbull
returned to London, he found Morris there. Morris
writes of him: "He says Mr. Monroe found it difficult
to change principles fast enough so as to keep pace
with the changes in the French government" — a mere
bit of wit of Morris's caustic kind.[3] The French looked
askance upon Trumbull. It seemed to them as though
Jay and Monroe were up to mischief. To Monroe, at
times, it must have appeared as though Jay's chief

[1] American State Papers, Foreign Relations, Vol. I, p. 518.
[2] Johnston's Correspondence and Public Papers of John Jay, Vol. VI, p. 179.
[3] Morris's Diary, Vol. II, p. 113.

reason for being born was to harry him. If he had such a whimsical thought one moment, he must have laughed at himself for it the next.

It was evident that Jay's Treaty of Amity, Commerce and Navigation was going through. It did go through. It was signed November 19, delivered to Randolph, March 7, 1795, and ratified August 18. Next day Randolph resigned. He was succeeded by Timothy Pickering, December 10. Meantime, Thomas Pinckney had gone out as minister to Spain; had visited Monroe in Paris, and had negotiated a treaty at Madrid. Monroe was perhaps of some help to Pinckney, as he had been in correspondence with various well-informed persons in relation to Spanish, Algerian and Malta affairs. Don Diego de Gardoqui had sought to open negotiations with France through Monroe.[1] In fact the fall of 1794 and winter and spring of 1795 were busy months with Monroe. The Consul-General at Paris was Fulwar Skipwith of Virginia; and he, too, had his hands full.

From the beginning of the French mission one observes in Monroe's letters an excellent access of the spirit of statesmanship — more clarity, directness, force. Most of the letters in Volume II of his Writings will repay reading, as contemporary chapters on the terrible days in France. His history of the Jacobins made an impression in Randolph's office. Washington was denouncing the Democratic Societies in America, and extracts from Monroe's account were published "as from a letter of a gentleman in Paris to his friend in this city." Monroe resented this misuse of his matter. He wrote to Judge Jones, June 20, 1795, that he regarded it as an "unbecoming and uncandid thing" to reproduce what he had said about "the misfortunes of that misguided club"— the least important of the

---

[1] See Letters from Monroe to Randolph, Jefferson, Madison and to the French Committee of Public Safety, in Writings of Monroe, Vol. II, p. 55, *et seq.* A thorough study of "The Monroe Mission to France" by Beverly W. Bond, Jr., appeared in the Johns Hopkins studies for February-March, 1907, and may be found in Vol. XXV, pp. 5-104.

many subjects he had dwelt upon in his correspondence.

But what of troubled Paris all this time — what of the La Fayettes, what of Tom Paine, what of the Monroes themselves?

One interesting incident was the presentation of an American flag to the National Convention. Monroe entrusted this duty to his good friend Joshua Barney, then Captain, later Commodore, in the United States Navy. Barney, too, received the *accolade*. He it was who, with Monroe's nephew, carried the same flag at the head of the column of Americans when the body of Jean Jacques Rousseau was borne to the Pantheon.

Meantime Monroe was active in behalf of General La Fayette and his family. La Fayette himself was in Olmutz dungeon, in Austria. Mme. de La Fayette was in Paris. At first she was in Le Petit Force prison, but at this time was five stories up in a garret at Le Plessis. She had lost three of her family by the guillotine — grandmother, mother and sister — the Duchesse d'Ayen, the Vicomtesse de Noailles and the Marechale de Noailles, who had gone to their death together. The Monroes visited her and gave her all the comfort and care they could. It was a terrible winter for her, but thanks to the Monroes and other friends, she survived and was allowed to revisit her home in Auvergne, subsequently sending her son George Washington La Fayette to General Washington at Mount Vernon and going herself, with her two daughters, to share her husband's prison at Olmutz. Monroe wrote to Washington concerning these things but especially about the American voyage of his namesake.

When Robespierre fell, Paine was almost at death's door. For a month his memory was a blank. A message from Monroe revived him. Monroe sent word of his solicitude. He would try to get Paine out of Luxembourg. Fifteen days later Peter Whiteside wrote to Paine and, on the strength of the Whiteside com-

munication, Paine addressed his celebrated Memorial
to Monroe.[1] Paine wrote to Washington: "Immediately upon my liberation, Mr. Monroe invited me
to his house, where I remained more than a year and
a half; and I speak of his aid and friendship, as an
openhearted man always will do in such a case, with
respect and gratitude."

It was on November 6, that Monroe rescued Paine
from Luxembourg prison. Monroe[2] "took him, half
dead, to his own abode; then the *Maison des Etrangers,
Rue de la Roi.* This is now (1899) *101 Rue de Richelieu,*
printing office of *Le Temps* and publishing office of the
Gironde. It is the same building as in Paine's time,
and several rooms retain traces of their former decora-
tions." Here Paine wrote much, including the second
part of his heretical work "The Age of Reason." This
book, Conway avers, was originally intended to combat
the French atheism of the Herbertists. It was to be
printed in French only. Lanthenas translated the first
part and sent a copy to Couthon. Paine says the
atheists "threatened his life." The pamphlet was
suppressed. Paine wrote to John Adams:

"The people of France were running headlong into atheism;
and I had the work translated in their own language to stop them
in that career and fix them in the first article of every man's creed,
who has any creed at all — I believe in God."

In Conway's "Life of Paine," we read: "A few
months after his going out of prison, he had a violent
fever. Mrs. Monroe showed him all possible kindness
and attention. She provided him with an excellent
nurse, who had for him all the anxiety and assiduity
of a sister. She neglected nothing to afford him ease
and comfort when he was totally unable to help himself. He was in the state of a helpless child who had
his hands and face washed by his mother. The surgeon

---

[1] Mémoire à M. Monroe, September, 1794, Paris. This memorial is printed in
full in Vol. III, Conway's Writings of Paine, pp. 175-212.

[2] Moncure D. Conway, Paris, March, 1899, to the London Athenaeum, April 1,
1899, No. 3727.

was the famous Dessault, who cured him of an abscess
which he had in his side." Conway continues: "The
Monroes, early in 1796, removed to 'The Pavilion,'
(*de la Buxiere*) *Rue Clichy*, where Paine continued with
them, having become an important, though unofficial,
attaché of the Legation. 'The Pavilion' was afterwards
turned into the famous Tivoli Gardens. The site is in
part built over and in part occupied by the *Rues del
Bruxelles* and *Ventimille*."

After the Monroes had left Paris, Paine lived with
Nicolas de Bonneville, printer and publisher, 4, *Rue
Théâtre Francais*, now *Rue de l'Oden*. Paine wrote
a great deal while with the Bonnevilles. "Napoleon
flattered Paine, telling him he ought to have a statue
of gold"; and also telling him that "the police had
their eye on him"— a kiss and a backhander, Napoleon
hinted that Paine had better put the sea behind him.
This he would have done long before but for his dis-
relish for British cruisers. One of them stopped
Monroe's packet, in search of Paine. However, he
accompanied the Bonnevilles to America. Mme. Bonneville was a motherly friend to Paine as long as he lived.
Her son was the General Bonneville concerning whose
adventures in the Rockies and on the plains Irving
wrote so charmingly. While in Paris Paine wrote
Washington a reproachful letter, but withdrew it at
Monroe's request. Monroe was sensitive on a point
of honor. He thought that Paine should not write
on American or English affairs, while living with
the American Minister. Then, suddenly, without
consulting Monroe, he wrote another — a very bitter
letter. Whether this reached Washington, or fell in
the hands of Secretary Pickering is not clear. Paine
did not hear from Washington.[1] His next move was

---

[1] Washington, for his part, was careful as to what he wrote. The Duc
d'Aumale, son of Louis Philippe, told E. B. Washburne this story: Washington was
a very early riser, and always dressed himself most carefully, wearing knee-
breeches and the like, and the first thing he did was to look into the negro cabins
to see that everything was in good condition. Louis Philippe said to Washington
on one occasion, "Why! you get up so early in the morning?" Washington

to issue the letter in printed form, and this not only reached its object but proved to be something of a winged shaft that pierced and hurt him. It is a huge pity that Paine did not do as Monroe advised. Conway surmises that Washington had been embittered against Paine by the Genet incident, by the studied enmities of Morris, and by his apprehensiveness that a friendly word for Paine would antagonize England — a most undesirable matter in view of the Jay negotiations. Monroe tried hard not to hurt Washington's feelings, or have them hurt; but by and by party spirit made him do what he was subsequently profoundly sorry for.

Monroe was Paine's friend to the last. Conway, speaking of James Cheetham, who, like George Chalmers (Francis Oldys), wrote a hostile life of Paine, quotes him as saying that when Paine was near his end Monroe "wrote asking him to acknowledge a debt for money loaned in Paris and that Paine made me no reply." "But before me," adds Conway, "is Monroe's statement, while President, that for his advances to Paine 'no claim was ever presented on my part, nor is any indemnity desired.'"

---

answered, "Yes, young man, because I sleep well, and I sleep well because I have never written a line with which I can reproach myself." "Lucky man!" said the Duc, "how many men are there who can say as much!"

CHAPTER X

Rise Of A Great Party

Washington's non-partisan experiment, well-meant and undoubtedly useful at the start, in the long run deepened party feeling.

By a paradox, Monroe, who was one of the victims of the experiment, also became one of its beneficiaries. His political martyrdom in Federalist times became an asset and an advertisement in Democratic days. He himself was an early partisan aggressor — hostile to Hamilton, to Jay, to Morris and, regretably enough, to Washington, whom he recognized, with veneration, as the foremost man of the age.

Some of Monroe's enemies were hardly as scrupulous as they should have been, considering that they especially classed themselves as high-toned gentlemen. Gouverneur Morris outdid all the others in subtle enmity. December 19, 1795, he wrote to Washington:

"Shortly after my successor arrived in Paris (viz., two or at most three days) a person who was in the habit of telling me of what passed called, and began a conversation by saying: 'This new Minister you have sent us will never do here.' 'Why?' 'He is either a blockhead himself or thinks that we are so.' 'I can't suppose either to be the case, as I know him to be strongly attached to your Revolution. I should think he would succeed very well.' 'No, it is impossible. Only think of a man's throwing himself into the arms of the first person he met on his arrival and telling them he had no doubt but that if they would do what was proper here, he and his friends in America would *turn out Washington.* . . .' 'I cannot believe the fact.' 'You may rely on it, 'tis true. . . . I own that I. . . did not believe it.''

But if Morris did not believe it, why did he worry Washington with an account of it? In so many words, he says, "I did not believe it"; yet it was outrageously slanderous against Monroe to repeat the alleged tattle

of an unnamed Frenchman. This method of pouring
poison into Washington's ear was *Iago's* own — subtle,
insinuating, provocative of hate. Morris wronged
Monroe; and what he said was all the worse because
he himself was in high favor with Washington.

As time proved, Washington, who "did not at all
like it," was wise in signing the Jay treaty. It was a
humiliating treaty, but it postponed "the second
American Revolution" until the United States had
doubled in population and had become so well-knit
and so thoroughly democratized as to render pro-
British sentiment less and less harmful.

Men of anti-British feeling like Monroe saw the
Anglo-American rapprochment with a different eye.[1]
They stigmatized the Jay treaty as a base surrender.
They resented England's domineering ways on the
water, and her arrogance on the land. She meant
mischief on the lakes and in the Mississippi Valley.
She exalted the aristocrats and kept her masses in
ignorance and poverty. High-handed, too, was this
England, with her Orders in Council. Was she so
privileged, then, that she could put a shot at her
pleasure across the bows of an American vessel, bring
her to, bobbing and ducking on the waves, board her,
and examine her crew in search of runaway British
sailors? When these sailors ran away and covertly
shipped on American merchantmen, wasn't it because
they had been flogged? Throw the cat into the sea!
Stop belaboring poor Jack with a marlinspike till he was
black and blue! Be as little of a brute as you can, not
as big a one. It is a bully that you are, John Bull, with

---

[1] Public protests were made at Boston (Fanueil Hall), New York, Philadelphia,
Baltimore, Richmond, Portsmouth, Wilmington and Charleston. Town-meetings,
as the Federalists called them, began in Boston, where 1500 persons met in protest
against the Jay treaty. In New York, "the meeting was numerous and tumul-
tuous." Hamilton tried to address it. He was stoned. In Philadelphia, the
meeting was general and numerous. Chief Justice McKean, Speaker Muhlenberg, Dr. Shippen and Blair McClenachan were its sponsors. And so the wave
passed from north to south until it reached Charleston. Anthony Wayne wrote:
"The man of straw," set up in Boston and which ran the seaboard gauntlet,
"was tossed over the Allegheny mountains into Kentucky." See Life of Timothy Pickering, Vol. III, p. 201, *et seq.*

no love for Jonathan. But let other people's ships alone on so wide a space as the ocean, which belongs to no particular flag, whatever one's illusions about it.

"Monroe's path in Paris was strewn more with thorns than roses," remarks John Joseph Conway,[1] in his comment on the French furore occasioned by the Jay treaty. Adolphe Thiers says:

"In the French government there were persons in favor of a rupture with the United States. Monroe, who was an ambassador, gave the Directory the most prudent advice on this occasion. 'War with France,' said he, 'will force the American government to throw itself into the arms of England and to submit to her influence; aristocracy will gain supreme control in the United States, and liberty will be compromised. By patiently enduring, on the contrary, the wrongs of the present President, you will leave him without excuse, you will enlighten the Americans, and decide a contrary choice at the next election. All the wrongs of which France may have to complain will then be repaired.'"[2]

Monroe's earnest plea for peace won over Rewbell, Barras, and Lareveillére, though it failed to win Lazare Carnot, grandfather of President Sadi Carnot, of more recent fame. In a letter to Pickering[3] November 5, 1795, Monroe told of the installation of this Directory; nor did he balk at praising its members. He reminded Jefferson, November 18, that the ordeal through which France was passing, in the establishment of a republican system, had given her enemies opportunities to contrast her convulsions (caused by unbearable misrule) with "the gloomy and sullen repose of the neighboring despotisms." He had been silenced neither by the hubbub of his enemies in America nor the suspicious coldness of the French. For that matter, he had not grown less watchful. That fall he wrote to Madison: "Gardoqui, when he returned to Spain, settled a secret service account for six hundred thousand dollars."[4]

---

[1] Footprints of Famous Americans in Paris, p. 37.

[2] Thiers, Histoire de la Révolution, tome IX, ch. I.

[3] Timothy Pickering, Secretary of War, was ad interim Secretary of State from August 20, 1795 to December 20, when he was regularly commissioned as head of the State Department.

[4] For Madison, Jefferson and Pickering letters at this period, see Writings of Monroe, Vol. II, p. 368, et seq.

But Monroe realized that he was in an untenable position — doubly so. He could not possibly please Pickering, who was much more censorious than the considerate Randolph, nor could he remain in the good graces of the French. John Quincy Adams says:[1]

"There are in the annals of all nations occasions when wisdom and patriotism, and the brightest candor and the profoundest sagacity are alike unavailing for success. . . . The difficulties of his (Monroe's) situation became much greater after the treaty had been ratified and was made public. The people of the United States . . . equally divided, were bitterly exasperated against each other."

John Spencer Bassett[2] says that when the treaty came out "Monroe was so dumbfounded that he could only gasp.[3] He did not try to set himself right, and thought himself lucky that the ministry did not call upon him to explain his position." Pickering wished him to defend the treaty. But Monroe let the sleeping dog lie. He pocketed his instructions, and kept them pocketed for two months. But, says Avery[4] "while Monroe thus failed to obey his instructions, he did not fail to keep the French Government informed as to the fight against the treaty that was going on at home and, for some months, the Directory refrained from 'ungentle remonstrance.'"

Pickering, Wolcott and McHenry of the Cabinet wrote a joint letter from Philadelphia, July 2, 1796, to Washington, at Mount Vernon, in reply to an inquiry by the President on the subject of the capture of the American vessel "Mount Vernon" by the French privateer "Flying Fish." Should an explanation be

---

[1] Lives of Madison and Monroe, p. 248.

[2] The Federalist System (Amer. Nation Series), Vol. XI, pp. 213-216.

[3] He wrote to Judge Jones: "Jay's treaty surpasses all that I feared, great as my fears were of his mission. Indeed, it is the most shameful transaction I have ever known of the kind."— Gouverneur Mss.

[4] The terms of the treaty, when first seen in American journals, declares Avery, "made Monroe stand aghast." "The French were greatly exasperated by what they considered the treacherous conduct of their old ally." There was no question that some of the articles of the Jay treaty controvened "at least the spirit of the treaty of 1778."— A History of the United States and Its People, by Elroy M. Avery, Vol. VII, p. 138, et seq.

asked of Minister Adet? Would it be within the power of the Executive and expedient "to send an extra character to Paris to explain the views of this government and to ascertain those of France?" The Cabinet officers thought that a direct explanation should be demanded; and that "the recall of Mr. Monroe, by creating a vacancy, can alone authorize the sending of a new Minister to that Country." They continued to animadvert upon the matter thus:

"On the expediency of this change we are agreed. We think the great interests of the United States require that they have near the French Government some faithful organ to explain their real views and to ascertain those of the French. Our duty obliges us to be explicit. Although the present Minister plenipotentiary of the United States at Paris has been amply furnished with documents to explain the views and conduct of the United States, yet his own letters authorize us to say that he has omitted to use them, and thereby exposed the United States to all the mischiefs which could flow, from jealousies and erroneous conceptions of their views and conduct. Whether this dangerous omission arose from such an attachment to the cause of France as rendered him too little remindful of the interests of his own country, or from mistaken views of the latter, or from any other cause the evil is the same."[1]

Pickering, Wolcott and McHenry thereupon advised Washington to recall Monroe and send in his place Patrick Henry, John Marshall, Charles Cotesworth Pinckney, or William Smith of South Carolina. The three Cabinet officers could not resist the temptation to have a final fling at Monroe. They added:

"Among other circumstances that will occur to your recollection, the anonymous letters from France to Thomas Blount and others

---

[1] Irving says, Life of Washington, Vol. V, p. 257, that whatever the cause of Monroe's nonaction "the result was the very evil he had been instructed to prevent." But the evil was not the result of anything Monroe did or failed to do. It was the result of making England a preferred nation against France previously preferred under the treaty of 1778. In his Life of John Adams, John T. Morse, Jr. (p. 274), says: "To cure the feeling which he [Gouverneur Morris] had wounded, Mr. Monroe of quite the opposite way of thinking was sent to supersede him. But Monroe was carried away by the Jacobinical excitement into behaviour so extravagantly foolish as to seriously compromise the National interests." Monroe's behaviour was less extravagant than this language — quite unmeasured and misleading.

are very noticeable. We know that Montflorence[1] was the writer and that he was the Chancellor of the Consul, Skipwith, and from the connection of Mr. Monroe with those persons we can entertain no doubt that the anonymous letters were written with his privity."[2]

They were not written with Monroe's privity. He had nothing to do with them — knew nothing about them. . . . The insinuation was slanderous, as was Morris's "I don't believe it" letter; and intended to blacken Monroe in Washington's mind.

Judge Jones thought that Pickering would have ordered Monroe home in time for him to have made a summer passage had it not been that the Federalist politicians feared lest his coming might set astir a campaign tempest adverse to them. The recall was dated August 22, and was received by Monroe after the elections; and also after stormy weather had set in. The untimeliness of the recall caused remark. Monroe and his family were obliged to pass another winter in Paris, where his household at this time consisted of fourteen persons.[3]

"During all his exciting residence in Paris," says Gilman, "it is interesting to trace the minute interest maintained by Monroe in whatever pertained to his domestic affairs. There are long letters in the Gouverneur collection devoted to his financial business, to the welfare of his brothers, Andrew and Joseph, and of his sister, to his land bought, near Mr. Jefferson's, his servants, fruit trees,[4] etc.; besides many a passage in regard to nephew Joseph, who was at school at

---

[1] Major J. J. Montflorence of South Carolina, a soldier of our Revolution long in France.

[2] Writings of George Washington (Ford), Vol. XIII, pp. 214-219; 253, 257, 330. In the Life and Correspondence of James McHenry, by Bernard C. Steiner, 1907, are thirteen references to Monroe, "envoy extraordinary of the tribe of Virginia." This 624-page book is full of Federal politics.

[3] "I shall decline a winter passage, and therefore most probably shall not embark till April or May." Monroe, Gouverneur Mss.

[4] Monroe sent the Madisons a box of china. In the same letter in which he wrote of the china he complained that Madison had not written to him in nine months. Mrs. Dolly, a bride, appears to have occupied some of the time formerly given over to things epistolary.

St. Germain, and young Rutledge, likewise placed
under the envoy's paternal care. His interest in the
progress of these American boys in the French school
betrays an unvarying kindness of heart in the midst of
pressing anxieties and cares."[1] Charles Cotesworth
Pinckney, Monroe's successor, appeared in Paris early
in December. Baron Pichon told George Ticknor[2]
that Paine prejudiced Monroe against Pinckney, as
an aristocrat, and that Monroe influenced the Directory in its determination to give him the cold shoulder.
But there is insufficient evidence that Monroe treated
Pinckney in that grudging and uncivil fashion. On
the contrary, Monroe and Pinckney got along very
well together. Pinckney's credentials were received at
the Foreign Office for transmission to the Directory.
The hitch was there — with "Monsieur Five Heads";
and a serious hitch it was. Monroe learned that no
American minister would be recognized.[3] He told
this to Pinckney who then expressed the wish to remain
until he could hear from home. Even this was denied,
and later he was threatened with arrest. But he
obtained his passports and made off. This it was
that brought French affairs to a head in the United
States.[4] In midwinter, 1796, Monroe learned that a
French envoy was about to be sent to America. This
aroused him, and he induced M. de la Croix, the French
Foreign Minister, to abandon the project. Yet the
French resentment was translated into several ominous
forms of activity. "They suspended the operations
existing between the United States and France; they
issued orders for capturing all American vessels, bound
to British ports, or having property of their enemies
on board; their diplomatic correspondence exhibited a
series of measures alike injurious and insulting to the
American government; and they recalled their minister

---

[1] Life of Monroe, by Daniel C. Gilman, p. 72.
[2] Life of George Ticknor, Vol. II, p. 113.
[3] American State Papers, Foreign, I, p. 746.
[4] McMaster, History of the United States, Vol. II, pp. 319-321.

from the United States without appointing a successor."[1]

This French Minister at Philadelphia was Pierre Auguste Adet, who, like his predecessors Fauchet and Genet, had made much politically of the Republicans. Adet ended his ministry about December 1, 1796. L. A. Pichon became *chargé d'affaires*, March 19, 1801; and it was as late as March 27, 1805, that General Louis Marie Turreau appeared as Napoleon's Minister to the United States.

Monroe took leave of the French Government on December 30, and left France by the Dublin packet, Captain Clay. The packet was brought to by a British frigate and searched down to her hold. The British were looking for Paine, who was not on board. As he had been voted into the Convention again and could not leave France without a passport from that body he foresaw that his arch-enemy would be informed by their spies of the granting of such a pass and would send a ship to seize him.[2]

Paine in Paris wrote a letter addressed to the editors of the *Bien-informé* on the recall of Monroe.[3] The charge that hurt Monroe was that he had been "the cause of the rupture between the two Republics." Paine declares: "The refutation of this absurd and infamous reproach is the chief object of his correspondence. . . . The observations of Monroe on the hidden causes of his recall are touching; they come from the heart; they are characteristic of an excellent citizen. . . . He will not suffer that a government, sold to the enemies of freedom, should discharge upon him its shame, its crime, its ingratitude, and all the odium of its unjust dealings. Were Monroe to find himself an object of public hatred, the Republican party in the

---

[1] J. Q. Adams, who exculpates Monroe. "He [Monroe] thought that France had a just cause of complaint."

[2] Paine was lucky that time and also lucky later on. Commodore Barney offered to carry him on a vessel he had secured, but Paine demurred. Barney's vessel sank at sea and all on board had to take a tossing in a small boat on tempestuous waves.

[3] Writings of Paine, M. D. Conway, Vol. III, pp. 368-370.

United States, that party which is the sincere ally of
France, would be annihilated, and this is the aim of
the English Government. Imagine the triumph of Pitt,
if Monroe and the other friends of freedom in America,
should be unjustly attacked in France."

Conway, commenting on this letter, says: "Monroe,
like Edmund Randolph and Thomas Paine, was sacrificed to the new commercial alliance with Great
Britain."

The great Washington, be it noted, was now out.
John Adams was President and Thomas Jefferson vice-
president. Washington city had become the seat of
government. But both Federalism and Hamiltonism
still prevailed. Adams had retained Washington's
cabinet; and Hamilton was able for a long while to
pull the strings whereby Federalistic politics and policies
were largely controlled. However, at this time it was
John Adams himself who took the French bull by the
horns. To Congress in extra session, May 15, 1797, he
declared that France was treating us "neither as
allies, nor as friends, nor as a sovereign state." It was
a crisis. We would try further negotiation but we
would put ourselves in a state of defense. Subsequently
he appointed C. C. Pinckney, John Marshall and
Elbridge Gerry as envoys to treat with the French
government.

"Monroe," says Bassett, "welcomed his removal.
He had felt for more than a year that Hamilton and
the politicians[1] behind the cabinet policies had used
him as a pawn to keep France quiet while the Jay
treaty was going through the formative processes.
He declared that if he were recalled he would publish
his instructions and show the whole affair to the public.
The Republicans approved of the project. Bassett
continues:

---

[1] Monroe himself was accused by the Federalists of playing politics. Writing
to Washington, July 21, 1796, Pickering hints that "the ominous letters of Mr.
Monroe composed a part of a solemn farce to answer certain party purposes in
the United States."

"They received him with feasts and justifications. During the summer he worked out a statement which was duly submitted to the inspection of Jefferson. It was based on documents connected and explained by an abundance of that casuistry for which the author was noted. It was not completed without bringing Adams into the controversy. In his recall he was told that it was because he had failed to obey Pickering's instructions in justifying the treaty and for concurrent reasons. On his return he asked Adams what the latter ground might be. In reply he was told that, as they concerned an administration which had gone out of office, the president did not feel at liberty to reply. He would have been glad to have had an avowal from the highest source that his recall was partly due to political causes, for it would have placed the controversy clearly in the realm of politics. He adroitly used Adams' refusal to charge that he was removed for secret reasons."[1]

Monroe "reached home full of wrath, but the opposition party gave him a cordial greeting, and he was entertained in Philadelphia at a public dinner where Jefferson, the Vice-President, Dayton, the Speaker, Chief Justice McKean, and other conspicuous men were present. Monroe's failure, it is clear, was not personal, it was a party affair."[2]

August 29, 1797, Washington wrote to Pickering: "Colo. Monroe passed through Alexandria last week but did not Honor me by a call. If what he has promised the public does him no more credit, than what he has given to it in his last exhibition, his friends must be apprehensive of a recoil." January 28, 1798, he asked McHenry: "What, as far as can be guessed at, is the public sentiment relative to Monroe's voluminous work? Which I have not yet seen but have sent for it."

Worthington C. Ford[3] in his Writings of Washington (Vol. XIII, pp. 452-490) gives in detail the General's remarks on Monroe's "voluminous work." Ford says:

"In the library at Mount Vernon was a copy of Monroe's View of the Conduct of the Executive in the Foreign Affairs of the United States, containing marginal notes in the handwriting of

[1] The Federalist System, by J. S. Bassett (American Nation Series), pp. 214, 215.
[2] Gilman's Monroe, pp. 63, 64.
[3] Writings of Washington (Ford), Monroe's vindication, Vol. XIII, pp. 415, 439, 447, 450.

General Washington. These are here brought together, with such extracts from the View as are necessary to afford a proper explanation of them. . . . The volume containing the autograph was presented by Judge Bushrod Washington to Judge Story, who left it to Harvard College. The President of Harvard, Edward Everett, placed it under seal, and it was only recently discovered by Mr. Justin Winsor, who courteously allowed me to copy all the annotations of Washington."

Gilman in his Life of Monroe (pp. 221-229) reprints Washington's annotations from the "copy by Mr. [Jared] Sparks now owned by the Library of Cornell University." This book of five hundred pages was intended to be its author's vindication. It contained the instructions given him by Secretary Randolph, official correspondence and various letters bearing upon the subject. Monroe touched upon fourteen points, as follows (Gilman pp. 65-66):

"(1) The appointment of Gouverneur Morris, a known enemy of the French Revolution.

(2) His continuance in the office until troubles came.

(3) His removal at the demand of the French Government.

(4) The subsequent appointment of Monroe, an opponent of the administration, especially in its foreign policy.

(5) The instructions given to Monroe, as to the explanations he should give the French in respect to Jay's mission, which concealed the power given him to form a commercial treaty.

(6) The strong expressions of attachment to France and the principles of the French Revolution given to Monroe.

(7) The resentment of the administration when these documents were made public.

(8) The approval of Monroe's endeavor to secure a repeal of the obnoxious decrees, and the silence which followed their repeal.

(9) Jay's power to form a commercial treaty with England, without corresponding advances to France.

(10) The withholding from Monroe of the contents of the treaty, an evidence of unfair dealing.

(11) The submission of this treaty to M. Adet, after the advice of the Senate, and before its ratification by the President.

(12) The character of Jay's treaty which departs from the modern role of contraband and yields the principle: 'Free ships shall make free goods.'

(13) The irritable bearing of the administration toward France, after the ratification, in contrast with its bearing toward England, when it was proposed to decline its ratification.

(14) Monroe's recall just when he had succeeded in quieting the French government for the time, and was likely to do so effectually."

Regretful, indeed, were Monroe's compunctions later in life when he thought of the way he had traveled past Mount Vernon without making a little detour of duty and paying his respects to the chief. He would have felt better the rest of his days. Tobias Lear,[1] in his account of the General's last illness, tells of a minor but painful incident of Friday evening, December 13, a snowy day when Washington was housed with a cold:[2] "He requested me to read to him the debates of the Virginia Assembly on the election of a Senator and a Governor — and on hearing Mr. Madison's observations respecting Mr. Monroe, he appeared much affected and spoke with some degree of asperity on the subject, which I endeavored to moderate, as I always did on such occasions."

Citing the case of an ancient worthy who "wished his enmities to be transient, and his friendships immortal," John Quincy Adams says: "Thus it was that the congenial mind of James Monroe, at the zenith of his public honors, and in the retirement of his latest days, cast off, like the suppuration of a wound, all the feelings of unkindness, and all the severities of judgment which might have intruded upon his better nature in the ardor of civil dissension. In veneration for the character of Washington he harmonized with the now unanimous voice of his country; and he has left recorded, in his own hand, a warm and unqualified testimonial to the pure patriotism, the pre-eminent ability and spotless integrity of John Jay."

---

[1] Letters and Recollections of George Washington, p. 129.

[2] Lear advised him to take something for the cold. He answered no; "you know I never take anything for a cold. Let it go as it came." He retired. Between two and three o'clock he awoke with an ague. He could hardly speak and breathed with difficulty. But he was afraid his wife would take cold if she got up. When a woman went in to light a fire, Lear was sent for. At Washington's request Overseer Rawlins bled him. This was at sunrise. Three doctors came and bled and dosed him. About five he said to Dr. Craik: "I die hard, but I'm not afraid to go." He was composed. He gave many orders. Between ten and eleven that night, he died without a struggle or a sigh.

In plain non-oratorical English, Monroe was sorry that he had thought so hard of those two great men whom he at times misjudged; just as he was sorry that he had figured in the Hamilton-Reynolds scandal.

It is necessary to touch upon this exceedingly disagreeable affair since Monroe was involved in it. Indeed, Bassett[1] asserts: "Shortly after his arrival in America Monroe gave a savage blow to Hamilton probably in retaliation for the latter's influence on his recall."

But is this view warranted? Let us state the case, so that the reader may not be offered either an apology for Monroe or a sweeping condemnation:

Two scamps, James Reynolds and Jacob Clingman were arrested in Philadelphia in 1792 for frauds, on the government. The charge was that they had procured a false adjustment of claims. Clingman countered. He said that the Secretary of the Treasury had been "engaged in corrupt speculation with Reynolds as his tool." High as Hamilton was, politically and socially, husband of General Philip Schuyler's daughter Elizabeth, who with her five children lived at the Hamilton place "The Grange" on the Hudson, there nevertheless had been partisan accusations against him with respect to his handling of the public funds. He worked hard, often till midnight; and he earned a great deal. But the reliable William Maclay, Republican Senator from Pennsylvania, in his Journal (1789-1791), has repeated references to Hamilton's "speculations." We are, of course, to remember that Hamilton's enemies said all sorts of unverifiable things about him. We have no monopoly of lies in this, our own age; and what the honest Maclay put into his Journal may have been but seeming truths. Congress, of course, was obliged to take cognizance of Clingman's charge. James Monroe, Abraham Venable and F. A. Muhlenberg, Speaker of the House, were named as a committee to call on Secretary Hamilton. This they

[1] The Federalist System (American Nation Series), pp. 215, 216.

did on the evening of December 14, 1792. Hamilton
told a strange story. By his own words he had been
approached by Mrs. Reynolds, who, on the plea that
she was from Hamilton's State and was in distress,
thus made her way with him. The illicit affair put
him at the mercy of Reynolds, a blackmailer, who
mulcted him of $1200. The astonished committee
accepted the explanation. Some letters bearing upon
the matter were also gone over. Hamilton had been
victimized — so it appeared; but what had the committee of Congress to do with the scrape, unless it
involved the accused in frauds on the government?
Next day the Committee wrote out a statement, signed
it, and left it with Monroe. Apparently the interview
satisfied the Committee. It was understood that
Hamilton regarded his frankness as of a confidential
nature, entitling him to the protection of the Committee. And so the scandal slept for nearly six years.

When Monroe sailed for France he left the documents in the Hamilton-Reynolds case "in the hands
of a respectable character" in Virginia. Hildreth
(Vol. V, p. 111) thinks Jefferson "the respectable
character." Schouler (Vol. I, p. 363) says: "These
papers, however, like some others which served for
party ammunition, seem to have circulated confiden-
tially among a conclave of Virginia Republicans which
included Jefferson, Madison, Giles and possibly
Edmund Randolph or Beckley. (See 7, John C.
Hamilton's Republic.) Beckley had recently lost his
re-election as clerk of the House."

Now who gave the documents to Callender? In
the fall of 1797, he published them in his "History
of the United States for 1796," Numbers V and VI.
Hamilton blamed Monroe for the publication. Many
historians since that time have accepted this assertion
and censured Monroe. But Monroe denied that he
brought about the publication. He might, therefore,
be censured for letting the papers pass from his own
hands to those of irresponsible politicians; but the

blame should end there[1]. We cannot assume that he
deliberately drew the incriminating papers from their
pigeon-hole and procured their publication in order
to get even with his maligners. He was a man of his
word; and so we take his word for it when he denied
all agency in the publication. One might, after reading
the animadversions of some of the historians, almost
believe that Monroe was the head-villain in the whole
affair, speculator, peculator and what-not. By a
strange process of onus-placing and odium-casting they
shift Hamilton's burdens away from him and fasten
them on the man sent by Congress to see what was
wrong. By raising a great "how-dy" on a minor point,
they divert the public from the real issue. In any
event, this was a discreditable case all around, and
quite modern in its disgustingness.[2]

[1] A number of them Federalistic. Randall's Jefferson goes into the case.
Gilman's Monroe avoids it. Hildreth, II, 104, speaks of Callender's "undigested
and garrulous collection of libels." A Study of Alexander Hamilton, by Fon-
taine T. Fox, 1911, is extremely anti-Hamiltonian.

[2] An extraordinary incident in Monroe's life is thus set forth in Allan McLane
Hamilton's "Intimate Life of Alexander Hamilton," pp. 116, 117: "Mrs. [Elizabeth
Schuyler] Hamilton could never forgive the behavior of Monroe when he, with
Muhlenberg and Venable, accused Hamilton of financial irregularities at the time
of the Reynolds incident. Many years afterwards when they were both aged
people, Monroe visited her and an interview occurred which was witnessed by
a nephew, who was then a lad of fifteen. 'I had,' he says, 'been sent to call upon
my aunt Hamilton one afternoon. I found her in her garden and was there with
her talking, when her maid servant came from the house with a card. It was
the card of James Monroe. She read the name and stood holding the card, much
perturbed. Her voice sank and she spoke very low, as she always did when she
was angry. 'What has that man come to see me for?' escaped from her. 'Why,
Aunt,' said I, 'don't you know, it's Mr. Monroe and he's been President, and
he is visiting here now in the neighborhood, and has been very much made of,
and invited everywhere, and so — I suppose he has come to call and pay his
respects to you.' After a moment's hesitation, 'I will see him,' she said.
"The maid went back to the house, my Aunt followed, walking rapidly, I after
her. As she entered the parlor, Monroe rose. She stood in the middle of the
room facing him. She did not ask him to sit down. He bowed, and addressing
her formally, made her rather a set speech — that it was many years since they
had met, that the lapse of time brought its softening influences, that they both
were nearing the grave, when the past differences could be forgiven and forgotten
— in short, from his point of view, a very nice, conciliatory, well-turned little
speech. She answered still standing and looking at him, 'Mr. Monroe, if you
have come to tell me that you repent, that you are sorry, very sorry, for the mis-
representations and the slanders and the stories you circulated against my dear
husband, if you have come to say this, I understand it. But, otherwise, no lapse
of time, no nearness of the grave, makes any difference.' She stopped speaking,
Monroe turned, took up his hat and left the room." It was Nemesis. Burr killed
Hamilton in 1804; Mrs. Hamilton died in 1854; she was fifty years a widow.

As for Callender there should be a few words more
about him; but we ought first to say that Monroe's
recall from France, in so far from injuring him
politically helped him with the electorate in Republican
Virginia. He was chosen Governor in 1799 and was
twice re-elected, holding that office till 1802. The
esteem in which he was held is well shown in a letter
from St. George Tucker, Williamsburg, December 22,
1799, congratulating him on his triumph over slander
and malignity in being made governor.

Henry Adams,[1] in his notable history of the United
States, says: "Some weakness in Monroe's character
caused him more than once to mix in scandals which
he might better have left untouched." The special
reference is to Callender's relations with Jefferson.
And now who was Callender?

James Thompson Callender, a Scotch radical, author
of a tabooed book, "The Political History of Great
Britain," who had fled to Philadelphia in 1792, was
one of the anti-Adams writers to suffer under the
Sedition Act. Judge Chase convicted him of libeling
the President. Jefferson pardoned him. When he got
out of jail, he went to Richmond and started a paper
there, *The Recorder*, supporting Jefferson's ideas.
But because Jefferson would not countenance so unfit
a man as postmaster of Richmond, Callender turned
upon the Democratic leader and struck at him as
venomously as he had struck at Adams. Jefferson[2]
wrote a long explanatory letter to Governor Monroe,
July 16, 1802, and another the next day, in which
he defended himself against Callender's attacks. He
had bought books and pamphlets of Callender in order
to help the persecuted writer to his feet; but the
Federalists made out that Callender was in Jefferson's

---

[1] Vol. I, p. 325. This work in nine volumes, by the author of "The Education
of Henry Adams," covers the administrations of Jefferson and Madison. Adams,
with the intellectual brilliancy of his race, also had a bit of its bias. It is a fascinating piece of history, but allowance must be made. He dwells upon the seamy
side of his characters, stinting his praise.

[2] Life of Jefferson, by H. S. Randall, Vol. III, pp. 16-21.

pay. It was a petty incident of a quarrelsome time, a molehill made into a party mountain. Callender, somewhat beliquored, was drowned in the James, whither he had gone to bathe, July 17, 1803.

This summary of large events and petty personal incidents brings us well into the period of the genesis of the Jeffersonian party, of which Monroe was one of the founders and life-long adherents. For a popular party there was bound to be. We have indicated why Washington, of course, knew that the "outs" would criticize the "ins"; what he, a broad and moderate man, did not believe in was senseless partisanship. Referring to Jefferson and Hamilton he wrote: "Why should either of you be so tenacious of your opinions as to make no allowance for those of the other?" In his Farewell Address, he warned Americans of the terrible consequences of blinding sectional partisanship; and, "in the most solemn manner, against the baneful effects of the Spirit of Party generally." It had its root, he declared in the strongest passions of the mind. Restrain it. Parties in free countries are useful checks upon the administration of the government and serve to keep alive a spirit of liberty; but what if the fire get away? Keep it under control.

These were wise words; and it would have been well if they had been heeded not only by Jefferson, Madison and Monroe but by Hamilton and John Adams. Nay, we should heed them now. That we should " steer clear of permanent alliances" is not the only solemn injunction in the Farewell Address.

John Morley in his book on Burke makes a strange mistake. He has been telling of what Burke saw and heard in Paris in 1773 — of his surprise that Madame du Barry, in so far from seeming gross, should have powderless hair, rougeless, simple toilet and unassuming ways; of his vision of the young dauphinness, "Glittering like the morning star," and of "the busy ferment of intellect in which his French friends most exulted." "It was from the ideas of the Parisian Freethinkers, whom Burke so detested," adds Morley, "that Jefferson, Franklin and Henry drew those theories of human society which were soon to find life in American independence."

This is very wide of the mark. Liberty and a better humanity were watchwords in America long before Rousseau's day. Moreover, they constituted the creed of such practical and pushing leaders as David Lloyd in Pennsylvania and Nathaniel Bacon in Virginia. Republicans now are far less liable to attack than were Republicans then. Few now advocate monarchy; many at that time thought as Hume did. Jefferson resented this passage in Hume: "The Commons established a principle, which is noble in itself and seems specious, but is belied by all history and experience, that the people are the origin of all just powers." Such was Jefferson's resentment that he was on the point of throwing Hume's History out of the University of Virginia. He rejoiced that Brodie had "pulverized" Hume. He hated Hume, hated the king idea. Patrick Henry, Mason, Monroe, Jefferson and all men of their school abhorred the enormous millennial black-list of monarchial crime, cruelty and despotism. We feel less abhorrence because our own age is less tyrannized over (by royalty at least); but with Jefferson and with Monroe the cue was to further the cause of democracy whenever they could.

Jefferson called his followers "Republicans"; but the Pro-French partisans used "Democratic" as descriptive of their societies, and so the awkward phrase "Democratic-Republican" filled the mouths of friends and foes alike. The men of the new party, mortified as they were at the excesses, the appalling inhumanities of the French, nevertheless sympathized with La Fayette's constitutionalism, and regarded Monroe's course as justifiable. The men of the Federalist party, twelve years in power, looked with disfavor upon Monroe, and with disgust upon the increasing membership of the "Self-created societies" of the Democratic

Associations. Not that the whole electorate was Anti-British and Anti-French, and nothing more. The Federalists gave a free and loose reading to the letter of the constitution; the Democrats professed to construe it strictly. In many other matters were these parties at logger-heads; or soon to be so; but, roughly speaking, one was the party of the aristocrats and the other the party of the people.

The Federalists spoke of themselves as "friends of order"— a cant phrase in which they as firmly believed as they believed themselves destined to take a high place on earth, and still higher in heaven. For heaven, they were sure, was on their side. Voltaire was an atheist; Voltaire was French; all Democrats were attracted to the French; therefore all Democrats are atheists — ergo, they belong in the brimstone pit, and heaven speed them thither. As for that, the old original serpent that seduced Eve was an arch-Jacobin. And, as for "the two Toms"— Tom Paine and Tom Jefferson — they were no better than the wicked. Paine had fallen under the *odium theologicum*, and that was the thing that tainted him with multitudes of the orthodox.

On the other hand, "the poor ragged Democrats who meet in barns" did not admit that all the religion was on the Federal side.[1] How about the Nazarene? Was he not with the poor and downtrodden? The Democrats said: "Aristocracies sink the people." "Courts and Camps are hotbeds of immorality and infidelity." "They are well-born, you are base-born." How selfish they were — those "well-fed, well-dressed, chariot-rolling, caucus-keeping, levee-revelling Federalists." In the printed speeches of the time we come upon such phrases as "Aristocratic Federalism;"— "the reign of terror is no more; the Alien and Sedition Acts have expired."

These measures, indeed, brought about the ruin of the Federalist party. Adams had four years of trouble.

---

[1] Continental Republicanism by Abraham Bishop, 1800.

Paine said that his "head was as full of kings, queens
and knaves as a pack of cards;" but, aside from his
vanity and lack of depth and balance, he was an able
man. France menaced him throughout his administration. Headstrong as he was, he managed French
matters well. It was the time of the "X Y Z" episode,
when a bribe of £50,000 was demanded from the
American envoys "for the pockets of the Directory."
The Republicans sang small in Congress after that; a
naval war came on; an army was organized; but, by
and by, Oliver Ellsworth, William Vans Murray and
William Richardson Davie, Commissioners sent by
Adams, negotiated a treaty with France; and there
was peace. That was in 1800. The same year the
Federalist party split. Hamilton, who had opposed
the Alien and the Sedition laws, and who wanted to
be the army's head, attacked Adams in an anonymous
pamphlet.[1] But Burr got hold of it, and made the
most of it for the Republicans. Adams threw the
Hamiltonian politicians out of his cabinet. These
internal dissensions helped to break up a party already
unpopular. Adams felt his lack of trustworthy friends.
He was isolated. He said, "I am as much a solitudinarian as Frederick the Conqueror." He began a
letter to his good wife Abigail: "The Solitudinarian
of Market Street to his dearest friend." "The Federalists," says Hart,[2] had governed well; they had built
up the credit of the country; they had taken a dignified
and effective stand against the aggressions of both
England and France. Yet their theory was of a government by leaders. Jefferson, on the other hand,
represented the rising spirit of Democracy. It was not
his protest against the over-government of the Federalists that made him popular, it was his assertion
that the people at large were the best depositories of

---

[1] A chill came over Jefferson when he heard Hamilton praise Julius Caesar as
the greatest man that ever lived. Already he was a political dictator, even in
Adams' own State. "Ames, Sedgwick, Cabot, Pickering and the whole Essex
Junto were thorough Hamiltonians."— Randall's Jefferson, Vol. II, p. 231.

[2] Formation of the Union, 1750-1829, by Albert Bushnell Hart, 1892.

power. Jefferson had taken hold of the 'great wheel going up the hill.' He had behind him the mighty force of the popular will."

CHAPTER XI

MONROE AND THE LOUISIANA PURCHASE

By this time Monroe was well up in the ways of both politics and diplomacy; yet he was destined to travel even mirier mazes than those he had hitherto followed. There was a new human development. Nineteenth century politics took on subtler attributes. Burr, in New York, organized a system. Hamilton, at this time a private citizen, was as active politically as ever. There were strange happenings. For instance, one cannot but regard the Jefferson-Burr electoral episode as extraordinary. It was a crisis that set the country by the ears. Incidentally it put Monroe to a fresh test.

The intent of the Republican voter in the autumn of 1800 was to elect Jefferson, President, and Burr, Vice-President; but, under the clumsy electoral system then in use, there was a dangerous hitch. Nowadays an elector has no free choice; then he had. It was his duty to name two persons; but he was not to say which was to be President and which Vice-President. When it came to the count, the man ahead was to be President; the next man, Vice-President.[1]

The count in this case gave Jefferson and Burr seventy-three votes each; to sixty-five for Adams, sixty-four for Pinckney and one for Jay. It was a Republican tie; and, accordingly, the election was thrown into the Federalist House of Representatives — Sixth Congress, second session, which met November 17, 1800, but which did not begin to ballot for President until the second week of the following February. John Adams was to go out on March 4. The feeling was tense, the

---

[1] This experience was enough for everybody. The twelfth amendment, adopted in 1804, so changed the system that each elector thereafter voted separately for the two offices. A tie was thus prevented.

situation dramatic. What a temptation was here for
honest men to become cunning casuists overnight and
argue themselves and their acquaintances into a state
of downright sophistication! Stories went around that
the Federalist majority in the House meant to continue
the deadlock till after March 4, so that there would be
an interregnum. In that event, it was proposed to
pass a bill devolving the government on the Chief
Justice, the Secretary of State, or the President *pro tem.*
of the Senate. This could only be done by "a stretch
of the Constitution." So, at least, Jefferson wrote to
Madison. This was putting the matter mildly, considering that the pending battle was what Muzzey calls
"the central fact of his career." He believed that
there was "a deliberate plot to subvert the Constitution
and nullify the Declaration of Independence. For him
the victory of 1800 was the vindication of the principles
of 1776. He was not overscrupulous in his methods";
he encouraged Freneau, Bache, Duane and Callender,
"whose slanderous articles on the Federalist leaders
tried their patience to the utmost . . . but for all these
faults of disposition or judgment, there was nothing
mean or base in Thomas Jefferson." [1] Burr, for his
part, "remained at Albany shrouded in mystery." [2]
Judge William P. Van Ness, "the confidant, newspaper
champion and instrument of Burr," was one of his
wire-pulling agents, and Jonathan Dayton, Federalist
Senator from New Jersey, was another. Van Ness it was
who subsequently "egged on the fatal duel which
terminated forever the fierce rivalries of Burr and
Hamilton." Meantime, as we shall see, Hamilton was
as busy as Burr. Indeed, every one was on the *qui vive.*
Gouverneur Morris and Wolcott found in the situation
fresh opportunities for intrigue. Cabot and Otis, seeing
with Federalist eyes, preferred Burr. Charles Carroll of
Carrolton feared "a Jacobinical President." He spoke

---

[1] Thomas Jefferson by David Muzzey, 1918, pp. 211-212.
[2] Randall's Jefferson, Vol. II, p. 604; Hammond's Political History of New
York, Vol. I, p. 149.

of "the insidious policy of Virginia" and "hoped the
[Maryland] Legislature would choose *pro hac vice* the
electors of President and Vice President." One has but
to read the letters of the period to discover for himself
that the high-toned gentlemen of the Federalist school
trusted the people very little, and Senates and Courts
a great deal. Luckily for Jefferson, his ablest opponent
thought him the lesser of two evils. Hamilton, who
had made Jefferson Vice-President, now wished to see
him President in preference to Burr. How could
Hamilton adumbrate that dark duel at Weehawken?—
how could he know that he was digging his own grave.
He felt that Burr would attempt "to reform the government à la Bonaparte." Again he said of Burr: "He is
as unprincipled and dangerous a man as any country
can boast — as true a Cataline as ever met in midnight
conclave." [1]   Thus, though the Republicans were
divided, the Federalists were likewise ripe for factional
manipulation. This is what happened:

Both Houses met in the Senate chamber, February
11, and Vice-President Jefferson opened and handed to
two tellers the certificates of the electors of sixteen
States. Then the Representatives returned to their
own chamber and began to ballot. Seven successive
ballots were taken, each like the other — eight states
for Jefferson; six for Burr, and two — Maryland and
Vermont — divided. Maryland stood four to four;
Vermont one to one. Then there was a recess. The
"hero" of the play was constantly in evidence; the
"villains" were still in the cellar with the trap-door
down. The "hero" was Joseph Nicholson of Maryland — a sick man, who, with a violent snow-storm
raging, was brought to the Capitol in order that he
might keep his State out of the Burr column. It was he
alone who kept Jefferson in the lead. He remained
abed in one of the committee-rooms, his wife attending
him; and the tellers took the ballot-box to him so that
he could vote with a minimum of exertion. As for the

[1] Hamilton's Works, Vol. VI, pp. 453-514.

"villains," Jefferson wrote in his Ana, February 12:
"Edward Livingston tells me that Bayard applied
today or last night to General Samuel Smith, and represented to him the expediency of his coming over to the
States who vote for Burr; that there was nothing in
the way of appointment which he might not command,
and particularly mentioned the Secretaryship of the
Navy."[1] He wrote to Monroe, February 15:

"If they (the Federalists) could have been permitted to pass a
law for putting the Government into the hands of an officer, they
would have certainly prevented an election. But we thought it
best to declare openly and firmly, one and all, that the day such
an act passed, the Middle States would arm, and that no such
usurpation, even for a single day, should be submitted to. This
first shook them. . . .[2] I have declared to them unequivocally,
that I would not receive the government on capitulation, that I
would not go into it with my hands tied."

"Monroe," says Henry Adams,[3] "was certainly
privy to these warlike preparations; for in the year
1814, Randolph attacked in debate the conscription
project recommended by Monroe, then Secretary of
War, and said: 'Ask him what he would have done,
whilst Governor of Virginia and preparing to resist
federal usurpation, had such an attempt been made by
Mr. [John] Adams and his ministers, especially in 1800!
He *can* give the answer.'" "The two great States of
Pennsylvania and Virginia, with their Republican
governors, McKean and Monroe," says Muzzey,[4]

---

[1] This is all the more curious when we consider that Jefferson himself by and
by made General Samuel Smith Secretary of the Navy, and that he served until
his brother Robert Smith was appointed to that place. The Smiths seem to have
had more than a common hold on the administrations of Jefferson and Madison.

[2] In Vol. XLII of the Massachusetts Historical Society Publications are Monroe's
letters to John Tyler, Sr., with other Tyler letters. Samuel Tyler, a nephew of
Judge John, was one of Governor Monroe's council. Monroe sent him to New
York to watch the progress of the difficulty regarding the election of Jefferson.
Samuel writes, February 9, 1801, on the subject. John Tyler wrote to Monroe,
December 27, 1799, from Greenway, congratulating him on "the triumph of
Democracy over Tyranny all over the world. *Vive la République.*"

[3] John Randolph, by Henry Adams, pp. 27,28.

[4] Life of Jefferson, p. 208.

"were ready to appeal to arms rather than see Jefferson
cheated out of the presidency."[1]

But Hamilton was soon heard from. His detractors
dwell upon his military ambition. Was he not a
peaceful manipulator now? He worked underhandedly
through Bayard of Delaware, leader of the House.
James Asheton Bayard, "a handsome, florid, fashion-
ably-attired man of thirty-five"; "an aristocrat with
a lofty scorn of all things Republican,"[2] who had a
great liking for cards, statecraft and diplomatic deals,[3]
was advised by Hamilton that it would be well to give
Burr the go-by. So Bayard called on Representative
John Nicholas, of Virginia, and told him what the
Federalists would do if Jefferson or his party should
choose to hearken. But Nicholas declined to serve as
a go-between. Then Bayard saw the same complaisant
General Samuel Smith whom Burr's agents are said to
have approached. Would Smith see Jefferson? Would
he? Smith saw Jefferson; but, of course, dared not
hint at what he was after. Jefferson talked freely as
to what he would do and what not do. Theirs was not
an "agreement among gentlemen," but simply a casual
conversation. Yet Jefferson must have known that
Smith was sounding him. He knew that the Federalists were playing into his hands in order to procure
protection for certain of their office-holders and certain
of their policies. As Muzzey says: "Jefferson, without
making any 'capitulation to the Federalists,' seems to
have let it be understood among them that he would

---

[1] McKean was a robust character. Randall, in his Jefferson, contrasts him with
Monroe. "Governor Monroe was of milder frame, but was as resolute a man as
there was on earth when his judgment bade him act. . . . It would be vain to
deny that both parties had the arbitration of arms distinctly in contemplation."
Cobbett in Porcupine's Gazette declares that menaces were thrown out at a Republi-
can festival at Petersburg, Va., when Monroe himself made one of the party.
Jefferson, writing to McKean, said that "Virginia was bristling up, he believed.
He should know the particulars from Governor Monroe."

[2] Beveridge's Marshall, Vol. III, pp. 78, 79.

[3] Grandfather of Senator Thomas F. Bayard and father of Senator James A.
Bayard. William Plumer (Plumer Mss., Library of Congress) wrote of J. A.
Bayard, Sr., that he was "a lawyer of high repute"; "a man of integrity and
honor"; "very attentive to dress and person," "who drinks more than a bottle of
wine each day" and "lives too fast to live long."

not disturb the main institutions of the government if elected (bank, tariff, army and navy)."[1]

But on the surface, the accommodation remained a mystery. What happened was: On the thirty-sixth ballot, Maryland was still divided. Bayard voted blank. Lewis Morris, Federalist, having absented himself, Matthew Lyon, an ardent Republican, cast the vote of Vermont for Jefferson. Thus the ninth State was in line, and Jefferson was President.

Jefferson, be it said, felt his responsibilities. The country was growing; it already had in it more than 5,000,000 people; its centre of population was within a morning's ride of the White House. It was a new century, with the new government in new hands; but it was not likely that there would be any violent new departures. So much depends on the point of view. When the "outs" are in, they look about them, cease to advocate extreme measures, weigh their words and measure their acts, realize the magnitude of difficulties hitherto unduly considered and proceed to adapt themselves to the practical situation.[2] Hamilton had foretold that Jefferson would pursue "a temporizing, rather than a violent system"; and that is precisely what he did. In fact, he kept on doing some of the very things he had objected to under Washington and Adams. In this he was wise. He was surprisingly wise in his leniency toward office-holding Federalists. Of three hundred and eighty-five men whom Jefferson might

---

[1] Life of Jefferson, p. 612. For letters and documents on this matter, see Randall's Jefferson, Vol. II, pp. 571-623. The depositions of Bayard and Smith in 1806 also appear in Randall.

[2] The Jeffersonian System (Vol. 12, American Nation Series), by Edward Channing, p. 15. "The third volume of the Writings of James Monroe" (pp. 300, 301), says Channing, "contains twenty-two letters from that personage to the new President. Fourteen of these have something to do with appointments. For instance, among the applicants to be indorsed by Monroe was Mr. Arthur Lee, of Norfolk. On September 25, 1801, Monroe wrote to Jefferson that Lee was a young man of merit, but three days later it occurred to him that he had been too complacent, and that Mr. Lee's object in going to Washington was to seek an office. Thereupon, he sat down and wrote to Jefferson that he did not know what Mr. Lee's object might be but that he was not well acquainted with that gentleman. . . . . If his object is the attainment of an office, the President should have much better information than his present correspondent could give. That letter settled the case of Mr. Arthur Lee of Norfolk." Monroe was conscientious, evidently

have removed, one hundred and eighty-three still held their jobs at the end of his first term.

Monroe, long with the "outs," was now so fortunate as to be with the "ins" all the rest of his life. He was past forty-one when, by this epochal turn, democracy came into its own. Jefferson was fifty-eight—"a loose-jointed man," in manner "shy and stiff," accustomed to sit "cornerwise on his chair, with one shoulder elevated above the other."[1]   He took the oath of office March 4, 1801. In the act of so doing, as it happened, he stood between two of his antipathies— Burr, Vice-President, who was to put an end to himself politically when he slew Hamilton; and Marshall, lately appointed Chief Justice, who by his Supreme Court decisions would make the country less and less a congeries of States and more and more a centralized nation. Like Hamilton, he was a great consolidator. Indeed, when years after,[2] Jefferson wrote to Spencer Roane, whom he wished to make Chief Justice: "The revolution of 1800 was as real a revolution in the principles of our government as that of 1776 was in the form," he could hardly have had Marshall in mind. John Adams declared that this country was "an empire of laws not men"; and many tried to make it so. Democratic as Marshall was personally — careless and lounging, like Jefferson — his mind was conservative. He was essentially un-Jeffersonian in mental method. He never mixed his metaphors. He never dreamt dreams. The principles of Federalism survived through him. Federalism had received a body blow; its soul lived because Marshall read it into constitutional law. Once a dear friend of Monroe, much controversy and much politics made Marshall draw away from him. Mason, Henry and Monroe had called for checks and balances to protect the people; Marshall devised checks and balances of another sort. John Adams thought Marshall a sounder Virginian than any of

[1] The Jeffersonian System.
[2] September 6, 1819. Works of Thomas Jefferson. Vol. VII, p. 133.

them and abler than all of them put together. It was unfair on the part of Adams to embarrass the incoming administration with partisan enactments embodying ultra-Federalistic ideas on the judiciary. Jefferson wrote to John Dickinson, December 19, 1801: "The Federalists have retired into the judiciary as a stronghold . . . and from that battery all the works of republicanism are to be beaten down and erased." But the Federalists were desperate. Were they perversely or patriotically desperate? Adams was both perverse and patriotic. He thought he was doing America a great service in putting up fortifications manned with Judges to save the country from the "excessive" democracy of the Jeffersons, Madisons, Monroes and John Randolphs. James Bradley Thayer[1] insists that "Jefferson had ludicrous misconceptions as to Marshall's real character." He spoke of the Judge's mind as "being of that gloomy malignity which will never let him forego the opportunity of satiating it upon a victim."

A close reasoner was Marshall. Intellectually, he hewed to the line. As an interpreter of the Constitution, his opinions were of weight and consequence, and grew more and more valuable when put together in a coherent and comprehensive doctrine. It was a strong union that he stood for and argued in behalf of. What his opponents objected to was that, in logical pursuit of his subject, he went beyond the letter of the Constitution. His interpretation was of its intent and spirit. Being a master-logician, as well as a simple and sincere patriot, unafraid of Jefferson or anybody else, he impressed himself upon the attentive public as few other Americans have ever done.

Let us glance at some of the causes and consequences. Perhaps we may thus start right in seeking to understand the quarrel. Reaction against democracy, begun abroad, had also made some progress here. Ultra-republican editors, driven hither, wrote with such

[1] Thayer's Marshall, p. 52.

venom as to bring down on their heads alien and
sedition laws similar to laws lately passed in England.
These harsh and un-American, as well as un-republican
laws drove Jefferson and Madison back from their
advanced position of accepted nationalism. They took
a stand on modified States' rights. They did it reluct-
antly, not meaning to do other than bring the power
of the State legislatures to bear in defense of
democracy. Why did they not take their case to the
Courts? Because the Courts were Federalist. What
other defense had they? English reactionaries had
suspended habeas corpus; would the Federalists in
America do so too? In their appeal to States' rights,[1]
they meant to defend the rights of man; not to establish
a nullification doctrine. But the large result, unfore-
seen, was to afford the mid-century successor of the
Republican party a constitutional doctrine upon which
to defend the secession of the slave States. Madison
lived to see this, and the old man repudiated it as best
he could. Monroe was spared the experience. Such, in
outline, was the sequence of events in the great quarrel.

What John Adams did was to impose his will on the
nation after he had been voted out. That Marshall
condoned it excuses some of Jefferson's feeling against
that very great man. Marshall, too, imposed his will —
not upon one administration merely, but upon all succeeding administrations. When he held questionable
acts of Congress and the Executive alike subject to
review and reversal, he put a bridle upon each. In the
case of Marbury vs. Madison,[2] the Supreme Court

---

[1] "Neglected or rejected by the other States, they (the Virginia and Kentucky
Resolutions) were passed again by their legislatures in 1799, and were for a long
time the documentary basis of the Democratic party. The leading idea expressed
in both was that the Constitution was a 'compact' between the States, and that
the powers (the States) which had made the compact had reserved the power to
restrain the creature of the compact, the Federal Government, whenever it undertook to assume power not granted to it. Madison's idea seems to have been
that restraint was to be enforced by a second convention of the States."— The
United States by Alexander Johnson, pp. 131, 132.

[2] Two days before his term expired Adams appointed William Marbury and
forty-one others Justices of the Peace in the District of Columbia. The Senate
confirmed all. Jefferson thought that there were too many of these Justices and
directed Madison to withhold seventeen commissions. Marbury's happened to

decided that an act of Congress was invalid. In the Burr case, Marshall sent a subpoena for Jefferson to appear before him. In other cases, one sees the rise of a new Federalism, or nationalism, which strengthened the central power, but gave cloak and cover to monopolies as well as to cankering officialism.[1]

Of course much was said in Congress against Marshall's decisions and the consolidating tendencies of the Federalist Judiciary. Breckenridge's speech was one of the notable utterances on the protesting side. In his "Life of Marshall" (Vol. III, p. 59) Beveridge says:

"James Monroe, then in Richmond, hastened to inform Breckenridge that 'your argument is highly approved here.' But, anxiously inquired that foggy Republican, 'do you mean to admit that the legislature (Congress) has not a right to repeal the law organizing the Supreme Court for the express purpose of dismissing the Judges when they cease to possess the public confidence?' If so, 'the people have no check whatever on them . . . but impeachment.' Monroe hoped that 'the period is not distant' when any opposition to 'the sovereignty of the people' by the Courts, such as the application of the principles of the English common law to our Constitution, would be 'considered good cause for impeachment.'[2] Thus early was expressed the Republican plan to impeach and remove Marshall and the entire Federal membership of the Supreme Court so soon to be attempted."

Thus we find ourselves apparently, though not

---

be one of the seventeen. Marbury and three others applied to the Supreme Court for a writ of mandamus, compelling Madison to issue the commissions. Meantime a great debate took place in Congress on a motion of Senator John Breckenridge, of Kentucky, to repeal the Federalist National Judiciary Act of 1801. For a good report of this significant debate see Beveridge's Marshall, Vol. III, pp. 1–222, under the chapter heads: "Democracy, Judiciary," "The Assault on the Judiciary," "Marbury versus Madison" and "Impeachment." The repeal bill passed at midnight, March 3, 1802, by a vote of fifty-nine Republicans to thirty-two Federalists. April 23 a bill suspending the June session of the Supreme Court was passed. The Republicans seemed to have the upper hand. Judge John Pickering of the New Hampshire District was impeached. High crimes and misdemeanors were charged against Judge Samuel Chase. But Marshall and his associates, Chase, Paterson, Cushing, Moore, and Bushrod Washington countered in a decision declaring the act of Congress in the Marbury matter invalid.

[1] Among such cases may be cited Fletcher *vs*. Peck; Dartmouth College *vs*. Woodward and the State of New Jersey *vs*. Wilson.

[2] Monroe to Breckenridge, January 15, 1802.   Breckenridge Mss., Lib. Congress as quoted by Beveridge.

actually, at the end of a friendship that had lasted
since Marshall and Monroe had gone to school together
to Parson Campbell of Campbellton back in the days
when the birds sang of other things than politics.[1]

Party feeling spent itself during the debate over
the Judiciary Act. This was in the winter of 1802,
Madison was Secretary of State and Gallatin Secretary
of the Treasury. Not infrequently now the Republicans
found themselves on old Federalist ground. But the
most complete reversal was soon to come. Jefferson,
indeed, was about to step deliberately out of the constitutional bounds, while Madison and Monroe were
to follow him with as little apparent compunction as
though they actually had turned Federalists. If the
gods aloft mocked them, those satirical ones must also
have laughed at the Federalists for revamping Republican arguments they had once despised. The grand
matter that made them all swing about and go contrari-
wise in spite of themselves was the Louisiana purchase,
involving empire on the Gulf of Mexico and in that
vast region stretching westward from the Appalachies.
States' rights? — Oh, yes; but how as to the nation's
future? Should the republic be cooped up between the
Atlantic and the Alleghenies, making it a mere seaboard
region — a long corridor? Should it be delimited on
the west by the Mississippi River, or should it expand
with an expansiveness as wide as the continent itself?
With Spain to the south, France to the west and
England to the north, we should be as in a vise; with
no chance to grow, and constantly menaced by alien
powers. Monroe and Patrick Henry had been disturbed by some such thought back in the days of Don
Diego de Gardoqui; here now, twenty-one years later,
Jefferson called upon Monroe, in a newly arisen emergency rendered all the more acute by the extreme

---

[1] Years after Monroe sent enclosures to Marshall bearing upon the imminent war
with Great Britain. Marshall replied enigmatically and without a sign of friendliness. Monroe apparently wished to sound Marshall on the war, and maybe also
to renew the cordial relations of their youth. Beveridge prints Marshall's matter-
of-fact letter in Vol. IV, p. 41. In their latter days they were friends again.

restlessness of the multitudes of people who had gone
west. We have here in fact a tremendous new drama
interesting alike to the trans-Allegheny settlers, the
people along the Gulf, the King's ministers in London,
the Court Circle of Don Carlos at Madrid and to that
manipulator of empires, the First Citizen of France.
In the *dramatis personae* are kings, queens, princes,
ministers and statesmen of high and low degree,
plotters and counterplotters, a host of participants
of many races and many tongues. The stake was a
region out of which we have formed twelve of our
fairest States under the free sky of the West.

John Randolph of Roanoke was not the only truth-
teller with respect to the defensive preparations in
Virginia during the threatening period of '98 and '99.
Howison[1] says that the cloud of mystery thrown around
the matter "is not dispelled by contemporary records."
January 23, 1798, the Legislature passed an act providing for two new arsenals and an armory at Richmond
big enough to hold ten thousand stand of muskets.
Equipment was made ready for a considerable cavalry
force. Cannon were mounted. The idea was that if
things should continue to go from bad to worse Virginia
ought to be prepared. But there was a vigorous party
that defended the "Laws" as against the "Resolutions." Marshall's brother-in-law, George Keith Taylor
of King George, General Henry Lee, and Patrick
Henry belonged to it. Henry, then about to die, again
thrilled the people with his grand plea for peace and
union. Another episode of the period was Callender's
trial for sedition, with the uncompromising Federalist,
Luther Martin, on the bench. At this time William
Wirt, George Hay (afterwards Monroe's son-in-law)
and William B. Giles, all destined to be of prominence,
came to the front.

More exciting even than these political episodes was

---

[1] History of Virginia, by Robert R. Howison, 2 vols., Vol. II, p. 347, *et seq.*
He quotes Statutes-at-large (new series) II, 87, 88 and Ms. Journal of the House
of Delegates for 1799.

the Gabriel slave rising which caused as great a stir in the fall of 1800 as did the Nat Turner rising in the summer of 1831. Gabriel, twenty-four years old, tall, strong, long-faced, with scars, a gloomy and frowning fellow, was a slave on the plantation of Thomas Prosser near Richmond. Another negro giant, six feet five, who wore his hair in a queue, was Jack or "Jack Bowler." These two organized a plot, involving a thousand slaves, who were to attack Richmond at night, seize the arms at the armory, kill all the men, and divide the women among them. Howison tells of the sequel: On the evening of the day near the close of August, a number of the conspirators had assembled in the country, several miles from Richmond, where they prepared for an attack during the night. A tremendous summer storm came on, attended by torrents of rain, and while it was yet raging, a slave named Pharaoh, the property of William Mosby, escaped without being observed by his fellows and hastened to Richmond. He swam an intervening creek which was then rising, arrived safely in the city, and communicated his information, which was regarded as so important that it was carried immediately to Governor Monroe. Forthwith the alarm was given, the drums beat, volunteer companies were called out, the militia were under arms and all things were made ready to give the assailants a proper reception.[1] Meantime the storm continued. Prosser, warned by a servant, escaped from his dwelling, by leaping through a window. Looking back he saw lightning flashes on the blades of innumerable scythes borne by the black insurgents. But these could make little headway in the storm. Some were drowned in the swollen streams and the rest dispersed. Of the ringleaders many were tried before the Justices of Henrico County, sitting in Oyer

---

[1] Howison's authority was Obadiah Gathright, who lived in Richmond at the time. The *Richmond Examiner*, September 30, 1800, contains Governor Monroe's Proclamation of September 17.

and Terminer, and hanged. Gabriel and Jack hid for weeks, but were seized finally and were hanged.

Louisiana [1] was not then a small area as now, but a wide region of wilderness, plain and mountain, home of numberless natives and grazing ground for herds of wild horses, deer and buffaloes. It stretched from the mouth of the Mississippi to its far-away fountain-heads. All the Missouri Country belonged to it, even to the bounds of Oregon.

Four capitals figured in the drama of retrocession of Louisiana to France,[2] and its speedy transfer to the United States — Washington, New Orleans, Madrid and Paris. Each had a group of characters. Those at Washington we know. Let us note some of those at New Orleans.

The Spanish Governor of Louisiana was Juan Manuel de Salcedo, who had succeeded the Marques de Casa Calvo (1799-1801); successor of General Gayoso de Lemos (1797-1799); successor of the active and astute Baron de Carondelet (1792-1797); himself the successor of that much-talked-of Don Estevan Miro (1785-1792). Miro it was who plotted with Wilkinson to break the American Union west of the Alleghenies. Miro sailed for Spain, and there won fame as a brilliant *Marescal de Campo.* Carondelet continued Miro's tactics of corrupting Kentuckians. He offered a bribe of $100,000 to Judge Benjamin Sebastian, District Attorney Harry Innes, Attorney General George Nicholas and others, to subvert American interests in Kentucky and bring about disunion. This, be pleased to note, was some time before Burr's more notorious Blennerhasset adventure

---

[1] Discovered by De Soto, 1539; explored by Marquette and Joliet, 1673; taken possession of by La Salle, 1682, and named by him in honor of Louis XIV; it was first settled by the brothers Iberville and Bienville, 1699. The grant to John Law of "Mississippi Bubble" fame was in 1718. New Orleans was founded in 1722. Louis XV grumbled at the great expense of the colony; and, February, 1763, ceded it to Spain.

[2] There is no lack of data on this theme. The sources in the Library of Congress and Bureau of Rolls and Library, Department of State, Washington, are the papers of Jefferson, Madison and Monroe; the Henry Adams Transcripts of English and French State papers from the Spanish Archives, and the Claiborne papers, Vols. I and II, collected by Governor William C. C. Claiborne

in treason. It was Carondelet who sent $9000, hidden in sugar barrels, which Philip Nolan delivered to Wilkinson.[1] Carondelet, with characteristic finesse, was frank on the surface and smooth below it. During his incumbency, Pinckney and Godoy signed, October 20, 1795, a treaty between Spain and the United States, opening the Mississippi River to the Americans, giving them a three-year right to New Orleans as a place of deposit, conceding the Natchez district and establishing the Spanish-American line at the thirty-first parallel. As for Salcedo, he was "an impotent old man in his dotage";[2] the "soul of the government" was Don Andres Lopez de Armesto, secretary, who, with "a great fund of cunning towards his superiors and much arrogance outside," had known "all the intrigues of the colony for twenty years." So much for the Louisiana Dons. They married Creole wives; they raised sugar and indigo, and got along well with the honest Governor of the Mississippi Territory, William C. C. Claiborne, until the intendant, Juan Buenaventura Morales, precipitated sudden trouble.

As we have noted, it was Pinckney in Madrid who secured the Spanish-American arrangement known as the Treaty of San Lorenzo el Real, and the man with whom he dealt was Manuel de Godoy (1767-1851), Duke of Alcudia, Prime Minister of Spain. Don Carlos IV was King — "a Bourbon," says Henry Adams,[3] "but an ally of the French Republic and, since the

---

[1] See the Spanish Conspiracy, by Thomas Marshall Green; Humphrey Marshall's Outline History; Gayarre's Spanish Domination; and, for Philip Nolan, Edward Everett Hale's Reminiscences.

[2] Laussat, the French prefect, to Duc Denis Decres, July 18, 1803. Pierre Clement Laussat was a man of character and consequence. His letters to Decres are clean-cut and of illuminating quality.

[3] History of the United States by Henry Adams, Vol. I, Chapter XIII, "The Spanish Court"; XIV, "The Retrocession"; XV, "Toussaint Louverture" XVI,; "Closure of the Mississippi"; XVII, "Monroe's Mission." A documentary work of great value in this connection is James Alexander Robertson's Louisiana Under the Rule of Spain, France and the United States, 1785-1807. Adams, in his nine-volume History, covers the period from the point of view of the States; Robertson's two volumes supplement Adams, covering the period from the New Orleans side. Robertson gives a great deal of essential matter and presents a translation of Dr. Paul Elliot's Reflexions.

eighteenth Brumaire, a devoted admirer of the young
Corsican who had betrayed the republic." He was a
truly devout man and an excellent gunsmith, unmindful
of smutty hands. Adams says he dined alone, ate
enormously, drank only water, "and in his whole life
never so much looked at any woman but his wife."
She, for her part, was quite the opposite. This incon-
tinent queen was Dona Maria Luisa de Parma. One of
her favorites had been the same Godoy who gave us the
good treaty. He had brought about another treaty;
that between France and Spain in 1795 and so was
called "the Prince of Peace." Rich and profligate
though he was, Godoy has been pronounced "quite the
equal of Pitt, or Talleyrand, in diplomacy; and their
superior in resource." [1]

But Godoy certainly had a long way to go when he
sought to circumvent Charles Maurice de Talleyrand-
Perigord, Prince of Benevento (1754-1838). He was
lame from boyhood.[2] When known as Abbé Perigord,
he was a Bourbon favorite; when Bishop of Antun, he
was a revolutionist, cynical enough to wink at La
Fayette on the joyous day of the Feast of the Federation. An emigré perforce, he nevertheless played the
part of foreign minister — and a corrupt one, too —
under the Directory; served Napoleon in the same
office; made himself useful to Napoleon's Bourbon
successors; and, finally, lent his wisdom and cunning to
Louis Phillippe. What a record in revolution and
counter-revolution! All his life, however far he fell, he
got up unbruised to become a somebody in state
affairs.

To Mirabeau he was "this vile, base trickster"; but
forty years after Mirabeau's death he was still a

---

[1] H. Adams' History, Vol. I, p. 348. *Mémoires du Prince de la Paix*, III, 36-
38. For Godoy's relations with Queen Luisa, see the Spanish Journal of Lady
Holland, edited by the Earl of Ilchester, 1910.

[2] He fell from the top of a cupboard and hurt his foot. This made him unfit
for military service. His father and grandfather had been generals in the King's
armies. His wife, a native of Pondichery, who had been Catharine Noel Worlee,
later Mme. Grant, spoke of him as "*L'Abbé Piebot*"— clubfoot.

power.[1] "The first man of his period" — "for half a
century the first man in Europe" — Talleyrand "served
in all eight known masters, not to reckon a great number of others who were, at one time or another said to
have him secretly in their pay." Napoleon said he was
"a stocking filled with filth." Carnot declared: "He
has all the vices of the old regime and none of the
virtues of the new" — "he has no fixed principles, he
changes them as he does his linen." Gouverneur Morris
said: "This man appears to me polished, cold, tricky,
ambitious and bad." Nevertheless most of his biographers agree with Whitelaw Reid: "The evil that Talleyrand did was chiefly to individuals. The good he did was
to France." In a codicil to his will, Talleyrand made
the claim that he had been true to France, and therefore true to Europe.

Was it by luck or design that Talleyrand spent the
bloodiest days of the Terror in England? He had to get
out of that country because of the alien law of 1794;
so he sold his library to obtain funds, and came to the
United States. He was here for thirty months, and they
must have been long ones to him, as he had no particular love either for our Constitution or cuisine. He
said: "I found thirty-two different religions in the
United States, but only one dish." If, perchance, he
encountered our General James Wilkinson he looked
upon a man of his own precious kind and kidney.
Jefferson was slow to wrath against the Wilkinsons of
that period of plots, chicane, and venality. He saw fit
to look upon Wilkinson with politic indulgence, just
as he did upon Burr. Only when Burr came out from
cover was he made to feel the pinch of the law. Which
was the more like Talleyrand — Burr, or Wilkinson?
Or is it incongruous to bring up either in the same
breath with the incomparably cunning diplomat whom
only Napoleon could master and Godoy outwit? Burr
was great as a politician. Wilkinson was not great at

---

[1] Memoirs of Prince de [Talleyrand, by the Duc de Broglie, introduction by
Whitelaw Reid.

all; yet he, too, had that cat-like quality of always landing on his feet. Associate of Arnold, hand-in-glove with the plotters of the Conway Cabal, in the pay of Don Carlos — this Talleyrand of the wilderness finally bluffed Burr at the critical moment of their conspiracy and lived to cover himself with other clouds in the War of 1812. Talleyrand missed much if he failed to look into the Spanish conspiracy during his American visit. Probably he made a close study of the whole Louisiana situation; for upon his return to France,[1] after the axe had ceased to drip, and upon his restoration to power as foreign minister of the Directory (July, 1797), he proceeded to carry out his scheme to re-acquire the region south of Natchez and west of the Mississippi.[2] This scheme was as simple as it was big. He sent Citizen Guillemardet as Minister to Madrid, May, 1798, with instructions to procure the retrocession of Louisiana and Florida to France.[3] As *quid pro quo*, Don Carlos was to have three districts lately taken by French troops from the Papal State, so that he might unite them to the Duchy of Parma, of which his son-in-law would be Duke. Thus did Talleyrand sugar the pill that Citizen Guillemardet was to give the Spanish King. But Carlos demurred. He had a conscience. His religion was real. He was a devotee. He was averse

---

[1] Talleyrand reached Paris on his return in September, 1796. November 28 he succeeded Charles Delacroix at the Foreign Office. There are many lives of Talleyrand, including the two-volume Life by Lady Blennerhassett (Grafin Leyden) translated from the German by Frederick Clarke.

[2] It was while Talleyrand served the Directory that the X Y Z incident occurred. Talleyrand's agents, Hottinguer, Bellamy and Hauteval, tried to exact a doceur of 1,200,000 livres ($250,000) from the American envoys. Sainte Beuve in his Talleyrand makes much of his venality. Whitelaw Reid says, in his introduction to the Duc de Broglie's book: "When the American Commissioners resented Talleyrand's demand for a bribe of $250,000 for himself and a bigger one called a loan, for the Directory, (32,000,000 Dutch florins) his representatives said naively: 'Don't you know that everything is bought in Paris? Do you dream that you can get on with this government without paying your way?'" A detailed statement of bribes received by Talleyrand appeared in Louis Bastide's "Life of Talleyrand," 1838. Talleyrand made no denial with respect to these specific charges. When Napoleon asked him how he had become so rich Talleyrand replied: "Nothing could be more simple, General; I bought Rentes the day before the eighteenth Brumaire and I sold them the day after."

[3] Instructions to Guillemardet, May 20-June 19, 1798, in the French Foreign Archives.

to annexing papal land. Events, too, balked Talleyrand, who ceased to be foreign minister, July 20, 1799.
Napoleon, at an impasse in Egypt, ran the British
blockade, landed at Frejus, October 9; and, one month
later executed his *coup d'état* known as that of the
Eighteenth Brumaire.

Though Napoleon had said "pitch the lawyers into
the river," he had no such thought as that with respect
to Talleyrand, whom he soon reintroduced into the
foreign office. They had this thought in common: the
restoration of the colonial power and glory of France.
Hence in July, 1800, Napoleon instructed Talleyrand
to send Citizen Alquier to Madrid. Alquier was to
regain Louisiana. In August he was displaced by
General Louis Alexander Berthier, who was to ask not
only for Louisiana but for the two Floridas and six
sloops of war. Berthier was Napoleon's "right-hand
man in matters of secrecy and importance." September 30, Berthier and Godoy at San Ildefonso signed a
secret treaty providing for the Louisiana retrocession.
Next day was signed the Treaty of Morfontaine whereby
friendly relations were re-established between France
and the United States. But, as Henry Adams points
out, the retrocession treaty spoiled the treaty of friendship. However, one was secret, the other open. There
was another open treaty — that of Amiens, March,
1801, between Great Britain and France. It was a two-
year truce; and gave Napoleon time to work out his
project for the reconquest of St. Domingo and the
restoration of French colonial power at New Orleans.
Had Leclerc, husband of Napoleon's beautiful sister
Pauline, succeeded in establishing a great French base
on the Island of St. Domingo it is likely that the other
part of the project might have been carried out. But
there were obstacles in the way. There was a black
Napoleon across the white Napoleon's path. Toussaint
L'Ouverture, imbued with ideas of the French Revolution, fought to the death, (or to the dungeon, which was
just as bad) rather than see slavery reinstituted on the

island; and, in so doing, he broke the military arm sent
to seize him. Fever swept the French soldiers into their
graves. Leclerc went speedily to his; and such terrible
things happened as must have made Napoleon shudder
to think of.

Nor did his negotiations with Godoy go through
quite as smoothly as Napoleon had anticipated. There
was an irritating hitch. By the treaty of Luneville,
February 9, 1801, the old Duke of Parma was dispossessed of his Duchy and the son-in-law of Don
Carlos was made ruler of Tuscany. Now Napoleon's
brother Lucien, who had gone to Madrid to arrange for
the erection of the kingdom of Tuscany and the American territorial transfer, permitted himself to be egre-
giously overreached. He was bribed with gold by the
bold Godoy; and in his brother's name, approved the
Treaty of Badajos, June 6, 1801, between Don Carlos
IV and Don Juan, Prince Regent of Portugal. This
was a spoke in Napoleon's wheel, balking as it did his
design in that direction. Coincidently there were other
happenings of a grave character, and Napoleon was
forcèd to acquiesce. Meantime Godoy continued to
thwart him. "I am long suffering," wrote Napoleon
to Talleyrand; Godoy's conduct was insolent — "ce
misérable," said he.[1] Godoy exacted from the new
French minister, General Gouvion St-Cyr, July, 1802,
"a formal written pledge in the name of the First Consul
that France would never alienate Louisiana." [2] Never
is a long while. Godoy also managed to resist Napoleon's demand for the Floridas, which, as the King
insisted, were not French at all. Talleyrand, let us
interject, wanted East Florida to remain Spanish as
a buffer against the United States. Napoleon sent out
Prefect Laussat, to take possession of Louisiana; but
it must have dawned upon the First Consul that he was
exhausting himself to no purpose. The gallant Leclerc

---

[1] Correspondance de Napoleon Premier, VII, 225-227.
[2] Adams, History of the United States, Vol. I, p. 400; St-Cyr to Don Pedro
Cevallos, July 12, 1802; Yrujo to Madison, September 4, 1803; State Papers, II, 569.

dead! An army of ten thousand veterans sacrificed as completely as though every ship in the fleet had sunk with the poor soldiers to the bottom of the sea! England again insolent! Yes — with Napoleon the very thought of Louisiana must now have caused a shrug or a shudder. But how if he should end that Amiens truce? — how if he should attack England? Why, then, he would need all the money he could raise in both hemispheres. He would sell Louisiana.

All this time Jefferson had been cultivating the friendship of both France and Spain. As early as May 26, 1801, he wrote to Monroe:[1] "There is considerable reason to apprehend that Spain cedes Louisiana and the Floridas to France. It is a policy very unwise in both, and very ominous to us." The cession of Louisiana and the Floridas by Spain to France "works most sorely on the United States," he wrote, April 18, 1802, to Minister R. R. Livingston in Paris. He continued:

"On this subject the Secretary of State has written to you fully; yet I cannot forbear recurring to it personally, so deep is the impression it makes on my mind. It completely reverses all the political relations of the United States, and will form a new epoch in our political course. . . . There is on the globe one single spot, the possessor of which is our natural and habitual enemy. It is New Orleans, through which the produce of three-eighths of our territory must pass to market, and from its fertility it will ere long yield more than half of our whole produce and contain more than half of our inhabitants. France, placing herself in that door, assumes to us the attitude of defiance. Spain might have retained it quietly for years. Her pacific disposition, her feeble state, would induce her to increase our facilities there, so that her possession of the place would hardly be felt by us, and it would not perhaps be very long before some circumstance might arise which might make the cession of it to us the price of something of more worth to her. Not so can it ever be in the hands of France. . . . The day that

---

[1] Writings of Jefferson, Ford, Vol. VIII, p. 58. He again referred to it May 29. November 24 he wrote a long letter to Monroe on the subject of a "receptacle" beyond the limits of the United States for deported blacks of dangerous character. November 14 he wrote introducing Eli Whitney, inventor of the cotton gin. Monroe's letters to Jefferson and others in regard to the "purchase of lands without the limits of the State to which persons obnoxious to the laws or dangerous to the peace of society might be removed" are in Vol. III of the Writings of Monroe. Much of the correspondence in Vol. III relates to Virginia affairs and is from the Letter-Book in the State Library at Richmond.

France takes possession of New Orleans fixes the sentence which is to retain her forever within the low-water mark. It seals the union of two nations who, in conjunction, can maintain exclusive possession of the ocean. From that moment we must marry ourselves to the British fleet and nation."[1]

This explicit letter was sent secretly by the hand of du Pont de Nemours, who was asked to see Napoleon and treat with him unofficially. He was to "impress on the First Consul the idea that if he should occupy Louisiana, the United States would wait 'a few years' until the next war between France and England, but would then make common cause with England."[2]

That spring and fall alarming news came from other directions. Madison had sent Tobias Lear to see what Leclerc was doing in St. Domingo. Lear had been given an uncivil congé and returned to Washington with reports indicative that Napoleon meant mischief. Americans were no better than Arabs, Leclerc had said; they were the scum of the nations. Louis André Pichon, the French chargé at Washington endeavored to mollify Madison, but Talleyrand sent Pichon a rebuke. Then on top of the French trouble came that other of which we have hinted — the trouble at New Orleans, precipitated by Intendant Morales, "a man of low extraction . . . evil by nature,"[3] who, October 16, 1802, issued a decree that New Orleans should no longer be a place of deposit for Americans. This fired the West. To Jefferson it seemed like a peal of thunder, betokening a tempest. The Spanish Minister at Washington hastened to repudiate the intendant's act. This was Don Carlos Martinez d' Yrujo (Spanish, Marques de Casa Irujo) who had married a daughter of Jefferson's friend and follower, Governor Thomas McKean of Pennsylvania. Yrujo wrote much; and with a peppery vigor unusual among diplomats. "Half Don and half Sans Culotte," Cobbett called him. He was bitter against

---

[1] Writings of Jefferson, Ford, Vol. VIII, pp. 143-147.
[2] H. Adams, History, Vol. I, p. 411.
[3] *Voyage dans les deux Louisianes* (Travels Through the Two Louisianas) by F. M. Perin du Lac.

Napoleon and fought the retrocession of Louisiana.[1]
Such were some of the excitements of a long period of
anxiety. Historian Adams, always severe upon Jefferson, lays stress upon Jefferson's inconsistencies.

" 'Peace is our passion!' This phrase of President Jefferson[2] . . .
expressed his true policy. In spite of his frequent menaces, he
told Livingston in October, 1802, that the French occupation of
Louisiana was not 'important enough to risk a breach of peace.' "

Jefferson was inconsistent in this particular, as in
many other matters involving the safety of the young
republic; but he was doing the best he could. Edward
Thornton, in charge of the English legation, wrote to
Lord Robert Hawkesbury (Earl of Liverpool) who had
signed the peace with France, that the storm had dispersed for a short time only. Jefferson was well aware
of this. It took a long while to communicate with
Livingston. With an extraordinary man, a restless
genius, experimenting as Napoleon was in the reconstruction of kingdoms, it was hard to tell one day what
would happen the next. We do not excuse Jefferson or
apologize for him — he needs neither excuse nor apology
— yet it is well to remind the reader of the immaturity
of the American republic in his day, of the difficulties
of communication then as compared with the facilities
of the present time, and of the exceptional nature of the
chief character on the world's stage following a revolution that shook mankind. Two political considerations
influenced Jefferson: He felt himself under the hostile
eye of the clerical conservatives of New England ("the
clergy had always hated Jefferson," says Adams); and
he felt himself under the scrutiny of certain common
people in all sections who knew that wars beget taxes.
Livingston wrote to Madison, January 13, 1802:

"There was never a government where less could be done by
negotiations than here. There are no people, no legislature, no

---

[1] Subsequently this proud Don quarreled with Madison and Jefferson. Long
in favor at the White House, he at last became *persona non grata.* He sought to
promote Burr's schemes in the Mississippi Valley.
[2] Jefferson to Sir John Sinclair, June 30, 1803, Writings IV, 490.

counsellors. One man is everything. . . . He seldom asks advice
and never hears it unasked. His ministers are mere clerks, and
his legislature and counsellors parade officers."

Jefferson had named Robert R. Livingston as Minister to France the day after his inauguration.[1] Aside
from Philip, the Signer, nearly a score of Livingstons
made their mark in early American history. They were
of romantic lineage, descendants of Robert, a fugitive
Scotch parson, who having sailed for the Western
world, found himself, by stress of furious storms, driven
back and doomed to die in Holland. But the hand of
heaven seemed in it; for his son Robert acquired the
Dutch tongue and Dutch culture; and, being a handsome youth, made his way among the Van Rensselaers
and Schuylers[2]. This Robert R. had a famous son,
Judge Robert R. — "a lover of liberty" — father of
Chancellor Robert R., "the rebel," graduate of King's
College (now Columbia University), law-partner of
John Jay, Chairman of the Committee to draft the
Declaration of Independence, Chairman of the New
York Constitutional Convention (1788), the man who
administered the oath at Washington's first inaugura-
tion, Robert Fulton's friend and patron, and now
Jefferson's minister to France. He was a very rich
man, a very generous man, fond of books, a good writer
and something of an orator. He was up and out every

---

[1] Edward, brother of the Livingston who "made the initial move in the purchase
of Louisiana," was the most noted Republican of the family. He was twenty years
younger than Robert. He was District Attorney and Mayor of New York. He
favored the Burr scheme, and defended its participants in the courts. He also
defended the LaFitts, identified with New Orleans. General H. B. Livingston was
another brother of Robert R. "The New York Republicans," says Henry Adams
in his History, Vol. I, p. 230, "were divided into three factions, represented by
Clinton, Livingston and Burr interests; and among them was so little difference in
principle or morals, that a politician as honest and an observer as keen as Albert
Gallatin inclined to Burr as the least selfish of the three." Gallatin to Jefferson,
September 14, 1801. Life of Gallatin by Henry Adams, p. 288.

[2] When Nicholas Van Rensselaer was on his deathbed he pointed to this immi-
grant Livingston, who had been brought into the room to draw up his will, and
cried out to his wife: "Take him away! Take him away. I know. That young man
shall not make my will; he will be your second husband." And he was; and became
first lord of Livingston Manor. He fitted out a ship for Captain Kidd before Kidd
turned pirate. It was his third son Robert who, when an Indian hid in a chimney,
seized the savage by the leg and pulled him down. The Indian confessed that a
massacre had been planned. It was prevented by this discovery.

morning at five. Tall and of gracious manners, he would have been a better figure in company but that he was hard of hearing. He was seven years older than Monroe.[1] Livingston and Jefferson were not quite in accord on the subject of retrocession. Livingston thought that "so long as France conforms to existing treaties" between the United States and Spain, we should not oppose the transfer of the Louisiana territory to her."

Thus it happened that Jefferson felt the need of some one in Paris other than Livingston. Besides, Jefferson could instruct this other diplomat by word of mouth instead of by labored correspondence, liable to misinterpretation. To him, Monroe was the man for the mission. He had just ended his term as Governor of Virginia. He "had many qualities," said Frederick Austin Ogg, "to recommend him for the task. He was genial, conscientious, patriotic and well-versed in the art of diplomacy. His former residence in Paris, while not wholly of glorious memory, had nevertheless prepared him in no small degree for the work now committed to him." [2] Moreover, he was as near to Jefferson personally and politically as any one, except Madison — obviously Monroe must be sent. So Jefferson wrote[3] to him about it and on January 10, 1803, nominated him Envoy Extraordinary to France. On the same day General Samuel Smith introduced a resolution in the House of Representatives, appropriating $2,000,-000 to defray any expenses which "may be incurred in relation to the United States and foreign nations."[4] On the eleventh, the House voted to apply the $2,000,000 to the purchase of West Florida and New Orleans.

On February third Jefferson wrote to Livingston "to

[1] Napoleon gave him a gold snuff-box, on which was his own portrait by Isabey. Stuart's portrait of Chancellor Livingston was used on the one-cent stamps commemorating the Louisiana Purchase.

[2] The opening of the Mississippi, by F. A. Ogg, 1904, p. 501.

[3] Jefferson to Monroe, January 10 and 13, 1803. Writings of Jefferson (Ford), Vol. VIII, p. 188.

[4] Annals of Congress (1802-1803), pp. 370-374.

work diligently for the cession of New Orleans by France to the United States." It was not Louisiana territory that was to be purchased, but "a barren sand six hundred miles from east to west, and from thirty to forty and fifty miles north to south, formed by the deposition of the sands by the Gulf Stream in its circular course round the Mexican Gulf."[1]

Monroe went from Richmond to Albemarle; and thence westward, in order to look after his interests in that quarter. He might be gone for years. He wrote from New York to Madison, February 22: "I arrived here on Saturday so much overcome with the fatigue of the journey that I kept my bed yesterday and was attended by a physician." He was still housed, but expected to be out in a few days. He had engaged passage on a ship for Havre, detained at his expense; but, as his final instructions were not at hand, he had to let her sail without him. March sixth he wrote to George Clinton:[2]

"I am now embarking on a new mission, which I neither sought or expected, but which I undertook with pleasure, as it is to act on an interest I have always had much at heart, on the principles of general right and policy. Of the result I can say nothing but I promise zeal in the undertaking and a certainty that if I do not improve the condition of our country I will not make it worse. It is uncertain how long I shall be absent, but the probability is, especially if I go to Spain, that I shall not be back till spring twelve month. I have the cabbin of a good ship, take my family with me, and expect to sail to-morrow morning."

Next day he received his instructions[3] and necessary

---

[1] Jefferson to du Pont de Nemours, February 1, 1803. Writings of Jefferson (Ford), Vol. VIII, p. 206.

[2] Clinton Papers, No. 7113; see also Writings of Monroe, Vol. IV, for this letter and others of the Louisiana Purchase Period; see Writings of Madison, edited by Gaillard Hunt, Vol. VIII, for Madison's letters to Monroe.

[3] Madison's instructions to Livingston and Monroe, March 2, 1803, American State Papers, Vol. II, p. 540; Annals of Congress (1802-1803) pp. 1095-1107. In his chapter on "Monroe's Mission" (Vol. I) Henry Adams tells of the activities of Thornton for Great Britain and Pichon for France. Pichon wrote to Talleyrand that Monroe had threatened to "receive the overtures which England was incessantly making." Monroe would hardly have done anything of the sort. Adams indicates the instructions. They were to bid rather than lose New Orleans and the Floridas. But if they should be unobtainable, take the right of deposit. Should that be denied "the commissioners were to be guided by instructions especially adapted to the case." "The essence and genius of Jefferson's statesmanship," comments Adams, "lay in peace."

documents, together with a letter from Jefferson;[1] but his ship, the Richmond, four hundred tons, was held in port by a snowstorm and head winds: finally she put to sea with bright skies and a good breeze on the morning of the ninth.

"Monroe," says Merwin, "had not a word in writing to show that in purchasing Louisiana — if the act should be repudiated by the nation — he did not exceed his instructions."[2] Monroe trusted Jefferson. "Jefferson's friends always trusted him perfectly," says Henry Adams.

While Monroe was crossing the Atlantic things were happening in Paris; and in London likewise. War was brewing. Napoleon had made up his mind to abandon Louisiana and attack England. It was no whim on his part. The St. Domingo disaster had grown into a horror — a colonial debacle, bringing down discredit upon his own head and upon Talleyrand's too. The Dominican war had devoured more men than the guillotine and here was Rochambeau (son of our York-town Rochambeau) asking for more — thirty-five thousand more.

On March 12, Talleyrand at Mme. Bonaparte's drawing-room heard Napoleon say to Lord Whitworth, the British Minister: "I find, Milord, that your nation wants war again." "No, Sir," replied his lordship, "we are desirous of peace." "I must either have Malta or war," said Napoleon.

Whitworth repeated the words to Livingston, who lost no time in forwarding them to Madison. Rufus King, the American Minister at London, also sent Madison a little story. Henry Addington (Lord Sidmouth), Lord of the Privy Seal, had said to him:

---

[1] In reply to Jefferson's letter, Monroe said: "The resolutions of Mr. [James] Ross prove that the Federal party will stick at nothing to embarrass the admn and recover its lost power. They nevertheless produce a great effect on the public mind and I presume more especially in the western country." Senator Ross wanted Jefferson to take New Orleans by armed force. Monroe added: "I accept my appointment with gratitude and enter on its duties with an ardent zeal to accomplish its objects."

[2] Thomas Jefferson, by Henry Childs Merwin, pp. 127, 128.

"If you can obtain Louisiana — well! If not we ought
to prevent its going into the hands of France."

Nevertheless no such news was coming from Livingston. He gave Jefferson little encouragement. "Do
not despair," was one of his messages. He knew Monroe
to be approaching the shores of France; and that
knowledge spurred him to fresh endeavor. Could he
settle the business before his colleague's ship should
come to anchor at Havre? That was very much in his
thought. It was natural that he should wish to do a
good piece of work; and, that, too, all by himself.[1]
Why share such an honor with an interloper? But
the greater Livingston's anxiety to consummate the
deal the less Talleyrand conceded. Adams says:
"Monroe arrived in sight of the French coast April
7, 1803; but while he was still on the ocean, Bonaparte
without reference to him or his mission, opened his
mind to Talleyrand in regard to ceding Louisiana to the
United States. The First Consul a few days afterward
repeated to his Finance Minister, Barbe Marbois, a part
of the conversation with Talleyrand. . . . 'He alone
knows my intentions,' said Bonaparte to Marbois. . . .
In reality the cession of Louisiana meant the overthrow of Talleyrand's influence."

Talleyrand had more than one motive in wishing to
mulct Livingston out of a large sum. As we have seen,
he himself was involved in the collapse of the grand
scheme of colonial reconstruction. His prestige was
suffering as well as Napoleon's; and so if he could go
to Napoleon and say: "Behold, General, we have not
done so badly after all!" the sore would be salved —
his own and his master's. Or, possibly, he meant to
pocket as much of the money as Livingston would let
him. . . . That motive is suggested by Edward

---

[1] Monroe wrote to Madison, April 13, 1803: "I was informed on my [arrival here
by Mr. Skipwith, that Mr. Livingston, mortified at my appointment, had done
everything in his power to turn the occurrences in America, and even my mission
to his account, by pressing the government on every point with a view to show that
he had accomplished what was wished without my aid." Monroe's Writings, Vol.
IV, p. 9.

Channing, in "The Jeffersonian System," when he says that Napoleon hesitated to trust Talleyrand with the money. Napoleon wanted to fill his war-chest. Albert Bushnell Hart says: "In reality, the province was thrown to the United States, as the Caliph Harun-al-Raschid might have given a palace to a poor merchant who had admired the portico." Rather was Napoleon a caliph, out of cash, in search of a pawnbroker. Nevertheless the act of cession stands out as something prodigal and Napoleonic. The ruler who could throw away the lives of a million men could find it in him to throw away a million, or very nearly a million square miles of the earth's surface. Perhaps Napoleon's geography was at fault, as Livingston's seems to have been. Monroe knew the great West better than either.[1]

Livingston did not grasp the full situation. Apparently he did not realize that Napoleon had been seized with deep disgust and that now, when his gorge had risen, was the time to take the whole of Louisiana off his hands. He hesitated, and so was lost; or rather he failed to advance the negotiations beyond the inconclusive preliminaries. Let us cite Adams, who says:[2]

"Easter Sunday, April 10, 1803, arrived, and Monroe was leaving Havre for Paris, when Bonaparte, after the religious ceremonies of the day at St. Cloud, called to him two of his ministers of whom Barbe Marbois was one. He wished to explain his intention of selling Louisiana to the United States; and he did so in his peculiar way. He began by expressing the fear that England would seize Louisiana as her first act of war. 'I think of ceding it to the United States. I can scarcely say that I cede it to them, for it is not yet in our possession. If, however I leave the least time to our enemies, I shall only transmit an empty

---

[1] Morris continued to write disapprovingly of Monroe. "It is possible I am unjust to Mr. Monroe," he wrote to R. R. Livingston, in Paris, "but I really consider him a person of mediocrity in every respect. Just exceptions lie against his diplomatic character, and, taking all circumstances into consideration, his appointment must appear extraordinary to the Cabinets of Europe. . . . The pretext that he is only joined with you in the commission is mere pretext, and every discreet man with you will naturally consider him as the principal and the chief, and, in fact, the sole minister."

[2] H. Adams, History of the United States, Vol. II, p. 26, et seq.

title to those republicans whose friendship I seek. They ask me only one town in Louisiana; but I already consider the colony as entirely lost; and it appears to me that in the hands of this growing power it will be more useful to the policy, and even to the commerce of France than if I should attempt to keep it.' "

Marbois agreed; the other minister demurred. Next morning at daybreak Napoleon summoned Marbois and said to him:

"Irresolution and deliberation are no longer in season. I renounce Louisiana. It is not only New Orleans that I cede; it is the whole colony, without reserve. I know the price of what I abandon. . . . I renounce it with the greatest regret; to attempt obstinately to retain it would be folly. I direct you to negotiate the affair. Have an interview this very day with Mr. Livingston."

But Talleyrand it was who saw Livingston first.[1] "He asked me," reported Livingston, "whether we wished to have the whole of Louisiana. I told him no." Livingston added that it would be better if France should give up the territory north of the Arkansas, so that she could have a barrier against Canada. Talleyrand wanted to know what America would give for the whole. Livingston named 20,000,000 francs as a possible sum. But Monroe, he said, would soon be in Paris. Talleyrand told him to think it over. "The next day, Tuesday, April 12," says Adams, "Livingston, partly recovered from his surprise, hung about Talleyrand persistently for his chance of reaping alone the fruit of his labors," vanishing with every minute that passed. "Monroe," continues Adams, "had reached St. Germain late Monday night, and at one o'clock Tuesday afternoon descended from his post-chaise at the door of his Paris hotel.[2] From the

---

[1] Livingston to Madison, April 11, 1803; State Papers, Vol. II, p. 552. It is said that when Bonaparte gave instructions to M. Marbois in regard to the cession, he stated that from the nature of the new combination forming against him in Europe, he was forced to sell the entire province or hold it at a great sacrifice of men and money, and probably be compelled to see it captured. He preferred to transfer it to the United States, adding that whatever nation held the valley of the Mississippi would be eventually the most powerful on earth, and that consequently he preferred a friendly nation should possess it rather than an enemy of France.— The Public Doma n, Thomas Donaldson, p. 95.

[2] Memoirs of James Monroe, 1828; Col. Mercer's Journal, p. 55. Henry Adams, History, Vol. II, p. 29.

moment of his arrival he was sure to seize public attention at home and abroad."

Monroe sent Livingston a note, and that evening
visited him. Next day they spent together. In the
afternoon they entertained a party at dinner in Livingston's apartments.[1] Adams continues:

"While sitting at table Livingston saw Barbe Marbois strolling
in the garden outside. Livingston sent to invite Marbois to join
the party at the table. While coffee was served, Marbois came in
and entered into conversation with Livingston, who began at
once to tell him of Talleyrand's 'extraordinary conduct.' "

Marbois here dropped a hint. If Livingston would
see him at his house, he would explain. Monroe left,
by and by; and soon Marbois was closeted with the
other at the Treasury Office. Livingston acted as
though he had reassured himself on essential points;
as if doubts were dissipated. But he had not lost his
desire to win a single-handed victory. Since Monroe
was already in confidential touch with him, his talk
with Marbois that night smacked of self a wee too much.
It was a bit disingenuous. After Monroe had disabused
him of all sorts of diplomatic dubieties; had reassured
him; had given him the cue, so to say, Livingston might
have acted more ingenuously, might have collaborated.
It was not Monroe's fault that he had been associated
with the resident minister; he had been sent across
the sea on a mission of the utmost gravity and he
should have been consulted at every step, including
that of the evening of the twelfth of April.

Monroe said that the account given by Marbois[2] in

---

[1] Livingston finally had a talk with Talleyrand that day — Tuesday — but to
no purpose. Talleyrand was evasive. He actually told Livingston, who had seen
it, that there was no treaty between France and Spain.

[2] Monroe had known the Marquis of Barbe Marbois personally a long while.
Marbois was *Chargé d'Affaires* at Philadelphia in the days of the Congress of the
Confederation. Gaillard Hunt says that Marbois was a fellow-lodger with Madison
when he had his love affair with Catherine Floyd. This was in Philadelphia in
1783. Catharine, a daughter of General James Floyd, a Signer of the Declaration
and a member of Congress from New York, was engaged to Madison, but jilted
him for a young parson who "hung around her at the harpsichord." She sealed her
letter, dismissing Madison, "with a piece of rye dough!" See Hunt's Madison, also
Gay's.

his book was correct in the main, though faulty in a few particulars. However, Marbois in his midnight talk with Livingston did not stick to facts. He was oblique. He gave an account of his Easter Sunday interview with Napoleon. As he put it, Napoleon had said to him: "Well! You have charge of the Treasury. Let them give you 100,000,000 francs and pay their own claims, and take the whole country." Bonaparte had said 50,000,000; but he wanted the Americans' claims to be paid in America. These claims amounted to about 20,000,000 francs. Livingston told Marbois that he did not want the region to the west of the Mississippi. Marbois came down to 60,000,000 francs, plus 20,000,000 for the claims. "I told him," said Livingston,[1] "that it was vain to ask anything that was so greatly beyond our means; that true policy would dictate to the First Consul not to press such a demand; that he must know it would render the present government unpopular. . . . I told him that I would consult Mr. Monroe but that neither he nor I could accede to his ideas on the subject." Near three that morning Livingston was writing to Madison that "without Monroe's help he had won Louisiana."

At the Tuileries this mid-April, there were some little scenes good enough to go into comedy. One especially: Lucien Bonaparte, who was ambitious, who took himself seriously, knew nothing of the project to sell Louisiana until bluntly told of it by his disgusted brother, Joseph. Joseph[2] had been employed by Napoleon in the preliminaries of the Louisiana sale and no doubt some of his chagrin arose from the subsequent use of shrewder agents. But Lucien was angry. He went to the Tuileries early in the morning; "by his brother's order he was admitted, and found Napoleon in his bath, the water of which was opaque

---

[1] Livingston to Madison, April 13 and 17, 1803; State Papers, Vol. II, pp. 552-554. H. Adams, History, United States, Vol. II, pp. 30-32.

[2] This extraordinary incident was reproduced by Henry Adams, in his History of the United States, from Theodore Jung's *Lucien Bonaparte et ses Mémoires* (Paris 1882), Vol. II, pp. 128-154.

with a mixture of *eau de cologne.*" So says Henry
Adams, who adds:

"They talked for some time on indifferent matters. Lucien
was timid and dared not speak until Joseph came. Then Napoleon
announced his decision to sell Louisiana, and invited Lucien to
say what he thought of it.

'I flatter myself,' replied Lucien, 'that the Chambers will not
give their consent.'

'You flatter yourself!' repeated Napoleon, in a tone of surprise;
then murmuring in a lower voice 'that is precious, in truth!'
(*'c'est precieux, en vérité.'*)

'And I too flatter myself, as I have already told the First Consul!'
cried Joseph.

'And what did I answer?' said Napoleon, warmly, glaring from
his bath at the two men.

'That you would do without the Chambers.'

'Precisely! That is what I have taken the great liberty to tell
Mr. Joseph, and what I now repeat to the Citizen Lucien. . . .'

At this, Joseph came close to the bath, and rejoined in a vehement tone: 'And you will do well, my dear brother, not to expose
your project to parliamentary discussion; for I declare to you that
if necessary I will put myself first at the head of the opposition
which will not fail to be made against you.'

The First Consul burst into a peal of forced laughter, while
Joseph, crimson with anger and almost stammering his words
went on: 'Laugh, laugh, laugh, then! I will act up to my promise;
and though I am not fond of mounting the tribune, this time
you will see me there!'

Napoleon, half rising from the bath, rejoined in a serious tone:
'You will have no need to lead the opposition, for I repeat there
will be no debate for the reason that the project which has not
the fortune to meet with your approval, conceived by me, negotiated by me, shall be ratified and executed by me, do you compre-
hend? — by me, who laugh at your opposition!'

Hereupon Joseph wholly lost his self-control, and with flashing
eyes shouted: 'Good! I tell you, General, that you, I and all of us,
if you do what you threaten may prepare ourselves soon to go and
join the poor innocent devils whom you so legally, humanely, and
especially with such justice, have transported to Sinnamary.'

At this terrible rejoinder, Napoleon half started up, crying
out: 'You are insolent! I ought —' then threw himself back in
the bath which sent a mass of perfumed water into Joseph's flushed
face, drenching him and Lucien, who had the wit to quote, in a
theatrical tone, the words which Virgil put into the mouth of
Neptune reproving the waves.

'*Quos ego.* . .'

Between the water and the wit the three Bonapartes recovered their temper, while the valet who was present, overcome by fear, fainted and fell to the floor.' "

The worst of the storm was now over, since Joseph had to change his clothes; but Lucien, who was in earnest brought on another wordy gust of anger. From jesting about what he called his "Louisianicide," Napoleon again fell upon Lucien. "You lay it on handsomely!" he cried. "Unconstitutional is droll from you. Come now let me alone! How have I hurt your Constitution? Answer!" Lucien attempted to do so. Napoleon interrupted him: "Go about your business! Constitution! Unconstitutional! republic! national sovereignty! — big words! great phrases! . . ." "If I were not your brother I would be your enemy." "My enemy! Ah! I would advise you! — My enemy! That is a trifle strong! . . . You my enemy! I would break you, look, like this box!" And he "flung his snuff-box violently on the floor."[1]

Thus whether splashing bath water with oceanic violence on one brother's clothes, or scattering snuff in a manner likely to make another brother sneeze, Napoleon was not to be browbeaten. He had plenty to think of. On April 17, he announced to the Pope that he was at war with England. Exciting events in Europe would put Louisiana out of the popular mind. Sooner or later, Frenchmen would bemoan the loss of Louisiana — how could they help it? but now they were too busy to weigh the matter. Napoleon, April 23, handed Marbois a project of a secret convention with the United States[2] "providing for the cession of Louisiana, in return for the granting of several cessions

---

[1] "In taking Louisiana," says Edward Channing, "we were the accomplices of the greatest highwayman of modern history." D. S. Muzzey sums up against Napoleon thus: (1) "Napoleon had not taken possession of Louisiana when he sold it to us. (2) He had never fulfilled his part of the bargain with Spain. (3) He had promised Spain never to transfer Louisiana to a foreign power. (4) He was forbidden by the French Constitution to alienate any territory of the French Republic."

[2] Correspondance de Napoleon Premier, Vol. VIII, p. 289; Gilman, p. 82; Adams, History, Vol. II, pp. 40, 41; The Opening of the Mississippi, F. A. Ogg. p. 529.

of the United States, including the free navigation of
the Mississippi, perpetual right of deposit at six points
on the river, the payment to France of 100,000,000
francs, and the liquidation of American claims unpro-
vided for by the Convention of 1800."

Marbois placed this *projét* before Monroe and Livingston on April 28. Monroe had been sick, so the meeting was held in his hotel. Even now he was unable
to exert himself. He was obliged to stretch himself
out at his ease on a sofa. The only known record of the
conference is to be found in Monroe's Memoranda.[1]
There was a long discussion. Livingston pressed the
claims. Monroe overruled him. Marbois substituted
his own *projét* for Napoleon's. By this the price was
to be 80,000,000 francs, including 20,000,000 to cover
claims. Marbois withdrew. Monroe and Livingston
then drew up a *contre-projét* offering a total of 70,000,-
000 francs; and this they submitted to Marbois. But
Marbois convinced them that his minimum was
80,000,000; and they agreed to give this sum —
$15,000,000.[2] Part of the money, $3,750,000, was to go
to the American creditors of France, and was to be paid
to them by the United States Government. On April 30,
Napoleon approved of the arrangement, although he
scolded Marbois in the matter of the claims. It was
"wasting money" to pay them. He wanted it for
gunpowder.

All this time Monroe had been awaiting his formal
presentation. Talleyrand is said to have delayed it
purposely; perhaps he thought that some sort of lightning might strike, out of the Napoleonic sky, and that
the sale of Louisiana might be abandoned overnight.
Monroe accompanied Livingston to the palace of the

---

[1] Journal, or Memoranda Louisiana, April 27, printed in full in the Writings of
Monroe, by S. M. Hamilton, Vol. IV, pp. 12-15; also Addenda to the Journal,
Appendix I, Vol. IV, pp. 499, 500.
[2] Or $15,000,000 in money and stocks; the interest on the stocks to time of
redemption, $8,529,353; claims of citizens of the United States due from France
paid by the United States, $3,738,268.98, a total of $27,267,621.98, and added to
the public domain 1,182,752 square miles or 756,961,280 acres.— The Public
Domain by Thomas Donaldson, 1884, p. 12.

Louvre, Sunday, May 1; and here is his account of his first meeting with Napoleon:

"When the Consul came around to me, Mr. Livingston presented me to him, on which the Consul observed that he was glad to see me. *'Je suis bien aise de le voir.'* 'You have been here fifteen days?' 'I told him I had.' 'You speak French?' I replied: 'A little.' 'You had a good voyage?' 'Yes.' 'You came in a frigate?' 'No, in a merchant vessel charged for the purpose.' Col. Mercer was presented. Says he: 'He is the Secretary of the Legation?' 'No, but my friend.' He then made enquiries of Mr. Livingston and his Secretary, how their families were, and then turned to Mr. Livingston and myself and observed that our affairs should be settled. We dined with him. After dinner when we retired into the saloon, the First Consul came up to me and asked whether the Federal City grew much. I told him it did. 'How many inhabitants has it?' 'It is just commencing; there are two cities near it, one above, the other below, on the great river Potomack, which two cities if counted with the Federal City would make a respectable town; in itself it contains only two or three thousand inhabitants.' 'Well, Mr. Jefferson; how old is he?' 'About sixty.' 'Is he married or single?' 'He is not married.' 'Then he is a garçon.' 'No, he is a widower.' 'Has he children?' 'Yes, two daughters, who are married.' 'Does he reside always at the Federal City?' 'Generally.' 'Are the public buildings there commodious, those for Congress and President especially?' 'They are.' 'You, the Americans, did brilliant things in your war with England; you will do the same again.' 'We shall, I am persuaded, always do well when it shall be our lot to be in war.' 'You may probably be in war with them again.' I replied I did not know; that was an important question to decide when there should be occasion for it."

That evening Monroe and Livingston and Marbois again met. Monroe says in his Memoranda:

"May 2nd. We actually signed the treaty and convention for the sixty millions of francs to France in the French language; but our copies in English not being made out we could not sign in our language. They were however prepared and signed in two or three days afterwards. The Convention respecting American claims took more time, and was not signed till about the 8th or 9th. All the documents were antedated to the thirtieth of April."[1]

---

[1] American State Papers, Foreign, Vol. II, pp. 507-509; select Documents by William MacDonald, pp. 160-165, contains treaty in full. Monroe's Journal of the Negotiations for the Purchase of Louisiana, April 27-May 2, 1803, published from the original Ms. in the Library of Congress, may be found in Monroe's Writings, Vol. IV, pp. 12-19; in Louisiana Purchase Papers, 1903, pp. 165-172; and in the Library of Congress, Notes for the Louisiana Purchase Exposition, St. Louis, Mo. 1904, No. 5, pp. 9-16.

Livingston wrote:

"We have lived long, but this is the noblest work of our whole lives. The treaty we have just signed had not been obtained by art or dictated by force; equally advantageous to the two contracting parties, it will change vast solitudes into flourishing districts. From this day the United States will take their place among the powers of the first rank; the English lose all the exclusive influence in the affairs of America."

Would Livingston have bought without Monroe? He had said that he had no such authority. Both ministers, for that matter "were embarrassed by the fact that the tender of the territory was beyond their instructions to buy or receive. Sometimes an army is unequal to a given task; it is re-enforced; thus strengthened it wins a victory. So it was when Monroe re-enforced Livingston.

In his "Century of American Diplomacy," John W. Foster, speaking of the Louisiana Purchase, said: "It made the acquisition of Florida a necessity. It brought about the annexation of Texas, the Mexican War, the thirst for more slave territory to preserve the balance of power, the Civil War, and the abolition of slavery. It led to our Pacific Coast possessions, the construction of the transcontinental lines of railway and our marvelous Rocky Mountain development, the demand for the Isthmus Canal, the purchase of Alaska, the annexation of Hawaii . . . . It fixed our destiny for world power."[1]

The purchase of Louisiana was not strictly constitutional — extra-constitutional, rather than unconstitutional as one of Jefferson's biographers, Merwin, reminds us. Jefferson thought the Constitution ought to be amended so as to constitutionalize it; but this was never done.

Jefferson wrote to Breckenridge, August 12, 1803:

"The Constitution made no provision for our holding foreign territory, still less for incorporating territory into our union. The Executive in seizing the fugitive occurrence which so much advances the good of their country, have done an act beyond the Constitution."

---

[1] Compare Gilman's thought in Monroe, p. 92.

Jefferson called Congress in extra session, October 17, 1803; on the nineteenth, the Senate ratified the treaty; on the twenty-first, ratifications were exchanged with Pichon, French *chargé d'affaires;* and, on the same day the President sent in a special message. John Randolph of Roanoke moved that provision be made for carrying out the treaty. This was passed, October 25. Various acts to this end were adopted by Congress. On November 30, at New Orleans, Prefect Laussat received the province from the Marques de Casa Calvo, Spanish commissioner; and twenty days later it was transferred to the American commissioners, William C. C. Claiborne and James Wilkinson. C. C. Robin[1] witnessed the transfer of Louisiana to the United States. He says:

"I saw the French flag slowly descending and that of the United States gradually rising at the same time. Soon a French officer took the first to wrap it up and bear it silently into the rear. The American flag remained stuck for a long time, in spite of the efforts to raise it, as if it were confused at taking the place of that to which it owed its glorious independence. An anxious silence reigned at that moment among all the spectators who flooded the plaza, who crowded against the galleries, balconies and windows; and it was not until the flag had been hoisted up that suddenly piercing cries of 'Huzza!' ¦burst from the midst of one particular group, who waved their hats at the same time. Those cries and that movement made more gloomy the silence and the quietness of the rest of the crowd of spectators scattered far and wide — they were French and Spanish and were all moved and confounded their sighs and tears."[2]

"The Anglo-Americans," wrote Laussat, "are extravagant in their joy. Most of the Spaniards . . . have the stupidity to show themselves satisfied. The French, that is to say, nine-tenths of the population, are stupefied and disconsolate . . . . The Louisianian . . . saw himself with regret rejected for the second time from the bosom of his ancient mother country." Claiborne was

---

[1] Voyages, Vol. II, pp. 128-141; as cited in Robertson's Louisiana, Vol. II, pp. 225, 226.

[2] Similar ceremonies for Upper Louisiana occurred at St. Louis, March 9 and 10, 1804. See "France in America" by R. G. Thwaites, 1905, Chapter XVIII. See Gayarre's "Louisiana under Spanish Domination." Also "Mississippi" by J. F. H. Claiborne, 1800.

invested with the powers "heretofore held by the governor-general and intendant of the province." He said to the Louisianians: "The American people receive you as brothers." March 26, 1804, Congress passed a territorial act; but there were complaints from the natives who had been brought up under different laws; and on January 28, 1805, Congress passed a second and better act. April 10, 1812, Louisiana was admitted as a State.[1]

---

[1] Albert Bushnell Hart, in his "Foundation of American Foreign Policy," reviews the various arguments, in Congress and out, on annexation and Statehood. Some thought it would be the ruin of America to take so much territory into the Union. Imperialism was feared. To the difficulties of immense distance and lack of cohesion was added the argument that the territory and its inhabitants were distinctly undesirable. The sectional argument was used. In fact, the wisdom of the purchase was questioned by all sorts of malcontents who succeeded in demonstrating their own lack of foresight, and the good statesmanship of Jefferson and Madison and Monroe. Hart adds: "This was not the first or last time that the United States sought a small territory and got a large one. Just as George Rogers Clark's capture of two frontier posts gave rise to the occupation of a vast territory between the Mississippi and the mountains, and just as the expedition to Cuba led to the annexation of the Philippine Islands, so Monroe and Livingston sought for 20,000 miles of barren sand and brought home 600,000 miles of empire."

CHAPTER XII

Monroe in England and Spain

"Since the conclusion of the business with France," Monroe wrote to Jefferson,[1] "I have doubted whether it would be best for me to remain here till I heard the result of the deliberations in the United States on what is already done, or proceed directly to Spain to treat for the Floridas; and after much reflection have decided in favor of the latter opinion. . . . I shall set out for Spain in a week or ten days, and hope to be back in three or four months at most. I leave my family at St. Germain in my absence, where my daughter is at school."

When the Monroes first went to Paris in 1794, their daughter Eliza, then seven, became a pupil of Madame Campan at St. Germain. Eliza, who was a well-grown girl[2] when her only sister, Maria, was born, now re-entered this celebrated school.

Madame Campan (born in Paris, October 6, 1752, died at Mantes, March 16, 1822) played a part in so many historic scenes that a veritable literature has grown up about her. One finds scores of books containing mémoires, anecdotes and gossipy references on the Campan shelf. She was Jeanne Louise Henriette Genest, or Genet, sister of Edmond Charles Genest, who under Louis XVI was *chargé d'affaires* at St. Petersburg, Girondin, minister to the United States and subsequently a citizen of New York. She married Pierre Bertholet, of the Valley of the Campan, near Tarbes, Bearn, a comely young soldier who served Marie Leckzinska, Queen of Louis XV, as page of the

---

[1] Paris, May 18, 1803, Writings of Monroe, Vol. IV, p. 28.

[2] The Children of James Monroe, by Harriet Taylor Upton, Widewake, July, 1888. Mrs. Upton thinks that Maria was born in Paris in 1803. If so, Eliza was sixteen years older. See also, Our Early Presidents, their Wives and Children, by Mrs. Upton, Boston, 1890.

backstairs. Madame Campan came to court after the Queen's death; won the liking of Marie Antoinette, and shared with her the sorrows, thrills and excruciating experiences of the French Revolution. As first lady of the bed-chamber, she knew intimately the gay life and final tragedies; so that her "Memoirs of the Court of Marie Antoinette" is read today. She escaped the guillotine, endured persecutions by the Directoire and in Napoleonic times found herself at the head of a boarding-school of sixty pupils. This was in the Hotel de Rohan, at St. Germain, "a huge place with a beautiful garden, situated in the rue de Poissy on the edge of the forest." It was called the Seminary of Montagne de Bon-Air. "Maman" Campan here became governess of the Bonapartes — Hortense and Emilie de Beauharnais and Pauline and Caroline Bonaparte.[1] We have many references to the Monroes in the volume entitled "The Celebrated Madame Campan" by Violette M. Montagu.

"Madam Campan used in her old age to tell an anecdote of how, while walking in the beautiful forest of Saint-Germain with Mr. Monroe and his little daughter Eliza in those days [in the time of the Directory] when France seemed drifting hither and thither at the mercy of any stray adventurer with a gift for despotism, the future President of the United States remarked: 'Fortune lies in the gutter; anybody who takes the trouble to bend down can pick it up!' He then went on to say what a much finer country America was than France, whereupon little Eliza burst in with: 'Yes, papa, but we haven't any roads like this'— pointing to the fine smooth road bordered with magnificent trees along which they were then walking.

---

[1] In December, 1801, General Claude Perrin Victor, Duke of Bellino (1764-1841), who was to have commanded for Napoleon at New Orleans, brought his little daughter Victorine to study with Mme. Campan. "Among her fellow pupils," says Violette M. Montagu in "The Celebrated Mme. Campan," "were Nelly Bourjol:e (later maid-of-honor to Stephanie de Beauharnais, when the latter became grand-duchess of Baden); Antoinette de Mackau (later Mme. Wathier de Saint-Alphonse); Eliza Monroe, the daughter of the originator of the celebrated Monroe doctrine, a great friend of Miss Paterson, Jerome Bonaparte's first wife, and one of Mme. Campan's most grateful pupils; Mlle. Hervas de Menara, the daughter of the rich banker of that name, and at that time 'the prettiest little creature which had ever been confided to my care; she is witty, sensible and good natured.' Mlle. de Menara married Duroc; ('Hortense's first love, and perhaps the only man for whom Hortense ever really cared')."

MADAME JEANNE LOUISE HENRIETTE GENEST CAMPAN

From a life-sized oil painting, executed on Napoleon's order, by Baron François Pascal Gérard and presented to the Monroe family, in whose possession it remained for more than a hundred years. Photographed from the original.

'That's true,' replied Mr. Monroe; 'our country may be likened to a new house, we lack many things, but we possess the most precious of all — liberty!' "

In the heyday of Napoleon's regime Madame Campan was appointed directress of the Imperial Educational Establishment of the Legion of Honor at Ecouen. "Be quicker to praise than to blame" was her Ecouen motto. She wrote *De l'Education.* Hortense de Beauharnais married Louis Bonaparte, and became the mother of Napoleon III. She was fond of her former school friends but "some of them expected her to do too much for them; great was Eliza Monroe's disappointment when she discovered that Hortense could not get her an invitation to the balls given by Caroline Murat at her chateau at Neuilly, because her sister-in-law was a great respecter of etiquette, and, as the sister of an Emperor, could not be expected to receive the daughter of an honest republican."[1]

Mrs. Monroe, who thoroughly appreciated the finer side of the social, artistic and literary life of Paris, making many life-long friends while there, accompanied her husband when he left for another capital. This other capital was not Madrid, as he had hoped, but London, where his living expenses were so great as to cause him to sigh for Virginia. He wrote that, whereas he could live well on $2000 a year in Virginia, it cost him £2000 in London. His salary was $9000 a year, leaving a deficit in his private purse of $1000. Even this he could ill afford to spare. Madison befriended Monroe in the matter of money accommodations, both at home and abroad.[2]

---

[1] In 1814 Mme. Campan fell under the ban of the Bourbons. "All her friends rallied around her; foremost among these were M. de Lally-Tollendal and Eliza Monroe's father, both of whom interceded for her with Louis XVIII." Later, in 1818, "Eliza Monroe, now happily married in America to a Mr. Hay and the mother of a little daughter baptized Hortense Eugenie after Eliza's two playmates at Saint-Germain, did not forget her old governess, and many were the letters which she wrote to Mantes, although she found that for some reason or other, they frequently miscarried or were intercepted."

[2] Madison Correspondence, Bureau of Rolls; see letters from Littleton W. Tazewell, Norfolk, on a loan obtained at the bank for Colonel Monroe, p. 669. Madison had lent money to Monroe in 1800; p. 535.

Before beginning his new mission, Monroe, though lacking in health, busied himself with many matters. He saw La Fayette and Kosciusko often. "They are the men you always knew them to be," he wrote to Jefferson. But one day he was shocked to learn that La Fayette, having dislocated his thigh, had suffered torture through over-pressure in a leg-and-hip machine devised by the famous surgeons, Boyer and Deschamps. La Fayette, after that, always walked lame. As for Kosciusko, Monroe and Colonel Mercer found that old knight of liberty near the barrier of St. Andre. He had a garden there and when his visitors greeted him was busy carrying his water pots. Monroe saw Houdon, too, and sent to Virginia that sculptor's receipt for 2800 livres — a balance due him on the noble statue of Washington now in the rotunda of the Capitol at Richmond. While in Paris, Mrs. Monroe sat for a portrait, as she had done during her first visit, in 1794, when Semé executed a beautiful miniature of her.

But why did Monroe go to London, instead of to Madrid? He wanted to negotiate for the Floridas. Jefferson was eager to acquire them. Livingston was of the opinion that West Florida was actually bought in with Louisiana, and Monroe adopted this view. But the acquisition of the Spanish possessions, whatever might be their metes and bounds, could only be arranged at Madrid. Marbois had promised that the support of France should be given to the United States in treating with the Spanish Government; therefore, on May 19, Monroe applied to Talleyrand for reassurance in the matter, prior to his departure for Madrid. Here, as told by Monroe himself, in a letter to Madison, is a bit about the result of the application:

"On the Sunday following, three or four days afterwards, I dined with the Consul Cambacéres,[1] who had been with the First Consul in council at St. Cloud, whence he returned late to dinner. He said to me soon after entering the room: 'You must

----

[1] Jean Jacques Regis, duc de Cambacéres (1753-1824). He was President of the Convention in 1794. He was one of Napoleon's Councillors.

not go to Spain at present.' I asked his reason. He replied: 'It is not the time; you had better defer it.' I revived the subject repeatedly but he declined going further into it."

Monroe again questioned Cambacéres; and, next day, sought to penetrate the mystery by interviewing Consul le Brun, who had also been in the council at St. Cloud; but he could make neither head nor tail of an affair that seemed to signify so much. Napoleon, of course, had originated the suggestion. Soon, however, Monroe's suspense ended. He received letters from Madison notifying him that, on April 18, he had been commissioned Minister to England, in place of Rufus King,[1] who had filled that post for nearly seven years, and who had asked permission to return to New York. Did this explain the mysterious hint of Cambacéres? Only partly, perhaps. But a big war between France and England was on; and there was need of an American minister in London. Monroe at once communicated with Chevalier d'Azara, Spanish Minister in Paris, and Ambassador Pinckney at Madrid, announcing his change of program; and arranged to quit Paris. Talleyrand wrote him on the evening of June twenty-third, inviting him to his house at noon the next day for the purpose of visiting St. Cloud, that he might take his leave of the First Consul. The presentation was at one o'clock.

"You are about to go to London?" was Napoleon's greeting.

Monroe replied that the resignation of the American minister there had made it necessary for him to supply the vacancy, adding that he had been instructed to call at St. Cloud and give assurance of the greatest respect, esteem and friendliness of the United States toward the First Consul and France.

No one, said Napoleon, wished more than he to preserve a good understanding. The Louisiana cession

[1] When King went to take leave at St. James, George III asked what he intended to do with his boys who were at Harrow. The answer was that they were to finish their studies there and then go to Paris. "All wrong, Mr. King," commented His Majesty: "boys should be educated in the country in which they live."

he had made was not so much "for the price as for the policy." He regarded "the President as a virtuous, enlightened man, a friend of liberty and equality."

Monroe left Paris, with his family, on July 12 and reached London on the eighteenth. He had expressed a desire to occupy the house vacated by Minister King. This we gather, with other data about Monroe, from the unfriendly letters of Christopher Gore, Federalist, whom Rufus King, Federalist, left as his friend in London. The ocean had not washed out their politics. Gore was a member of the Commission in London to consider claims under the Seventh Article of the Treaty between the United States and Great Britain.[1] At this time King and Monroe were far apart in feeling, as compared with their pleasant relations when they were together in the Congress of the Confederation. In a letter to Jefferson, which he wrote but never sent, Richmond, Va., April 30, 1801, Monroe had expressed the sentiment of Republicans there with respect to Rufus King, to wit: that "our present Envoy at London should be withdrawn." He continued:

"They think nothing is done unless that is done; that, as every calamity foreign and domestic we have experienced from Great Britain, a person known to be friendly to her interests, acquainted with our interior, able to guide her councils and plan her measures against us, ought not to be left there, under the present Administration."[2]

Doubtless Monroe was expressing his grudge against the pro-British Federalists rather than against King personally; nevertheless, his strictures were unfair and he did well to put the letter aside. It would have been better if he had burnt it, just as his own enemies, should have done with their letters when they were criticising him for his course in France. At London, few indeed were the mortals who looked upon American

---

[1] While Monroe was in London, Gore offended George W. Erving, U. S. Consul at London, who sent him a challenge to fight a duel. Monroe and William Pinkney, Gore's associate on the commission, endeavored to make peace.

[2] J. C. Hamilton, in his Life of Alexander Hamilton, Vol. VII, p. 585.

affairs as Americans themselves did. Monroe said that
the great majority of people in England misunderstood
the people of the United States. On the other hand:
"Monroe knows little that passes in London," wrote
Gore, August 24. "He has seen Hawkesbury twice;
once on his arrival and once on his introduction to the
King. [August 17.] He has also seen Hammond
once. . . . He appears to have a sort of creed that it is
improper to know what is passing in relation to European Powers, unless the United States are directly
interested. He will, therefore, have a quiet time in
England, for you know they do not press their knowledge, no more than their civility, on any man."

Lord Hawkesbury was Robert Banks Jenkinson
(second Earl of Liverpool, 1770-1828) and the same
man, who, as Lord Liverpool led the Tory ministry
during the War of 1812, as well as during Monroe's
administration, until succeeded by George Canning
in 1822. So, in seeing his lordship, Monroe was seeing
a future antagonist who, though not a great statesman,
had many of the solid qualities and much of the tact
of his famous forbear. This was old Anthony Jenkinson,
who, in Shakespeare's day, under privilege of Solyman
the Great, penetrated the Tartar depths of Asia and
laid the foundation of the family fortune.

But in this year of grace 1804, Hawkesbury was
friendly enough. Whatever may be said of Minister
King's politics, he had smoothed out debt and boundary
difficulties; and when Monroe arrived in London there
was a cordial feeling, and really not much to do. In
fact he probably understood his own business even
better than Gore who lost no opportunity of slurring
the new Minister for the delectation of the old. King,
too, referred to Monroe, in his answer to Gore. "Monroe
is authorized to buy the Floridas from Spain or whoever
is the owner provided he can make the purchase in a
certain sum in six per cent bonds." Again he referred to
"the unsound as well as unwise and impolitic" memorial
of Livingston to Bonaparte. In the same letter he said:

"In regard to Monroe, P. Porcupine will make him uneasy and in some degree put him out of good company by republishing with comments an article from his unwise and stupid performances." Nevertheless Gore, being in the vein of gossip, could not resist writing to King[1] of something the rich Philadelphia merchant, William Bingham, then in England, had sent from Tunbridge Wells to Sir T. B.: "He did not, till he met Monroe in Paris, know he was so able and so moderate a man."

In seeking to make themselves agreeable, the Monroes suffered from certain of those British attributes so humorously caricatured by Jane Austen in "Lady Catharine de Bourg." They were snubbed and insulted in a most outrageous manner, partly out of aristocratic superciliousness of the sort set forth in "Pride and Prejudice," and partly in retaliation for Jefferson's inconsiderate treatment of the new British Minister at Washington. Monroe, in a long letter to Madison, March 3, tells of his experiences with the lords and ladies of the diplomatic circle with whom he and his wife dined.[2] Mrs. Monroe was snubbed quite as often as "Elizabeth Bennett." When Mrs. Monroe called, her calls were not returned. There seemed to be a studied attempt to humiliate the republican Monroes, and, strange to say, Gore and King appear to have been rather pleased at it. Moreover, when King wrote to

---

[1] For the King-Gore letters with pin-pricks at Monroe see Life and Correspondence of Rufus King, Vol. IV.

[2] "At the first state dinner to which he was asked, Mr. Monroe found himself seated at the foot of the table between two representatives from German principalities. 'James Monroe doesn't care where he eats his dinner,' he said, 'but to find the American Minister put at the bottom of the table between two little principalities no bigger than my farm in Albemarle made me mad.' So angry, that when the first toast, 'The King' was given and all rose to drink it, Mr. Monroe in reseating himself put his wine-glass down in the finger-bowl — splashing the water. This made his German neighbors exchange sarcastic smiles, and he was rapidly getting too angry when the Russian Minister, who was at the right hand of the presiding Minister of State, rose and offered his toast, 'A health and welcome to our latest-comer, the President of the United States.' 'Then I saw clear again,' said Mr. Monroe. 'And when my country and General Washington had been honored, I rose and thanked the Russian Minister, as I offered mine: "The health and prosperity of our friend, the Emperor of Russia." ' "   Souvenirs of My Time, by Jessie Benton Fremont, 1887, p. 9.

HORTENSE EUGENIA BEAUHARNAIS

Baron François Pascal Gèrard painted this life-sized oil portrait of Hortense by order of her step-father, Napoleon I. With the companion "Gèrard" of her brother Prince Eugene, it was presented to the Monroes. In 1802 Hortense married Louis Bonaparte, King of Holland. She was the mother of Napoleon III. King Louis abdicated in 1810. Queen Hortense, separated from her husband, returned to Paris, and in 1814 was created Duchess of Saint-Leu. She died in 1837. Queen Hortense was the school friend of Eliza Monroe and godmother of Eliza's daughter, Hortensia Hay.

Gore about the trouble at Washington, Gore was at pains to tell his news to Hawkesbury and Hammond and the underlings, who made the Monroes pay for Jefferson's incivilities to the very unmerry Merrys.

Anthony Merry, who succeeded Edward Thornton as British ambassador, arrived in Washington, November 4, 1803. Rufus King had chosen Merry in preference to Francis James Jackson, who was said to be "positive, vain and intolerant"; and Prime Minister Addington,—Henry Addington, later Lord Sidmouth — out of complaisance and friendliness, had appointed him. Henry Adams says of Merry: "He was a thorough Englishman, with a wife more English than himself." Jefferson, who spoke well of Merry, had no good word to say of his more aggressive mate. We are sorry to add that he called her a virago. Now Jefferson felt himself to be the pioneer of official democracy. He planned to eliminate all those niceties and nonsensical ceremonies of the European Courts and to set an example of plain and unconventional intercourse such as a Virginia gentleman was used to in his daily life at home. Henry Adams in the second volume of his "History of the United States," pages 360-388, has a whole chapter concerning Jefferson's "Canons of Etiquette to be observed by the Executive," and the troubles that grew out of the new code. Merry, a punctilious man and a stickler for precedence, did not understand this new principle of pell-mell, or social equality, which Jefferson wished to establish. No exceptions were to be made in favor of a gentleman like himself and ladies like his wife, who took themselves much to heart and who sincerely believed that Great Britain was by right the first and foremost nation on earth. The Merrys were in a bad humor because of the inconveniences of life in the crude capital. Merry in full uniform, at the appointed hour for his first official call, went to the White House, Madison accompanying him. The audience hall was empty,—where was Jefferson? Merry met him in so narrow an entry that he had to back out in the most undignified manner. It did not become the representative of his Britannic Majesty to walk backwards on an official occasion. And when he was introduced, Merry's eyebrows went up. Jefferson was in undress. He wore slippers and Connemara stockings, and, to Merry's horror, the slippers were heelless! But this was not the last straw. He and his wife dined at the White House. Jefferson, he thought, would take Mrs. Merry into the dining room. Instead, he took Mrs. Dolly Madison. Similarly, at a dinner at the Madisons, the Merrys were again shamed by the odious pell-mell. In fact, the Minister, flushing with anger because the Secretary of State had not offered Mrs. Merry his arm, took her in himself. Jefferson was scandalizing the British world in his effort to simplify and democratize the manners of such of the great as happened to be in close contact with his official family.

Less parade of democracy and pell-mell and the exercise of more common sense, not to mention tact, might have saved Jefferson and Madison a deal of trouble, and, incidentally prevented the discomfiture of the Monroes. In one sense the whole affair was petty, yet it was by no means inconsequential. Did not Pichon write to Talleyrand, Yrujo to Cevallos and Merry to Hammond? In the manuscript departments of the Spanish, French, and British Archives are numerous well-yellowed but piquant letters telling of a cloud no larger at first than a tempestuous teapot, out of which finally came an international blow. It is hardly too much to say that the episode served to reawaken in England the feeling of hostility toward America and perhaps had something to do with the war that broke out a few years later. When Gore dined at Hawkesbury's: "His Lordship took me aside," he wrote to King, "and mentioned the unpleasant accounts they had received from Washington. . . . In this silly business, they probably see here a disposition to affront England, and it will, with others increase a growing discontent with us."

In a letter to Monroe, January 8, 1804, Jefferson, as was his wont, covered many points. He proffered him the office of Governor of Louisiana, but at the same time told him that he probably would have to go to Spain. To him Pinckney's continuance at Madrid was a continual reproach.[1] Monroe might advise him to resign. Jefferson spoke of the Merry incident. Mrs. Merry, he said, was "absurdly pretentious."

Madison also wrote. He requested Monroe to bring forward the plan of a convention covering impressment, blockade and search.

Monroe in his reply to Jefferson said that his proposed service in Louisiana seemed incompatible with his convention work in London and his important affair with Spain. It would take two months at least in London, six in Madrid and two more to get home. He was frank to say that he hoped to extricate himself speedily from his disagreeable English situation. Thereupon he unbosomed himself of many details concerning the incivilities of the British towards himself and his wife. Here for example:

"At Ld. H's table when speaking with his Lady,[2] who appears to me to be an amiable woman, on the subject of our climate, of its variety, etc., I mentioned that while the northern parts were perhaps in snow the southern enjoyed the bloom of Spring; that in Feby at Charlestown they had the *course*, and from want of other topicks of conversation, I added that on such occasions there was always a great concourse of people with gay equipages, etc. Ld. Castleray asked me what kind of equipages had they? I co'd

---

[1] Pinckney had "compromised" Madison and "adopted a high tone with Cevallos." These indiscretions and the awkward situation brought about by them had caused his recall to be asked for. See Adams, History of the United States, Vol. II, Chapter 11, "Quarrel with Yrujo."

[2] In "The Journal of Elizabeth, Lady Holland" (1791-1811), edited by the Earl of Ilchester, 2 vols., 1908, we find many references to the official characters of the time, including Monroe. She was Elizabeth Vassall of Jamaica. She married first Sir Godfrey Webster, then Henry Richard, third Lord Holland, nephew of Charles James Fox. She had separated from Sir G. Webster. She was "the domineering leader of the Whig circle"; and "gave orders" to such guests as Macaulay and Sydney Smith. Page 209, Vol. II, she says: "Monroe has had a conversation with Ld. H. about Spanish America; he wishes nothing to be attempted without a concert with the U. S., the country to be declared independent, and free ports to be opened to both countries." This shows that even thus early Monroe had the germ of the Monroe Doctrine in mind.

not be but surprised at the enquiry, nevertheless replied, such as I saw here. Sir Wm. Scott then remarked that he had lately read an acct. of a grand fête at the Cape of Good Hope which concluded with that all 'the beauty, taste and fashion of Africa were assembled there.' This occasion'd some mirth, as you will suppose, at our expense, in which I could not well partake."

Even an expert in pell-mell could not have been ruder than this wit who made a butt of the American ambassador. If he had not been such, Monroe might well have kicked the great Sir William; as it was, the best he could do was to swallow the insult with his soup.

No wonder the maltreated Americans were homesick and unhappy! No wonder Mrs. Monroe thought of her friends in Paris, and Eliza sighed for her Hortenses and Paulines and Carolines at the Hotel de Rohan! As for Monroe, he wrote his uncle[1] just as he used to write to him in the days of Trenton, Brandywine and Valley Forge. He was gathering up law-books he said; they would be of use to him in his practice. Perhaps he would accept the governorship of Louisiana after all. His wife was suffering from the moist climate. The expenses were dreadful. He longed to be home.

But he went to see Lord Hawkesbury, as Madison had directed; and was on the point of proposing a convention such as had been outlined in his instructions when the Addington government gave way for the return of Pitt. It was a stormy time in British politics. Lord Sheffield, champion of the British navigation laws, was protesting against their relaxation. "The existence of the United States," says Adams, Volume II, page 410, "was a protest against Lord Sheffield's political religion; and therefore in his eyes the United States were no better than a nation of criminals, capable of betraying their God for pieces of silver. The independence of America had shattered the navigation system of England into fragments, but Lord Sheffield clung the more desperately to his broken idol. Among the portions that had been saved were the

---

[1] Monroe to Judge Joseph Jones, May 16, 1804. Gouverneur Mss.

West Indian colonies. . . . To Lord Sheffield these
islands were only a degree less obnoxious than the
revolted United States." British tonnage was
decreasing. Stop American neutrals from glutting the
European market. Coincidently there was a cry
for younger statesmen and George Canning was heard
from. Pitt returned to power and Lord Harrowby
succeeded Hawkesbury as foreign secretary. With
respect to the Sheffield agitation against American
neutrals, Monroe, says Adams, "might count on having
some day to meet whatever mischief the shipping
interest of Great Britain could cause. No argument
was needed to prove that the navy would support
with zeal whatever demands should be made by the
mercantile marine." His first meeting with Lord
Harrowby made a deep impression upon Monroe, as it
did upon Madison to whom he gave a full account of
it in a letter dated June 3.[1] His Lordship was "far
from being conciliatory." The remarks he made were
"not in the spirit of amity." In fact, the British
foreign secretary was highly displeased with the United
States. In Monroe's own words:

"The conduct of Lord Harrowby thro' the whole of this conference was calculated to wound and irritate. Not a friendly
sentiment toward the U. States or their govt. escaped him. In
proposing a postponement of the interests in which we were a
party, he did not seem to desire my sanction, but to assume a tone
which supposed his will had settled the point. . . . Everything he
said was uttered in an unfriendly tone, and much more was
apparently meant than was said. I was surprised at a deportment
of which I had seen no example before since I came into the
country, and which was certainly provoked by no act of mine. . . .
I now consider those concerns as postponed indefinitely. . . .
Whether the conduct of Lord Harrowby was produced by any
change of policy towards us, or by any other cause, transient or
otherwise, it is utterly out of my power to ascertain at present.
My most earnest advice, however, is to look to the possibility of
such a change."

"An approaching contact of opposing forces," comments Adams, "always interests men's imaginations.

[1] Writings of Monroe, Vol. IV, pp. 191-199.

On one side, Pitt and Harrowby stood meditating the details of measures, which they had decided in principle, for taking from the United States most of the commercial advantages hitherto enjoyed by them; on the other side, stood Monroe and Jefferson, equally confident, telling the Englishmen that very much greater advantages must be conceded. That one or the other of these forces must very soon give way was evident; and if ever an American Minister in London needed to be on the alert, with every faculty strained to its utmost, the autumn of 1804 was such a moment. Monroe, aware of his danger, gave full warning to the President."

Monroe sent Harrowby a draft of Madison's plan. Harrowby was too busy to consider it. So he said. Monroe then informed his Lordship of his route to Spain, through Holland and France. His mission, he explained, was "extraordinary and temporary." On October 8, 1804, he sailed for Rotterdam, and did not return to London until July 23, 1805. No doubt he was glad to be on the continent again, and Mrs. Monroe was rejoiced to be able to live awhile at St. Germain, where Eliza re-entered Madame Campan's school.

We now come to a tale of many diplomats; indeed, we enter upon a veritable geographical and diplomatic maze. If we follow the Monroe thread we shall be able to go in and come out of this labyrinthine history without undue bewilderment.

But let us first fix in mind a few facts as to the Atlantic side of the world — the world of Pitt and Bonaparte, as well as of Jefferson, now entering upon his second term as President.

Jefferson talked peace and wanted it. If he made a threat of war it was for effect, not with an idea of actually going to war. He believed in fighting with such unexplosive weapons as the embargo. War to him was abhorrent, none of his impulses were martial or heroic; he was a philosophical manipulator of men; and he readily could stoop to politics, for which, like most Virginians, he had a strong inclination. He had done so well, up to 1805, as to have high hopes of matching his initial successes with a second series — a Louisiana with a Florida. He had sent Lewis and Clarke as far as the Oregon country. Clearly, it was the age of expansion — not only in territory, but in the letting out of constitutional garments, that chafed or choked or smothered by their strict-construction tightness. With a little war won against Barbary pirates, there was, also, some satisfaction on the sea. But on the sea were the British, and they seemed to think it theirs. There was something to be said on that score — even in their favor; for they were islanders in a titanic struggle with Napoleon, who would surely overrun their country and make vassals of them if by hook or by crook he could break their naval defense and cross the Channel. It was, indeed, Napoleon's day on the land, and Nelson's on the sea. Bitter as was the blow given him at Trafalgar, Napoleon won at Ulm and Austerlitz; and, at Jena, he saw himself master of the Continent of Europe. Jefferson's plans were to be frustrated throughout his second term by the grim struggle for supremacy between the warring nations. They reached and jarred the White House like successive seismic shocks. In following Monroe, we will do well to keep in mind this jarring of the earth and the lurid Napoleonic background.

As we have seen, it was Napoleon who had diverted Monroe from Madrid to London. He did it because he felt that he had already goaded Don Manuel Godoy and Don Pedro de Cevallos as much as they would stand. Even the hornless Spanish bull would turn. Their Louisiana anger must be given time to cool.

Now Napoleon had told his New Orleans prefect, Laussat, that Louisiana extended on the west to Rio Brava, or Rio Grande del Norte. Texas, therefore, must have been transferred with Louisiana to the United States. But neither Napoleon nor Talleyrand, when appealed to by Monroe and Livingston with respect to delimitations, had intimated the existence of any such western boundary — so few Americans thought of Texas as a part of the purchase. It is true that in a letter from Jefferson to John Dickinson, August 9, 1803, mention was made of the Rio Brava on the west and the Rio Perdido on the east as possible demarcations. There were "some pretentions" with respect to the Texas region, and greater ones to the Mobile country — the West Florida strip along the Gulf.

Now as to East Florida, it was Spain's; no one questioned that fact; but the greatest confusion existed in regard to West Florida. And no wonder. "Exploration, occupancy, conquest, treaty and revolt," says Henry E. Chambers, "have caused the region in question to change ownership and jurisdiction no less than six times. Perhaps this can be said of no other portion of American soil."[1] There were three separate and distinct West Floridas; British West Florida, Spanish West Florida and the Independent State of West Florida. Spain owned Florida from the time of Ponce de Leon, 1512, and Fernando de Soto, 1539, until she traded it with Great Britain for Cuba. This was in 1736. There were a few French families along the coast. After the French and Indian War, France gave up Louisiana to Spain and East Louisiana to England. So after February 10, 1763, Great Britain owned the Floridas from the Mississippi to the Atlantic; but not the Island of New Orleans.[2] The British were active in West Florida. Big land grants were given to veterans. They took in fertile Yazoo lands; and, when John Elliot succeeded Captain George Johnstone as Governor (1767), the northern boundary was set down as on the line thirty-two degrees, twenty-eight minutes, instead of thirty-one degrees, the line familiar to us as

---

[1] West Florida and its relation to the Historical Cartography of the United States, by Henry E. Chambers; Johns Hopkins University Studies, Series XVI, No. 5, 1898, pp. 1-59.

[2] It was on the east bank of the Mississippi from the Gulf to Bayou Manchac, or Iberville River, which has been filled up and exists only as a name.

the present north bound of Florida and that portion of the present State of Louisiana which touches the State of Mississippi. Thus the British shouldered themselves up to the vicinity of the Vicksburg parallel, whereas they should have held back some thirty miles below the Natchez parallel. This British extension of West Florida caused confusion in the minds of statesmen and historians. Peter Chester (1770) was the last British Governor. In 1783, Great Britain retroceded to Spain the two provinces of East and West Florida. In the definitive treaty of that year with the United States, there was a secret clause under which the boundary was put back to thirty-one degrees. Spain resented this as an Anglo-American subterfuge; but in the treaty of Madrid, October 27, 1795, accepted the line below Natchez. As to the third West Florida, the Independent State, so called, that was not organized until September 26, 1810, long after the period with which we are dealing.[1]

Livingston insisted that West Florida was actually included in the purchase of 1803.[2] Monroe, too, believed West Florida to be "comprised in the cession." Jefferson came to this view; so did Madison. Finally, in 1804, Congress passed the Mobile Act, declaring the Mobile country to be a collection, or customs district, with Fort Stoddert as its port of entry. This enactment angered Yrujo as nothing else had done. He "overwhelmed Madison with reproaches." General Louis Marie Turreau, the full-fledged French minister who had got out of France to escape his enemies and especially his wife[3] tried without avail to make peace between Yrujo and Madison. Yrujo's day in Washington was done. He was recalled. Mean-

---

[1] With Monroe's former Paris friend Fulwar Skipwith, late of the Consular service as Governor.

[2] Without warrant, according to H. E. Chambers in "The Madison-Livingston Theory of West Florida Acquirement" (Part II of West Florida, in Johns Hopkins University Studies). Accompanying this monograph is a chronology of the Floridas and a bibliography of the subject.

[3] She followed him, however, with the result that the Turreau conjugal quarrels scandalized Washington.

time there was trouble for Madison in Madrid. He "complained to the President," says Adams,[1] "that his Minister at Madrid teased the Spanish Government on the subject of Florida, which he had been ordered not to touch without the presence or the advice of Monroe." Moreover, "Livingston at Paris, equally restive under the imposed authority of Monroe, could not resist the temptation to stimulate Pinckney and offer advice to both France and Spain." Now a Spanish claim convention, negotiated by Pinckney, having been ratified by the United States Senate, was returned to him so that he might secure due ratification by Don Pedro Cevallos. Don Pedro "made difficulties"; and, when Yrujo sent him the Mobile Act, declared that if it were not revoked he would not ratify the convention. At once Pinckney took a violent tone. Pierre de Ruel Beurnonville, the French Minister at Madrid, wrote to Talleyrand that "Pinckney had terrified the secretary beyond reason," "he positively threatens war." When Madison heard of Pinckney's conduct, he recalled him, and "wrote to Monroe ordering him in haste to Spain." "Madison," adds Adams, "undeterred by Pinckney's disaster, still persisted in advising him to place his main reliance, 'in a skilful appeal to the fears of Spain.'"[2] Livingston was also recalled; and, shortly after Monroe's arrival in Paris, General John Armstrong, the new American Ambassador to France, reached that capital. "Thus it happened," says Adams, "that three American Ministers — Monroe, Livingston and Armstrong — met at Paris in November, 1804, to cope with Talleyrand, in whose hands lay the decision of Jefferson's quarrel with Spain: Cevallos looked to him for help; and so did Monroe who had been instructed to offer $2,000,000 for Florida east of the Perdido. As for West Florida, Spanish acknowledgment of American right to it was to be *sine*

---

[1] H. Adams, History of the United States, Chapter XII, "Pinckney's Diplomacy," Vol. II, pp. 264-287.

[2] Madison to Monroe, November 9, 1804.

qua non; and nothing was to be paid for it. Napoleon, whom the Monroes saw crowned at St. Cloud, was full of business; but by Livingston's hand, Monroe sent a long letter to Talleyrand, asking the Emperor's good offices with Spain. It was a well-worded letter, full of courtesy, but it is said to have irritated Napoleon. Marbois gave Monroe a hint that money might help him to win what he wanted. "Spain must cede territory," said another of Napoleon's men, M. Hauterive; "the United States must pay money." Armstrong subsquently wrote to Madison to that effect. It explained, he said: "the marked incivility with which Mr. Monroe was treated by Talleyrand."

Just before leaving Paris, Monroe made an effort to see Talleyrand personally. He went alone to Talleyrand's house. Carriages stood in line in front of it. As it happened, Talleyrand was giving a reception in honor of the Ambassadors. With marked civility, the Cerberus at the door offered to go see the Prince in behalf of the unexpected guest; but Monroe, diffident as he was, hesitated; and finally went away.

The outlook for friendly aid from the hand of power — a hand that seemed to itch, as it had done in X Y Z days — was indeed dubious. Venality ruled. "With Napoleon in this frame of mind," says Adams, "with Godoy and Cevallos in a humor far worse, and with Talleyrand in such a temper as not to allow his treating Monroe with civility, the American Ambassador departed to Madrid, hoping that something might occur to overcome his difficulties. During his journey Charles IV declared war against England."

As for Talleyrand's report on Monroe's letter it was dated November 19, and "lay some weeks in the Emperor's hands." Monroe left Paris for Madrid December 8, and still no answer had been sent to his note. He wrote from Bordeaux, December 16, a long and interesting letter to Madison, and resumed his journey. He could hardly have crossed the Bidassoa when Armstrong received from Talleyrand, December

21, "the long expected answer which, by declaring the claim to West Florida emphatically unfounded, struck the ground from under his feet and left him to repent at leisure his defiance of Talleyrand's advice."

Monroe wrote to Jefferson and Madison in friendly fashion concerning the difficulties and dangers of traveling in Spain. A man was not unlikely to be beset as well as upset. He had been seven days between Paris and Bordeaux and had sent forward to Bayonne for mules to take him to Don Quixote's country. "With a relay of mules," he wrote to Madison,[1] "the journey may be made without halting, as I presume a moment, in five or six days. With the same set it requires twelve or fifteen." He traveled through a beautiful part of France and through the passes of the Pyrenees. According to Alexander de Laborde,[2] a friend of his, who wanted to hire a servant and who asked for credentials, was rather astonished when the man brought him "authentic documents of nobility from King Ordonius II." Thanks to his mules, Monroe was soon in the elevated region of the Castiles. He would spend part of the time at Aranjuez, the royal resort, seven leagues to the south of Madrid, as that other famous treaty town, St. Idlefonso, was fifteen leagues to the north. Aranjuez, watered by the Tagus, was in a verdant valley of tall trees and rippling brooks — all the more beautiful because in contrast with the naked plain to the north of it. At the time of Monroe's visit, it was alike famous for its gardens, avenues, cascades and numberless fine fountains. Originally a royal hunting-lodge, it was laid out like a Dutch town and became the favorite play place of the Court of Spain. The palace, designed by Herrera, was built of brick and white marble, and looked like a great castle.

It was the day after New Year's, 1805, when Monroe rode into Madrid. Pinckney was apprehensive lest he

---

[1] Letter-Book, Library of Congress.
[2] A View of Spain, 1809. Vol. I, p. 51 (introduction). The experience was that of Count de Froberg.

should be barred by Monroe from the new negotiations, but the fear was groundless; the two Americans worked together, and, on January 28, addressed Cevallos[1] in a joint note. Accompanying the note was a *projét.* What did Monroe propose? That Spain should hand over the Floridas and as much of Texas as lay east of the Rio Colorado; that she should create a claims commission to pass upon French and Spanish spoliations, as well as upon losses due to the closing of the entrepot at New Orleans; and that she should seal all this in solemn treaty. Cevallos agreed to take up matters point by point. Monroe replied, January 31, that the whole subject must be dealt with, or else nothing. Adams calls it his ultimatum. If so, it was an honest one. Cevallos took up the Mobile Act, agreeing to withdraw the demand for its repeal. Monroe suggested that they take up the boundaries. Cevallos came back with a note on the French spoliation claims, which Napoleon had said, through Talleyrand, July 27, 1804, were undiscussable; and on the harm done by Intendant Morales in suspending the deposit of American goods at New Orleans. "As for this," said Cevallos, "it was *nil.*" Thus the diplomatic duel proceeded day by day — a keen combat in which Cevallos, backed by the masterful Godoy,[2] handled his weapons with all the skill of an accomplished disputant. Monroe, in a strange capital, with two other capitals — Washington and Paris — constantly in mind, was at manifest disadvantage. Another drawback: he had taken up Pinckney's lost battle. But he, too, handled himself like a supple duelist, a clever dialectician. On the subject of Morales, he was not to make any ado; as to Napoleon's inhibition with respect to the spoliation claims, he got over that difficulty with much grace not untinctured with the flattering, if ironical, intimation that Spain and the United States, being independent

---

[1] Pedro de Caballos y Guerra was born in 1764. He served Fernando VII as well as Carlos VII, retired in 1820 and died in 1840.

[2] Godoy began life as a private in the Royal Guards. A book about him is "The Queen's Favorite," by Edmund B. D'Auvergne.

nations, were at liberty to think for themselves.
"Every nation," he said, "is the guardian of its own
honor and rights; and the Emperor is too sensible of
what is due to his own glory, and entertains too high a
respect for the United States, to wish them to abandon
a just sense of what is due their own." But Cevallos
could or would not discuss the claims. There was a
cessation of sword-play. Monroe felt the shadow of
Talleyrand as perceptibly in Madrid as in Paris. In a
letter to Armstrong, March 1, Monroe wrote: "She
(France) must clearly understand that the negotiation
is about to break up without doing anything, and that
the failure is entirely owing to the part taken against
us." There were reasons, and good ones too, why
France should not quarrel with America. He was
inclined to think that "a rupture with us is an event
which of all others, she least seeks at the present time."
These passages show that Monroe knew the men he
was fighting — not Cevallos and Godoy merely, but
Talleyrand and Napoleon. Since, with his long arm
reaching all the way from Paris, Talleyrand was holding
him down, he would rap his knuckles as best he could.
It was a timely and justifiable threat; and, having
made it, he waited. Armstrong replied, March 12 and
18, that those in power had declared "that our claim,
having nothing of solidity in it, must be abandoned."
"To the question 'What would be the course of this
government in case of rupture between us and Spain?'
they answered: 'We can neither doubt nor hesitate —
we must take part with Spain; and our note of the
thirtieth Frimaire was intended to communicate and
impress this idea.'"[1] Meantime March passed.
West Florida was the theme for a while, and then
Cevallos brought up the western boundary of the ceded
region. Talleyrand had put it in his head that the true
line of demarcation should be between the French and
Spanish settlements. So the subtle old diplomat had

---

[1] This was Talleyrand's letter of December 21, 1804. Monroe's diary at Aranjuez, March 16, 1805; Monroe Mss.

served Spain again. When Monroe talked of the Rio
Colorado, Cevallos talked of a line — the Sabine line —
that would cut off a segment of what is now the State
of Louisiana. Although as early as April 9, Monroe
notified Cevallos that the negotiation was "essentially
terminated," it was prolonged until May 12 when the
American ultimatum was sent. May 15 Cevallos
replied. May 18 Monroe wrote for his passports.
Taking leave of Cevallos next day, Monroe, with no
treaty in his portmanteau, quit Madrid, May 26, for
Paris and London. Pinckney lingered until October,
when George W. Erving was transferred from the
London Consulate as *Chargè d'Affaires* in Spain. As
Adams has it,[1] when Erving called on Godoy to protest
against the seizure of American ships, the Prince of
Peace received him with good-natured courtesy: " 'How
go our affairs?' he asked; 'are we to have peace or
war?' Erving called his attention to the late seizures.
The Prince replied that it was impossible to allow
American vessels to carry English property. 'But we
have a treaty which secures us that right,' replied
Erving. 'Certainly, I know you have a treaty for I
made it with Mr. Pinckney' . . . . Then he continued,
with laughable coolness: 'You may choose either
peace or war. 'Tis the same thing with me! I will tell
you candidly that, if you go to war this certainly is the
moment, and you will take our possessions from us.
I advise you to go to war now, if you think that is best
for you; and then the peace which will be made in
Europe will leave us two at war.' Defiance could go
no further. Elsewhere the Prince openly said that the
United States had brought things to such a point as to
leave Spain indifferent to the consequences. In the
war the President could only seize Florida; and Florida
was the price he asked for remaining at peace."

But Godoy would not always be so confident, so
daring. One is strangely impressed with this Spanish
Talleyrand — cunning, corrupt, profligate, reputed

[1] H. Adams, History of the United States, Vol. III, pp. 37, 38.

father of the Queen's children. The day of reckoning would come for him, for the vicious and criminal Queen, for the deluded King and for the unspeakable Prince Ferdinand who, instigated by Napoleon, intrigued for his alleged father's crown. At the palace in Aranjuez, March 8, 1808, perished the old monarchy. Godoy fled; Don Carlos placed the crown on the head of the Prince of the Asturias; and, by and by, that unworthy one gave way to Joseph Bonaparte. So there was a reason why Talleyrand and Napoleon wished the Floridas to remain a Spanish possession. But, anon Wellington took a hand, and the Bourbons were restored. But the Spanish empire had gone to pieces; and its South American dependencies became sister republics of that elder republic which by and by would publish to the world a great doctrine with respect to them.

When Monroe reached Paris, Napoleon was in Italy, where, at Milan, May 26, he received the iron crown of Lombardy. Talleyrand was with Napoleon. Monroe and Armstrong conferred. Armstrong suggested a change of plan. It was to occupy Texas. West Florida was to be let alone. "A stroke of this kind," said Armstrong, "would at once bring Spain to reason, and France to her rescue, and without giving either room to quarrel." "Armstrong," says Adams, "saw the weak point of Napoleon's position, and wished to attack it. He had no trouble in bringing Monroe to the same conclusion, although in yielding to his arguments, Monroe tacitly abandoned the ground he had been persuaded by Livingston to take two years before — that West Florida belonged to Louisiana."

Monroe was in Paris from June 20 to July 17, when he left for London by way of Antwerp. "During a century of American diplomatic history," says Henry Adams, "a minister of the United States has seldom if ever within six months suffered, at two great courts, such contemptuous treatment as had fallen to Monroe's lot. That he should have been mortified and anxious for escape was natural. He returned to England, meaning to sail as quickly as possible." The date of Monroe's arrival in London was July 23. He wrote to Madison that he hoped to leave for home by the first of November; and to Jefferson he confessed that, but for the recent seizure of American ships, he would no longer have remained. One of his daughters — Eliza, no doubt — was ill; and by the advice of a physician, he took her to Cheltenham. At that resort were mineral springs of some celebrity, the waters being "compounded of sulphur and steel." Mrs. Monroe was ailing too. She had suffered from rheumatism ever since the fête of the coronation at Paris. "I leave Mr. Purviance in town," he added, "and shall keep an apartment to which I shall repair occasionally." Purviance was to notify him whenever he should be needed. He was even willing to risk a winter voyage rather than linger in unpromising and inhospitable England. Had he known of the extreme illness of his much loved uncle, Judge Jones[1] (born in 1727) who died at Fredericksburg, Va., October 28, he would have been all the more anxious to reach home.

Monroe's English letters at this period are to Jefferson Madison, Armstrong, John Randolph and others, and usually bear the London date. One is to Charles James Fox. A letter to Madison, February 2, 1806 shows Monroe in an unusual light — that of a critic of his political assailants. His protests against misrepresentation were due to an account he had read of a New York fête in honor of Livingston, at which Morris and King were present. Monroe discloses considerable irritation, if not a wee bit of spleen — most unusual with him — in this letter. His opinion of the diplomatic services of the three ex-ambassadors could not have been high.

---

[1] In a later letter Monroe expressed himself most affectionately about Judge Jones. "He held the place and was always regarded by my family as a parent." A son of Judge Jones went abroad with the Monroes. Monroe had under his care St. George, a deaf and dumb nephew of John Randolph of Roanoke. He placed the youth with Braidwood, an instructor.

In a letter to Madison, October 18, Monroe said:

"I have no doubt that the seizure of our vessels was a deliberate act of this Government. . . . On a review of the conduct of the Government towards the United States, from the commencement of the war, I am inclined to think that the delay which has been so studiously sought in all these concerns is the part of a system, and that it is intended, as circumstances favor, to subject our commerce at present and hereafter to every restraint in their power. It is certain that the greatest jealousy is entertained of our present and increasing prosperity, and I am satisfied that nothing which is likely to succeed, will be left untried to impair it."[1]

Henry Adams declares[2] that Pitt had made good use of Monroe's absence in Spain to strengthen the British merchant marine. But would not Pitt have done the like if Monroe had remained in London? It did not seem to make a great deal of difference to the British what they said or did with respect to America at that time. It was an age when only frigates counted. Pitt was for England — he was working himself to death for England. Sir William Scott who could insult America's ambassador at a dinner party as flippantly as he could condemn batches of American vessels in his Admiralty Court was for England, first, last and all the time. British arrogance had been intensified by Bonaparte's violence, which Canning was willing to equal if not surpass. Adams is hardly just to Monroe in expecting him to succeed among venal intriguers on the Continent, and then among the war-hardened Tories of London who knew very well that Thomas Jefferson was as much enamored of peace as the veriest Quaker since the days of George Fox. Nor does Adams's harsh criticism of Monroe tally with his subsequent suggestion that Jefferson and Madison had set an impossible task for Monroe with the purpose of eliminating him as a coming presidential

---

[1] Writings of Monroe, Vol. IV, pp. 303-495. Writings of Monroe, Vol. IV, p. 361.
[2] H. Adams, History of the United States, Vol. III, p. 48, *et seq.* Adams devotes three chapters to Monroe in this volume: "Monroe's Diplomacy," pp. 22-56; "Monroe's Treaty," pp. 392-412; and "Rejection of Monroe's Treaty," pp. 413-440.

candidate. And when Pitt "died of old age at forty-six," being succeeded by the Grenville Ministry, with Charles James Fox, ever friendly to America, as Foreign Secretary,[1] why did Madison hasten to send William Pinkney of Maryland as Monroe's associate? Did it not seem as though, fair weather having come at last, Madison feared lest Monroe might make a good treaty after all? Was it not the politic thing to thrust in a colleague to share in whatever honors might be forthcoming? News of Pinkney's appointment to work jointly with him in negotiating a new treaty reached Monroe, May 31, 1806. The object of the treaty was the restoration of trade with the West Indies and the indemnification of vessel-owners for losses by decisions of Admiralty Courts. Great Britain was to be asked to abandon impressment. Monroe had been sent to aid Livingston in Paris and Charles Pinckney in Madrid; so he could not consistently object to that turn of fortune whereby he, too, was thus yoked to another. Nevertheless, "the blow to Monroe's pride was great, and shook his faith in the friendship of Jefferson and Madison. . . . The nomination of a colleague warned him that he had lost influence at home, and that Jefferson, however well-disposed, no longer depended on him. . . . Monroe was well informed of the efforts made to raise or depress his own fortunes at Washington and could see how easily his rival, the Secretary of State, might play a double part. Nothing could be simpler than such tactics. Madison had only to impose on Monroe the task of negotiating a treaty under impossible conditions. If the treaty should fail, the blame would fall upon Monroe; if it should succeed, the credit would be with Pinkney. No one would suppose that Madison would make any great effort to secure the success of a negotiation when success might make the negotiator

---

[1] After his first interview with him Monroe wrote of Fox as one "who in half an hour put me more at my ease than I ever felt with any person in office since I have been in England." — Monroe to Madison, February 12, 1806; Mss. State Department Archives.

the next President of the United States. . . . Monroe could not doubt the President's coldness toward the treaty; he could not fail to see that the Secretary's personal wishes were rather against than for it; and when he studied the instructions he could not but admit that they were framed, if not with the intention, at all events with the effect, of making a treaty impossible. No harder task could well have been imposed than was laid upon Monroe."[1] Jefferson's claim was that concessions would be made either by England or France, as the case might be, under the fear that America, which could equip "fifty Frigates," would otherwise join the other side. Moreover, "we begin to broach the idea that we consider the whole Gulf Stream as of our waters." So Jefferson wrote, forgetful of the fact that the British had outraged us at the very gateway of New York. If fifty frigates had thundered within earshot of Gravesend, instead of in the Quaker-like President's letter, they would have impressed Monroe and the British negotiators in a very different degree. These negotiators were Fox's alternates, Lord Holland and Lord Auckland. But Fox, ill of dropsy, unfortunately, died September 13; and Lord Howick (Charles Grey, later Earl Grey) became Foreign Secretary. Monroe and Pinkney knew exactly what they now had to face. They put their instructions and Jefferson's fifty paper frigates, behind them; and negotiated a treaty to which they affixed their signatures December 31, 1806 — a treaty, says Adams, with unction, "remarkable for combining in one instrument every quality to which Jefferson held most strenuous objection." Impressments were set aside; no indemnities were obtained for American losses in 1805; and, in regard to the colonial trade,

---

[1] Adams, History of the United States, Vol. III, pp. 400, 402, 403. Adams says, truly: "If America wanted such concessions she must fight for them, as other nations had done since mankind existed. England, France and Spain had for centuries paid for their power with their blood, and could see no sufficient reason why America should take their hard-won privileges without a challenge. Jefferson thought otherwise."

"a compromise was invented which no self-respecting government would admit."[1] News that a treaty had been made by Monroe and Pinkney reached Washington on March 3, 1807. David Montague Erskine who had succeeded Anthony Merry as British Minister went at once to Madison, who asked him "what had been determined on the point of impressment of seamen." When Madison learned that nothing had been done he "expressed the greatest astonishment and disappointment." That night a joint committee of Congress waited on the President and asked him whether the Senate would be called upon to consider the treaty; "certainly not," said Jefferson. General Samuel Smith wrote to Wilson Cary Nicholas that the President was angry about the treaty; that he meant to send it back for revision. Smith added: "Will not M. and P. both conceive themselves insulted, and return to make war on the administration?" Again Smith wrote: "What a responsibility he [Jefferson] takes! By sending it back he disgraces his Ministers and *Monroe is one.*" He wanted to know what people would say: "Jealousy of Monroe and unreasonable antipathy by Jefferson and Madison to Great Britain! — this will be said, this will be believed. And Monroe will be brought forward, new parties will arise and those adverse politically will be brought together by interest. . . . Monroe will be called a martyr, and the martyr will be President. And why? Because he has done right, and his opponent has advised wrong."[2]

"To Monroe," says Adams, "the President wrote with the utmost forbearance and kindness. Instead of reproaching, Jefferson soothed the irritation of his old friend, contradicted newspaper reports which were calculated to wound Monroe's feelings, and pressed

---

[1] For the British view of the treaty and Lord Howick's retaliatory Order in Council, January 7, 1807, see H. Adams, Vol. III. Chapter XVIII; "American State Papers," Vol. III, pp. 153, 158, 267; Cobbett's Debates, Vol. VIII, p. 632 *et seq.* Edinburgh Review, Vol. XXII, p. 485 and T. P. Courtney's Additional Observations on the American Treaty, p. 89.

[2] S. Smith to W. C. Nicholas, March 4, 1807; Nicholas Mss. as quoted in Adams, History of the United States, Vol. III, pp. 431, 432.

upon him the government of New Orleans Territory."
Jefferson reminded Monroe[1] that it was "the second
office in the United States in importance." "I am still
in hopes you will accept it," said he; "it is impossible
to let you stay at home while the public has so much
need of talents." On May 20, Madison sent further
instructions to Monroe and Pinkney. But just then
the 38-gun frigate "Chesapeake," Commodore Barron,
bound as a relief ship to Barbary waters was made to
heave to off the Virginia capes and, after a trumpet
parley, raked by the British two-decker "Leopard,"
50 guns. Three Americans were killed; eighteen
wounded. The "Leopard" was after three deserters
from the British "Melampus." There was a profound
sensation and, of course, no more treaty-making for a
long while.

Let us now take Monroe's own testimony as to his
work in England.

"The failure of our business with Spain and the knowledge of
the renewal of the negotiation and the manner of it, which were
known to every one, were sensibly felt in our concerns with
England. She was not willing to yield any portion of what she
called her maritime rights, under the light pressure of the non-
importation law, to a power which had no maritime force, nor
even sufficient to protect any one of its ports against a small
squadron, and which had so recently submitted to great injuries
and indignities from Powers that had not a single ship at sea.
Under such circumstances, it seemed to me highly for the interest
of our country and to the credit of our government to get out of the
general scrape on the best terms we could, and with that view to
accommodate our differences with the great maritime Power on
what might be called fair and reasonable conditions, if such could
be obtained. I had been slighted, as I thought, by the Administration in getting no answers to my letters for an unusual term, and
in being subjected to a special mission, notwithstanding my remonstrance against it on thorough conviction of its inutility, and by
other acts which I could not but feel, yet believing that my service
in England would be useful there, and by means thereof give aid to
the Administration and to the Republican cause at home, I
resolved to stay, and did stay for those purposes. The treaty
was an honorable and advantageous adjustment with England.

[1] Jefferson to Monroe, March 21, 1807; Jefferson's Works (Ford), Vol. V, p. 52.

I adopted it in the firm belief that it was so, and nothing has since occurred to change that opinion."[1]

This clear and manifestly sincere statement of Monroe's difficulties, motives and accomplishments might well have been weighed more trustingly by Henry Adams, who reads into the character of the negotiator traits that do not belong there. When he says that Monroe "was often called a very dull man" and adds that "people suspected him of thinking more of the Federalist vote than he did of Madison's political promotion," he makes him a dullard and a sharper in the same contradictory sentence. He was neither. In New England once, somebody asked Monroe a question upon his arrival at a town, after many hours of fatiguing travel and because the poor man, weary with many receptions and much hand-shaking, took his time in answering it, started a story that he was "dull." This anecdote went the rounds of the Federalist papers and finally got into the phrase-book of the historical writers. That probably explains its use by a grandson who might have profitably read his grandfather's "Monroe."[2] Henry Adams's documents relating to Monroe are of the greatest value and so are his facts about him; but some of his conclusions are open to question.

Monroe never worked harder or with more ability than when in Spain seeking the acquisition of the Floridas or in England endeavoring to insure future peace. He was clear and forceful in logic and language. He let nothing drag. He preserved the amenities, so that no Don of Castile could question his courtesy. In a word, Monroe was at his best during these years of negotiation. He failed in Spain and his British treaty was pigeon-holed by the President. But in each case conditions were against him. Only by the lavish use of bribes could the Floridas have been acquired at

---

[1] Monroe to Colonel John Taylor of Caroline, September 10, 1810. Monroe Mss. State Department Archives.

[2] See eloquent estimate of Monroe's work in England and Spain by John Quincy Adams; Eulogy, pp. 257-268.

that time; and Monroe was both clean-minded and clean-handed. As for the British treaty, it was the half-loaf or nothing. But, by a strange twist, some of those who warmly defend Jay as coldly criticise Monroe.

Here is how Monroe impressed Lord Holland:[1]

"We found the two American Commissioners fair, explicit, frank and intelligent. Mr. Monroe (afterwards President) was a sincere Republican, who, during the Revolution in France had imbibed a strong predilection for that country, and no slight aversion to this. But he had candor and principle. A nearer view of the consular and imperial government of France, and of our Constitution in England converted him from both these opinions. 'I find,' said he to me 'your monarchy more republican than monarchical, and the French republic infinitely more monarchial than your monarchy.' He was plain in his manners and somewhat slow in his apprehension; but he was a diligent, earnest, sensible, and even profound man.

His colleague, who had been partly educated in England and was a lawyer by profession, had more forms and readiness of business, and greater knowledge and cultivation of mind; but perhaps his opinions were neither so firmly rooted nor so deeply considered as those of Mr. Monroe. Throughout our negotiation, they were conciliatory, both in form and in substance." With regard to the putting aside of impressment, Lord Holland says: "Upon this omission, and upon other more frivolous pretexts, but with the real purpose and effect of defeating Mr. Monroe's views on the presidentship, Mr. Jefferson refused to ratify a treaty which would have secured his countrymen from all further vexations and prevented a war between two nations, whose habits, language, and interests should unite them in perpetual alliance and good-fellowship."

Lord Holland's excellent pen-picture of Monroe may be supplemented by another view of him as he appeared while in England. William Dillwyn[2] wrote under date of Higham Lodge, third month, tenth, 1806, to Samuel Emlen, West Hill, near Burlington, West New Jersey:

"Monroe, the American Ambassador, having taken a good house at Leyton adjoining this parish for his temporary accommodation, I paid him a visit this morning and was much pleased with his friendly, republican, unassuming manners. He seemed quite

---

[1] Memoirs of Lord Holland, Vol. II, pp. 98-103.

[2] Letter-Book of William Dillwyn. Ridgway branch of the Philadelphia Library, Mss. collection.

MARIA MONROE AT FIFTEEN.

MARIA HESTER MONROE (Mrs. Gouverneur)

pleased with my Freedom in calling on him and readily engaged to dine here with his wife and two young Daughters this Day se'night. In conversation he rather increased my Hope that the present existing uneasiness between our country and this government will be dissipated by a more conciliatory Disposition in the present ministry than appeared in their predecessors. Be it so — for a war would unavoidably add to the irksomeness of our separation in many respects; and of selfish opponents this nation already has an ample share. Buonaparte is repeating his threats of Invasion and the preparations to repel it are no less active on every point deemed accessible. Happy for the nation as for Individuals would it be had we solid grounds for Reliance on a better Protection than human effort can afford. Some seem to think the Corsican too wicked to be employed even as an Instrument of Punishment, but altho' I have never felt much alarmed by any Ideas of his succeeding in his ambitious Designs on these Kingdoms I cannot easily appreciate the strength of an argument of that kind."

On the day appointed (third month, seventeenth) Dillwyn adds:

"Our four girls, etc, etc, are as busy in their Preparations to entertain them [the Monroes] as if they thought Republican & Spartan Manners were not necessarily sinonymous, and Lydia deprecates my censure by hinting that she means the compliment as much to her father as to the minister. . . . I have often had occasion to remark that the lower orders of people here are more ignorant than the same class in my native country. I find a notion prevails among our poor neighbors that the Greatest Man in America, by them y'clept a King, is expected as our guest.

19th. Our expected Guests came, accompanied by a Purviance of Baltimore (of the Philadelphia family of that name) probably attached to the Embassy. Monroe married a Cartwright [Kortright] of New York. She knows a good deal of our friends there, and is herself of a friendly social disposition. Several hours passed in as much Freedom and Ease as if we were assembled on the banks of the Hudson, the Delaware, or Potomack. Monroe's general information and particular knowledge of American affairs, render his conversation very interesting, and I believe we parted mutually pleased with the opp° of such a joint excursion to our native shores. Our young folks were highly delighted with it, the elder Daughter, about 18, much resembling Lydia in the artless Frankness of Her Manners."

On fifth month, twelfth, Dillwyn writes:

"The day before yesterday, with my three younger daughters (Judy being not then well enough) I dined with Monroe, the

American Ambassador, and could collect nothing from him discovering the hope that the Ministers were disposed to settle matters in dispute by amicable negotiation. It was an agreeable afternoon."

CHAPTER XIII

Monroe and the War of 1812

Just as we can see why Monroe and Pinkney were
unable to secure a more favorable treaty, so, with the
same glance, we perceive why Jefferson was unable to
establish a workable peace policy.

It was a vicious — a desperate situation. November
21, 1806, Napoleon sent forth his Berlin decree. After
that, no American vessel that had touched at an English
port could enter a French port. November 11, 1807,
came the retaliatory British Order in Council, closing
all Napoleon's ports, whether in France or elsewhere.
Next, Napoleon, December 17, issued his Milan decree,
authorizing the seizure of any vessel that had paid
British port-dues, or had permitted herself to be
searched. Here, then, was a joke for the gods — Ho-
meric their laughter, sardonic their smiles. The British
would search us, whether or no; and, because the
British searched us, the French would seize us. It was
a *reductio ad absurdum*. Could Jefferson extricate himself from so illogical a situation?

One way out of the difficulty was to keep our ships
at home.[1] Then, nobody could search them or seize
them. December 22, 1807, Jefferson's Embargo Act
was passed by Congress, and various enabling measures
were subsequently adopted. Sure enough, the seizures

---

[1] One effect of the British Orders in Council and French Imperial decrees was
to cause the failure of American shipping houses. For instance, that of Beckford
& Bates, Boston. Joshua Bates then went to Europe as an agent of William Gray.
In the counting-room of Hope & Co. at Havre, he won the confidence of Peter
Caesar Labouchere, of Hope & Co., and, subsequently through Labouchere,
founded the house of Baring Bros. & Co. Bates was trying to get two cargoes of
cotton sold on a lower commission than another Havre house had offered. In
the course of the talk, it developed that he himself, being on salary, would not
profit by the lower commission. Old Mr. Labouchere, behind his newspaper
heard it all. When Bates asked how he could get a conveyance to Paris, Labouchere
offered him his own chaise. The young American had quite won him.

ceased. But were the French hurt? Not in the slightest; and the British had the ocean and its trade all to themselves. We were the victims. Like a modern siren, wailing in the fog, sounded the protest of the New England vessel-owners. The Federalists added their curses to the anti-Jeffersonian chorus. Jefferson clung to his embargo, as a device preferable to war; but, it had to go by the board. Congress repealed it, and passed the Non-Intercourse Act, March 1, 1809, thus stimulating home manufactures. So, after all, England would get the worst of it, in one way at least — she would sell America less; she would cease to supply many articles customarily sent hither since early colonial times.

On the whole, Jefferson had reason to feel that his first administration was good; but his second was far below the mark. Its lapses were due to his singular belief that the peaceful republic could get along without a navy, and yet send its merchant ships out upon the seas, dominated by a fighting nation with high ideas of its own primacy. Sir James Mackintosh spoke of a statesman as "a philosopher in action." Burke, to him, was "the greatest philosopher in action that the world ever saw." But John Randolph said: "I do not wish another philosopher for President." He wanted Monroe, he added. Henry Adams is altogether too hard on Jefferson, whose inconsistencies were as apparent to his friends as to his opponents. Madison advised that "allowances be made for them."[1]

Like the astute politician General Samuel Smith, many another man thought Monroe in line for the presidency as Jefferson's immediate successor. Knowing ones regarded Monroe's recent experiences as excellent lessons that would be of value to him should Napoleon continue to keep the British on edge. They understood why he had not come home with the

---

[1] Julius Melbourn, edited by a late member of Congress, 1847, p. 92. According to Melbourn, Monroe was "mild and moderate." Without brilliancy of talents, he "seemed rather to float than to swim." "Undoubtedly, however, he possessed much prudence and sagacity." As a politician, he was "cautious and wary." p. 96.

Floridas in his pocket, and why he had sought to pacify British belligerency. On the other hand, Monroe had disappointed Jefferson. We have already referred to the suggestion that Madison might have pre-arranged Monroe's diplomatic failure by setting a task and imposing conditions impossible to carry out. If so, the time-clock was well set to go off just as Jefferson, troubled with racking presidential pains, would be looking about him for some one of his own stamp to take his place. Madison loved Monroe but he also loved Madison; and who can blame him? "Jefferson," says Edward Channing,[1] "affected neutrality as between Madison and Monroe. . . . Monroe had for a long time been a political pupil of Jefferson's; but of late years Madison had been in such close official relations that he had the first chance. Besides, Monroe had coquetted with John Randolph and the irreconcilables, and, by breaking his instructions, had brought his diplomatic career to an unpleasant close, and in so doing had greatly disturbed Jefferson. Under these circumstances, the administration phalanx in Congress rallied to the support of Madison."

But is it a fact that Monroe coquetted with Randolph? We find nothing in Monroe's letters to warrant the assertion. As for Randolph, he flattered Monroe, cajoled him, and finally tried to make a tool of him. Henry Adams in his life of the Roanoke eccentric, in the chapter headed "John Randolph's Schism," in the third volume of his history (1805-1809) and on various other pages of his extraordinarily vigorous and impressive works, brings out the relations of the two Virginians with edifying completeness. John Randolph of Roanoke can hardly be understood unless we take into account his environment — some of the characteristics of the age he lived in. Very human, very vengeful were the gentry of the period. John James Audubon tells us of a voyage to America in a motley company of refugees

---

[1] The Jeffersonian System (American Nation Series, Vol. XII), pp. 220-223. See Jefferson's letters to Monroe, Jefferson's Works (Ford), Vol. IX, p. 176 et seq.

in 1806. A lady's bonnet blew overboard. A French officer plunged into the sea after it. That night the passengers were startled by shots on deck. It proved to be a duel — and the gallant rescuer was dead; shot by the lady's lover. Nor were our diplomatic frictions unheeded on this side of the sea. Heated controversies grew out of them — deadly disputes, indeed. It was still the day of the duel. Dr. J. Marion Sims,[1] speaking of a still later period, declared the duello to be "the bane of life." In Petersburg, John Daly Burk, author of an excellent history of Virginia, lawyer, poet, playwright, an ardent liberty-lover and Anglophobe, became a victim. He was in the dining-room at Powell's Tavern, and was denouncing the French, in connection with the Armstrong-Champagny[2] episode. He said they were "a pack of rascals." M. Felix Coquebert, a Frenchman, overheard him and cried out, protesting. "Who are you, sir?" asked Burk[3]; adding: "you can interpret what I said as you like." "Very well, sir";

[1] Story of My Life, Dr. J. Marion Sims, 1884, edited by his son, H. Marion Sims. Also see Life and Times of Walter Addison, for an account of the duel of Mason and Jack McCarty. McCarty, a dead shot, proposed that the two should take hold of hands and jump from the top of the Capitol.

[2] Jean Baptiste de Champagny took Talleyrand's place as Foreign Minister. Napoleon wrote him, February 2, 1808, to let Armstrong know that if America should become his ally he would make Spain give her the Floridas. He would also arrange the western boundary of Louisiana to suit America. Armstrong wrote to Madison, February 15: "With one hand they offer us the blessing of equal alliance against Great Britain; with the other they menace us with war if we do not accept this kindness; and with both they pick our pockets with all imaginable diligence, dexterity and impudence."—Adams, History, "The *Dos de Maio*," Vol. IV, p. 295.

[3] Burk's story is romantic. On the steps of Trinity College, Dublin, he saw British soldiers taking a man to drum-head execution. He called other students, and his party bowled the soldiers over and rescued the captive. Burk fled to a book-seller's shop. His Irish wolf dog at the door kept his pursuers back until he escaped in woman's clothes at the rear of the house. He was "Miss Daly"; and that is how the "Daly" got into his name. He was caught in Boston and was about to be hanged at the yard's-arm when Colonel Aaron Burr saved him. He wrote "Bunker Hill," a play. President John Adams went to see it. "Sir," said he to Burk, "my friend General Warren was a scholar and a gentleman, but your author has made him a bully and a blackguard." Jefferson encouraged Burk, and John Randolph of Roanoke liked him. Poets wrote of him in *The Portfolio*. He was buried in a beautiful garden by the Appomattox. His son, John Junius Burk, was a noted judge in Louisiana. Skelton Jones, connected with Burk's History of Virginia, also lost his life in a duel. In the spring of 1800, there were twenty-one duels within six weeks. Six men were killed and eleven were wounded.

and at sunrise next day, in a piney grove, Burk, a handsome, fine man, tore open his waistcoat as he leaped in the air and fell; shot through the heart.

Not only were those our duelling days, but it was a period of contentiousness, of hot-blood, of bravado, of peppery resentment. One had to show spirit or slink out of the circle of gentility. Manhood resentment of a noble sort was common enough on the border; and your Indian was as apt to bristle on a point of honor as was a white man. At Vincennes, in 1811, General Harrison ordered a chair to be brought for Tecumseh. The man who fetched it bowed and said: "Warrior, your father, General Harrison, offers you a seat." "My father!" said Tecumseh, lifting his long arms aloft; "the sun is my father, and the earth is my mother; she gives me nourishment and I repose upon her bosom." And down he sat, with grace enough to excuse his fine old grandiloquence. We shall soon hear from him. He stuck his tomahawk into history's tree, and it is still there.

John Randolph of Roanoke was a product of these days of Tecumsehs, duelling-pistols, and stormy factional democracy. If he had no Tecumseh in him, he at least had some of the blood of Pocahontas, as well as plantation aristocracy. He had his slaves, his thoroughbreds and his expansive acres. He often rode breakneck, mile after mile; and is said to have nearly killed William H. Crawford of Georgia, who accompanied him on one of these mad cross-country dashes.

Such was the man who selected Monroe as a favorite, and Madison as anything but a favorite. He was quick to criticize Jefferson, too; and, at last, worked up an opposition both to the President and Secretary of State. For a long time Randolph's schism seemed to be a mere whim. Everything was done in secret at the Capitol and White House; but Randolph said such cutting things, his sarcasms were so keenly true, that people began to suspect a split in the Republican party. Randolph's real purpose was to keep Madison

out of the presidency. So when the Administration
asked Congress to pass the two-million act, and Madison
told Randolph, chairman of the Ways and Means
Committee, that we must give that sum to France for
Florida "or have a Spanish and French War," Randolph saw his opportunity to begin a quarrel. He said
that "his confidence in the Secretary of State had never
been high, but now it was gone forever." The issue
was joined. Jefferson and Madison won in the House
by seventy-six to fifty-four. Henry Adams[1] says: "The
malcontents felt that for the first time in the history of
their party the whip of Executive power had been
snapped over their heads." Madison wanted to coerce
England through restrictions in trade — "peaceable
coercion," Jefferson called it. In the Senate, the
ambitious General Samuel Smith[2] introduced three non-
importation resolutions. They embarrassed Jefferson,
who "disliked and dreaded the point in dispute with
England." The resolutions were modified. Henry
Adams[3] adds:

"The reason of this halting movement had been explained by
Merry to Lord Mulgrave nearly two weeks before. The Senate
stumbled over the important personality of James Monroe. The
next Presidential election some three years distant, warped the
national policy in regard to foreign encroachment. Senator Samuel
Smith, ambitious to distinguish himself in diplomacy, having
failed to obtain the mission to Paris, wished the dignity of a special
envoy to London, and was supported by Wilson Cary Nicholas.
The friends of Madison were willing to depress Monroe, whom John
Randolph was trying to elevate. Even Mrs. Madison[4] in the
excitement of electioneering allowed herself to talk in general
society very slightingly of Monroe, and there were reasons which
made interference from Mrs. Madison peculiarly irritating to

---

[1] H. Adams, History, Vol. III, p.139.
[2] The Baltimore Smiths who figure in the Senate and Cabinet were Samuel and
Robert — sons of John, merchant, ship owner and Revolutionary patriot. "Sam"
it was who fought so well at Mud Island in the Delaware, aided by the Frenchman
Fleury.
[3] H. Adams, History, Vol. III, pp. 151-152. Anthony Merry, British Minister,
to Lord Mulgrave; Mss. British Archives.
[4] Diary of John Quincy Adams, March 14, 1806, Vol. I, p. 420: "Mr. Bayard
told me he had last evening some conversation with Mrs. Madison upon the
presidential election now so warmly carried on, in which she spoke very slightingly
of Mr. Monroe."

Monroe's friends. Dr. Logan, the Senator from Pennsylvania, while helping Madison to satisfy Napoleon in regard to St. Domingo, was prominent in suggesting that it would be well to set Monroe gently aside.[1] This coalition of Madison, Smith, Logan, and Wilson Cary Nicholas was so strong as to control the Senate."

From the Senate, the non-importation question got into the House. Chairman Randolph would not report on British relations, but one day, when he was sick in bed, the House voted to take the matter out of his hands. A debate followed. It lasted many days. Finally, in came Nemesis with the sarcastic mouth, pale as a ghost. He was "manacled, handcuffed, and tongue-tied," he said, but he would "hobble over the subject as well as his fettered limbs and palsied tongue would enable him to do it." Then he uttered his memorable philippic against Jefferson, Madison and their adherents in Congress. He paid his respects to Representatives Gregg and Crowninshield who had just spoken: "The proper argument for such statesmen are a strait-waistcoat, a dark-room, water-gruel and depletion." Crowninshield wanted to confiscate British property. "God help you if these are your ways and means of carrying on war." He protested against "secret, irresponsible, over-ruling influence," against an "invisible, inscrutable, unconstitutional Cabinet, without responsibility, unknown to the Constitution. I speak of back-stairs influence — of men who bring messages to this House, which, though they do not appear on the Journals, govern its decisions."

Henry Adams thinks that, if Randolph had contented himself with this first assault, he would have done actual good; but he kept up the assaults, day after day, attacking Madison for the manner in which he had managed affairs. "I do not speak of the negotiator [Monroe] — God forbid! — but of those who drew the instructions of the man who negotiated." On April 7; he cut loose from the administration, carrying with

---

[1] Diary of John Quincy Adams, February 1, 1806, Vol. I, p. 395.

him "some twenty-five or thirty of the ablest Republicans in Congress." "Meanwhile," says Adams,[1] "the President busily conciliated opposition; and his first thought was of Monroe in London, certain to become the centre of intrigue." Randolph likewise wrote to Monroe "that the Republican party was broken to pieces and that the 'old Republicans' were united in his support against Madison for the Presidency."[2] April 22, he wrote: "A decided division has taken place in the Republican party." Other letters followed. In a long one from Bizarre, Randolph flattered Monroe with lavish brush — "laid it on thick," as the phrase goes; too thick, of course, since Monroe was a man of discernment, and modest withal. Again Randolph wrote: "We don't want a Yazoo president." He harped on the corrupt Yazoo land deal in Georgia, when the Legislature of that State let millions of acres go at two and one-half cents an acre.

Nathaniel Macon,[3] Speaker of the House, and Joseph H. Nicholson, of Maryland, were among Randolph's "Old Republicans." So were Joseph Clay of Philadelphia, Colonel John Taylor of Carolina and Littleton Tazewell — all "unshaken friends of Monroe" all excellent men. Jefferson adroitly made Nicholson judge. Randolph wrote from Richmond to Nicholson, during the Burr trial, expressing astonishment that Burr's partner in the big plot, Wilkinson, should be "on the very summit of Executive favor, whilst James Monroe is denounced." Randolph might well have felt disgust; for Monroe's treaty had served to eliminate him from the presidential contest; Jefferson had smothered it; Monroe was coming home humiliated and with the feeling that he had been scurvily treated

---

[1] H. Adams, History, Vol. III, p. 165. Jefferson to Monroe, March 16, 1806; Jefferson Mss.

[2] Life of John Randolph by Henry Adams, pp. 199-202.

[3] Macon wrote to Nicholson, April 21, 1811: "Can you tell me how the change in the Department of State was brought about? The office of State seems to be the path to the Presidency and the mission to Russia a port of political deathbed." He thought Monroe would be hard pressed with British negotiations on account of the treaty he made.

by the very men whom he had served with an eye to
the success of the administration and the good of the
country.

Monroe left London, October 29, 1807; and, after a
long wait for a fair wind, on November 14 sailed in
the ship "Augustus" from Portsmouth for home. His
family remained oversea. Henry Adams[1] notes that,
during our diplomat's five years abroad, he had been
"insulted by every Foreign Secretary in France, Spain
and England." He adds, with severity, if not injustice:

'In many respects Monroe's career was unparalleled, but he
was singular above all in the experience of being disowned by
two Presidents as strongly opposed to each other as Washington
and Jefferson, and of being sacrificed by two secretaries as widely
different as Timothy Pickering[2] and James Madison. . . . Doubtless only personal friendship and the fear of strengthening Federalist influence prevented President Jefferson from denouncing
Monroe's conduct as forcibly as President Washington had
denounced it ten years before; and Jefferson's grounds of complaint were more serious than Washington's. Monroe expected
and even courted martyrdom, and never quite forgot the treatment he received. In private, George Hay, Monroe's son-in-law,
who knew all the secrets of his career, spoke afterward of Jefferson
as 'one of the most insincere men in the world; . . . his enmity
to Mr. Monroe was inveterate, though disguised, as he was at the
bottom of all the opposition to Mr. Monroe in Virginia.' "[3]

No doubt Judge Hay knew some of Monroe's secrets;
but in that time of many troubles he may have made
unwarranted assumptions; just as Adams appears to
do in this chapter. The cold facts are: Monroe exercised
unusual skill and admirable judgment in France and
Spain. In England he gave in on impressment, it is
true; but what happened after a bloody war when eight
wise peacemakers put their heads together at Ghent?
They also put aside impressment — for a later treaty.

---

[1] In his chapter headed "Insults and Popularity," Vol. IV, History of the United
States, pp. 126-151.
[2] For Pickering's commendation of Monroe, see H. Adams, Vol. IV, pp. 129, 130;
Pickering to Thomas Fitzsimmons, December 4, 1807.
[3] Diary of John Quincy Adams, May 23, 1824, Vol. IV, p. 348.

John Bull, cousin of Squire Western, was own brother to Sir Giles Overreach.[1]

Charming, indeed, is the chapter in which Adams reviews Monroe's diplomatic disasters, but what he says is mainly speculation. Monroe's efforts to acquire Florida involved an immense deal of intelligent labor; his Louisiana success cost him little, and won him enough glory to offset the discredit of the most censorious of his critics.

Monroe reached Norfolk on December 13; Washington on the twenty-second, where he had a talk with Madison; and probably spent Christmas at his home in Albemarle. Though there were signs that he meant to go into the opposition, he appears to have realized the futility of such a course. He soon witnessed the complete discomfiture of his Randolphian friends. January 21, 1808, Madison was nominated by a caucus of the Virginia Legislature. January 23, Congress held its caucus. Of the one hundred and thirty republican members of the House and Senate, but eighty-nine attended it. Madison received eighty-three votes; Monroe three and George Clinton, three. For a long while thereafter, Randolph worked on Monroe's wounded pride; but later turned on him. His letter to Monroe dated Bell Tavern, Monday night, January 14, 1811, shows clearly his realization that it was useless to court a man so unwilling to be manipulated.

Nevertheless Monroe's return from London was in sackcloth, if not in ashes; just as his return from Paris had been ten years before. History was repeating itself

---

[1] Students of Henry Adams would do well to follow his "Insults and Popularity," Chapter on Monroe (Vol. IV) with an examination of Monroe's letters to Colonel John Taylor of Caroline in Vol. V of Writings of Monroe. In these Monroe goes over the ground of his discomfiture and reasons out the ethical questions involved. What does a man owe to his party? Should he not be very careful, indeed, before harboring factional spirit? There was a patriotic course, as a rule; this course a man should find and take. It would hurt him sorely to feel that, in attacking the administration, he should play into the hands of the enemy. Let his smarts heal themselves. Taylor, says S. M. Hamilton, differed with Monroe. What he wanted for the minority was "a manly avowal of principle; Monroe should adopt the course he took in 1797; the true motive for guidance is to take office if good can be done thereby."

in his case, surely. He had then busied himself writing his "View"; now he wrote a defense of his diplomacy in England. Dated April 5, 1808, it occupied ten folio pages of the State Papers.[1] Nor does the parallel end here. He was elected Governor in 1799; and now, having been elected to the Virginia House of Delegates (for the third time) in the spring of 1810, he was again chosen Governor[2] of the State, serving from January to November, 1811. We have a good glimpse of him at this period in a letter by Nicholas Biddle printed in a book[3] about a contemporary, W. S. Shaw, who was secretary to President John Adams. "While I was in Virginia," wrote Nicholas Biddle, "I saw Mr. Monroe who is calmly sitting down to the culture of tobacco, near Charlottesville. His estate is very good, but has been out of order during his absence. However he has received another handsome estate left to him by an uncle." He was Judge Jones's executor and his duties as such, with other family matters, kept him employed for a considerable time.

It was not long before Madison had to pay a penalty for suppressing the Monroe-Pinkney treaty. He received one hundred and twenty-two electoral votes in a total of one hundred and seventy-five,[4] and succeeded Jefferson as President, March 4, 1809. He regarded the British outlook as favorable, since young Mr. Erskine was friendly, sanguine and zealous in

---

[1] While Monroe's letters to Jefferson and Madison during the winter and spring of 1808 are couched in friendly terms, there is a reserve that bespeaks a grievance. These letters are to be found in Writings of Monroe, Vol. V, pp. 20 *et seq.* The memoranda sent to Madison may be found in the same volume, pp. 39-46. Most of the letters bear the Richmond date. Monroe returned to Albemarle late in April. In midsummer he was in Bedford county and in September in Albemarle. It was much the same in 1809.

[2] Jefferson wrote to Monroe congratulating him on his election as Governor. It was a testimony to his fidelity in principle.— Jefferson to Monroe, January 25, 1811.

[3] Memorials of William Smith Shaw, by Joseph B. Felt, 1852. Biddle's letter was to Colonel George Gibbs, the Boston mineralogist. Biddle wrote in a friendly way to Monroe, November 18, 1808; and in his reply, January 7, 1809, Monroe confessed that it pained him to touch upon his differences with his old associates. Works, V, 85.

[4] George Clinton, Vice-President, had 113 votes. The Federalist vote was Charles C. Pinckney, 47 and Rufus King, 47.

his efforts to put aside difficulties. Erskine[1] promised
that the Orders in Council should be withdrawn if the
United States would hold fast to its rule of non-intercourse with France, pending the repeal of the French
decrees. He also agreed that an adjustment of the
Leopard-Chesapeake affairs should be undertaken.
Accordingly Madison (April 19, 1809) lifted the non-
intercourse act as far as Great Britain was concerned;
and, on June 10, "a thousand ships . . . spread their
wings like a flock of long-imprisoned birds, and flew
out to sea." [2] But soon Madison wrote to Jefferson:
"Erskine is in a ticklish situation with his government."
Foreign Minister Canning, in fact, repudiated Erskine
just as Jefferson and Madison had repudiated Monroe.
It was tit for tat. Erskine was recalled (August 9,
1809); Francis James Jackson sent in his place. This
was "Copenhagen Jackson" who was with the British
fleet at the time of the outrage at that capital. When
Madison learned that the British were still stubborn
he proclaimed non-intercourse again, August 9. March
23, 1810, Napoleon issued his Rambouillet decree,
confiscating a hundred American craft.

In England, meanwhile, the Grenville Ministry had
fallen — not on account of Lord Grenville's "reckless
foreign policy," but on the issues of the abolition of
the slave trade and Catholic emancipation. The union
of aristocratic Grenville Whigs and Sidmouth Tories
was a thing of the past; from this time until Waterloo,
and long after, the Tories alone would hold sway.
With the Duke of Portland as the titular chief, the
real brains of the Ministry were lodged in the head of
George Canning, Foreign Secretary. Now, it so happens

---

[1] Erskine was the son of Lord Erskine, and owed his appointment to Charles
James Fox. He was half Republican by education, half American by marriage;
and, probably, like all British liberals, he felt in secret an entire want of confidence
in Canning and a positive antipathy to the Tory commercial system. . . . The
course of his [Canning's] own acts and Perceval's measures, suggested that he did
not intend to offer any terms which the United States could accept. H. Adams,
History, Vol. V, Chapter 3.

[2] James Madison, by Sydney Howard Gay, 1884, p. 286 — a book that is criticized as having too strong a tincture of Federalism.

that Canning not only played a famous part as an
anti-American in the events leading up to the War of
1812 but as a pro-American ten years later. He did all
he could to down Madison and Monroe while the war
was threatening, and favored the formation of the
Monroe doctrine after the war was over. Canning,
then, is an especially large figure in our story. Who was
he?

George Canning was born in the parish of Mary-le-
bone, London, April 11, 1770. His branch of the
Cannings had been identified with Ireland since Queen
Elizabeth granted George Canning a manor in the
county of Londonderry. His father, also George, had
married a dowerless beauty, all for love's sake, and
had been set adrift with a pittance and the stern
reminder that it would not be augmented on the death
of his father. Called to the bar in London, he went in
for poetry and politics, but "died of a broken heart on
the very first birthday of his illustrious son, who with
his mother, was left in such circumstances of destitution
that she was obliged, for her maintenance, to attempt
the stage." She appeared as Jane Shore to Garrick's
Lord Hastings. But she was not successful in London
and went to the provinces, where she married an actor.
She was a beautiful and accomplished woman and in
her later years was happy in the attentions of her son
who was educated at Eton through the generosity of
an uncle.[1] A pupil under Pitt, Canning's "brilliant
rhetoric gave him power over the House of Commons,
while the vigor and energy of his mind gave a new
color to the war." So says Green, who reminds us that
at no time had opposition to Napoleon seemed so
hopeless. Whatever Canning did to check France at
sea, he could do nothing to arrest her progress on land.
Napoleon was drunk with success. He was absolutely
master of Western Europe, "and its whole face changed

---

[1] Memoirs of George Canning, by Samuel F. Lea, 1829, 2 vols. An old playbill
of the Theatre Royal, August 23, 1771, announces "Othello," followed by the farce
"Like Master Like Man." "Mrs. Reddish, who played Leonora in the farce, was,
we presume, the mother of George Canning."

as at an enchanter's touch." Napoleon placed three
of his brothers on three thrones. Only when after the
Treaty of Fontainebleau, October, 1807, he seized first
Portugal and then Spain, did his luck fail him. Wellington arose. Austria allied herself with Spain. Affairs
went somewhat better for the Allies until Wagram
and the failure of the British expedition against
Antwerp. This failure caused the fall of the Portland
Ministry. Canning laid the blame on Lord Castlereagh[1]
and they subsequently fought a duel. A new ministry
was formed under Spencer Perceval, "an illustrious
mediocrity of the narrowest type." An elder brother
of Wellington, the Marquis of Wellesley, became Foreign
Secretary.[2]

Let us bear in mind that there was fear in England
lest Napoleon should land in America and "take the
lead of those who have money, talents, audacity and
despair."[3]

Canning thought he had a just grievance against
America. "Who," he asked, "would have expected to
see this favorite child of freedom leagued with the
oppressor of the world?"[4] But he could not see how
the injustice of search and impressment rankled in the
American mind. Gallatin said of his dexterity in the
Leopard-Chesapeake affair: "He applied the curb and
the spur at the same moment with marvelous audacity."
He sent George Henry Rose to Washington "to amuse
Jefferson"; and at the same time did all he could to
suppress American shipping. Rose was to smooth
over the Chesapeake affair. He sailed from Portsmouth
ahead of Monroe, who, however, beat him in the race.
Behind the British Minister's carriage when he rode

---

[1] Robert Stuart, Viscount Castlereagh (Marquis of Londonderry) (1769-1822);
enemy of the French Revolution; soul of the coalition against Napoleon; furnished
subsidies to the Powers; at the Congress of Vienna in 1815, he sacrified Poland,
Belgium, Saxony and Genoa. The strain was too great for him. His mind gave
way. He opened his carotid artery with his penknife.

[2] There were three of these Wellesleys (or Wesleys): Richard Colley, b. 1760;
Arthur, b. 1769; and Henry, b. 1773.

[3] Croker's Correspondence and Diaries, Vol. I, p. 88.

[4] Speeches of Canning.

to church, within sight of representatives of American democracy in Washington, were two liveried servants with drawn swords.[1]

Monroe soon rejoined this democratic group at the national capital where he was very much needed. When Madison formed his cabinet, Gallatin, who should have been Secretary of State, was found to be unacceptable to the Smith senatorial faction of the Republican party; so Robert Smith was given that post. Randolph said that Madison was "president *de jure* only. Who exercises the office *de facto*, I know not, but it seems agreed on all hands that there is something behind the throne greater than the throne itself." Madison failed to support Gallatin in his effort to re-charter the first bank of the United States.[2] Gallatin wanted to resign. "The Administration," asserts John Austin Stevens, "was going to pieces by sheer incapacity. The leaders took alarm and the Cabinet was reconstructed."[3] In February, 1811, Pinkney took "inamicable leave" of London, and came home. After the affair of the "President" and "Little Belt" in May, 1811, the young men of the country thought more and more about war. The election demonstrated that. Madison bought the secret papers which a certain John Henry had prepared for sale in London, but which the British refused to take, although the Governor-General of Canada, Sir James Craig, had sent the spy down into New England. Henry Adams says that Madison got a poor bargain; nevertheless the spy's account served as newspaper ammunition in the spring and summer of 1812. Madison told England, that, as Napoleon had revoked his decrees (November 1, 1810), the British orders ought also to be cancelled. The British made difficulties.

---

[1] Walter Dulay Addison, St. John's Church, Georgetown, 1809.

[2] The second bank of the United States was authorized under a law approved by Madison, April 10, 1816. "Three men," says Dr. K. C. Babcock in "The Rise of American Nationality" "were prominent in the debates on the bill — Calhoun, Clay and Webster." Clay had voted against re-chartering the first bank.

[3] Life of Gallatin, p. 301.

Finally, they withdrew their orders, June 23, 1812 —
just a little too late, just four days after something had
happened that made the withdrawal a superfluous
proceeding. The King, poor soul, had gone mad; a
regent ruled; Perceval was assassinated, and Lord
Liverpool was Prime Minister.

When the Twelfth Congress met, November 4, 1811,
young men, whelps of the earlier war time, held sway
in the House. This was the autumn when Henry Clay,[1]
six times Speaker, made his debut. He avowed himself
in favor of a war against England. What was America
obliged to do? "To bear the actual cuffs of arrogance,
that we may escape a chimerical French subjugation.
We are called upon to submit to debasement, dishonor
and disgrace; to bow the neck to royal insolence."
There spoke the West. By and by Calhoun would
voice the South, logically, without a stammering note.
Clay's utterance may have been declamatory, but it
had the merit of dissipating the fog — especially the
French fog. It was the time of Felix Grundy, Langdon
Cheves and William Lowndes. According to an old
Federalist assertion, Clay headed a committee that
proceeded from the Capitol to the White House and
notified Madison that he must either send a war
message to Congress or fail to succeed himself. The
story ends with the surrender of the elder statesman
to the young men who had the audacity to go coerce
him in his den. It is an interesting story, but not true.[2]
Clay himself denied it. Of his own accord, Madison
saw that the commercial devices used by him while in
Jefferson's Cabinet and since he himself had become
chief, were inadequate. He had been his own Secretary
of State practically; for Smith could not write the
necessary papers, much less direct the affairs of the
department. Time had come for a change. Monroe

---

[1] Clay was at the front for forty years. He wrote to Monroe that he preferred
the turbulent House to the solemn Senate; November, 1810, Schouler, Vol. II, p. 336.

[2] Hunt says, Life of Madison, p. 317: "Mr. Henry Adams, in his Life of Albert
Gallatin (p. 456 *et seq.*) gives all the proofs of this charge that the Federalists could
produce and pronounces it unfounded."

was the most trustworthy man. He and Monroe had
almost ceased to write to each other. But they must
come together. Smith must go. Madison summoned
Smith and frankly told him what he thought of him.
Smith wanted to go to England as Minister, or to be
elevated to the Supreme Court. Madison said he would
send him to St. Petersburg. This did not suit Smith,
who, being thus dismissed, attacked his former chief.

There are several letters in the Bureau of Rolls[1]
that tell of Monroe's transfer from the gubernatorial
chair at Richmond to the office of Secretary of State
at Washington.

Monroe wrote from Albemarle, February 25, 1810,
to Senator Richard Brent of Virginia, telling of a visit
from Jefferson, who suggested that Monroe should
take the governorship of Louisiana or else a military
position. Monroe replied that he wanted neither; but,
said he, had Mr. Madison offered him a seat in the
Cabinet he would have accepted it. As a matter of
fact, he was not desirous of any office. In course of
time Brent replied, suggesting that Monroe should
take the portfolio of State. Writing from Richmond,
March 18, 1811, Monroe expressed doubt as to whether
he should embrace the opportunity offered him. What
did Brent think? March 18, he wrote to Brent again.
By whom had Brent been consulted, the President, or
Mr. Gallatin, or both? Would the President write
such a letter (that might be read to the Legislature)
as would justify his retirement from the executive office
in Virginia? His State had treated him so well, so
appreciatively, that this much was due to her. Madison
wrote on the twentieth, and Monroe replied on the
twenty-third, saying that he was disposed to take hold.
The promotion of the public happiness would be his
aim. On the twenty-ninth he accepted outright; he
would be ready, he said, to leave Richmond the day

---

[1] Bureau of Rolls, letters to Brent, pp. 267, 268; Monroe to Madison, pp. 307,
308; there are many letters from Madison to Monroe relating to the war, pp. 146-
156.

after the commission and documents should be received.

This commission soon reached him; and, on April 2, 1811, he began his duties in the State Department. As the change was made during the recess of the Senate, the nomination was not sent in until November 13. On the twenty-fifth of that month he was confirmed. At once Madison felt his arm strengthened for a conflict. which he had almost ceased to evade — which was bound to come. It is true that a newly appointed British Minister, John Augustus Foster, — who had arrived at Washington, still endeavored with some skill to sustain various British contentions. But "the diplomatic insolvency inherited from Merry, Rose, Erskine and Jackson became more complete with every year that passed."[1] Such was the case with the general situation. "Awkward as Madison's position was, that of Monroe was many degrees worse. . . . In July he found himself in painful straits." He was obliged to blame Jonathan Russell, of the American Legation at Paris, for questioning the revocation of the French decrees. When Foster protested against the seizure of West Florida, Monroe had to resent "the assertion that West Florida belonged to Spain, for his character as a man of sense, if not truth, was involved in the assertion that he had himself bought West Florida in his Louisiana purchase." Monroe "pained" Foster[2] by calling his attention to the fact that "the United States showed sufficient forbearance in not assisting the insurgents of South America." Was Monroe even then mulling the Monroe Doctrine in his mind? "Foster," says Adams, "was obliged to ignore the meaning of this pointed remark, while his inquiries how far the American Government meant to carry its seizures of Spanish territory drew from Monroe no answer but a laugh. The Secretary seemed a transformed man. Not only did he show no dread of interference from England in Florida, but he took an equally

---

[1] H. Adams, History, Vol. VI, Chapter 2, "The Little Belt."

[2] H. Adams, History, Vol. VI, pp. 25-45.   Foster to Wellesley, July 5, 1811.

indifferent air on every other matter except one. He had not a word about impressments; he betrayed no wish to trouble himself about the 'Chesapeake affair'; he made no haste in apologizing for the 'Little Belt'; but the Orders of Council — these and nothing else — formed the issue on which a change was to depend." The more ground Foster lost the more threats he made. July 18 he wrote that England would retaliate for the non-importation act. "While this threat," adds Adams, "was all that England offered for Monroe's friendship, news arrived on the same day that Napoleon, May 4, had opened his ports to American Commerce. Not till then did Monroe give way, and turn his back upon England and his old political friends. July 24 Monroe sent his answer to the British Minister's argument.[1] In substance this note, though long, contained nothing new; but in effect it was an ultimatum which left England to choose between concession and war." "Your Lordship," wrote Foster to Wellesley, "cannot expect to hear of any change till Congress meets." As for Serurier who had succeeded Turreau as Minister for France, he likewise was writing home. Hugues Bernard Maret, Duc de Bassano, had supplanted Champagny in Paris, and to him Serurier addressed a remarkable note concerning Monroe.[2] It had come to his ears that Napoleon had instructed French Consuls in the United States to issue certificates to the American vessels about to sail for France. Monroe sent for Serurier, who wrote:

"Mr. Monroe's countenance was absolutely distorted (*tout-a-fait decomposée*). I could not conceive how an object apparently so unimportant, could affect him, so keenly. He continued thus: 'You are witness, sir, to the candor of our motives, to the loyalty of our principles, to our immovable fidelity to our engagements. In spite of party clamor and the extreme difficulty of the circumstances, we persevere in our system; but your Government abandons us to the attacks of its enemies and ours by not fulfilling on its side the conditions set forth in the President's proclamation. . . .

---

[1] State Papers, Vol. III, p. 439.
[2] Serurier to Maret, June 30, 1811, as quoted by Adams.

The Administration finds itself in the most extreme embarrassment (*dans le plus extreme embarras*); it knows neither what to expect from you, nor what to say to its constitutents."

Adams ironically hints that Monroe had caught the European tone. He satirizes at Monroe's expense. Very different was the estimate of the satirist's grandfather[1] who declares that Monroe's duties at this critical time — "a time full of difficulty and danger" — were "performed with untiring assiduity, with universally acknowledged ability, and with a zeal of patriotism which counted health, fortune and life itself for nothing in the ardor of self devotion to the cause of his country."

If Monroe's countenance were "distorted" on the occasion just mentioned, it was frigidly composed when Serurier saw him next — after the arrival of the "Essex" with dispatches: "I found him icy. . . . 1 was heard with politeness, but coldly. . . . Already, within a few days, I notice a change in the manners of every one about me." Monroe's high tone caused Serurier to reflect it. July 4, Monroe sent Joel Barlow, the new minister, off for France; next day, he called Barlow back. July 9 Monroe had "a striking" interview with Serurier, "in which the Secretary of State became more impassioned than ever." And now we come to Serurier's report of the interview which we feel obliged to give for what it is worth. Monroe is reported to have said: "People in Europe suppose us to be merchants, occupied exclusively with pepper and ginger. They are much deceived, and I hope we shall prove it. The immense majority of citizens do not belong to this class, and are, as much as you Europeans, controlled by principles of honor and dignity. I never knew what trade was. The President is as much a stranger to it as I; and we accord to commerce only the protection that we owe it, as every government owes it to an interesting class of citizens."

---

[1] Life of James Monroe, by John Quincy Adams, p. 270.

Viewed in the cold light of these present days of
looming commercialism these were unfortunate words
in the mouth of Spence Monroe's son; but when spoken
into the ear of Monsieur Serurier, the accomplished
diplomat, they served a purpose. Monroe wished to
stress a new and significant matter. At last a new
spirit was rising. An American could be as proud as
Tecumseh upon occasion. Besides, there was such a
thing as stretching patience and continuing to stretch
it until, by and by something happened. Madison and
Monroe were at the end of patience. France continually tried to fool them. England was ceaselessly
irritating. Adams says: "Under such circumstances,
Monroe needed more than common powers in order to
do his part. Talleyrand himself would have found his
impassive countenance tried by assuring Foster in the
morning that the decrees were repealed, and in rating
Serurier in the afternoon because they were in force."
Not that such double-dealing actually happened; but
the opportunity for appositeness was too good to miss.
We have the word of John Quincy Adams for it that
duplicity was foreign to Monroe's nature. He knew
Monroe well. He appreciated, too, the perilous situation of the whole country, with New England clamorous,
and vengeful enemies talking of a Tippecanoe just
passed and òther Tippecanoes to come. "The Constitution" he said, "had never before been subjected
to the trial of a formidable foreign war." But Monroe
has had many severe critics. For instance, Edward
Everett Hale.[1] His contention is that the country
got along in spite of Jefferson, Madison and Monroe.
"The people of America govern America," he avers.
Hale has a chapter on Monroe, following one on "The
Virginian Dynasty." He says:

"Undoubtedly Thomas Jefferson, without meaning to inflict
a serious injury on the fortunes of the young Nation, really thought

---

[1] In his Memories of a Hundred Years (1902), a sprightly but exceedingly partisan budget of reminiscences and opinions in two volumes. He condemns the
ante-bellum historians, and lauds Adams,

he was to be a sort of a King. But the young Nation was so much stronger than he was that, after he became President, he really fills the place in history which a fussy and foolish nurse fills in the biography of a man like Franklin, or Washington, or Goethe, or Julius Caesar, of whom the nurse had the charge. . . . To tell the whole truth the history of what I call the Virginia Dynasty, their failures and follies, their fuss and feathers and fol-de-rol, for the first quarter of a century, never got itself written down until twelve years ago. Mr. Henry Adams (1890) published his very entertaining history of the years between 1801 and 1817. . . . He is the son of a great statesman, who is the son of another great statesman, who is the son of another great statesman, and all his ancestors have left behind them full materials for history. . . . With a charming and pitiless impartiality, he draws curtains back and reveals to us the frenzies, the follies, the achievements, and the failures of what people call the 'government' between 1800 and 1817."

The three Adamses — John, John Quincy and Charles Francis, Sr. — are "great statesmen"; but the author of the Declaration of Independence, the father of the Constitution and the promulgator of the Monroe Doctrine are really to be pitied as mere bunglers who only failed to ruin the people because the people were not of the mind to let themselves be ruined. Of course Hale was a good man, a patriot who made his mark, but his ante-bellum history is woefully distorted. History and biography are not to be made a family matter of, or aggrandized by a section of the country whether east of the Hudson or south of the Potomac. As we have said, with much more reiteration than is agreeable either to us or to our readers, the prime, the vital struggle of the period was in behalf of American democratic government as against the aristocratic rule of the few.

But both threats and cajoleries soon ceased to be of value. Indeed, as Gaillard Hunt[1] says "war was practically existent; New York was blockaded; American ships were seized by British ships; American sailors were impressed." Madison's war message was sent to Congress, June 1. On June 3, Calhoun's committee

---

[1] Life of Madison, p. 322.

reported in favor of war. On June 4 the House adopted
the war report, seventy-nine to forty-nine. On June 18,
the Senate acquiesced by a vote of nineteen to thirteen.

For a long time this war report of the Committee on
Foreign Relations was thought to be the work of John
Caldwell Calhoun (born March 18, 1782; died March
31, 1850) then new to Congress — an erect, thin-faced,
six-footer, with bushy brown hair, bushy brown eyebrows, deep set gray-blue eyes of remarkable brilliancy,
and manners that were at once "simple, gentle and
sympathetic."[1]   But did he really write the war
manifesto of 1812? His early biographer, John S.
Jenkins[2] who gives his speech in the House on the
war resolutions, does not attribute it to him. But
several of the later biographers and historians do —
John Randolph Tucker, H. von Holst, Sydney Howard
Gay and even Henry Adams.[3]

Apparently "the message and the report came from
sources so closely allied as to be almost intermingled."
So insists Gaillard Hunt, who, in a convincing study
of the subject, in the *American Historical Review*
(Vol. XIII, pp. 303-312) and in his " Life of Calhoun "
(p. 25) says :

"it (the manifesto) had, in fact, been prepared, when the message
was prepared, or before, and by the hand of the Secretary of State,
James Monroe. Both the message and the report emanated from
the same source, the administration of James Madison."

Now by the way of historical reminiscence, Joseph
Gales for fifty years editor of *The National Intelligencer*, published in that journal as late as January 3,
1853, the speech made by John Randolph of Roanoke
in the House, on January 12, 1813. At the same time,
Gales commented upon the speech. Randolph had

---

[1] John C. Calhoun, by Gaillard Hunt, 1907.
[2] Life of John C. Calhoun, by John S. Jenkins, 1850; pp. 39-47.
[3] Tucker, Appleton's Cyclopedia of Biography, says: "He [Calhoun] drew a
report which placed before the country the issue of war or submission to wrong."
Henry Adams says, Vol. VI, History, p. 226: "Calhoun's report was admirable,
and its clearness of style and statement forced comparisons not flattering to the
President's message."

referred to the rejection of the treaty negotiated by Monroe and Pinkney, and had said that the subsequent placing of "one of these Commissioners of the United States — these very missionaries of peace and conciliation — into the Executive Councils of the country has been the signal of war with Great Britain." He meant Monroe. Gales[1] takes this passage as his starting point and proceeds to tell of the treaty, its summary rejection, Monroe's protest against "this harsh proceeding on the part of the Executive, implying an undeserved reproach upon him as a Statesman and a Minister"; and then comes to Randolph's attempt to "place that distinguished citizen in the field as a candidate for the presidency." He continues:

"Eventually, however, things took a different turn. Before the election came on, Mr. Madison became the sole candidate of the Republican (Jeffersonian) party; and, long before the election actually took place, Mr. Madison and Mr. Monroe were brought together, during the summer vacation, at Monticello, or elsewhere in Virginia[2] — through the instrumentality, as it was then generally understood, of Mr. Jefferson — and whatever of coldness existed between them was entirely removed by amicable explanations. We do not know that the friendship of Mr. Randolph and Mr. Monroe was by this latter incident turned to enmity, but it was sensibly abated. Nor was it at all restored by the acceptance by Mr. Monroe of the office of Secretary of State, offered to him

---

[1] Joseph Gales, Jr. (born at Eckington, England, April 10, 1786; died at Washington, D. C, July 21, 1860) was educated at the University of North Carolina; learned the printer's trade in Philadelphia and became owner of *The National Intelligencer*. He was joined by his brother-in-law William Winston Seaton (born in King William County, Va., January 11, 1785; died at Washington, December 31, 1864). A. K. McClure in his "Recollections of Half a Century," 1903, has a chapter, "The Eras of Good Feeling and Convulsion," in which he tells of Gales, Seaton and another great editor of the first half of the nineteenth century, Francis Preston Blair. Gales, a good stenographer, reported the proceedings of the Senate; Seaton, of the House.

[2] Gales is not backed up in this particular by the letters of Jefferson, Madison or Monroe. Indeed, he appears to have been misinformed as to the meeting of the three statesmen in Virginia. Jefferson and Monroe met (Writings of Monroe, V, 110) but Madison was not with them. April 23, 1811, Monroe wrote to Dr. Charles D. Everett: "The conduct of the P. since my arrival has corresponded with my previous anticipation; it is perfectly friendly, and corresponding with our antient relation, which I am happy to have restored. On publick affairs we confer without reserve, each party expressing his own sentiments, and viewing dispassionately the existing state, animated by a sincere desire to promote the public welfare. I have full confidence that this relation will be always preserved in the future."

by President Madison, midway of his first term of the Presidency to fill the vacancy occasioned by the resignation of Mr. Secretary Smith, in the Spring of 1811.

"The passage in Mr. Randolph's speech upon which we are now remarking was hardly intended in kindness to Mr. Monroe — perhaps not in a hostile spirit — but certainly must be taken to convey a reflection upon his consistency in regard to the questions in controversy between the United States and Great Britain, out of which the existing war had sprung. However intended, it is due to the truth of history to say that Mr. Randolph hardly overstated the 'fact' when he said that the accession of Mr. Monroe to the Cabinet had been the 'signal of war with Great Britain.' The connexion of the two events cannot, indeed, be well denied. We ourselves do not doubt that the opinions and exertions of Mr. Monroe greatly influenced the great event. We have ever believed, also, that his course in that trying emergency was most honorable to his discernment as well as to his patriotic and fearless spirit; and that, therefore, no disparagement could be inferred from it to his consistency as a true American statesman. This is not the place, nor have we now the time, to undertake to indite the unwritten history of that declaration of war. It would make a volume itself."

Gales contents himself with citing a pertinent passage from Crittenden's memorial oration on Henry Clay, in the course of which the eulogist touched upon the position occupied by Monroe when he accepted the office of Secretary of State. Monroe had come home "thoroughly disgusted with the contemptuous manner in which the rights of the United States were treated by the belligerent Powers, and especially by England. England had reduced to a system "a course of conduct calculated to debase and prostrate us in the eyes of the world." Crittenden adds:

"Reasoning thus, he had brought his mind to a serious and firm conviction that the rights of the United States, as a nation, would never be respected by the Powers of the Old World until this Government summoned up resolution to resent such usage, not by arguments and protests merely, but by an appeal to arms. Full of this sentiment, Mr. Monroe was called, upon a casual vacancy, when it was least expected by himself or the country, to the head of the Department of State. That sentiment, and the feelings which we have thus accounted for, Mr. Monroe soon communicated to his associates in the Cabinet, and in some degree, it might well be supposed, to the great statesman then at the head of the Government."

Monroe had gone dutifully along with Jefferson and Madison as a peace man until he realized that peace had become dishonorable. He was for war because war was the way out — the last resort. He asserted himself against Jefferson and Madison. In a different manner, he asserted himself as against Randolph, who whimsically defended England.

The chapter of reminiscences in *The National Intelligencer* was a chapter of history; and it is strange that it should have been unappreciated until brought out by Hunt. Gales heard from it. "A gentleman who was a confidential member of the Government at the time the speech was made entirely confirmed" what Gales said. Gales lost the use of his hand; so William W. Moore of *The National Intelligencer* answered his letters for him. One of these letters was addressed to Richard K. Crallé, "a wealthy planter in Virginia," chief clerk of the Department of State under Calhoun in 1844. Ten years later he was gathering material for a life of Calhoun; and, accordingly, wrote to Gales concerning his statement that Monroe, not Calhoun, had written the war manifesto of 1812. Crallé's grandson, J. Lawrence Campbell, of Bedford City, West Virginia, supplied Hunt with a letter dictated by Gales to Moore in reply to Crallé. Moore signed it. Gales says:

"The war manifesto reported in the House of Reps. on the third of June, 1812, was the production of Mr. Monroe. Of this Mr. Gales is positively certain, as well from other knowledge as from his familiarity with the handwriting in which the report is written, being that of Mr. Monroe's Private Secretary and Confidential Clerk. The Select Committee by which this report was made had the subject referred to them at the close of the day's sitting on the first of June, and submitted their report on the opening of the House on the third of June, which fact, taken in connection with the importance of the subject and the conciseness of the statements of the report, sufficiently indicate the improbability that the committee could, within the brief time that intervened after the reference, have deliberated upon the subject, prepared the report and had it copied.[1]

Moore, the amanuensis, sent Crallé some "extracts from an unpublished article of Mr. Gale's":

"When Congress assembled in November, 1811, the crisis was upon us. . . . The message (Nov. 5) was of the gravest cast, reciting the aggressions and aggravations of Great Britain as demanding resistance. . . . Whilst Mr. Clay, Mr. Calhoun, and others, within the walls of the Capitol were breaking lances with the opponents of the preparation for war, there was in operation at the further end of the avenue an influence less publicly exerted, but not less potent, upon the hearts and understandings of the younger Members of the House of Reps, and especially upon those who composed the Com^ee on Foreign Relations. Comparatively young and inexperienced in National affairs, they naturally resorted to Mr. Monroe, who might be termed, without hyperbole, the Nestor of the day, for information and advice as to the affairs of which, as Secretary of State, he was the official depository and for the lessons of experience he had acquired by long service abroad. To these gentlemen, in frequent private consultations, principally at his own abode on the long winter nights, he constantly repeated the deep conviction of which I have already spoken, of the infinite disgrace which would infallibly attend a longer submission to foreign insult and outrage; replying, night after night, to every suggestion of postponement, delay or renewed attempts at negotiation, 'Gentlemen, *we must fight.* We are forever disgraced if we do not; disgraced in our own estimation, in the eyes of our adversary, and in the opinion of the world'. . . . Chiefly through the fearless influence of the counsels of these ardent patriots, the House of Reps., on whose decision as originator of all measures of revenue the prosecution of war must depend, was gradually warmed up a war spirit. . . . At length, after private conference, a deputation of Members of Congress, with Mr. Clay at their head, waited upon the President, and, upon the representations of the readiness of a majority of Congress to vote the war if recommended, the President, on the first Monday in June, transmitted to Congress his message submitting the question to their decision. The agency of Mr. Monroe in this measure was not yet at an end; for the Com^ee on Foreign Relations, to whom the President's message was referred, had prevailed upon the Secretary as being more fully possessed than themselves of the facts and merits of the question, to prepare a

---

[1] The members of the Committee were Calhoun, Grundy, Smilie, Harper, Desha, Seaver, Republicans; and Porter, Randolph and Key. Porter was home, sick.

Report upon the message; which Report was presented to the House of Reps. by the committee, as their report, on the second day after the reception of the message, and had been (from its length) evidently prepared, if not adopted, by the Committee before the message was sent in. It was an elaborate Manifesto filling ten or twelve printed pages."

The Federalists protested in the press and at public meetings against the war. They had the sympathy of Randolph's followers and of the factional Republicans. Altogether they made an imposing show of opposition. It was more than a show — it was actual; it was chillingly oppressive; it was almost enough to take the heart out of those who were responsible for the conduct of the war. Madison, in his letters, repeatedly speaks of the sinister influence of the New England opposition. As Parke Godwin[1] expresses it: "The scenes of battle on the ocean, or on the frontier, were scarcely more fiery than those in Congress and the popular assemblies." William Cullen Bryant, then a law student in the office of Congressman William Baylies, of Bridgewater, Conn., betrayed "an insatiable curiosity in regard to the progress of events." He writes of the President as "His Imbecility," and tells Baylies in Washington that "the subject of the separation of the States is more boldly and frequently discussed." He himself wants to go into the army — not for the defense of the General Government but of the State of Connecticut. In reading the letters of so true a man and genuine a patriot as Bryant, we begin to understand what at first flush is hardly understandable — the threat of disunion at the Hartford Convention. "From the origin of the government," says Godwin, "the Republicans had professed themselves the opponents of Nationalism or Centralism and the particular defenders of the rights, or, as it was called, the sovereignty of the States. On the other hand, the Federalists, as their name imports, were sticklers for central supremacy and local subordination."

---

[1] Life of William Cullen Bryant, by Parke Godwin. 2 vols., Vol. I, pp. 126,127.

Now all was whirled about, so that the very opposite was the case.

The Federalist contention was that Madison went to war because he hoped thus to keep his party in power; that war was begun with undue preparation; that if we must fight we should fight France, not England, whose extreme measures were excusable since she was in the throes of combat with the mad Napoleon.

The Republican reply was that things had come to such a pass[1] as to make peace a hissing and a by-word; that America ought to fight both France and England, but that to wrestle with one at a time was the dictate of common sense; that the Federalists would see, if they were not as blind as bats, that the British meant to monopolize the ocean to the detriment, yea, absolute destruction, of New England's shipping; and that, though it was a pity to be obliged to draw the sword that Jefferson had allowed to rust, the rust would soon wear off and the sword be as bright and glorious as in the Revolution. Thus said the "War Hawks" of Congress. According to Benjamin Perry, when Madison sent in his message, Clay, Calhoun, Cheves, Bibb, Grundy and Lowndes who messed together and were called the "War Mess," joined hands, à la ring-around-the-rosy, and then and there danced all over the floor. They were eager to wipe out all American stains, all contumelies due in part to the pacifism of the Monticello philosopher and in part to the pressure of what Jefferson called the Federalist "anglomen," or as we would call them Anglomaniacs. "Party politics were inexpressibly violent." It was Theodore Parker who, in 1852, in his discourse on the death of Daniel Webster, said:

"An eminent lawyer of Salem [Mass.], afterwards one of the most distinguished jurists in the World, a Democrat, was on

---

[1] Some 2500 Americans, held on British vessels, were sent to Dartmoor prison at the outbreak of the war. "Over 6000 cases of impressment were recorded in the Department of State."

account of his political opinions, knocked down in the street, beaten and forced to take shelter in the house of a friend, whither he fled, bleeding and covered with the mud of the streets. Political rancor invaded private life; it invaded the pulpit; it blinded men's eyes to a degree almost exceeding belief; were it not now a fact we should not believe it possible at a former time."

With the Federalists there was a great veneration for England. Said Fisher Ames: "The immortal spirit of the wood-nymph Liberty dwells only in the British Oak. . . . Our Country is too big for union, too sordid for patriotism and too democratic for liberty."

But, in spite of the opposition, Madison was re-elected. His opponent was De Witt Clinton, a factional Republican, whom the Federalists supported. Madison was given one hundred and twenty-eight of the two hundred and eighteen electoral votes. Elbridge Gerry was chosen Vice-President.

There were surprises for each side from the very start. The British had no idea that the Americans would challenge them on the wide ocean. What happened was: that in an eight-minutes' fight, August 13, the "Essex," Captain David Porter, captured the British sloop "Alert;" the forty-four-gun "Constitution," Captain Isaac Hull, August 19, captured the thirty-eight-gun "Guerriere," and so it went like a thrilling sea serial, with a victory in every chapter. The Yankee "Wasp," October 13, finished the British "Frolic," and she disported herself tauntingly on the waves no more. So, too, with a great thundering off Madeira, October 25, the frigate "United States," Captain Stephen Decatur, took the frigate "Macedonian." By this time the "Constitution," now under Captain William Bainbridge, was off the coast of Brazil and there, December 29, she fell in with and demolished the British frigate "Java." This long series of victories on the sea was marred for the Americans by but one heavy blow. After Captain Lawrence, in the "Hornet," had sunk the "Peacock" and had been transferred to the "Chesapeake," he lost that frigate, June 1, 1813, to the "Shannon," Captain Philip

Broke. By reason of his victory, Broke[1] became a
baronet; by reason of his last command: "Don't give
up the ship," the dying Lawrence became one of
the immortals. It was all the more gratifying to the
Americans to learn of these naval victories because the
sea had been the scene of their humiliations. They
heard with astonishment and delight of the cruise of
the "Essex" in Pacific waters, where David Farragut was
making his heroic debut; and the news of the victories
of "Old Ironsides" under Captain Stewart gave them
great joy.[2]

Now America's declaration of war had seemed "sheer
madness" to the English when they first heard of it;
but by and by Wellington said: "I have been very
uneasy about the American naval successes. I think
we should have peace with America before the season
for opening the campaign in Canada if we could take
one or two of those d——d frigates."[3]

But it was quite a while before any one felt the
significance of the sea victories.[4]   On land the war
dragged; and, as we have said, the Americans had a
surprise, too. Clay and the sanguine Westerners had
anticipated an easy conquest of Canada. Neither
Jefferson nor Clay had read Revolutionary history to
advantage or they would not have talked in such a
sanguine vein about Canada. Jefferson declared its
acquisition would be a mere matter of marching. The
querulous Randolph said that he was tired of hearing
"but one word, like the whippoorwill, but one eternal
monotonous tone — Canada, Canada, Canada!" The

[1] Memoirs of Admiral Sir P. B. V. Broke, Bart., by Rev. F. G. Brighton, M.D.
Captain James Lawrence, by Albert Gleaves, 1804. Secretary Monroe, in Washington, July 4, 1813, gave this toast: "To the memory of Captain Lawrence whose
last words were 'Sink the ship sooner than surrender her!' (Sic), p. 235.

[2] See the Naval War of 1812 by Theodore Roosevelt, 1882, 2 vols.; and Sea
Power in its Relation to the War of 1812, by Captain A. T. Mahan, 2 vols., 1905.
Mahan says that Monroe had advanced views for one of his party concerning the
utility of the navy.

[3] Duke of Wellington to Marshal Beresford, February 6, 1813.   Wellington's
Despatches, 1838, Vol. X, p. 92.

[4] George Coggeshall in his "History of the American Privateers," 1856, lists
250 sail sent out from various ports. He says that the British lost about 2000
ships during the war.

French-Canadians, said the "War Hawks," would seize
the opportunity to rise. The six hundred thousand
Canadians would gladly join their seven million
American neighbors. But nothing of the sort happened.
The Canadians got rid of their cannon-balls and
musket-balls fast enough, but not of their British yoke.
Instead of gaining Canada, it looked as though the
Americans might lose the whole northwestern territory.
The British began by taking Michillimackinac. This
was a mere outpost, of little seeming account, but to
the watchful Indians it was significant. Tecumseh,
his brother the Prophet and their numerous chiefs and
warriors would now let themselves loose. This thought
must have been in the mind of Captain William Hull,
a Revolutionary soldier, who, in obedience to orders,
built a road two hundred miles long through the forest
to Detroit, the keypoint of the Michigan region, only
to surrender that post, without a fight, to Sir Isaac
Brock.[1] Hull, by no means blameless, was unhardened
to his task. He was "cankered by a long peace," just
as were many others — officers of the old war, in which
they had served when in their heyday. They were
politicians who had been honored and often over-
honored for past services and who, when suddenly
called upon to live up to their exaggerated reputations,
collapsed under pressure of stern and bloody require-
ments. War is no soft, chivalric thing, as hero-tales
often lead us to imagine, but essentially mathematical,
strategical, hard and death-dealing. Hull, Dearborn
and most of the other incompetents of 1812 and 1813
were of this description. Hull was court-martialed and
sentenced to be shot;[2] thanks to Madison, the sentence
was not executed. Hull's plea was that if the Indians,

---

[1] Major-General Sir Isaac Brock, born in the Isle of Guernsey in 1769; in the
British army before he was sixteen; died in battle October 13, 1812.

[2] If a Hull had disgraced America at Detroit, another Hull, his nephew, Commodore Isaac, had won a most glorious victory at sea; and would continue to win
victories. The Hull side of General William Hull's discomfiture is told in "The
Revolutionary Services and Civil Life of Gen. Wm. Hull," prepared from his Ms.
by his daughter, Mrs. Maria Campbell, together with a history of the surrender
of the Post of Detroit, by his grandson, James Freeman Clarke, 1848.

Monroe (by Vanderlyn)

who surrounded Detroit, had taken it, tomahawk in hand, they would have massacred the women and children who had sought refuge there. But nobody thought of this. All they knew was that disaster had overtaken them in that part of the Canadian border, which was a thousand miles long. Doubts arose. There were but ten regular regiments, and these were short of men. People realized the country's unpreparedness — that it was beset with enemies. Before news came in from the ocean, the outlook was blue indeed.

In less than two months, all doubts resolved themselves into downright disasters. The war was unsupported in Massachusetts, Connecticut and Rhode Island, which declined to send their quotas of troops. Federalists there proclaimed it a party, not a national, war.[1] There was lack of vigor among those whose bounden duty it was to be alert. There was misjudgment in the selection of both high officials and high officers. William Eustis of Boston was Secretary of War. Ex-surgeon, ex-congressman, he was fifty-six years old — two years older than Monroe. Paul Hamilton, gentleman, of South Carolina, was also an "ex" — ex-governor. Seeing that the Jeffersonian "cankers of a long peace" had eaten away the strength of both army and navy, the responsible heads of those departments should have been men of force and initiative. But neither Jefferson nor Madison had the soldier instinct, and political considerations, rather than fitness, too often influenced them in their choice of those who held the war and naval portfolios.

Major-General Henry Dearborn was in chief command of the American Army. He had failed to cooperate with Hull. The Fort that bore his name, now Chicago, was abandoned on the day Detroit was surrendered. Dearborn, as we have intimated, was

---

[1] It was contemptuously called "Mr. Madison's War." Chancellor Kent, Federalist, wrote that "the surge of Jacobinism which had swept over the country, and under the leadership of Madison had plunged the United States into War with England, had made him weary of judicial life." Memoirs and Letters of Chancellor James Kent, by William Kent, 1898.

unequal to his task, which, for that matter, few men could have executed since there was so small and so ill-disciplined a force. He was sixty-one years old. He had but sixty-seven hundred regulars. Nor were these model troops. General Winfield Scott, in his Memoirs, speaks disparagingly of officers and men. Sloth, with the handy flask, had made for flabbiness of character as well as muscle. Dearborn[1] was a highly respectable and much esteemed man; but he was lacking in the chief qualities of vigorous leadership. "His movements were sluggish and his plans hazy," says Babcock;[2] "and for a time he seemed to be on the eve of an accommodation which would end the war.[3] He lingered long in New England and longer still at Plattsburg when he should have been at Niagara. The plans contemplated a double invasion of Canada — on the Detroit frontier and on the Niagara frontier. The first was already a failure. For a long time, most of the fighting would be in the vicinity of Niagara Falls.

General Stephen Van Rensselaer was in command in that pivotal quarter. Monroe spoke of him as "a weak and incompetent man of high pretensions." At Queenstown Heights, October 13, Van Rensselaer lost a thousand men. But this loss was offset by the

[1] Major-General Henry Dearborn was born at North Hampton, New Hampshire, in 1751. He was tall, sinewy — an unmatched wrestler. A Captain in Stark's regiment at Bunker Hill, he accompanied the Quebec Expedition and killed his dog, a fine animal, that his starving comrades might have food. He served with Scammell and fought shoulder to shoulder with Dan Morgan at Saratoga. He was at Germantown, Valley Forge, Monmouth and Yorktown. Talleyrand, while Dearborn's guest at Pittston, Mass., "fell into the river while fishing at Hallowell and was saved by a little boy holding to him his fishing rod." Fort Dearborn, (Chicago) was named in General Dearborn's honor. A log cabin and fort stood there in 1803. The cabin was owned and occupied by Pierre Le May, a French Canadian trader, and his Indian wife. Capt. John Whistler and company of the First Regiment, U. S. A., first occupied the fort. General Dearborn married the widow of the excellent Governor Bowdoin, patron of Bowdoin College. Bowdoin mansion stood in Milk Street, Boston, on the site of Bowdoin block. R. C. Winthrop was born in this house. The younger Henry A. S. Dearborn, son of General Henry, was likewise distinguished.

[2] The Rise of American Nationality, by Kendrick Charles Babcock, 1906. "American Nation Series, Vol. 13."

[3] Suggested by Sir George Prevost (made Governor-General, September 14, 1811) when he heard that the British Ministry had withdrawn the objectionable Orders in Council. But Madison put an end to the proposed truce. Monroe "explained the situation to the British Minister."

loss to the British of their very best commander on the
American continent — Sir Isaac Brock. General Alexander Smyth succeeded Van Rensselaer, but was even
less fitted for the work. One of the "War Hawks,"
Peter B. Porter, who had left Congress for the front,
called him a coward; so they fought a duel, and Smyth's
name was speedily thereafter dropped from the roster.
As for Dearborn, whose futile attempt to organize a
Montreal expedition had brought him only discredit,
that unfortunate officer again failed in his operations
along the southern shore of Lake Ontario. What is
now Toronto was then York. This place Dearborn
took, but when the magazine there exploded, General
Zebulon M. Pike was killed. The Government building,
too, was burned — an incident that was to have a
smoky sequel by Potomac side. Dearborn's day was
done; and who should succeed him but Wilkinson?
Though not in the pay of the King of Spain at this
particular time, nor plotting with Burr, he was blundering as usual; and by and by he was up before a court-
martial. His day was done, as well as Dearborn's.
Monroe, watching the progress of events, wrote as
helpfully as he could to Dearborn and others; but his
letters about Wilkinson[1] were addressed to the man at
Monticello. The newspapers were reviewing Wilkinson's treason, and Monroe had seen references to
Jefferson concerning which that worthy ought to
know. It was one of his many friendly acts toward
Jefferson.

Let it not be thought that Madison, Monroe and
other responsible officials remained unconcerned while
the blunderers were blundering. Their letters indicate
how keenly they felt the reverses on the Canadian
border — how shocked they were at such tragedies as
that at Raisin River, January 22, 1813, when but forty
of six hundred and sixty frontiersmen escaped the
scalping knife, and that at Fort Mims, Ala., in August

---

[1] Works of Monroe, Hamilton, Volume V, pp. 197, 199, 200, 273.

of the same year, when four hundred souls were massacred by a thousand Creeks.

As early as August 8, 1812, Madison wrote to Monroe from Montpelier suggesting that he take general command. In the "Monroe Correspondence" of the Bureau of Rolls, pages 146-156, are many letters from Madison to Monroe relating to the conduct of the war. September 6, 1812, Madison insisted that a suitable head was required. Monroe, said he, was the best man for the big work. Madison realized, as did others who were brought into contact with Monroe, that he had been broadened by his experiences oversea.

Cabinet reorganization was proposed. Monroe was to be made Secretary of War, and Gallatin was to succeed him as Secretary of State. But Madison feared that the Senate would not accept this re-arrangement.[1]

In December, 1813, Paul Hamilton was relieved of the Navy portfolio which was given to a Philadelphia ship-owner, William Jones. General John Armstrong, whom we but lately met in France, succeeded Eustis as Secretary of War. Manifestly, Madison was injudicious in his choice of such men as James Winchester, of Tennessee, when General William Henry Harrison was at his service to command in the Northwest. He was forced to take Harrison finally. Adams, in his "Gallatin" shows that Madison had doubts from the start with respect to Armstrong. "Monroe," says K. C. Babcock,[2] "desired the War portfolio since the State Department did not furnish sufficient scope for his talents while the most active field of diplomacy was closed by the war. Although, for political reasons, Madison did not comply, jealousy and suspicion between Monroe and Armstrong had a detrimental effect upon the military service."

---

[1] "Monroe's service at the head of the State Department was interrupted by four assignments to act as Secretary of War" Gaillard Hunt, Life of Madison, p. 339.

[2] Rise of American Nationality, p. 97.

Let us give Gaillard Hunt's estimate of Armstrong:

"The objections to him were fatal to his usefulness. Long diplomatic service in which his ability was conspicuous had not fitted him for duty as an executive officer when quick decision and action were needed. He was an indolent man and energy was needed, and he was a member of the Clinton faction in New York, and loyal co-operation in the cabinet was essential. He was unpopular in the West, and his nomination was confirmed by a majority of three votes only, both Kentucky Senators voting against him; and Kentucky under Henry Clay's leadership was the most enthusiastic State in the Union in support of the War. Monroe, Gallatin and Jones, the new Secretary of the Navy all distrusted Armstrong."[1]

In a letter to Jefferson, June 7, 1813, Monroe told him what he had said to Madison when Madison proposed to make him commanding general:

"I stated that if it was thought necessary to remove me from my present station in the idea that I had some military experience, and a change in the command of the troops was resolved on, I would prefer it to the Department of War in the persuasion that I might be more useful. In the Department of War a man might form a plan of campaign and write judicious letters on military operations; but still these were nothing but essays — everything would depend on execution. I thought that with the army I should have better control over operations and events, and might even aid, so far as I could give aid at all, the person in the Department of War. I offered to repair instantly to the Northern army, to use my best efforts to form it, to promote the recruiting business in the Eastern States, to conciliate the people to the views of the Government, and unite them so far as it might be possible in the war. The President was of the opinion that if I quitted my present station, I ought to take the command of the army. It being necessary to place some one immediately in the Department of War to supply the vacancy made by Mr. Eustis's retreat, the President requested me to take it *pro tempore*, leaving the ultimate decision on the other question open to further consideration. I did so."

His son-in-law, the able Judge George Hay, wrote from Richmond, September 22:[2]

"It is rumored here that you are to be appointed lieutenant-general. Such an appointment would give, I believe, universal

---

[1] Hunt's Madison, p. 329.
[2] Monroe Mss., State Department Archives.

satisfaction. . . . This is indeed a critical moment. Some great
effort must be made. Unless something important is done,
Mr. Madison may be elected again, but he will not be able to get
along. But Mr. Madison ought not to exact any further sacrifices
from you. If you go into the army, you ought to go with the
supreme power in your hand. I would not organize an army for
Dearborn or for anyone else. Mr. Madison ought not to expect it,
and if he did I would flatly and directly reject the proposal.
Everybody is looking forward to an event of this kind, and I do
not believe that any man calculates that you are to go in a subordinate character. The truth is that Dearborn is laughed at, not
by Federalists but by zealous Republicans. I do not give on this
subject a reluctant, hesitating opinion. I am clear that if you go
into the army (about which I say nothing), you should go as
commander-in-chief."

"The only member of the Cabinet who had any
knowledge of military matters," says Colonel Thomas
Wentworth Higginson, "was Colonel James Monroe,
Secretary of State; and it was subsequently thought
that he knew just enough to be in the way." The tart
reference is to a minor incident at the Battle of Bladensburg, to which we shall come by and by. As to Monroe's
military knowledge, it must have been considerable;
but he had never managed large bodies of men; he
had never planned or executed a strategical campaign;
nor had he ever been in a critical situation with the fate
of other commands than his own depending upon his
orders. He had doffed his uniform in his early twenties;
he was now fifty-six. It was probably fortunate for him
that he remained in the cabinet instead of following the
impulses of his patriotism and his honorable ambition
which, undoubtedly, were to proceed to the front.
Others in civilian clothes have wished for uniforms.
For example, one brings to mind Jefferson Davis.
He had been a soldier in the Mexican war, and a good
one. Therefore, he itched to be out of Richmond and
with the army. That was why he ventured upon the
battlefield of the first Bull Run. Again on the morning
of the battle of Mechanicsville, when Lee had set afoot
his series of combats designed to drive McClellan out
of the Peninsula, Davis rode with his imposing staff

to the spot where Lee stood busy with his pressing duties. Lee gave one over-the-shoulder look at the party, but no more. "Take those people to the rear!" said he. After that Davis never interfered on the field.

Now at last, however, had come a change in the untoward run of events. The change was due to the energetic carriage of iron, canvas, cordage and armament all the way from the seaboard through the wilderness to Presque Isle (Erie); the transfer thither of Atlantic Coast shipwrights and sailors; the construction and manning of a fleet of ten war vessels, and, finally, to the genuine seamanship and fighting genius of Captain Oliver Howard Perry. Commodore Isaac Chauncey, operating against Sir James Yeo, had done considerable good for the American cause on Lake Ontario; but, on Lake Erie, Perry now made a masterstroke. He engaged the British fleet, under Captain R. H. Barclay, Monday, August 5, 1813; and by and by sent word to General William Henry Harrison: "We have met the enemy, and they are ours; two ships, two brigs, one schooner and one sloop." "It was Perry," says John Fiske, "who turned the scales of war." The multitudes of hostile Indians were startled to see the King's "big canoes" swept from the lake. Harrison realized his opportunity to win back the Detroit frontier; and, indeed, the whole Northwest. Harrison, a Hampden-Sydney man, (Wayne's aide in 1792) was tall, slender, with high forehead and dark eyes. He had gone through much that was arduous and bloody on the border, then the scene of dramatic and thrilling incidents.

No sooner had Perry opened the way for him than Harrison entered Canada on the heels of the British General, Henry Proctor. Babcock says that Tecumseh felt contemptuous toward Proctor because he retreated when Harrison, with Governor Shelby of Tennessee and Perry at the head of his sailors, started in pursuit of him. Fearless men were Tecumseh (the Crouching Panther), Chief of the Shawnees, and his brother Olliwacha, the prophet. Their word flew like a spark along the border and fired the fuse for such disasters as Fort Mims and Raisin River. But Proctor was skulking away and Tecumseh likened him to "a fat animal that carries its tail upon its back, but when affrighted it drops it between its legs and runs off."

Harrison overtook Proctor near Moraviantown on the River Thames.[1] The Johnson brothers led Harrison's two columns — Colonel Richard M., the left, and Colonel James, the right. It was Colonel "Dick" who encountered Tecumseh and slew him with his own hand.[2] Tecumseh, on foot, shot at Johnson on his white horse (by this time stung with many bullets) and then raised his tomahawk to hurl it, but the Kentuckian was too quick for the Shawnee chief. He pistoled him ere his tomahawk left his hand.

Which was the greater loss to the British — Brock or Tecumseh? One might speculate interminably on the question. Brock had the gift of leadership; so had Tecumseh, who was possessed of an inveterate hostility to our people from the Lakes to the Gulf. The elimination of these men seemed like a heaven-send.

Younger and more spirited men had revivified Congress; why not rejuvenate the army? The answer was the appointment of two major-generals — Izard and Brown — and six brigadiers, among whom were Scott, Macomb and Gaines. Brown and Scott proved to be the very commanders the country had been praying for. Major-General Jacob Brown was a Bucks County, Pennsylvania, Quaker. To show how courageous he was, though in bed at Buffalo, badly wounded, during a critical week of his campaign, he issued his orders with unmitigated pugnacity and prevision.

---

[1] Harrison helped himself toward the Presidency by this battle and Col. **R. M.** Johnson, who served in the Thirteenth Congress toward the Vice Presidency.

[2] The old rhyme ran:

Rumpsey dumpsey
Col. Johnson killed Tecumseh.

Life of Ben Hardin, by Lucius P. Little, 1887. Doubt has been thrown on the story as to Johnson's act. He slew a powerful chief in the fight, but his victim may not have been Tecumseh.

Scott, a big-bodied Virginian, famous for fifty years of his soldier life — spanning as he did the stretch of time from Washington to Lincoln — was at the head of Brown's First Brigade; and Eleazar Wheelock Ripley, of New Hampshire, was at the head of the Second. Scott was impetuous; Ripley, wary. With them marched Porter's brigade of six hundred warriors of the Six Nations, under Chief Red Jacket, and six hundred militia from Pennsylvania. Colonel Hindman, with four companies of artillery, handled the field-pieces. On the open plain of Chippewa, hard by Niagara Falls, July 5, Brown won a three-hour battle over Riall's Royal Scots and Dragoons. On July 25, the British Major-General, Gordon Drummond, having meantime joined Riall with fresh regiments, was fought the seven-hour battle of Lundy's Lane, also near the Falls of Niagara. Though it was a drawn battle, with nearly all the chief officers wounded, people rejoiced over it as evidence that once more our troops were up to their old mark of dauntlessness. Similarly, at Fort Erie, in August and September, Brown met with deserved success.

The fall of Napoleon set free tens of thousands of British troops. It was decided by the British Government to use three powerful contingents of these highly disciplined soldiers in a final effort to dictate a strong peace in America. Some were to proceed to Canada to invade the States from the north; some were to attack the cities along the Atlantic Coast, and others were to proceed to New Orleans, with the idea of relieving the Americans of their recent Louisiana bargain. The thrust from the north was to be vigorous and vicious, in a military sense, and so was that from the south, but the expedition against the coast cities was to have a light military, yet heavy punitive, touch. Sir John Borlase Warren,[1] Admiral of the Blue, with headquarters at Halifax, had long blockaded these

---

[1] For Warren-Monroe Correspondence see American State Papers, Vol. III, pp. 595, 596.

ports to the detriment of their trade, and since February, 1813, had been especially active in the Chesapeake. Through him and in other ways, the directing heads in London had learned of the inadequate defenses in this bay, which marauding parties had penetrated from the Virginia Capes to the mouth of the Susquehanna River.

Let us note first the attack along the line of Lake Champlain — Burgoyne's line. In 1777 the British plan was to cut New England off from the rest of the country. In 1814 the strategy was similar; though the Hartford Convention did not meet until December 15 of that year, sedition was ripe.[1] The British hoped that they could help separate the sections by a successful occupation of the Hudson River Valley.

But these great expectations came to naught. General Alexander Macomb and Lieutenant Thomas MacDonough, a hero after the American's own heart, balked the efforts of Sir George Prevost with his army of eleven thousand men and Captain George Downie who commanded on Lake Champlain. MacDonough with an eighty-six-gun flotilla beat the British fleet carrying ninety guns. Downie was killed. General Prevost precipitately retreated, his campaign collapsing over night. Perhaps, in his dreams, he thought himself another Burgoyne. As it was, his failure must have been much in the minds of those who put their heads together at Ghent.

As for General George Izard, it was his misfortune to be withdrawn from Prevost's front, and dispatched

---

[1] Babcock in the Rise of American Nationality says, p. 165: "To the more advanced Republicans like Grundy and Calhoun, the Federalist opposition, culminating in the Hartford Convention amounted to moral treason, while John Quincy Adams passionately asserted, in 1829, that the Hartford Convention was unconstitutional and treasonable, wholly abnormal, hideous and wicked." William Wirt said of Madison (Kennedy's Wirt, Vol. I, p. 339): "He looks miserable, shattered and woebegone. . . . His mind is full of the New England Sedition. He introduced the subject and continued to press it, painful as it obviously was to him." "Monroe, however," adds Babcock, "was less pessimistic. Late in December he wrote (Writings, IV, p. 305): 'The gentry will, I suspect, find they have overacted their part. They cannot dismember the Union, or league with the enemy. . . . I hope that the leaders will soon take rank in society with Burr, and others of that stamp.'"

by Secretary Armstrong on a needless march to Sackett's
Harbor. According to Henry Adams:

"Izard was a friend of Monroe's,[1] and was therefore an object
of Armstrong's merciless criticism. Brown was a favorite of
Armstrong, and shared his prejudices. The position of Izard at
Buffalo was calculated to excite jealousy. He had implicitly
obeyed the wishes of Armstrong and Brown; in so doing he had
sacrificed himself, yielding to Macomb the credit of repulsing
Prevost, and to Brown, who did not wait his arrival, the credit
of repulsing Drummond. As far as could be seen, Izard had acted
with loyalty toward both Armstrong and Brown; yet both distrusted him. . . . Izard felt the mortification of his failure."

General Izard resigned; and, though his resignation
was not accepted, he was practically out of the operations thereafter on the Canadian border. Izard wrote
many letters to Monroe, during the fall of 1814.[2]

Very different was the attack on the Atlantic seaboard. The stroke was directed at the Chesapeake
country, and one of the objectives was the American
capital. Baltimore, too, was to be taken; and then, if
the nest of pernicious frigate-builders at Philadelphia
could be broken up, so much the better. It may be
said, in passing, that the Philadelphians, whether soft-
handed or hard, volunteered by the thousand and,
working without pay, put their port and river in a
complete state of defense.

Bermuda was the British base for the Chesapeake
operations. General Robert Ross, who had been with
Sir John Moore at Corunna, sailed from Bordeaux with
thirty-five hundred of Wellington's veterans. Gleig,[3]
the literary chaplain and Wellington's biographer, was
with the expedition; so that we have the British side
of the story both with respect to the adventure of Ross
in the Chesapeake and the equally tragic last act of
Sir Edward Packenham's New Orleans drama. The
British squadron was under Sir Alexander Cochrane.

---

[1] H. Adams, History, Vol. VIII, p. 114, *et seq.*

[2] Izard Correspondence, Izard to Monroe, October 16, 23, November 20, December 18; as quoted in H. Adams, History Vol. VIII.

[3] The Campaign of the British Army at Washington and New Orleans, by G. R.
Gleig, Chaplain.

The lower Chesapeake was soon white with British sails. A thousand marines under Admiral George Cockburn joined Ross, whose force seemed very large indeed to one of the two Joshuas then in the bay. The fighting Joshua was Commodore Joshua Barney with a considerable flotilla, which took itself off and hid under the timbered banks of the beautiful Patuxent. The praying Joshua was Joshua Thomas, "Parson of the Isles," who welcomed the thousand of redcoats ashore on the beach of Tangier. He preached to the heroes of the Peninsular campaign; told them of their sins; and advised them not to try to go to Baltimore. Why? For one thing, they couldn't. For another, they had better hurry home, where they belonged. But the British ships spread their sails again and, like Admiral Lord Howe's fleet thirty-seven years before, passed up the Chesapeake and entered the Patuxent. August 18, Admiral Cochrane wrote to Monroe that he had been called upon by the Governor-General of Canada to retaliate upon the United States for damage done by American troops in Canadian territory. He had been obliged to issue to the naval force under his command "an order to destroy and lay waste such towns and districts as may be found assailable." This did not look as though the "Parson of the Isles" had made much impression upon the vengeful Admiral. On the nineteenth, twenty-four vessels, with four thousand men, proceeded up stream to Benedict, forty miles southeast of Washington. Sir Henry Smith, one of the officers,[1] found the Patuxent "serpentine and wooded." Coincidently, other British ships were passing up the Potomac

But what were Madison and Monroe and the "War Hawks" doing all this time? The "War Hawks" were absent, as it was in the summer recess of Congress. Madison was at the White House with his wife. On August 20, Monroe took a party of dragoons — some twenty-five or thirty — and reconnoitred in the direc-

---

[1] Autobiography of Sir H. Smith, 1901.

tion of Benedict. He must have thought of the time when he scouted in the pleasant company of Captain William Washington. Evidently, Monroe had not forgotten how to gather information. He wrote to the President from Horse Road, on the twenty-first:

"I quartered last night near Charlotte Hall, and took a view this morning at eight o'clock, from a commanding height, below Benedict creek, of all the enemy's shipping near the town, and down the river the distance of at least 8 or 10 miles. I counted 23 sq: rigged vessels. Few others were to be seen, and very few barges. I inferred from the latter circumstance that the enemy had moved up the river, either against Com. Barry's [Barney's] flotilla, at Nottingham, confining their views to that object, or taking that in their way and aiming at the city, in combination with the force on the Powtowmac, of which I have correct information. I had, when I left Aquosco Mills last night, intended to have passed over the Powtowmac, after giving you an account of the vessels from the height below Benedict; but on observing the very tranquil scene which I have mentioned, I was led by the inference I draw from it to hasten back to take a view of the enemy's movements in this quarter, which it might be more important to the Govt. to be made acquainted with. I am now on the main road from Washington to Benedict, 12 miles from the latter, and find that no troops have passed in this direction. The reports make it probable that a force by land and water had been sent against the flotilla.'

Next day Monroe notified Madison that "imminent danger threatened the Capital," advised the removal of the Government records and suggested that materials be in readiness for the destruction of the bridges.[1] It seems strange to us at this day that no considerable army was available for the defense of Washington. Citing a letter from Winder to Armstrong[2], Adams says: "A thousand determined men might reach the town in thirty-six hours, and destroy it before any general alarm could be given. . . . Armstrong neglected to fortify. After experience had proved his error, he still argued in writing to a committee of Congress that fortifications would have exhausted the

[1] Gilman's Monroe, p. 117.
[2] Dated July 9, 1814, State Papers, Military Affairs, I, 543; Adams, History, Vol. VIII, Chapter V, "Bladensburg," pp. 120-148.

Treasury; 'that bayonets are known to form the most efficient barriers.' He did not even provide the bayonets. . . . Being an indolent man, negligent of detail, he never took unnecessary trouble; and, having no proper staff at Washington, he was without military advisers whose opinions he respected. The President and Monroe fretted at his indifference, the people of the District were impatient under it, and every one except Armstrong was in constant terror of attack," but he would do nothing. He was sure that Baltimore was the city the British wanted. At a Cabinet meeting, June 23, after Armstrong, Jones and Campbell had agreed to "abandon impressment as a *sine qua non*" in the negotiations at Ghent, the subject of putting the capital under adequate military protection was discussed. It was agreed that a corps should be organized. Armstrong suggested General Moses Porter as the commander, but Madison overruled him and appointed General William H. Winder. Madison's idea was to mollify the Maryland Federalists, since Winder was of that stripe and related to the Governor of Maryland. Armstrong carried out the Cabinet programme, but did it with bad grace and "left further measures to Winder, Monroe and Madison." His conduct "irritated the President," what he did was "passive," and perfunctory.

General Winder could muster but three hundred regulars and four thousand militia, under General Samuel Smith, a man politically at odds with Madison and Monroe; General Tobias E. Stansbury of the Eleventh Maryland Brigade, and General John Stricker of the Third Maryland Brigade. The Virginia militia had been summoned, but could not report for duty since they were without flints for their firelocks. Later, militiamen flocked down from the Maryland and Pennsylvania counties in the region between the Potomac and Susquehanna. Ross said that he "didn't care if it rained militia," but he underrated the prowess of the citizen soldiery. Winder should have had a force

of militia at least thrice as large as that which he
brought together at Bladensburg to dispute the advance
of "Wellington's invincibles." Just wherein Monroe
was to blame in this state of affairs is not clear. He
had expressed himself as frankly as he could on the
subject of Armstrong's shortcomings. We are no
apologist for Madison and Monroe, nor yet their critic.
That there was something much amiss when, after a
long-continued menace, the British could land five
thousand troops and take an unobstructed road to the
Capital goes without the saying. We use the word
"unobstructed," yet are reminded of the rather curious
fact that Prince George County used to be full of
plantation gates.[1] The high-roads were shut off by
them. But there was plenty of tall timber too, and,
if the defense had been even ordinarily energetic, this
timber would have been felled across the roads. And
now what of Commodore Barney — our fighting Joshua?
He kept the British back much longer than did the
gates. But by and by he blew up his gunboats at
Nottingham and, with five hundred sailors and marines,
retreated from the Patuxent toward Washington.

Winder, unsparing of himself but unequal to his task,
blundered from the start. He mistook the real spot
for his battle. He thought the British would be so
foolish as to approach by the road leading to the Navy
Yard. He himself retreated by that road and reported
at the White House that night. Next morning he
heard that the British were marching by way of
Bladensburg. Adams[2] says:

"Monroe notified Serurier Monday evening that the battle would
be fought at Bladensburg. . . . Everyone (except Winder) looked
instinctively to that spot. . . . No sooner did Winder receive
intelligence at ten o'clock on Wednesday morning that the British
were on the march to Bladensburg, than in the utmost haste he
started for the same point, preceded by Monroe and followed by
the President and the rest of the Cabinet. Monroe was earliest

---

[1] See Life of William Winston Seaton, pp. 115,116.
[2] H. Adams, Hist. Vol. VIII, p. 138 *et seq.* He cites Rush's Narrative, Winder's
Narrative, Review of J. Q. Adams, by Kosciusko Armstrong, and William Pinkney's
Statement; State Papers, Military Affairs I, pp. 542-572.

on the ground. Between eleven and ten o'clock he reached a spot where hills slope gently toward the Eastern Branch, a mile or more in broad incline, the little straggling town of Bladensburg opposite, beyond a shallow stream, and hills and woods in the distance. Some Maryland regiments arrived at the same time with Monroe. About three thousand were then on the field, and their officers were endeavoring to form them in line of battle. General Stansbury, of the Baltimore brigade, made such arrangement as he thought best. Monroe, who had no military rank, altered it without Stansbury's knowledge."[1]

This is the incident mentioned by Higginson, already cited in connection with Monroe's "penchant for military affairs," as Babcock[2] characterizes it. Other writers refer to it, and not a few magnify its importance. It was noon of a hot day before Winder reached the field. "At the same time the British light brigade made its appearance, and wound down the opposite road, a mile away, a long column of redcoats, six abreast moving with the quick regularity of old soldiers, and striking directly at the American centre. They reached the village on one side of the stream as Winder's troops poured down the hill on the other.

Madison, Monroe, Armstrong and other officials watched the preparations for a fight. Just before it began Madison said to Monroe: "It would now be proper for us to retire in the rear leaving the military movements to the military men."[3]

A little more and they would have been captured. "A volunteer scout warned them of their danger."[4] They left the field. Winder had no time to improve

---

[1] H. Adams, Hist. Vol. VIII, p. 140. He refers to Stansbury's Report; Monroe's Letter; State Papers. Millitary Affairs I, p. 596. Rossiter Johnson in his History says that Monroe moved three of Stansbury's regiments five hundred yards further up the slope.

[2] Rise of American Nationality, by K. C. Babcock, p. 137; State Papers Military I, 524; Armstrong's Notices, II, 140.

[3] "Come General Armstrong, come Colonel Monroe; let us go and leave it to the Commanding-General"; "and," adds Rossiter Johnson, in his History of the war of 1812, "it was not long before the militia followed their illustrious example." It was the day of Scott's "Marmion;" and a New York paper said:
"Fly, Monroe, fly! Run Armstrong, run!
Were the last words of Madison."

[4] Letter of William Simmons, State Papers, Military Affairs, I. p. 596; quoted by Adams.

the dispositions made by his subordinates. That was one cause of the trouble that now came on. Thornton's eighty-first regiment dashed across the bridge in the face of fire. It was checked, but only momentarily; and pushed on till it met fiercer fire when it sought cover. A fresh regiment, fording the branch above, turned the American left. Winder's men then broke. Thereafter, it was a rout. There was fast going at the Bladenburg races.

But Barney? Barney was heading for Bladensburg on the run to get into the fight. He was on the main road, within a mile of the field, when first the fugitives came at him; then, the British. Seeing Barney, with his battery, the British took notice, halted, formed and advanced. Barney sent them back with his fire. They again advanced, but he smashingly cleared the road with his eighteen pounder. A third and fourth attack found him still there. They then tried to flank him on the right; but he sent Captain Miller, with three twelve-pounders, and stopped them. But with the militia gone, the British did finally flank Barney, whose men were quick as cats and fought to the last. Gleig says that some of them were bayoneted with fuses in their hands. Barney, wounded, "ordered his officers to leave him where he lay." The British took him to their hospital at Bladensburg and treated him " with the most marked attention, respect and politeness as if I was a brother."[1]

It was now four o'clock and battle dust was no longer visible. The British were used up with the heat and fight. They rested for two hours. It was six before their advance reached Washington.

Mrs. Madison, meantime, was having an unhappy experience. Tuesday, August 23, she wrote to her sister Anna, Mrs. Richard Cutts: " Disaffection stalks around us. . . . I am determined not to go myself till I

---

[1] Barney's Report, State Papers, Military Affairs, I, p. 579. See the Campaigns of the British Army at Washington and New Orleans, by Rev. G. R. Gleig, chaplain-general, p. 126; "The Subaltern," by Gleig; James' History (British) II, p. 499

see Mr. Madison safe." Penciled notes came from him. "I lived a lifetime in those last moments," she said, waiting for Mr. Madison's return, "and in an agony of fear least he might have been taken prisoner." She pressed as many Cabinet papers into trunks as could be bestowed in one carriage. French John wanted to lay a train of powder so as to blow up the British as soon as they should enter the White House; but she, a sensible woman, would have none of it. Wednesday noon, August 24, she wrote: "Since sunrise I have been turning my spy-glass in every direction. . . . Three o'clock — Will you believe it, my sister, we have had a battle, or a skirmish near Bladensburg, and here I am still within sound of the cannon. Mr. Madison comes not! May God protect us!" A messenger came to bid her to seek a safer place. Then, another. He, too, was dust-covered, with panic in his eye. Finally, with the British in sight, she withdrew. Jean Sioussat, the French porter, cut Stuart's Washington from its frame and saved it. He was the last of Mme. Dolly's entourage to leave the White House.[1] He handed the key to the Russian Minister appropriately named Andre de Daschkoff (Mr. Dashoff) who was hurrying away to Philadelphia.[2]

British soldiers were already in the city. Ross arrived about dark. A shot from Gallatin's house killed his horse. The house was burned, and soon the victors began to set fire to other places. Admiral Cockburn, on horseback, rode through the town. He said he wanted to find the office of *The National Intelligencer,* "as his friend Gales had honored him with some hard rubs." Two women who lived in an adjoin-

---

[1] She went off in a carriage with Mrs. Anna Cutts — the "Sister Cutts," of an ungallant Federalist lampoon, somewhat in this style.

"Sister Cutts and Cutts and I,
    And Cutts' children three
Shall in the coach, and you shall ride,
    On horseback after we."

Sioussat gave the precious painting to Jacob Barker and Mr. de Peyster who hid it.

[2] Memoirs and Letters of Dolly Madison, 1886, pp. 108-115.

ing house begged him not to burn the place lest their dwelling too should be destroyed. "Be tranquil, ladies," said he; "you shall be as safely protected under my administration as under that of Mr. Madison." Cockburn, followed by a rabble, entered the House of Representatives, and took his seat in the Speaker's chair. With mockery, he put the motion: "Shall this harbor for Yankee democracy be burned." It was burned; and so were the White House, the Treasury Buildings and all other government structures except the Patent Office. Secretary Smith had already destroyed the Navy Yard. "I never saw a scene at once more terrible and more magnificent," wrote Serurier to Talleyrand; "your Highness knowing the picturesque nature and grandeur of the surroundings can form an idea of it. A profound darkness reigned in the part of the city that I occupy, and we were left to conjectures and to the lying reports of the negroes as to what was passing in the quarter illuminated by those fearful flames."

A tempest arose next day and helped to finish the work of the flames. Roofs were torn off, cannon lifted by the wind, soldiers buried under the debris. It was "a tremendous hurricane."

According to the contemporary British claim, Washington was sacked and burned because the Canadian Government buildings at York (now Toronto) had been put to the torch. The soldiers who set fire to the York buildings said they did it on impulse when they saw a human scalp hanging on the wall in the legislative chamber. There had been a British premium on scalps, and when the soldiers saw the scalp they saw red. What these soldiers did under such provocation was no excuse for the deliberate retaliatory outrage suggested by Sir George Prevost; threatened by Admiral Cochrane, in his letter to Monroe, and executed with alacrity by General Ross. When the French Minister sent a request for a guard, so that his house might not be pillaged, his messenger found "General

Ross[1] in the act of piling up the furniture in the White House drawing-room preparatory to setting it on fire."

Adams dwells upon the mortification of Madison and Monroe. They left the battlefield at two and reached the White House at three. Madison had been in the saddle since eight. The Cabinet was to reassemble at Frederick; but he and Secretary Jones and Attorney General Richard Rush, instead of riding north, crossed into Virginia and took a carriage westward. "Monroe's adventures," says Henry Adams, "were not less mortifying. . . . He did not return to the White House with Madison, but joined Winder and rode with him to the Capital, where he assented to an evacuation, and retired after the flying troops through Georgetown, passing the night on the Maryland side of the Potomac. The next morning he recrossed the river and overtook the President. After an interview with him, Monroe recrossed the river to Winder's headquarters at Montgomery Court House, where he resumed the military function." Adams is merciless toward Winder; he could neither "organize, fortify, fight nor escape." He was "worse than Hull, Smythe, Dearborn, Wilkinson or Winchester." If Winder, then, were so superlatively bad, why also abuse Monroe for trying to make the best of the bad Winder bargain? With respect to Winder, the simple truth is that he had no head for the business in hand. With respect to Monroe, he certainly conducted himself with good sense, courage and a patriotism that is ready to take the rub however raw it may be. He should have kept hands off at Bladensburg, but even that act of superrogation was due to excess of zeal. He was willing to invite even a century of invective, some of it almost humorous, if he could keep the enemy out of the Capital. As if in prescience of unctuous exaggeration, Monroe left a memorandum as to the President's movements and his own.

---

[1] "Serurier lived then in the house built by John Tayloe in 1800, called the Octagon, a few hundred yards from the War and Navy Departments and the White House." Adams, Hist, Vol. VIII, p. 145.

According to Monroe's narrative[1] Madison, with Attorney General Rush and General Mason, crossed into Virginia on the twenty-fourth and remained a few miles above the lower falls all next day. On the twenty, sixth he recrossed the Potomac and went to Brookville with the idea of joining General Winder. Monroe was with Winder, whose rendezvous was Montgomery Court House. On the twenty-sixth Winder marched toward Ellicott's Mills but in the evening pushed on in person to Baltimore, then menaced by British movements. Monroe remained with Generals Stansbury and Smith. The narrative continues:

"On the 27th, the Secretary of State, having heard that the enemy had evacuated the city, notified by express, to the President, and advised immediate return to the city for the purpose of re-establishing the government there. He joined the President on the same day at Brookville, accompanied by the Secretary of State and Attorney General; set out immediately for Washington, where they arrived at five in the afternoon. The enemy's squadron was then battering Fort Washington, which was evacuated and blown up by the commander on that evening, without the least resistance. The unprotected inhabitants of Alexandria in consternation capitulated, and those of Georgetown and the city were preparing to follow the example. Such was the state of affairs when the President entered the city on the evening of the 27th. There was no force organized for its defence. The Secretary of War was at Fredericktown, and General Winder at Baltimore. The effect of the late disaster on the whole Union and the world was anticipated. Prompt measures were indispensable. Under these circumstances, the President requested Mr. Monroe to take charge of the Department of War, and command the District *ad interim* with which he immediately complied."

Monroe learned that certain citizens were about to send a deputation to the British commander. This he forbid: but planted some batteries and ordered Winder on the Virginia side to co-operate with the Maryland

---

[1] Gilman's Monroe, p. 119-122. Gilman says of this narrative: "It belongs to the class of *Mémoires pour servir*, or semi-official memoranda, and will serve to give prominence as to the Secretary's proceedings at this time, as he would like to have them remembered."

batteries. Colonel Winder would not recognize his authority, preferring to leave the field.[1]

"Monroe's act," says Adams, "whether such was his intention or not, was a *coup d'état*. The citizens, unable to punish the President, were rabid against Armstrong. Monroe, instead of giving to Armstrong in his absence such support as might have sustained him, took a position and exercised an authority that led necessarily to his overthrow. . . . All the President's recorded acts and conversation for months after the capture of Washington implied that he was greatly shaken by that disaster. He showed his prostration by helplessness. He allowed Monroe for the first time to control him; but he did not dismiss Armstrong." That same day Armstrong returned. He offered to resign. Madison suggested "temporary retirement." "Between conscious intrigue and unconscious instinct," adds Adams, "no clear line of division was ever drawn. Monroe, by one method or the other, gained his point and drove Armstrong from the Cabinet; but the suspicion that he had intrigued for that object troubled his mind to the day of his death." [2]

As we have just seen, Madison appointed Monroe Secretary of War, on the thirty-first.[3] On September 29, Governor Tompkins of New York was offered the State portfolio. He declined it; so as the President searched no further, Monroe was both Secretary of State and Secretary of War.

General Ross said that he had selected Baltimore as his winter-quarters. He left Washington by night and reached Marlboro, on the Patuxent, August 29. He descended that river to the bay and went up it. After sacking Alexandria, Gordon of the Potomac Squadron also returned to the Chesapeake. One of the marauding Potomac ships was the "Minelaus," Sir Peter

---

[1] Monroe Mss.— In the Gouverneur Mss. is a corroborating letter by William Robinson.

[2] McKenney's Memoirs, p. 44, as cited in Adams.

[3] Monroe demanded a commission as Secretary of War and received it September 27.

Parker, who led a fresh expedition to the "Sassafras" on the Eastern Shore. There two colonial towns were burned — Georgetown and Fredericktown. Sir Peter stirred up the hornets, and was killed.[1]

Ross, too, got into a hornets' nest. When the British fleet entered the Patapsco, Ross landed on the night of the eleventh and by daybreak had nine thousand men on shore at North Point. Then Cochrane with the ships went up toward the city and bombarded Fort McHenry, Major Armistead defending, from six o'clock Tuesday morning, September 12, till six o'clock Wednesday morning, September thirteenth, when Francis Scott Key thrilled to see the star-spangled banner still afloat above the ramparts. He was a prisoner on one of Cochrane's ships, which hurled fifteen hundred two-hundred pound bombs.

On shore the defenders did just as well as the men in the fort. It was the reverse of Bladensburg. But this time there were fourteen thousand men under arms; including the picked companies of the city. General John Stricker led thirty-two hundred of these — artillery, cavalry, infantry — out toward North Point and, when within five miles of the British landing-place, stood waiting.

General Ross and his aides slept that night at the Gosage dwelling. In the morning Gosage asked his guest if he should prepare supper for his party. "No," said Ross; "I shall sup in Baltimore tonight, or in hell." He mounted his white charger and rode away. The charger helped to make a target for the Baltimore riflemen, who that morning heard someone cry out: "Remember, boys. General Ross[2] rides a white horse today!" In the skirmish preliminary to the actual clinch it so happened that these riflemen encountered

---

[1] Sir Peter was buried in Westminster Abbey. His epitaph would lead one to imagine that he died heroically. No doubt he was a hero; but not on that rather unseemly marauding occasion. Far from it.

[2] Life of John H. W. Hawkins by Rev. William George Hawkins, 1859. J. H. W. Hawkins, whose hat was pierced by a bullet, saw Ross fall. Wells and McComas, young Americans, fell at the same time.

Ross, who fell thus early in the battle. The onrush of hardened veterans made Stricker give way and go back a little; but the fight was so sharp and the British losses were so heavy that they drew off and returned to their ships. "Did I not tell you," said "the Parson of the Isles," when some of the survivors went ashore on Tangier Island, on their way home, "that you would not take Baltimore?" Cochrane sailed for Halifax; Cockburn for Bermuda. By December tenth, Cochrane with fifty sail and sixteen thousand veterans, with a thousand heavy guns, was at the mouth of the Mississippi.[1] There were a few fights in the preliminaries, and then the battle of January eight — Jackson's great victory, bringing balm for hurt feelings and introducing a new character who would soon make his presence felt in the affairs of the nation.

"At the moment of the declaration of war," wrote Monroe to Jonathan Russell, *chargé d'affaires* in London, August 21, 1812, "the President, regretting the necessity which produced it, looked for its termination and provided for it." Madison stipulated a repeal of the Orders in Council and the cessation of impressment. Russell made Lord Castlereagh acquainted with these stipulations. As Admiral Warren had left England with a proposition for an armistice in view of the repeal of the Orders in Council, Castlereagh would not take up Madison's points, Russell wrote to Monroe, September 17, 1812. Lord Castlereagh once observed somewhat loftily, that "*if the American government was so anxious to get rid of the war*, it would have an opportunity of so doing on learning of the revocation of the Orders in

---

[1] The biographer of Sir John Burgoyne says that the British plan to seize Louisiana originated with the Admiral on station, and adds: "It is a remarkable feature of English wars that so large a number of combined naval and military operations have been undertaken by English Ministers on information supplied by Admirals on foreign station." "Seamen," he adds, "are too apt to look upon the storming of a fortress in the same light as boarding an enemy's ship. Packenham was aware of a possible grand error of the sort, and was extremely anxious to get upon the ground ahead of his army; but the Statira, the frigate that bore him hither, landed him later than he had wished." Life and Correspondence of Field Marshal Sir John Burgoyne, Bart., by Lieut.-Col. George Wrottesley, 1873.

Council." Captain Mahan[1] sees an inamicable fling on his Lordship's part in Russell's italicized words, and a threat in Monroe's reminder of "the injuries which cannot fail to result from a prosecution of the war." "In transcribing his instructions," comments Mahan, "Russell discreetly omitted the latter phrase; but the omission, like the words themselves, betrays consciousness that the administration was faithful to the traditions of its party, dealing in threats rather than deeds." Through a great part of the final negotiations "the impression thus made remained with the British ministers."

On March 8, 1813, Monroe was gratified to learn that Czar Alexander of Russia, through his Chancellor, Count Roumanzoff, had offered to mediate between Great Britain and the United States. He at once accepted the offer; and associated Albert Gallatin and James A. Bayard with the resident minister at St. Petersburg, John Quincy Adams, as American Commissioners. But Lord Castlereagh sent Monroe an offer to treat directly. This invitation was accepted in January, 1814. Gottenburg was suggested by Lord Castlereagh as the place of meeting and Monroe agreed to this; but subsequently Ghent was selected instead. There were five Americans and three British Commissioners; for Henry Clay and Jonathan Russell, then Minister to Sweden, were joined with Adams, Gallatin and Bayard as envoys, while vice-Admiral Lord Gambier, Henry Coulbourn, of the Colonial Office, and Dr. William Adams, admiralty lawyer, served Great Britain.

The American envoys arrived at Ghent, July 6, 1814. Clay dined alone. The others, he wrote, "sit after dinner and drink bad wine and smoke cigars." He would do nothing of the sort. Cakes and ale? No, not for a virtuous Kentuckian. But Adams writes that, just before rising, he heard Clay's card-party breaking

---

[1] Sea Power in its Relation to the War of 1812, by Capt. A. T. Mahan, 1905, 2 vols. Vol. II, p. 410.

up. Adams and Clay were often at odds. Clay "waxed
loud and warm"; he was "peevish and fractious."
But it was a good thing to have him at Ghent. The
British were hard to deal with. They were extreme
in their demands,[1] could see only their side, until
Wellington rebuked them and brought them to reason.
The negotiations lasted five months. A. T. Mahan[2]
has reviewed them illuminatingly in an article on
Monroe and the Treaty of Ghent. Whatever Clay
might urge, peace was in order. What was the use to
continue a war that could only end in more bloodshed
and a big debt for posterity to pay? As Cobbett[3]
put it, in a letter to Lord Liverpool: "Have we not
generals of the first talents and the best of veteran
troops employed? What a Drummond, a Ross, a
Pakenham, a Gibbs, could not perform with a hundred
thousand men, who could? Had the Duke of Wellington
been at Orleans what would have prevented his sharing
the fate of Pakenham?" No doubt the long-headed
Duke foresaw the insuperable difficulties. It was he
who threw cold water on a war he did not relish.
Captain Mahan tells why he did not come to America.

It was high time that each side should sum up as
to its successes and shortcomings on land and sea,
and sign a treaty. In spite of the Corsican's overthrow,
the rich and powerful British backers of the war against
him were pocket-weary. They wished to be rid of the
income tax. What had been gained in America?
Nothing. As for the looting and burning at Washington,
they shook their heads about it. So the treaty of
Ghent was signed on Christmas Eve, which fell on
Saturday, December 24, 1814. The British Commissioners were true to form to the last. Like Minister
Merry they were sticklers for precedence and insisted

---

[1] For Monroe's letters and Gallatin's replies prior to these negotiations see
Gallatin's Works (Adams) Vol. I, on impressment, pp. 540, 1.2.

[2] In the American Historical Review, Vol. II, pp. 68-87.

[3] Letters of William Cobbett, Esq., 1815, p. 405. Cobbett wrote a little book
on the war entitled: "The Pride of Britannia Humbled, or the Queen of the Ocean
unqueened by the American Cock Boats."

upon signing all copies of the treaty before the American subscribers had affixed their signatures.[1] Henry Carroll son of Charles Carroll of Bellevue, near Georgetown, "one of the intimates of Madison and Monroe" sailed from England in the sloop-of-war "Favorite," January 2, 1815, bringing the American counterpart of the document, and landed at New York, February 11. He handed the treaty to Madison, Tuesday evening, February 13. "'Not an inch ceded or lost' were the first words we heard in Washington of the treaty," says Charles J. Ingersoll.[2]

Ratifications were exchanged, February 17, 1815, at Washington; and the welcome outcome was announced in Congress, February 20.[3]

---

[1] Clay signed the treaty "with a heavy heart." He called it "a dammed bad treaty." Henry Clay by Carl Schurz, Vol. I, p. 116.

[2] Historical Sketch of the Second War between the United States of America and Great Britain, by Charles J. Ingersoll, 1849, 2 vols., Vol. II, p. 311.

[3] For the text of the Treaty of Ghent see Select Documents of United States History, Macdonald, p. 191.

CHAPTER XIV

PRESIDENT OF THE UNITED STATES

Just, as in "Hudibras," "silence like a poultice came to heal the blows of sound," so now the peace of Ghent stilled the clamor of war and of the Federalist opposition. No doubt the happiest man in the United States, next to James Madison, was James Monroe.

We have realized by this time why Madison and Monroe go together. To speak of one is to speak of the other. With a single breath we utter both names. Though, as a fact, Madison was seven years older than Monroe, they appear in our imaginings as twin sons of Uncle Sam. Certainly, they were close contemporaries — these celebrated founders, both born on the Rappahannock, both identified with the Revolutionary struggle, both participants in the great task of Constitution-making, both followers of Jefferson[1], both President in the period when the foundations of democracy were laid and each destined to be memorialized cheek by jowl in histories, in paintings, in statues and in the names of the counties, towns, cities and villages in the majority of the States of the American Union. One who scans a list of counties is considerably edified at the great number of "Monroes," and "Madisons" to be met with. It is so with streets, squares and parks.

But there are points of difference, too. Monroe, blue-eyed and of light complexion, says Dr. T. T.

---

[1] Martin Van Buren, while visiting Patrick Henry's friend Judge Spencer Roane in his sick-room at Richmond, Va., noticed that busts of Jefferson, Madison and Monroe were arranged in the room in the order named. Van Buren remarked that if there had been anything of the courtier in his [Roane's] character he would have placed Mr. Monroe, he being the actual President, at the head, instead of the foot. He replied with emphasis, "No! No! No man ranks before Tom Jefferson in my house! They stand, sir in the order of my confidence and affection." Van Buren's Autobiography.

Moran, was "six feet tall, broad, square-shouldered, and impressive in personal appearance. He was a man of rugged physique, raw-boned and by no means handsome. . . . At one time during the War of 1812 . . . for a period of ten days and nights, he did not go to bed, or remove his clothing, and was in the saddle the greater part of the time." This sufficiently proves his "great physical strength and endurance." No doubt his hardening experiences as a campaigner served him well in after life. John Marshall, when asked in his old age to what he attributed his own continued vigor, said that he thought it due to the habit of walking acquired by him when as a youth he marched up and down the continent. Monroe "did not impress his contemporaries as a particularly cultured man. He was awkward and diffident; and without grace either in manner or appearance."

Small and bald, Madison was in contrast with Monroe. Madison is spoken of as "frail in body but powerful in mind — that prim little man who always appeared prematurely old." "He was so modest that the color came and went upon his cheeks as upon a young girl's." "He represented pure intelligence," says John Fiske, "which is doubtless why his popular fame has not been equal to his merit." Rufus Choate[1] speaks of "the calm, capacious intelligence of Mr. Madison — that great man among our greatest, the dead or living." Hugh B. Grigsby, who saw him, says that Stuart's likeness of Madison was true to nature. He always wore black "his coat being cut in what is termed dress-fashion; his breeches short, with buckles at the knees; black silk stockings, and shoes with strings or long fair top boots when out in cold weather, or when he rode on horseback of which he was fond. His hat was of the shape and fashion usually worn by gentlemen of his age. He wore powder on his hair, which was dressed full over the ears, tied behind and

---

[1] Works of Rufus Choate, with Memoir of Samuel Gilman Brown, 2 vols.

brought to a point above the forehead, to cover in some
degree his baldness."

No nineteenth century President, except Abraham
Lincoln, ever had a more trying time than Madison.
His humiliations were many, and the blow Admiral
Cochrane gave him nearly broke him down. But now
all was over — all was well. With the passing of the
acute foreign controversies, party animosity ceased —
the Federalist party perished. At least, no more was
heard of it as a party; though the vital ideas of its
supporters continued to reproduce themselves, as they
do to this day. A marked division began in the Republican party. There was what Alexander Johnston, in
his "United States," calls "a nationalizing tendency,"
due to the younger men, who constantly pulled Monroe
away from the older Republicanism. Some of these
were from the West. The country was growing fast;
and, with the war over, and the better part of the continent ours, the prospect was as bright as the sunset
skies — with but one dark cloud, slavery; and that, as
yet, had not begun to menace the life of the nation.
Indiana entered the Union in 1816, Mississippi in 1817,
Illinois in 1818, Alabama in 1819, Maine in 1820 and
Missouri in 1821. By 1830 the population would be
thirteen million. A new bank-act having been proposed
by Madison and put through by Congress, specie
payment was resumed by all the sound State banks on
February 20, 1817.

In a speech in the House of Representatives, in
February the year before, Ben Hardin of Kentucky
had spoken of Monroe as the "heir apparent." But
that the choice of Monroe was not quite a foregone
conclusion is indicated by articles in contemporary
newspapers, as well as by the figures of the Congressional caucus. Naturally there was a sectional protest.
Governor James Sullivan,[1] Republican, of Massachusetts, thought that the Virginians had held the Presidency "as often as they were entitled to"; so he

---

[1] Life of James Sullivan, by Thomas C. Amory, 1859, 2 vols. Vol. II, p. 254.

MRS. MONROE (Benjamin West)

advocated De Witt Clinton as Madison's successor. "Virginia," it was said later, "had eight out of the first nine presidential periods." Parton called these periods those of the "Secretary dynasty."

Monroe was nominated by a caucus of the Republican members of Congress, William II. Crawford of Georgia being his competitor. There were in Washington at that time, 141 Republican Congressmen, of whom 119 attended the caucus, either in person or by proxy. The vote was Monroe, 65; Crawford, 54. For Vice-President, Daniel D. Tompkins of New York was nominated by the same caucus. Of nineteen States, with a total electoral vote of 221, Monroe carried sixteen; and received 183 votes. Rufus King, his opponent, carried three States, with 34 electoral votes.[1]

On his first inauguration day, Tuesday, March 4, 1817, Monroe was favored with fine weather. In contrast with that of his second inauguration, it was truly "delightful."[2] Schouler speaks of it as "a day of spring sunshine unusual for early March in the latitude of our National Capitol"; and adds: "The softness of the air, the radiance of the noonday sun, the serenity of the rural surroundings, from wooded heights to the placid Potomac, carried a sense of tranquil happiness to the hearts of thousands of spectators who had assembled for the outdoor ceremonies on Capitol Hill."[3] But the ceremonies were not held out of doors. They began in the temporary Capitol, a brick building "erected by David Carroll and others, soon after the British invasion, and leased to the Government for the accommodation of the national legislature." This building was known later as the Capitol prison, frequently referred to in Civil War

---

[1] "Vacancies," as they were then termed, 4. For Vice President, D. D. Tompkins had 183 electoral votes; John E. Howard, 22; James Ross, 5; John Marshall, 4; Robert G. Harper 3. "Vacanies" 4.

[2] Thus described in The National Intelligencer, March 5, and in Niles' Weekly Register, Baltimore, March 8. For a contemporary account, with the inaugural address in full, see Niles, Vol. XII, No. 2.

[3] History of the United States under the Constitution, by James Schouler, six volumes, Vol. III, pp. 1-3.

histories. Just to the northeast, were the ruins of the old Capitol — fragments of marble, heat-cracked columns and a pile of debris that served as reminders to the thousands of visitors of Admiral Cochrane's vandal hand. The visitors found another reminder of the same sort at the White House, now in process of reconstruction. At this particular time, the Monroes occupied a private dwelling, and it was from this private house that President-Elect Monroe and Vice-President-Elect Tompkins, escorted by many citizens on horseback, under guidance of the Inaugural Committee, proceeded at half-past eleven to Capitol Hill. Madison rode with Monroe. As many as eight thousand people were in the Capitol grounds; "such a concourse," declares Niles' paper, as "was never before seen in Washington. The President was received on his arrival, with military honors, by the marine corps, by the Georgetown rifles, a company of artillery and two companies of infantry from Alexandria."

The saluting guns without notified those within of the presence of the new Executive. Everything was ready for his reception. The Senators had met in their own chamber at eleven o'clock, had organized and had gone thence to that of the Representatives. Here were assembled the members of the House, the Judges of the Supreme Court, the foreign ministers, the heads of departments, visiting dignitaries and as many ladies as could be accommodated with seats. The chamber was crowded. Vice-President Tompkins took the chair; Ex-President Madison and John Gaillard, President of the Senate, sat to the right, and Henry Clay, Speaker of the House to the left, along with the diplomatic corps. The Judges of the Supreme Court were at the table in front of the chair; beyond these sat the Senators; and, in the body of the house, the Representatives. At the conclusion of the Vice-President's address, the Senate adjourned, whereupon the ceremonies were transferred to a portico that had been erected out of doors. On this portico, with a host

of honorables gathered around, Chief Justice John
Marshall, in his black gown, administered the oath
of office to the President — an old schoolmate of his,
as we well remember, a comrade-in-arms, a near friend
when they first wooed the law and compared the
beauty of the belles of Richmond, but now of late
somewhat apart, owing to the political embitterments
of a stormy quarter of a century. "The oath," says
Niles' *Register*, "was announced by a single gun, and
followed by salutes from the Navy Yard, the battery,
from Fort Washington and several pieces of artillery
on the ground." Then the multitudes dispersed, many
of the dignitaries proceeding at once to the Monroe
dwelling where a reception was given. Madison and
his wife shared with their successors the honors of the
hour. At three the affair was over; and, in the quiet
of his study, the fifth President was enabled to dis-
engage himself from the exacting duties of the trying
day.[1]

It was Josiah Quincy who first alluded to Madison
and Monroe as "James the First and the Second."
The newspapers caught up the phrase and made much
of it. But even the Federalist comment was jocular
and friendly. The "Era of Good Feeling" had come.
Nathan Sargent [2]("Oliver Oldschool") informs us that,
throughout Monroe's eight years in the White House,
"tranquility pervaded the country like the placid
calm of an Indian summer." William J. Grayson
writes:

"There was a pause in politics. Federal parties and their distinctions and disputes were in abeyance. The great achievement
of Mr. Monroe's administration was to keep everything quiet,
to please everybody, and secure a second term of office. We were
all Federalists then, and all Republicans. The Missouri question

---

[1] An English paper, noticing the election of Mr. Monroe to the Presidency of
the United States, observes that he lost a leg in the Revolutionary War, and is
rather of the Washington school — Item in Niles' *Weekly Register*, May 31, 1817.

[2] In Public Men and Events from the Commencement of Mr. Monroe's Administration in 1817 to the Close of Mr. Fillmore's Administration in 1853, 2 vols.
Vol. I, p. 19.

excited some commotion but it subsided into compromise. The vexed question seemed to be settled, and everybody was again in a good humor. It was the reign of peace and dulness, of which Mr. Monroe was the happy representative."[1]

"This near approach to unanimity," says George Ticknor Curtis,[2] "evinces almost an obliteration of party distinctions. Mr. Monroe's personal popularity and the general confidence that was reposed in him had a considerable influence in producing what was called 'The Era of Good Feeling' which prevailed while he administered the government. The Federalists, who had been strongest in the North and East were conciliated by his first Inaugural, while his strength was not weakened among the Republicans (Democrats) of the South. In truth it was not until the war was over and some of the animosities which it caused had begun to fade that the attention of men began to be directed to the question of internal administration, which would involve the exploration of the Federal Powers and a discussion of policies applicable to a state of peace. No sectionalism disturbed the country." Did this placidity, this good feeling, develop of itself; or did Monroe promote it, by what Calhoun spoke of as his "intellectual Patience"?[3] No doubt Monroe was fortunate in coming into the Presidency at the very moment when the great quarrels with France and England were over, and when the Federalists had discredited themselves by unpatriotic lukewarmness,

---

[1] Memoir of James Louis Petigrew, by W. J. Grayson, 1866.
[2] Life of James Buchanan, 2 vols. Vol. I, p. 23.
[3] "He (Monroe) had a wonderful intellectual patience, and could, above all men that I ever knew, when called on to decide an important point, hold the subject immovably fixed under his attention till he had mastered it in all its relations. It was mainly to this admirable quality that he owed his highly accurate judgment. I have known many much more rapid reaching the conclusion but very few with a certainty so unerring." Schouler, Vol. III, p. 205, who refers to Monroe Mss. August 8, 1831, and adds: "This letter, not too laudatory, which was written to Gouverneur on the news of Monroe's death is in Calhoun's tenderest strain. He accords to Monroe a high station in the eyes of posterity. 'Though not brilliant,' he says 'few men were his equals in wisdom, firmness and devotion to his country.'" In these same Mss. may be found deserved tributes from Wirt and Richard Rush and others. See also Adams' Eulogy; Watson, Benton and others, cited in Gilman's Life of Monroe; 4 Madison's Writings (1831).

by seditious utterances and threats of disunion at a crisis in the life of the republic. We have seen that when the time was inopportune as, for instance, when at Madrid and at London, Monroe could do little; and we conclude that his administration must have been a stormy one had the winds of circumstance still blown a gale. But, with this said, we may add that Monroe took full advantage of his opportunities when in the White House and with great skill and painstaking sought to help along whatever promoted the continuance of a rational, prosperous and happy age.

There had been a great deal of pulling and hauling that winter as to his cabinet, a strong one, selected with great care. Monroe had aimed to put a fit man into each place, and he had kept in mind the desirability of avoiding heartburnings. To Jefferson he had written, February 23:

"On full consideration of all circumstances I have thought it would produce a bad effect to place anyone from this quarter of the Union in the dept. of State, or from the South or West. You know how much has been said to impress a belief on the country, north or east of this, that the citizens from Virga, holding the Presidency have made appointments to that dept. to secure the succession from it to the Presidency of the person who happens to be from that State."

He thought that in his own case his service in the war department had helped to take out the sting, or at least some of it.[1] However, the prejudice was still strong. Should he nominate a southern man the effect would be to antagonize the whole country north of Delaware. His wish was to forestall such a combination. He added:

"With this view, I have thought it advisable to select a person for the Department of State from the Eastern States, in consequence of which my attention has been turned to Mr. Adams,

---

[1] Schouler calls attention (Vol. III, p. 3) to the fact that, when conscription seemed inevitable, in 1814, Monroe frankly told his friends, who were preparing to nominate him for the Presidency, that as he must take the odium of proposing and executing so unpopular a measure they ought to put him aside. War ended suddenly and without conscription." Monroe Mss.

who by his age, long experience in our foreign affairs, and adoption into the Republican party seems to have superior pretensions to any there. To Mr. Crawford I have intimated my sincere desire that he will remain where he is. To Mr. Clay the department of war was offered which he declined. It is offered to Govr. Shelby, who will be nominated to it before his answer is rec'd. Mr. Crowninshield, it is understood, will remain in the Navy Department."[1]

He wrote in like vein, but with less particularity to General Andrew Jackson, March 1, 1817. "At this moment," he said, "our friend, Mr. Campbell, called and informed me not to nominate you (for the Department of War.)"[2]

The Cabinet consisted of John Quincy Adams of Massachusetts, Secretary of State; William H. Crawford, of Georgia, Secretary of the Treasury; John C. Calhoun, of South Carolina, Secretary of War; William Wirt of Virginia, Attorney General; and Benjamin W. Crowninshield, of Massachusetts, Secretary of the Navy, who in the fall of 1818, gave way to Smith Thompson of New York. The Postmaster General, not a cabinet officer, was Return J. Meigs of Ohio. Not only were these able men but the various sections of the country were considerately drawn upon.[3]

John Quincy Adams,[4] then Minister to England, records in his Memoirs, Volume III, page 497, under date of April 16, 1817: "Soon after rising this morning, I received four letters. One was from James Monroe, President of the United States, dated March 6 last,

---

[1] Writings of Monroe, Vol. VI, pp. 2-4.

[2] Parton's Life of Jackson; also Monroe's Writings, Vol. VI, p. 4.

[3] There were few changes in the Cabinet during Monroe's eight years. When Brockholst Livingston died, Monroe made Thompson a Justice of the Supreme Court; and Samuel L. Southard of New Jersey became Secretary of the Navy. Ex-Chancellor Kent's friends thought he should have had the Justiceship; but he became a law professor at Columbia and wrote his Commentaries. This, thinks Schouler, worked out well. There was another change in Monroe's cabinet when Meigs, who was out of health gave way to John McLean of Ohio. Postmastership disputes developed at this time. A New York case, involving the factions and most of the big politicians, including Van Buren and Tompkins, caused a Cabinet meeting. Monroe refused to interfere with Meigs' appointment of Van Rensselaer.

[4] Like Monroe, John Quincy Adams was, as Gilman puts it, "a participant in the diplomatic questions evolved by two wars." When but fourteen, a "mature youngster" he went as Francis Dana's secretary to St. Petersburg. He was Minister to Holland, Prussia, Russia and England. His diary covers many years. In Gilman's belief "the Eulogy which he delivered on the death of Monroe remains to this day the best history of his political standing."

informing me that he had, with the sanction of the
Senate, committed me to the Department of State.
He requests me, in case of my acceptance of the office
to return to the United States with the least possible
delay to assume its duties and mentions that he sends
a special messenger with the letter, and copies by
various conveyances. That which I received is a
quadruplicate, and came by a vessel from Boston to
Liverpool. . . . 17th, I answered the letter from the
President of the United States, and accepted the
appointment of Secretary of State. The manner in
which the President has thought proper to nominate
me was certainly honorable to himself, as it was without
any intimation from me, or, as far as I know, from any
of my friends, which could operate as an inducement
to him. His motives were altogether of a public
nature."

"It was taken for granted," says Carl Schurz in his
"Henry Clay," "that he [Monroe] would have two
terms and that then the competition for the presidency
would be open to a new class of men. As Madison had
been Jefferson's Secretary of State before he became
President, and as Monroe had been Madison's, the
Secretaryship of State was looked upon as the stepping-
stone to the presidency. Those who expected to be
candidates for the highest place in the future, therefore
coveted it with peculiar solicitude." Clay felt that he
was entitled to it. He had lifted his voice in behalf of
manly America — against further acceptance of con-
tumelious cuffs and kicks; he had "fired the popular
heart" while the war was on, and he had helped to
wrest from haughty England, "on the pinnacle of her
pride," such terms as were secured at Ghent. It is
true he had called it "a damned bad treaty" when he
signed it; but that was a little matter he could conveniently forget. America had been despised before
the war. "What," he exclaimed, "is our situation
now! Respectability and character abroad, security
and confidence at home." But Monroe merely offered

him the war portfolio, or the mission to Russia. He declined both. He was re-elected Speaker of the House in the Fifteenth Congress, which met December 1, 1817, one hundred and forty members voting for him and but seven against. We shall see presently how Clay opposed Monroe; or, as Thomas Hart Clay, a grandson, expresses it, became "a gadfly on his flank." It is enough to add here that when Monroe, to mollify New England, determined to put Adams into his cabinet, he hurt Clay in a tender spot. Clay and Adams could not be made bedfellows even by politics. While at Ghent, Clay was "the fighting antithesis" of Adams, who was "steeped in the Puritan traditions of New England, confident in his learning and tenacious of the niceties of speech and behavior to which he had been bred." [1] Clay was fiery and fearless and said what he thought. When it was proposed to put it into the treaty that the British might trade with the western Indians he walked up and down the room, repeating, "I will never sign a treaty upon the *status ante bellum* with the Indian article, so help me God." He was always losing his temper — always bickering, sometimes quarreling with Adams, who himself was no angel. And Clay was right a great deal of the time. For instance, when the British took advanced ground and assumed a peremptory tone, Adams said that they would not recede — it was "inconceivable" that they would recede. Clay insisted that they would do just that; and they did. In Vol. III of his Memoirs, Adams tells, in his precise way, of his own naggings of Clay and of Clay's outbursts. Sometimes, indeed, the differences of these able men breed humor; we smile; we understand Clay, the Kentuckian, the American; we understand Adams, too, who by and by would grow warm enough, on one subject at least, and become "the Old Man Eloquent." Monroe, let us add, was in great good luck when Clay refused to enter the Cabinet. Monroe had his troubles with it as it was constituted;

---

[1] Henry Clay, by Thomas Hart Clay, 1910, p. 75.

he would have had more if Adams and Clay had been associated in it.

Crawford was of "almost gigantic stature, portly, dignified in bearing and self-possessed." In an old play he would have been chosen to take the part of a potentate, or Lord Chancellor, or the like. But biographers are not drawn to him. Schouler, who calls him "a very Saul in appearance," finds that he repaid Monroe's magnanimity in inviting him into his inner circle not by good work for the government, but by scheming for the presidency. "His game was for himself; and though he played a bold hand he lost it." [1] Adams, Calhoun and Wirt were true; not so Crawford.

It was transition time from old to new. A different type was developing. Of the three C's in the Cabinet — Calhoun, Crawford, and Crowninshield, two at least would rise to considerable celebrity. Outside the Cabinet was Jackson, who, as the hero of the battle of New Orleans, was to be reckoned with, not only by Monroe, but by everybody else.[2] Already Jackson's characteristics were known. Already his vehemence and pugnacity caused cautious gentlemen to tread softly in their dealings with him — this duellist who had fought with Colonel Waightstill Avery,[3] who had killed Charles Dickinson and who had barely escaped with his own life when, in attempting to horsewhip Thomas H. Benton, he had drawn the quick pistol-fire of both "Tom" and his brother Jesse. Jackson wanted Monroe for president when Madison was first nominated; and at a Monticello dinner, when summoned north to help reorganize the army gave the toast — "James Monroe, Secretary of War," the

---

[1] Schouler says that in the main, "the unfavorable estimate which Adams formed of Crawford is confirmed by all trustworthy testimony of this period," Monroe Mss.

[2] Jackson worked in the shop of a Waxhaw, S. C., saddler; Andrew Johnson was a tailor; Grant, a tanner.

[3] After this duel, Avery said: "Jackson, don't you think we are both d——fools?" "Do you?" inquired Jackson. "I most certainly do." "Then Col. Avery, allow me to say I am glad there is one subject we can agree on." This is from Parton, who says that Avery shot six feet over the tall man's head and Jackson a yard to one side of his big-bodied opponent.

inference being that Monroe was still his man for the higher office. Monroe welcomed him to Washington, where he was lionized. The country was divided into the Northern and Southern Military divisions, with General Brown in command of one and Jackson of the other, his headquarters being Nashville. When Jackson returned to Tennessee he declared that he was for Monroe "First, last and all the time." The two corresponded for many years.[1] Jackson's letters are full of patriotic pith. Monroe wrote to him on the rise, progress and policy of the Federalists; Jackson replied:[2] "I am free to declare that had I commanded the Military Department when the Hartford Convention met, if it had been the last act of my life, I should have punished the three principal leaders of the party." Here is a forehint of what he would do with nullifiers, North or South.

Jackson was a forceful, self-willed man, who could not detach himself from his prejudices. Monroe could, and did. Schouler writes of him as a man conspicuous "for patient consideration to all sides." "He had a mind," said J. Q. Adams, "sound in its ultimate judgments and firm in its final conclusions." Jackson's personality was much more pronounced; his ego was an honest ego, but insufficiently disciplined, though he himself was a soldier and knew the necessity of discipline. He loved his friends, hated his enemies and worried both. His own best friend was Andrew Jack-

[1] "The subject-matter of the Monroe-Jackson correspondence is mainly statesmanship in the abstract with incidental reference to current problems of practical administration. It is marked throughout by a perfect reciprocity of confidence, respect and admiration. Its tone is lofty and it discloses throughout mutual aspirations of the purest patriotism."— History of Andrew Jackson, by Augustus C. Buell, 2 vols., Vol. II, pp. 106-108. Commenting on Gilman's assertion that Monroe made a good Secretary of War, Roosevelt in "The Naval War of 1812" (p. 456) makes this statement: "I think he was as much a failure as his predecessors and a harsher criticism could not be passed upon him. Like the other statesmen of his school he was mighty in word and weak in action. As an instance, contrast his fiery letters to Jackson with the fact that he never gave him a particle of practical help." The reference is to Jackson's offer to Armstrong, July 18, 1814, to go down into Florida and expel the mischief-making British at Pensacola. Armstrong did not reply. He was succeeded by Monroe, and Jackson thought Monroe would take up the plan. He was disappointed.

[2] Monroe to Jackson, December 14, 1816: Jackson to Monroe, January 6, 1817.

son and his worst enemy was Andrew Jackson.[1] His
resentments were unreasoning, though sometimes warranted. He resented the indifference of the bureaucrats
to his achievements in the Creek campaign, when he
forced his way through an almost impassable country in order to attain his objective. It was not Hercu-
lean, this labor of his, but it was a hard task, executed
with uncommon spirit and grit. His was the same sort
of resentment one nurses whether in mine, mill, factory
or field against those who profit by one's sweat and by
the risk one takes of life or limb and yet deny due
recognition of labor done. Crawford re-ceded some of
the land acquired by Jackson at the Creek cession.
Would Jackson stand for this? No, it was a personal
insult. He obtained a reversal of Crawford's act, and
regarded Crawford as his enemy. Monroe adroitly
handled the maladroit Jackson, but even Monroe by
and by would have something to explain in a Jackson
matter — on his very deathbed, as we shall see, he
would be obliged to take part in a Jacksonian controversy.

But, now, thanks to Monroe's appreciation and
guardedness, they were co-operating. Monroe was
both politician and statesman. Jackson, too, was
strongly drawn by politics. In spite of his wish to
chastise the sinners who met at Hartford, he advised
Monroe to appoint a Federalist as a member of his
Cabinet. He sent Monroe a letter[2] which ran: "Now

[1] Jackson's mother had advised him when he left her to go to Tennessee "not
to lie or sue anybody. Always settle them cases yourself," she said. "My mother,"
said Jackson, "was a little, dumpy, red-headed Irish woman." Memories of Fifty
Years, by W. H. Sparks, 1890.

[2] According to W. G. Sumner, Life of Jackson, 1882, p. 49: "In October, 1816,
a letter, signed by Jackson, was addressed to Monroe, in anticipation of his election
to the Presidency, urging the appointment of William Drayton of South Carolina
as Secretary of War. William B. Lewis, Jackson's neighbor and confidential friend,
husband of one of Mrs. Jackson's nieces, wrote this letter. . . . Drayton had been
a Federalist. He belonged to the South Carolina aristocracy. . . Jackson said
(in 1824) that he did not know Drayton in 1816." As we learn from "A Sketch
of the Life of Robert F. Stockton (Commodore Stockton) by S. J. Bayard, 1856;
"in the Middle States in 1824, especially in New Jersey, a large number of Federalists supported General Jackson. The grounds for this preference were the
celebrated letter of General Jackson to Mr. Monroe, advising him to appoint a
Federalist to his Cabinet." p. 57.

is the time to exterminate that monster called party spirit. By selecting characters most conspicuous for probity, virtue, capacity, firmness, without regard to party, you will go far to, if not entirely, eradicate those feelings which on ʝformer occasions threw so many obstacles in the way of government, and perhaps have the pleasure of uniting a people heretofore politically divided. The Chief Magistrate of a great and powerful nation should never indulge in party feelings." Van Buren (Autobiography, pp. 234 to 239) goes into the details of the political effects of the use made by Monroe of Jackson's letter, especially with regard to Senator Walter Lourie of Pennsylvania.

Nor should we lose sight of other rising men of the time. Revolutionary worthies, the Constitution-makers, the partisan champions of the last decade of the past, and first decade of the current century, were out of public life; new questions were up. Webster, who was to be among the giants, had begun to show his growth. In Ohio an old settler who had come from New Hampshire asked him: "Is this the son of Captain Webster?' "It is, indeed.' "What! Is this the little Black Dan that used to water the horses?" Speaking of Webster, B. F. Perry said:[1] "His eyes were the largest I ever saw in any human head." Calhoun said that when Webster was worsted in an argument, he felt it, and you saw he felt it, but that Clay[2] gave no such sign.

Though surrounded by such men as those we have just sketched, Monroe kept in mind the excellences of his elders. Schouler credits him with endeavoring to model his administration upon that of Washington. We get an inkling of this in a letter to Jackson, in which Monroe questioned the necessity of a division into

---

[1] Reminiscences by B. F. Perry, Ex-Governor of South Carolina, p. 47.

[2] Henry Clay succeeded General Adair in the United States Senate in 1806. Adair had resigned. Benjamin F. Perry, the South Carolina Unionist, makes this comment: "He was not then thirty years old and consequently not eligible to a seat in the Senate. How he took his seat and the oath of office, I have never seen explained." Clay was born April 12, 1777.

parties. He favored fusion. "I think," said he, "that the cause of these divisions is to be found in certain defects of those governments rather than in human nature; and that we have happily avoided those defects in our system." This bit of speculation was allowable in that era of good feeling; but he had not come to the golden age. Nor have we. "Taken in their natural course," says Schouler, "parties organize, disorganize and reorganize, as vital issues change. Within seventy-five years passed away the Anti-Federal, the Federal, the First Republican, the Whig, the Native American parties." [Monroe, with magnanimity, addressed himself to the task of exterminating old party divisions and giving new strength and direction to the government. Proud of Virginia, "a filial follower of the great Jefferson," regardful of Madison, Monroe did not confine himself to the old Republican circles./ Marshall he admired. "Nor," says Schouler, "could his heart cease to own its secret allegiance to Virginia's greatest of sons, the first President." His old resentment against him had dried up altogether; "by the time of his accession to the Presidency, the illustrious example of the first incumbent had become with Monroe an overpowering influence." Schouler adds:

"He sought the same high plane of unpartisan service. Without Washington's commanding presence, transcendant fame, or superb endowments, he nevertheless had grown to resemble him strongly in predominate traits of character, and, more especially, in an honest sincerity of purpose to administer well; in habits of patient and deliberate investigation, all contending arguments being weighed dispassionately; and in a fixed determination not to be influenced in a public trust by private considerations. Even in personal looks the last Virginian, with his placid and sedate expression of face, regular features and grayish-blue eyes had come to appear not unlike the first; so that in these years the names of Washington and Monroe became naturally coupled together.'"

Monroe tried to follow Washington's example as closely as he could. Because Washington had gone out to see the people and the country, Monroe thought

it incumbent upon him to do likewise. Accordingly
he planned an extended tour which lasted throughout
the summer. Edward Everett Hale, in his "Memories
of a Hundred Years," Vol. I, p. 221, says of Monroe's
tour:

"In my boyhood, this journey of his, which began on the 31st
day of May, 1817, and did not end until October of the same year
was called 'The President's Progress.' Washington's similar
journey in 1791 was always called 'Washington's Progress.' There
is a little touch of burlesque when one reads that President Monroe
arrayed himself in the old buff and blue of the Revolution with
an old-fashioned three-cornered soldier's hat. There is just a
touch of absurdity about this, because his military exploits were
of his whole life, the enterprises which his friends would have
most gladly forgotten."

Hale quotes Aaron Burr,[1] who, in 1815, slurred
Monroe as one who "never commanded a platoon
nor was ever fit to command one." As aide to General
Stirling, "Monroe's whole duty was to fill his Lordship's
tankard and to bear with indication of admiration
his Lordship's long stories about himself." This is
curious nonsense. Monroe would have been a Medal of
Honor man, if that order had been in existence in his
time. He offered his life in a pinch, and was within an
ace of death, his blood gushing from an artery at every
heart throb.[2] Nor do we share Hale's opinion as to
the impropriety of Monroe's use of the blue-and-buff.
He wished to bring on what he did bring on — the
Era of Good Feeling. He had a perfect right to wear it,
and he wore it with a great good grace.

As we learn from Waldo's book[3] about the tour, its
main object was "the advancement of the public

---

[1] Monroe was well acquainted not only with Colonel Burr but with his wife,
Theodosia's mother, with whom he had corresponded, addressing her as "my dear
little friend." When Burr married her, she was known as the Widow Prevost, and
lived in the Hermitage at old Hopperstown, now Hohokus. She was the widow of
Colonel Prevost, of the British army, who had died in the West Indies.

[2] Niles's *Register*, July 23, 1831, says: "In Colonel Trumbull's painting of the
'Capture of the Hessians' Monroe appears prostrate and bleeding on the field."

[3] The tour of James Monroe, President of the United States, through the
Northern and Eastern States in 1817; his tour in the year 1818, together with a
sketch of his life, with descriptive and historical notices of the principal places
through which he passed; by S. Putnam Waldo, Esq. Hartford, 1820.

interest." The official object was an inspection of defensive works in course of construction under General Bernard who had been recommended by the Marquis de La Fayette. So Monroe was accompanied not only by his private secretary, but by General Joseph G. Swift, Chief of the Corps of the Engineers and Superintendent of West Point Academy.[1] When he left Washington, he had it in mind to travel as a private citizen. He had hardly reached Baltimore before he was obliged to abandon the idea. People knew what he was about and some of them criticized him because he entered that city on a Sunday, albeit he went to church. Next day accompanied by Generals Smith, Stricker, Winder and Swift, he visited Fort McHenry and the spot where Ross fell, and reviewed the third brigade, under General Sterret, at Whetstone Point. The Mayor and City Council addressed him, and Monroe replied.[2] This was the custom in all the big towns and cities throughout his tour. It must have been something of a strain upon him to prepare the long string of addresses made up as they were of pleasant platitudes and those patriotic orotundities that occur to one when the fife sounds and the drum rolls. It is interesting to follow Monroe and his fellow-travelers by steamboat, June 4, up the Chesapeake to Frenchtown, and across Delaware to New Castle, whence, on the sixth, they proceeded to Wilmington, Fort Mifflin and the Philadelphia Navy Yard. His quarters at the Mansion House, Philadelphia, "were crowded every hour." The Pennsylvania Society of the Cincinnati addressed him,

---

[1] "Swift was a New Englander of New Englanders, the first graduate of West Point, and a friend of Eustis, late Secretary of War, whom he had accompanied from Boston to Washington in 1809, and 'inducted into the mysteries of his new vocation.' By his skill in protecting New York during the war he had gained the applause of 'Benefactor of the City,' and had received more substantial proofs of the gratitude of the people." Gilman's Monroe, p. 136. Also Gen. G. W. Cullum's Campaigns and Engineers of 1812.

[2] Monroe said in his Baltimore address, June 2: "Congress has appropriated large sums of money for the fortification of our coast and inland frontier, and for the establishment of naval docks and building a navy. It is proper that these works should be executed with judgment, fidelity and economy. Much depends in the execution on the Executive, to whom extensive power is given as to the general arrangement and to whom the superintendence exclusively belongs."

many celebrities, including Justice McKean, soon to die, waited upon him; and he took great pleasure in revisiting the shrines with which he had been familiar in times past. This was the case at Trenton, whither he proceeded, and where the volunteer companies, on the evening of the seventh, gave him a *feu de joie*, instead of a shower of bullets as the Hessians had done in '76. Next day being Sunday, he had time to go to his old battleground as well as to church. Mayor McNeely, the aldermen and the people of Trenton sped him on his way, past Princeton field; and Chief Justice Kirkpatrick welcomed him at New Brunswick, while bells rang and guns sounded.

At New York, Monroe was greatly honored. He was the guest of the Vice-President, Tompkins, on Staten Island, from which he went by steamboat, under escort, up the harbor, past saluting ships, to the Battery. It was a day of powder-burning, parades and addresses. That Rufus King and De Witt Clinton gave him welcome added to the piquancy of a zestful day. Many veterans of the old war, such as Colonel Marinus Willetts, and of the new war, such as General Winfield Scott, met him and honored him. He was loth to leave them, but soon took a steamboat for New Haven. He was in New England now, but found no abatement whatever in the warmth of his welcome. Whether at Durham, Middletown, Hartford,[1] on the Massachusetts State line, or at Springfield, the people turned out heartily, making his journey a "progress," wherever he went. He reached New London on the twenty-fifth, passed by boat to Stonington, and thence to Newport, in company with Commodore Oliver H. Perry. Talking over the late war was one of the pleasures of the tour. Another pleasure at Newport was Monroe's meeting with the venerable William Ellery, a signer of the Declaration of Independence.

It was in Boston, however, that Monroe was given

---

[1] Monroe said at Hartford that he was not at the head of a faction but President of the whole people. Such he now habitually thought himself.

his greatest New England greeting. The Massachusetts Legislature gave the signal in a resolution providing for an escort from the State line; so that, when Monroe passed to it from Providence, he was met by an imposing concourse and cavalcade, civil and military, and was escorted to Boston with a notable spirit and all the complimentary noise a man need wish to hear. "A cavalcade of citizens, arranged in sixteen divisions," says Schouler,[1] "was followed by one hundred and fifty truckmen, well mounted, and dressed in white frocks; this procession, more than a mile in length, defiled slowly down Washington and the other chief streets in presence of some forty thousand applauding spectators; there was a military escort, and the President was on horseback. Entering the green lawn of the Common, Monroe passed a long line of children from the public schools, youths of both sexes drawn up to meet him, many of whom wore roses, red and white together, in token that all civil feuds were happily ended." At Breed's Hill and Bunker Hill on the fourth of July, the tourist reached his apogee. It would take a chapter to tell of all the interesting happenings while Monroe was in Boston. His headquarters were at the Exchange Coffee House, then the largest hotel in America, where he received the congratulatory address and replied to it.[2] He paid his respects to John Adams, who, by this time, was most friendly toward him, as was Mrs. Abigail Adams. Indeed, that most capable of Presidents' wives honored Monroe with her correspondence. Other Federalist celebrities were likewise complaisant, notably Harrison Gray Otis, once an enemy, whose Beacon Street Mansion was thrown open to the Virginian "Jacobin." Otis[3] gave a fireworks display in Monroe's honor. He and Quincy, as well as General Dearborn, were at the Adams dinner to the Republican guest.

---

[1] History of the United States, by James Schouler, Vol. III, p. 9.
[2] Memorials of the Massachusetts Society of Cincinnati, pp. 54, 55.
[3] Life and Letters of Harrison Gray Otis (1765-1848) by Samuel Eliot Morison, 1903; 2 vols.; Vol. I, pp. 87-231; Vol. II, pp. 44-46, 128, 168, 202-11, 216.

The Dearborns gave a grand ball in the Bowdoin Mansion, Boston, July 3. According to Daniel Goodwin Jr:[1]

"The visit of President Monroe to Boston was a brilliant ovation, the whole city, without distinction of party joining in parades, balls, illuminations and receptions. General Dearborn was chairman of the Committee, Commodores Bainbridge, Hull and Perry were there with war vessels; also Generals Brooks, Sullivan, Sumner, Crane, Wells, Blake, Thorndike, Perkins, and a throng of other officers and military companies. A great meeting was held at Bunker Hill on the 4th of July, where Monroe expressed a sentiment similar to that of Lincoln at Gettysburg. 'The blood spilt here roused the whole American people and united them, in a common cause in defense of their rights. That union will never be broken.' He visited Cambridge and was welcomed by President Kirkland, and all the faculty and students of Harvard. Dearborn, Otis, and Quincy dined with the Monroes at Ex-President John Adams'."

We particularize thus since it is a joy to note that those who had once yearned to eat Monroe alive now loved him, as it were; or at any rate lavished their very best upon him whether of wit, wine or compliments.[2] Monroe wrote to Jefferson (July 27): "I have seen enough to satisfy me that the great mass of our fellow-citizens in the Eastern States are as firmly attached to the union and to republican government as I have always believed or could desire them to be."

John Greenleaf Whittier was nine years old when Monroe visited Haverhill. As it happened, a menagerie with circus attachment, was in town on the same day. His biographer says:[3]

"The Quaker boy was not allowed the privilege of seeing either the collection of wild beasts or the Chief Magistrate of the Nation. He did not care much for the former, but he was anxious to see a President of the United States. The next day he trudged all the

---

[1] The Dearborns, by Daniel Goodwin, Jr. (Chicago, 1884).

[2] As a case in point, the *Boston Centinel* gives this anecdote: "In the widow of the late President Wheelock, the President found the fair comforter who dressed the wound which he received in the memorable battle of Trenton. . . . As they had not before seen each other since that period, the emotions which the interview occasioned may be better conceived than described."

[3] Life and Letters of John G. Whittier, by Samuel T. Pickard, 2 vols. Vol. I, p. 25.

way to Haverhill, determined to see at least some footsteps in the street that the great man had left behind him. He found at last an impression of an elephant's foot in the road and, supposing this to be Monroe's track, he followed it as far as he could distinguish it. Then he went home, satisfied that he had seen the footsteps of the greatest man in the country."

But there were so many happenings during the prolonged tour, so many evergreen arches passed under, so many unexpected sights such as that of a majestic live eagle looking down from its roadside perch as the President passed (and then set free to soar aloft) that it is impossible to enumerate them, much less dwell upon them. The people of New England, thinks Schouler, "longed for a reconciliation, for unity, for a new national development." Monroe understood that longing and gratified it.[1] Why were Revolutionary flags and relics produced from old chests and wardrobes? What meant those arches of evergreens and festoons of roses, these pious visits to sires of '76 and the old battlefields; these gatherings of the Cincinnati and heroes of 1812, of soldiers and civilians, of Federalists and Republicans in mass? Their united honors were not paid merely to the accidental incumbent of the chief office. They were honors to the man, and indicated the general hope that under his administration national brotherhood would be restored." Lynn, Marblehead, Salem, Newburyport, Portsmouth, York, Biddeford, Scarborough, Woodstock, and finally Portland were visited in turn. At Portland, General Swift took his leave of Monroe and General Miller of New Hampshire joined his suite. Portland, July 6, was the easternmost point of the tour.[2] A feature of great interest to Monroe was the outpouring of grandsires. At York it was an octogenarian, Judge Sewell, who spoke the welcome. At Judge Thatcher's in Portland the

---

[1] According to Schouler, III, 12, The "Era of Good Feeling" was first used in Boston, at the time of Monroe's visit; *Boston Centinel*, July 7, 1817. See Niles' *Register*, July 12 and 19, 1817.
[2] For details of Monroe's Tour see Niles' *Register*, Vol. XII, from March to September, 1817; also the numerous local histories of New England cities and towns.

venerable Deacon Samuel Chase, then in his ninety-ninth year, gave him his blessing.

From Portland Monroe journeyed to Burlington, Vermont; Plattsburg, N. Y., by way of the wilderness known as Chateaugay woods to Sackett's Harbor; Niagara Falls and the battlefields of the vicinity; Buffalo; Detroit, and southward then through Ohio to Pittsburg, September 5; and, finally to Washington, September 18 — three and a half months after his departure. It was a great event in Monroe's life.

Next year Monroe traveled in the opposite direction; Secretary Calhoun accompanied him on his journey of five thousand miles through the South. Mrs. St. Julien Ravenel in "Charleston: The Place and the People" tells of the visit to Charleston. In the party were "Mr. Calhoun's lady and family, Major General Thomas Pinckney, Mr. Gouverneur, the President's private secretary, and Lieutenant Monroe, his nephew. Having spent the night at Colonel Jacob Bond I'on's plantation, about ten miles from the town, the party drove to Clement's Ferry, six miles up the river, near the present navy yard, and came thence in a large and handsome barge, rowed by twenty-five members of the Mariners' Society, steered by their President, Captain Thomas Jervey; the style very fine. The entertainments, inspections, reviews, fireworks, presentation of addresses, of societies, dinners, balls, etc., were much the same as those offered to Washington, with but two exceptions. On Friday, having visited the lines, 'he breakfasts at the villa of Joel R. Poinsett, Esqr.,' and on 'Saturday attends a grand concert and ball given in his honor by the St. Cecilia Society '." "It was the only occasion a St. Cecilia was ever given ' to any one man.' Its times and seasons are as fixed as if ordered by the heavenly bodies. Lent alone disturbs its dates! Saturday is unheard of! That would hardly be a real St. Cecilia which did not begin on a Thursday at 9 p.m." Monroe stayed a week in Charleston. Promising to sit to S. F. B. Morse for a

PRESENT APPEARANCE OF OAK HILL, MONROE'S HOME IN LOUDON COUNTY, VIRGINIA

(Photograph loaned by Mrs. Henry Fairfax)

portrait to be hung in the Charleston Council Chamber, he took his leave of the citizens at Ashley River Bridge, declining a salute.[1]

From Charleston, Monroe went to Augusta; thence through the Cherokee region to Nashville, and afterwards to Louisville and Lexington.[2]

These tours were talked of the country over. The people liked the idea. They felt that he was knitting the pieces together, in shuttling himself thus from one point to another. There was, then, this general good in addition to the particular good done in the communities where he showed himself — the last of the Fathers; the Chief Magistrate who thought enough of the people to come among them for actual hand-shaking and pleasant words. Here he actually was, this Virginian, said they; no longer a shadowy personage hidden under the mantle of authority but a man of flesh and blood, with kindness in his look.

Until Monroe's time the White House was called "the President's House"; now it became the "Executive Mansion." Cochrane and Ross had not quite destroyed it. Some of the vaulting was still good, and so were parts of the walls, arches and columns. Congress voted $500,000 to restore it and, fortunately, the work of restoration was in the hands of its original architect, James Hoban, born in Dublin, Ireland, who, having seen that it was erected according to his plans now superintended its re-erection. In 1819 Congress set aside $8,137 for enlarging the offices just to the west, at the spot where the executive offices now stand. Adams says in his Diary, September 20, 1817: "Monroe returned last Wednesday. He is in the President's

---

[1] Charleston — the Place and the People, by Mrs. St. Julien Ravenel, 1906. The St. Cecilia Society dates from 1737, Thursday being St. Cecilia's Day. Gen. C. C. Pinckney and Ralph Izard were members and performers in their youth.

[2] Monroe "made personal examination of the arsenals, naval depots, fortifications and garrisons along the northern border from Maine to Michigan, and passed down to Louisville, thence to Washington. He wore the undress uniform of an officer in the Revolutionary War — a blue military coat of homespun, light-colored underclothes and a cocked hat." History of Kentucky by Richard H. Collins. 2 vols. Vol II, p. 368.

House which is so far restored from the effects of the British visit in 1814, that it is now for the first time habitable. But he is apprehensive of the effects of the fresh painting and plastering and very desirous of visiting his family at his seat in Virginia. He is, therefore, going again to leave the city in two or three days, but said his absence would only be for a short time."

The *National Intelligencer*, of January 2, 1818, speaks of the fine weather on New Year's, adding: "The President's House, for the first time since its re-aerification, was thrown open for the general reception of visitors. It was thronged from two to three o'clock by an unusually large concourse of ladies and gentlemen." Diplomats, Congressmen, the whole official world of Washington attended; and the Marine Corps was out in force.

The outstanding events during Monroe's presidency may be counted on the fingers of one hand, if we use the thumb also to indicate the most important of all — the enunciation of the Monroe Doctrine.

These chief events are: the Seminole War (1817-1818); the acquisition of Florida (1819-1821); the Missouri Compromise (1820); the veto of the Cumberland road bill (1822) and the aforesaid Doctrine as set forth in the Presidential message of December 2, 1823.[1]

There were other considerable events to be sure — many of great interest. It was a time of notable changes. Napoleon, pacing his path on Longwood plateau at St. Helena, was caged for good; reforms were due in Great Britain, and, though reactionary elements had gained temporary power, there would be soon a return of liberalism in Europe.

Before we take up the chief American events, let us indicate a few of the multitude of other matters with

---

[1] For Monroe's annual messages, from the first to the eighth, his many special messages and his two inaugural addresses, see Messages and Papers of the Presidents, by James D. Richardson, Vol. II, pp. 4-287. These official communications also appear in Writings of Monroe, Vols. VI and VII.

which Monroe was concerned.[1] There were two serious boundary controversies — the Spanish and the British. Monroe settled the Northwestern dispute, *pro tem*, by a treaty with Great Britain, providing that "the disputed region should be jointly occupied."

As to the neutrality of the Great Lakes,[2] John Quincy Adams was instructed, January, 1816, to propose that steps be taken to prevent naval rivalry in that quarter. Madison wanted a "clean sweep" of all war vessels. The British Minister at Washington, Charles Bagot, received from Monroe, August 2, "a precise project for limiting the force." In January, 1817, Lord Castlereagh replied, accepting the proposal. But the actual reduction occurred in 1818. Monroe's proclamation on the subject was issued on the twentieth of April of that year. In justice to Gallatin, it should be noted that it was he who made "the first definite proposition of disarmament" — a wise and happy suggestion, indeed, fruitful of great good.[3]

American fishery privileges were defined in a commercial convention with Great Britain. This was made in 1818. But the West Indian trade privileges were withheld for several years. There was much trouble in that quarter. Commodore O. H. Perry was sent thither to break up piracy. He died of yellow fever there. Finally in 1822, owing to a retaliatory act, West Indian trade was restored.

Notwithstanding the heartiness with which Monroe had been received in New England, he understood that the kindness shown him there came from the

---

[1] Direct taxation was twice invoked prior to the Civil War — in 1791 to meet the demands of the new government, and in 1813 to provide funds for the war against Great Britain. "In both instances, however," says William Dana Orcutt in "Burrows of Michigan and the Republican Party," "direct taxation was abandoned at the earliest moment consistent with national honor and safety. The law of 1791 remained in force but nine years and was repealed at the earnest solicitation of President Jefferson, while the Act of 1813, after having been on the statute but four years was expunged upon the recommendation of President Monroe."

[2] Neutrality of the Lakes, by J. M. Callahan, Johns Hopkins Studies, Vol. XVI, 1898.

[3] H. Adams, "Gallatin," Vol. I, p. 640; J. Q. Adams' Memoirs, September 19, 1814.

people themselves, rather than from the old Federal leaders. According to the Monroe manuscripts, as cited by Schouler, the President was informed that of them all "only Webster and Lloyd could be trusted." But Webster, who had lately moved to Boston, was not in the Fifteenth Congress, which met December 1, 1817, adjourned April 20, 1818, re-assembled for its second session November 16, 1818, and expired March 3, 1819. "Among Western Representatives in this Congress," says Schouler, "two heroes of the late war, William Henry Harrison, of Ohio, and Richard M. Johnson, of Kentucky, seemed inclined at present to follow Henry Clay[1] into a sort of half opposition to Monroe's administration. Clay was constantly playing a larger part in affairs. He had his eye on the presidency. He thought of Monroe as the last of the old order, and of himself as the first of the new. He gave Monroe trouble with regard to the South American question. In the summer of 1817 Monroe appointed three commissioners[2] — Cæsar Augustus Rodney, John Graham and Theodorick Bland to go to South America "to obtain information of the actual condition and political prospects of the Spanish provinces which were contending for independence." When the bill came up, March 24, 1818, appropriating $30,000 for the expenses of the commissioners, Clay moved to

[1] Clay once advised Robert C. Winthrop what to do when in the Speaker's Chair: "Decide — decide promptly — and never give your reasons for the decisions. The House will sustain your decisions, but there will always be men to cavil and quarrel as to your reasons." Clay, says Winthrop, was a man of singularly fascinating address and magnetic qualities, attracting admirers and friends on every side. As he sometimes sauntered across the Senate Chamber, taking a pinch of snuff out of one friend's box and offering his own to another, he was a picture of affability and nonchalance. He had "the genial jaunty air of Lord Palmerston; but, like Palmerston, he could be 'lofty and sour,' too." But he was quick to apologize and was unresentful. When Randolph called him a "blackleg in contrast with Puritan Adams" and they had fought, Clay was quick to make up. He vastly preferred whist to dueling. Winthrop says that in Boston in 1818 while Clay was at the whist table in the Exchange Coffee House, the cry was raised that the hotel was on fire. "Oh, there will be time enough, I think, to finish our game," said Clay; and finish it they did. As for the hotel, it was burned to the ground.

[2] These Commissioners made a strong impression at Buenos Ayres and elsewhere in South America. Rodney, an able and energetic man took his whole family with him. His letters illuminate the times he lived in. His life has been ably written in Spanish by Dr. Enrique Loudet of Buenos Ayres.

amend by adding; "And one year's salary and outfit to a Minister to the United Provinces of Rio de La Plata, the sum not to exceed $18,000." Had this passed, the United States would practically have recognized the independence of the Spanish provinces. Schurz[1] says truly; "It was a step in advance, not only of the country and of the government but of the whole civilized world." He wanted the neutrality measure of 1817 repealed and everything done to help the insurgents. "South America had set his imagination on fire." Finally, his contemptuous flings at the President and Secretary of State displeased a large part of the House. It was well known that Monroe and Adams were not at all unfriendly to the insurgent colonies; only they wanted to be sure that the new governments had the necessary element of stability to justify recognition; they hoped to obtain the co-operation of England in that recognition; they desired to avoid the embarrassment which a hasty recognition would cause the negotiations between the United States and Spain concerning the cession of Florida; and, finally, they wanted to be assured that the public opinion of the country would sustain them in so important a step. The motion was defeated one hundred and fifteen to forty-five. "Monroe," says Schurz[2], "was terribly disturbed by Clay's attack. Monroe was perfectly right." He and Adams were acting like broad and thorough statesmen in the Florida and South American matters; Clay like a politician bidding for popularity. In the next session Clay and Jackson clashed; and we shall now see why.

We approach a new and curious drama, with plots and characters enough to work into a spectacular five-act historical play; and, for the sake of a short title, we call it "The Seminoles." Not to involve ourselves, we must go back to the point where we left the story of the Floridas and come forward in an

---

[1] Life and Times of Henry Clay, by Carl Schurz, 2 vols. Vol. I, p. 216.
[2] Life of Henry Clay, by Carl Schurz, Vol. I, p. 151, et seq.

orderly manner. Spain still owned what is now Florida
and still claimed the Mobile region or West Florida.
We also claimed it as a part of the Louisiana purchase. Apparently, the wish with us was largely father
to our claim. Not that Madison and Monroe were
merely covetous, and without justification. Reasons
why we should have the Gulf outlets to our Georgia,
Alabama and Mississippi rivers were so clear as to
hardly need enumeration. And was there ever worse
misgovernment than that of Spain, whose South
American provinces were in revolt? She could not
even put down an insurrection in West Florida. The
revolting people there applied to the American Secretary of State for annexation. "Here," comments
Babcock[1] "was the whole thing in a nutshell — a
desirable province, a convenient claim under the ambig-
uous treaty, a weak and troubled opponent, and a
shadowy 'third party' eager to snatch the prize away.
. . . The solution was Madison's remarkable proclamation of October 27, 1810." Madison acquiesced in
"the temporary continuance of Spanish authority over
West Florida," and declared "that friendly negotiation
and adjustment would be continued," but he directed
Governor W. C. C. Claiborne, of Mississippi Territory,
to take possession, nevertheless. Later, part of West
Florida was annexed to Louisiana and the rest to
Mississippi, May 14, 1812. Was there a violation of
Spanish rights in all this? There is a suggestion of self-
beguilement, of speciousness, in the whole affair, which
should only be defended on open ground, to wit: Ferdinand, King of Spain, was corrupt, vicious, and a hater
of republics. No one denies the right of the South
American republics to govern themselves — why should
not West Florida? And for that matter East Florida?
Don Luis de Onis, Spanish Minister at Washington,
understood the situation. He knew that the time was
near when Spain must withdraw from what may be
called the natural territory of the United States, and

[1] Rise of American Nationality, by K. C. Babcock, p. 24.

his policy was to bide his time until he could secure the best possible terms. His policy was one of delay. But the Georgians said they would no longer put up with the outrages on their southern border. As a case in point, we have the Amelia Island incident. This island at the mouth of the St. Mary's River, which flows into the Atlantic where Fernandina stands, a little way below the Georgia line, and therefore, at that time just without the jurisdiction of the United States, became the resort of Gregor McGregor's band of outlaws recruited in Savannah and Charleston. A similar gang of slave smugglers and freebooters was at Galveston on the Texas coast. When Monroe returned from his northern tour in the fall of 1817, he took up in Cabinet meeting the depredations of these gangs. Spain would not, or could not, suppress them. The thing to do was to send down naval vessels to break up the nests. It was an easy task in each case. Buccaneer Aury, who had succeeded McGregor, had but one hundred and fifty men all told at Amelia Island. Once more was it demonstrated that the arm of the Don no longer reached to Florida.[1] Spain threatened war, but the cloud vanished at the next smile of Don Luis de Onis.

The suppression of the buccaneers mended matters only a little while. There were other lawless ones in Florida. Runaways, cast-offs and refugees — black, white, red — sought safety among the Seminoles, or "Wanderers," or "Lost People," an offshoot of the Creeks, who had migrated into the long peninsula and who thought themselves beyond paleface reach. Listening to the mocking-birds in the Everglades, they hearkened also to Spanish and British adventurers who poisoned their minds against the Americans. Colonel Edward Nichols was an especially enterprising enemy of the United States. He had served as British commander in Florida during the War of 1812. Though

---

[1] See Schouler, III, p. 24, *et seq.*; Monroe's second annual message, November, 1818 and message of January 13, 1818; Adams' Diary, IV; Monroe Mss.

peace had come, Nichols built a fort fifteen miles from
the mouth of the Appalachicola — "Negro Fort,"
manned by three hundred negroes — and armed about a
thousand men, many of whom were Seminoles and
Creeks. He made a treaty with the Creeks and took
some of them to England with him. But Lord Bathurst
shrugged his civilized shoulders. He was more squeam-
ish than Nichols. He could not stomach such a treaty.
But he pleased the Creek chiefs with gifts and sent
them back. Meantime a United States gunboat ascending the Appalachicola, destroyed "Negro Fort" with
red-hot shot. Considering all these things — hostile
Indians, buccaneers and a fortified rendezvous for
runaways — no wonder the people of Georgia threatened to march into East Florida, seize it and annex it.
Somebody else was impatient likewise — Andrew Jackson, of "by-the-eternal" fame.

Jackson, as well as Jefferson, Madison and Monroe,
helped to build the Gulf side of the mansion of the
Republic. He had done a good job at New Orleans,
and now he proposed to do another. He knew fairly
well what was going on at Washington. Not only was
he in correspondence with Monroe, but he had his
friends in Congress, who wrote to him from time to
time concerning the secret sessions and secret acts[1]
of that body. He had reason to believe that the government was fingering the Floridian nettle with a great
desire to possess it, yet with the usual diplomatic
timidity. He had rebuked the War Department
because it had ignored him in transmitting an order
directly in the Nashville division, and had instructed
his subordinates to disobey such orders in the future.
He had also threatened General Winfield Scott with a
duel. In a word, the hero of New Orleans disbelieved
in fingering nettles. Monroe understood Jackson.
"He had a liking for him," says Schouler, "as a genuine
patriot, one of exalted traits; and wished to be a little

---

[1] For the Acts of January 15, and March 3, 1811 and February 12, 1813, see
United States Statutes at Large, III, 471.

blind to faults, while generously estimating his virtues.
. . . Jackson was strongly attached at the present
time to Monroe. He had supported him for President
and owned the kindliness and generosity of his nature.
But Monroe and Jackson were men of a different mould;
nor did the sycophants of the latter fail to excite his
ardor by flattering comparison with those of higher
station. . . . Monroe understood himself, however,
as Chief Magistrate, while Jackson and his intimates
had most likely expected to find him pliable. Why
otherwise should Jackson, warm friend though he was,
and ardent and impulsive in his own course of conduct,
have undertaken to tutor and push the President into
difficulties so confidently at the outset?''

In November, 1817, General Edmund Pendleton
Gaines, commanding on the Florida border, remon-
strated with the Seminole Chief at Fowlton near the
Georgia line. The chief threatened further violence.
Gaines [1] sent Colonel D. E. Twiggs, who, at Fowlton,
discovered evidence that its chief was allied with the
outlaws. Twiggs burnt Fowlton. Nine days later the
Indians retaliated. They ambushed and massacred all
but five of forty men who, under Lieutenant Scott,
with many women and children, were ascending the
Appalachicola to Fort Scott, a stockade on the Flint
above its junction with the Chattahoochee. But for
the few who escaped to tell of the horrors, the massacre
was complete. A shock passed over the country — and
then a thrill, when news came that Jackson had been
ordered to gather up re-enforcements and proceed from
Nashville to take command of the American troops.

Before Jackson left Nashville, he wrote to Monroe
his famous letter of January 6, 1818. This is the Rhea
letter[2] so much talked of. In it Jackson urged the

[1] For an account of Gaines's life see Robinson's Army of the United States, pp. 300
et seq.; for Twiggs, see Life of Twiggs.
[2] John Rhea was Representative in Congress from Tennessee from 1808 to 1815.
Webster tells how he and Rhea, on a House Committee, waited on Madison and
found "Little Jimmie" sick in bed. Rhea was in Congress from 1817 to 1823. In
1816 he was appointed United States Commissioner to treat with the Choctaws.
In the Diary of John Quincy Adams there are some references to Rhea. Edward

immediate seizure of East Florida.[1] "Let it be signified to me," he said, "through any channel (say Mr. J.
Rhea) that the possession of the Floridas would be
desirable to the United States, and in sixty days it
will be accomplished."

With that Jackson was off. Again was he in his
glory. Thin, sinewy, tall, he looked well when standing
but better still on horseback, as now he was, hurrying
to the far Appalachicola. His hollow-cheeked face was
long and narrow, his brow serious and lowering, his
nose high and long, his eyes "cold, grey, piercing in
the highest degree, with crowsfeet skinfolds beneath;
his mouth and chin expressive of stern decision."
Such was the old eagle.

With a thousand men, he marched four hundred and
fifty miles in forty-six days. It was winter; the rivers
ran high; and "the ground was so rotten" that even
pack-horses could not pass.[2]   But he entered Florida,
built a fort and investigated. He learned that Alexander Arbuthnot, a Scotchman, and Robert Christer

N. Vallandigham, author of many excellent studies in American politics, favors
the present writer with a letter on the subject of Rhea. The assumption that Rhea
lacked in some essential quality because he was spoken of as "Johnny Rhea" is
wrong. It was a custom in the Southwest thus to use a touch of familiarity in
referring to one's political leader. For instance William H. Crawford was "Billy
Crafford." In a letter to Dr. Vallandigham, Knoxville, May 9, 1903, John L. Rhea,
grandson of Congressman Rhea, said: "Mr. Rhea was the son of a Presbyterian
clergyman, Rev. Joseph Rhea, born in Donegal, Ireland, and educated at Glasgow,
Scotland. He married Elizabeth McIlvaine; and, in 1769, with his wife, four sons
and two daughters came to this country and located in Maryland. He had charge
of Piney Creek Church in said state; preached here until 1776. . . With his eldest
son John he visited the Holston country — now Tennessee. He was with Colonel
Christian fighting the Indians at the Battle of Long Island, near Kingsport. He
bought land on Beaver Creek in Sullivan Co." He returned to Maryland to get
his family but died at Piney Creek, September 20, 1777. John Rhea, born in
Ireland in 1753, moved his father's family to Sullivan County. The homestead
established by him is still occupied by the Rheas. John Rhea went to Princeton.
He began the study of law, but quit it to fight. With his brother Matthew he was
in Brandywine battle. Matthew was a Captain in the Seventh Virginia. John was
at King's Mountain, and a member of the Constitutional Convention of North
Carolina. In 1796 he helped to frame the Constitution of Tennessee.

[1] Schouler's History, Vol. III, p. 69 et seq.; Schouler's Historic Briefs, pp. 97-126.
Magazine of American History, October, 1884; Colton's Clay, "The Cause of
Great Effects," Vol. I, pp. 253-257; Life of General Abner Lacock, United States
Senator from Pennsylvania, from 1813 to 1819, and a friend of Monroe. Lacock
has a chapter on the Rhea letter.

[2] Parton, Vol. II, p. 442 et seq.; Niles's Register, XIV; Van Buren's Autobiography,
pp. 336, 383.

Ambrister of New Providence, an ex-British lieutenant of the Negro Marines, with one Woodbine and
others, had joined with the "prophets"— Francis, or
Hillis, Hugo and Peter McQueen — in stirring up the
Red Sticks against the United States.[1] Jackson tried
the white ringleaders. They claimed to be traders.
Arbuthnot[2] had a schooner at St. Marks. He was
hanged in her rigging. Ambrister was shot. Then
Jackson captured Pensacola. Florida now was his.[3]

Taking Spanish territory was one thing, executing
British subjects was another. Minister Richard Rush
reported from London what Lord Castlereagh had
remarked to him; "If the Ministry had but held up a
finger," said his Lordship, "there would have been
war."

Whatever the excitement in Great Britain, there
certainly was a great stir at Washington and throughout
the United States.[4] At a Cabinet Council held upon
receipt of the sensational news, Jackson was condemned by every member, except John Quincy Adams,
as having gone too far. It was decided to disavow the
proceedings. An order was issued restoring St. Marks
and Pensacola to Spain; and, as soon as it was learned
that Jackson had ordered Gaines to occupy St. Augustine, the occupation order was countermanded.

Congress too, reviewed the episode. Abner Lacock,
of Pennsylvania, was the chairman of a special Senate
committee, and Thomas M. Nelson of Virginia, chair-

---

[1] Variously referred to in the letters of the time. Francis Hillisihago and Hornot-
limot, or Hornot Henrico, participant in the Appalachicola massacre, were leaders
in the outrages. Gen. George Gibson, the Colonel and Quartermaster General in
Jackson's army, and Captain McKeever of the Navy, were the two Commanders
who hung the Seminole chiefs.

[2] Trial of Arbuthnot and Ambrister, Memoirs of Jackson by S. Putnam Waldo,
p. 304, et seq.

[3] Sixteen years later, the Seminoles began a hunt on their side of the line and
got across in the zest of the chase. The whites took some of them. This led to
retaliation, the massacre of Major Dade's men and the outbreak of the Seminole
War of 1836. Osceola, or Asseyahola, or Powell, son of a white father and a Muscogee
mother, was the hero of the war — a favorite theme of the novelists.

[4] For further facts see Niles's Register, Vols. XV and XVI; Parton's Jackson,
Vol. II; Sumner's Jackson: Buell's Jackson; Colton's Jackson; The Florida
Border, by Gen. Samuel Dale; and Lives of Eaton, Goodwin, Frost and Dusenbery.

man of a House committee, to take evidence and report.
A long debate followed. In the House, on the final vote,
Jackson's conduct was approved by one hundred to
seventy. In the Senate no vote was taken on the con-
demnatory report of the committee.

As for Jackson he was in his glory. Not only had
he no compunctions for what he had done, but he felt
that Monroe and Calhoun were secretly pleased at the
turn of affairs. His Washington friends assured him
that Calhoun had spoken up for him at the Cabinet
meeting. It did not matter what the government should
do for effect abroad — that was to be expected; he was
pleased to think that Calhoun was his backer as well
as Monroe. As a matter of fact, Calhoun was his
severest critic at the Cabinet council. Calhoun suggested that Jackson ought to be court-martialed.
What happened in the Cabinet meeting is set forth
in the Diary of John Quincy Adams. But not until long
after did Jackson know the truth. When he did learn
it there was trouble — as we shall see, for there was a
sequel to the Rhea letter and to Calhoun's utterance
in the Cabinet on the day news came of Jackson's
Seminole seizure.[1] On the way up from Nashville to
Washington, Jackson gave a toast at Winchester, Va.
It was: "John C. Calhoun; an honest man is the
noblest work of God." He would not permit himself
to be lionized at Washington, seeing that Congress was
investigating his conduct; but in Baltimore, in Philadelphia (where he had once been criticized for wearing
an eel-skin queue) and in New York, he was the man
of the hour. New York Common-Council voted him a
gold snuff-box. Doubly a hero, he found followers
elsewhere.

As we have said, Secretary Adams took Jackson's
side, defending him "on the high ground of international law as expounded by Grotius, Vattel and
Puffendorf. "Confound Grotius! Confound Vattel!
Confound Puffendorf!" said Jackson, when he heard

[1] See Chapter XV of this book, pp. 450-452.

of it; "this is a matter between Jim Monroe and me."[1]

No doubt the Seminole episode expedited the settlement of the Florida question. By the treaty with Spain, arranged between Secretary Adams and Don Luis de Onis, Spanish Minister, February 22, 1819, East and West Florida were secured for $5,000,000 in bonds similar to those issued for the purchase of Louisiana. With interest, $1,489,768, the total cost was $6,489,768. The territory acquired contained 59,268 square miles, or 37,931,520 acres. The cost per acre was seventeen and one-tenth cents.

There was a slight ruffle on the smooth surface of things because Spain was slow to deliver Florida and Clay in Congress grew vehement again, but the short session passed with Monroe as master of the situation. "Colonel Monroe has some enemies here," wrote Judge Spencer Roane from Richmond, February 19 1820; "and they have been at work." Other letters are extant bearing upon the same theme, and conveying the same information. "Such is the state of feeling" (on the Missouri question) wrote St. George Tucker, from Williamsburg, February 11, "that Mr. Monroe must, I am satisfied, make up his mind to retain his Southern friends or exchange them for those of the North. He cannot keep both." But, all things considered, Monroe was fortunate in having a clear field. The Congressional caucus was held in April. Only forty members attended it, and Monroe was put through in short order.

Twenty-four States took part in the ninth presidential election of 1820. Monroe with two hundred and thirty-one electoral votes as against one electoral vote for John Quincy Adams, carried all the States, as did Vice-President D. D. Tompkins with two hundred and eighteen votes. Richard Stockton for Vice-President received eight votes; Daniel Rodney, four; Robert G. Harper, one, and Richard Rush, one; "Vacancies," for both President and Vice-President, three.

[1] Ben Perley Poore's Reminiscences, Vol. I, p. 167.

But since the vote was so nearly unanimous, why was it not quite so? According to C. O. Paullin[1] here is the explanation: "That the one vote in the electoral colleges of 1820 withheld from James Monroe, for President, was that of William Plumer, of New Hampshire, is somewhat generally known among historical writers. The reason for Plumer's action is not so well known. Indeed, most historians attribute to him an erroneous reason. They usually state that one New Hampshire elector withheld his vote from Monroe in order to prevent that statesman from sharing an honor previously accorded Washington alone. . . . The true reason for Plumer's action is stated in a letter that he wrote to his son, William Plumer, Jr., on January 8, 1821, and that is now found in the Plumer papers, Division of Manuscripts, Library of Congress. From this letter the following extract is taken: 'I was obliged from a sense of duty and a regard to my own reputation to withhold my vote from Monroe and Tompkins; from the first because he had discovered a want of foresight and from the second because he had grossly neglected his duty.' Plumer voted for Richard Rush for Vice-President. Contemporary impressions of Plumer's action possess considerable interest. His son, who was a Representative in Congress, writes: 'I received many congratulations on this vote of my father, from such men as Randolph, Macon and other Republicans of the old school. Not that they like Adams; (Randolph assailed him with the fury of hereditary hate); but they disliked Monroe, whom they regarded as having adopted, chiefly from the influence of Calhoun, some of the worst heresies of the old Federal party.'"

But the New Hampshire *Sentinel* was not so flattering to old Governor Plumer, who, by the by, with inconsistency, wrote Monroe a welcoming letter when the President passed through New Hampshire on his northern tour. In its issue of December 16, 1820, The *Sentinel* said: "Every one who knows anything about

[1] In the American Historical Review, Vol. XXI, pp. 318-319.

that odd old gentleman would have guessed as much
and, as his propensity is to be singular and overwise
was probably ungovernable, it is well that he voted
for the man who would, on the whole, be most acceptable to the people of this State as the successor of
Mr. Monroe. But this vote is to be regretted, because
it will probably be the only one throughout the United
States in opposition to the re-election of the present
incumbent and thus to prevent a unanimous election
will be pronounced sheer folly."

For his part, John Quincy Adams deeply regretted
Plumer's act, "as it implied a disapprobation of
Monroe's administration."

Justice Joseph Story wrote to Ezekiel Bacon, Washington, March 12, 1818: "There is a great deal of
gayety, splendor, and as I think, extravagance in the
manners and habits of the city. The old notions of
republican simplicity are fast wearing away, and the
public taste becomes more and more gratified with
public amusements and parade. Mr. Monroe, however,
still retains his plain and gentlemanly manners, and
is in every respect a very estimable man. But the
Executive has no longer a commanding influence.
The House of Representatives has absorbed all the
popular feeling and all the effective powers of the
country. Even the Senate cowers under its lofty
pretensions to be the guardians of the people and its
rights."[1]

Judge Joseph Story wrote to his wife, Washington,
March 6, 1821:

". . . Yesterday was the day appointed for the
Inauguration of the President, upon his re-appointment
to office. The weather was very inclement in the
morning, a violent storm having set in. Towards noon,
however, it abated, and a vast crowd was collected in
the Capitol to witness the ceremony. It was, according
to arrangement, to be performed in the Chamber of

---

[1] Life and Letters of Joseph Story, Edited by his son, William W. Story, 1851;
2 vols. Vol. I, pp. 310, 311.

the House of Representatives. This is a most splendid and magnificent hall in the shape of a horseshoe, having a colonnade of marble pillars round the whole circular sweep, which ascend to, and support a lofty dome. The galleries for spectators are about midway the pillars, and the seats gradually rise as they recede. The hall was early thronged with ladies and gentlemen of the first distinction, who had come from the neighboring cities to witness the scene. The whole area was crowded to excess, and the galleries appeared to be almost weighed down by their burden. About twelve the President came into the hall, dressed in a plain suit of black broadcloth, with a single-breasted coat and waistcoat, the latter with flaps in the old fashion. He wore also small-clothes, with silk stockings and shoes with gold buckles in them. His appearance was very impressive. He placed himself in a chair usually occupied by the Clerk of the House of Representatives, facing the whole audience. On his right was the President of the Senate and on his left the Speaker of the House. The Secretaries of all the Departments sat in a row on the right, and, on the left, all the foreign ministers and their suites, dressed out in their most splendid court dresses, and arranged according to their rank. Immediately in front of the President, at a small distance, were placed seven chairs for the Judges, who, upon notice, after the arrival of the President, went into the hall in their judicial robes, attended by the Marshal. The Chief Justice was immediately requested to take the chair on the left of the President, who soon afterwards rose, and the Chief Justice administered the oath of office. The President then delivered his inaugural speech, the Chief Justice, the foreign Ministers, the President of the Senate and the Speaker of the House remaining standing. The rest of the audience wherever they could remained seated. As soon as the speech was concluded, the marine corps of musicians who were in the gallery played 'Hail Columbia,' which was succeeded by 'Yankee Doodle' and after some

hurrahs from the crowd, the President received the
congratulations of the assembly and retired. Altogether, the scene was truly striking and grand. There
was a simple dignity about it which excited very
pleasing sensations. The fine collection of beautiful
and interesting women, dressed with great elegance,
the presence of so many men of talents, character and
public services, civil and military — the majestic
stretch of the hall itself, the recollection of our free
and happy situation, all combined to produce a most
profound feeling of interest. I do not know that I
ever was more impressed by a public spectacle."[1]

After the ceremony at the Capitol, hundreds proceeded to the White House where they congratulated
the President and Mrs. Monroe on the happy auspices
under which his second term had begun. "All the
world was there," adds Judge Story: "hackney coaches,
private carriages, foreign ministers and their suites,
were immediately in motion, and the very ground
seemed beaten into powder or paste under the tram-
pling of horses and the rolling of wheels. The scene lasted
until three o'clock, and then all things resumed their
wonted tranquility." The Judge himself for instance,
could go back to his patient examination of cases or
read his Jane Austen, of whom he was one of the
first as well as most ardent admirers.

Monroe was now sixty years old. He had lived to see
the United States acquire great and noble expanses of
territory. He himself had been instrumental in enlarging and securing the boundaries of the land he loved.[2]
It is true Texas was still to come in, the Oregon claim
was unadjusted, and California was to be a prize of
the future, but Monroe's fears had been dissipated and
his hopes realized.

Yet there was a fly in the ointment. Monroe had

[1] Life and Letters of Joseph Story, Vol. I, pp. 339-401.
[2] In a reference to John Quincy Adams's despatch proving that the Rio Grande
was the western boundary of Texas, Clark E. Carr, in his Life of Stephen A.
Douglas, 1909, says: This was the opinion of Messrs. Monroe and Pinckney in
1805."

hardly felicitated himself upon the security of the republic in consequence of its territorial aloofness from foreign enemies when, like Jefferson, he was struck a-back by the menace of slavery. Abuse Jefferson as they may, his critics confess that he hoped in his heart for relief from this ominous evil. He wrote from Monticello: "This momentous question, like a firebell in the night, awakened and filled me with terror. I considered it at once the knell of the Union." Subsequently, he seemed to see with the eyes of a prophet, and said that, though the storm would lash us we should withstand and outride it. We take on prejudices easily while in this mortal clay; and no historical misjudgment is so common as the off-hand condemnation of Slave-State statesmen. The very fact that they came thence is deemed sufficient warrant to neglect them or minimize whatever merits they may be grudgingly allowed. This is not only unfair to them, but perverts history, injecting bias where truth should be. Many of those men — notably Jefferson, Madison and Monroe — labored as best they could, not only to prevent the extension of slavery, but to rid the country of it. Madison, in 1831, spoke of slavery as a "dreadful calamity." "In an old age rendered bright with optimism," says Gaillard Hunt, "slavery was the one dark object that hung over him." Harriet Martineau, who visited him at Montpelier, wrote: "With regard to slavery, he owned himself almost in despair."

Monroe wanted to repatriate the free blacks to Africa. Monrovia in Liberia is a namesake capital. He and Jefferson had corresponded on the subject as far back as 1801. The first colonization society was organized at Princeton in 1816. On December 23, of that year, the Virginia Legislature invited the attention of the United States Government to the matter. At this same Christmas time the National Colonization Society was organized at Washington. Judge Bushrod Washington, nephew of General Washington, was its first president and *The African Repository* became its

organ. Many of its members lived in the South; and
they laid the flattering unction to their souls that the
blacks could be deported to the region from which they
had come, taking with them what they had learned
and founding there a free and happy commonwealth.
They were idealists, with troubled consciences. As yet
they were unhectored; and their generous feeling was
spontaneous. The animating thought was to bring
about emancipation, without economic or political
violence.

At least that was the motive of many; but it is
equally true that others hoped to rid the country of
the free blacks and the free blacks only.[1] However,
as most of the emancipation leaders of the coming
decades began as colonizationists[2] — such as Benjamin
Lundy, James G. Birney and Gerrit Smith — it is
clear that the society was truly reformatory in character and not a sham or makeshift.

Sierra Leone, a British colony, was first used as a
colonization point; next, in 1820, Sherbro Island; and,
finally, December 15, 1821, Cape Mesurado.

It was Commodore Matthew Calbraith Perry who
selected the site of Monrovia. The first site on Sherbro
Island in the estuary of Sherbro River, as pitched upon
by the American Colonization Society was found to be
malarial. In 1832, Perry hoisted the American flag
over Cape Mesurado. "Shortly afterward," says
William Elliot Griffis, in his " Life of M. C. Perry,"
"Monrovia, the future capital, named after President
Monroe, began its existence. To this form of the
Monroe Doctrine European nations have fully ac-
ceded. Liberia is the only colony founded by the
United States." [3] John Quincy Adams — "hard as

---

[1] "The whole scheme was but a palliative, and in fact rather tended to strengthen
slavery by taking away the disquieting presence of free blacks among the slaves" —
Hart, Formation of the Union.

[2] American Political History, 1763-1876, by Alexander Johnston, 2 vols. Vol. II,
pp. 44, 45.

[3] Matthew Calbraith Perry, by William Elliot Griffis, 1887. For Commodore
Stockton's voyage to Liberia, see Life of Robert F. Stockton, by S. J. Bayard,
1856, p. 39.

a piece of granite and cold as a lump of ice "[1] — was not
in agreement with Monroe in respect to the colonization idea. He thought it visionary and compared it
with the project of John Cleves Symmes of going to
the North Pole and traveling within the nutshell of
the earth.[2]

The time had come (1818–1821) to take in the States
carved out of the Louisiana land, of which the upper
region was known as Missouri Territory. Now slaves
were held there under the old French and Spanish law
and continued to be held under American territorial
law. In December, 1818, a bill was introduced in the
House of Representatives providing for the government
of Arkansas Territory. Taylor of New York put in a
word. He wanted a proviso — let slavery be prohibited
there. McLane of Delaware got over the difficulty
with the suggestion that a line be drawn and fixed
west of the Mississippi "north of which slavery could
not be tolerated."

When Arkansas Territory was organized, March 2,
1819, no mention was made of slavery. Less easily
disposed of was the case of Missouri. The people there
sent a petition to Congress asking that they be allowed
to form a constitution. This petition was presented
in the House on March 16, 1818. On April 6, the committee to which the petition was referred reported an
enabling act; but nothing further was done in the
matter at that session of Congress. On February 13,
1819, Tallmadge of New York offered an amendment
to the enabling act prohibiting slavery in Missouri
except in the case of crime. At once, the great sections
showed their colors — the issue was drawn. The North
voted for, the South against, the Tallmadge amendment. Rufus King led the debate on one side, John
Randolph of Roanoke on the other. The House voted
for the proviso, but the Senate struck it out. The

---

[1] What I Remember, by Thomas Adolphus Trollope, quoting from a letter of
T. C. Grattan, p. 503.
[2] Memoirs of John Quincy Adams, Vol. IV, p. 355.

Aquarelle Portrait from Life of President James Monroe

This portrait was drawn from life during the time Monroe was Minister to France

bill was lost, but when Congress adjourned March 3, 1819, the battle of the sections was begun.

When the new Congress (the sixteenth) met on the sixth of December, Alabama was admitted, December 14, and the admission of Maine was agreed to by the House, January 3, 1820. But the Senate put a Missouri "rider" on the Maine measure, twenty-three to twenty-one. On February 17, Thomas of Illinois offered an amendment, suggested by McLane of Delaware, dividing the Louisiana purchase on a line between slave and free. The Senate voted yea, but the House disagreed. Then came the crisis, March 3, 1820, when Congress voted to admit Missouri without slave prohibition, but with the proviso that no slavery should be permitted north of 36° 30′. This was the first compromise. When the Missourians in their new constitution excluded free blacks another compromise was necessary. This, as suggested by Clay, was that "the Missourians were to agree not to deprive of his rights any citizen of another State." As thus shaped the Missouri bills reached Monroe for his signature. He submitted two questions to his Cabinet: "(1) Whether the prohibition of slavery was constitutional, and (2) whether the word 'forever' was a 'territorial' forever, or applicable to States formed from the Territory in future." There was no dissenting voice in the first question; but on the second there was a division. Calhoun thereupon combined the two into this: "Was the Thomas amendment constitutional?" All said yes; and Monroe signed the bill March 6, 1820.[1]

Monroe burned the midnight oil — a conscientious and laborious student of public questions. John Quincy Adams used to notice a light in the President's apartment long after others were in bed. The matter of internal improvements concerned him. How far ought the government to go?

The need of better roads was felt all the time, but especially while the war was on. Another reminder of

[1] Johnston, Political History, Vol. II, p. 116.

this need, and of the desirability of canals, was the country's great expansion. During the first year of Monroe's incumbency, twenty-two thousand immigrants, mostly Irish, arrived. Multitudes of people were moving west. The Erie Canal was begun a little after Monroe went in, and finished a little while after he went out. But the Erie Canal was constructed by the State of New York. Could Federal money be constitutionally used in such great works? There was the Cumberland Road, begun in 1806, and well known as "The National Turnpike." In Jefferson's time, with surplus in the Treasury, thanks to Gallatin, there had been little question as to the power of Congress to vote money for building this road from Cumberland to Wheeling. Jefferson had compunctions about it, however, and talked of the desirability of a constitutional amendment. Madison agreed with him, and, similarly, Monroe could not rid himself of strict construction ideas on the subject. Calhoun could; so could Clay; they had no scruples about it; how nonsensical to let great improvements be blocked for lack of specific authorization! Just before the end of Madison's second term, Congress set aside the bonus due the government from the United States bank for use in improving the Cumberland road.

Madison vetoed this measure, March 3, 1817, in his last message[1] to Congress. His point was that the Constitution did not specifically grant the power under which Congress could vote money for internal improvements. Could the general wellfare clause be stretched to cover the case? He thought not.

Monroe gave serious thought to the subject, consulted Madison and by and by marked out for himself a plan of procedure.[2] He let it be understood that he was heartily in favor of such improvements *per se;* yet he agreed with his predecessors as to the insuffi-

---

[1] Schouler, Hist., Vol. III, pp. 249-254; Monroe Mss.; Annals of Congress, 1817-1822. Messages and Papers of the Presidents, I, 584.
[2] First Annual Message. December 2, 1817.

cient powers of Congress. He accordingly urged Congress to consult the States with a view to the adoption of a suitable amendment. He said: "Disregarding early impressions, I have bestowed on the subject all the deliberation which its great importance and a just sense of my duty required, and the result is a settled conviction in my mind that Congress does not possess the right."

Clay, for his part, made two speeches, in which he claimed that Congress had a perfect right to vote money for such improvements. Other western Congressmen thought as he did. With some of them it was a burning question. They regarded the broad gravel-covered turnpike, with its substantial bridges, as the first great transcontinental highway equal to the historic Roman roads. So they felt they were justified, in the first session of the seventeenth Congress, in voting $9000 for repairing the road. The vote in the House, April 29, 1822, was eighty-seven to sixty-eight. The Senate passed the bill and it went to the President, who vetoed it. On May 6, the House failed to pass it over the veto, sixty-eight to seventy-two. Schouler says that Monroe was proud of the veto, "confident of the ground he had chosen." He "sent out copies of his veto message to the Judges of the Supreme Court, and to most of his political friends. He received in response many testimonials of approval from Wirt, Rush, Madison, Southard, and others. Madison approved. . . . Story was non-committal."[1] Since then the subject has been a favorite one with statesmen and historians.

---

[1] Schouler Hist., Vol. III, Monroe Mss.; Clay made two speeches on this subject. Buchanan's speech is in Vol. I of his Works. See also the Life of Reverdy Johnson, by C. B. Stenier, p. 111.

CHAPTER XV

THE MONROE DOCTRINE — LAST DAYS

On December 2, 1823, Monroe sent to Congress his seventh annual message. Embodied in it was what is now known the world over as the Monroe Doctrine. Monroe was then sixty-five years old. Many a day, both at home and abroad, had he gone to that school of experience which all of us agree is the best of schools. Ripe in statesmanship, his diplomatic practice in France, Spain and England, coupled with his varied labors at Washington, enabled him to see the necessity for what he was doing and to go about his international task in the right way. Lately he had been helped by his contests with Speaker Clay on questions connected with South American insurgency. Clay, grinding his own axe, had unwittingly sharpened Monroe's. Moreover, Monroe was aided not a little — perhaps more than we shall ever know — by the able men with whom he had surrounded himself. Many historians attribute the Monroe Doctrine to the influence of John Quincy Adams. Elihu Root speaks of him as the major force in formulating it. In his diary, indeed, Adams indicates clearly some of the things done by him in connection with the work. Undoubtedly, his part in the performance was greatly to his credit. He was an honest man, a sound American and an experienced diplomat.

As we go along we shall see that Adams's work shows as a distinct thread in the cloth, but we have the testimony of Calhoun that Monroe cut it and shaped it with his own hand. In the *William and Mary Quarterly*[1] is an article telling of Judge Francis T. Brooke (born August 27, 1763; died March 3, 1851), a lieutenant in the Virginian line during the Revolution and a member

[1] Vol. XVII, p. 4.

of the Supreme Court of Virginia, who left some
reminiscences entitled: "Narrative of My Life for My
Family." In the course of his narrative, he said: "I
knew Mr. Monroe, practiced law with him, and I think,
though a slow man, he possessed a strong mind and
excellent judgment. When I was at York [Yorktown],
in 1824, with General La Fayette, Mr. Calhoun, then
Secretary of War, was there; and I asked him whether
it was the President, Monroe, or his Cabinet, who were
in favor of that passage in his message which declared
to the Holy Alliance that America would not be indifferent to any attempt to aid the Spanish Government to
prevent the enfranchisement of the South American
Powers, then at war with Spain; and he replied that it
was the President's own sentiment, and, though he was
a slow man, yet give him time, and he was a man of
the best judgment he had ever known."

Napoleon's fall was followed by a Bourbon restoration and other reactionary phenomena betokening a
return to despotic government. The sovereigns who
were thus happy to be rid of the terrible Bonaparte
looked upon themselves not as despots but as privileged
potentates, ruling by the grace of God. They declared
that it was necessary to base the relations of the Powers
on "the sublime truths of the holy religion of the Lord
and Redeemer." Hence the name "Holy Alliance"
given to a league said to have been suggested by
Mme. de Krudener, wife of the Baron de Krudener,
the Russian diplomat, to Alexander I, during that
Emperor's residence in Paris. She was the daughter
of Baron Weitinghoff of Livonia; and was wont to
entertain the Czar at her house, being a woman with
intellectual as well as other charms. The document
instituting the Holy Alliance was prepared by Alexander
I, on September 26, 1815, and was signed by the
Emperor Francis of Austria, King Frederick William
III of Prussia and King Louis XVIII of France. The
Pope was not asked to join the Holy Alliance. England
refused to enter it; and with good reason, since it stood

for the suppression of democracy. A Congress of the
Allied Powers, held at Aix la Chapelle in 1818, took
preliminary steps toward the repression of liberalism.
In 1820 a similar Congress at Troppau declared that
the sovereigns of Russia, Austria and Prussia "regarded
as legally null all pretended reform operated by revolt
and open hostility." Naples was disciplined; so was
Spain, where, upon the restoration of the Bourbon
dynasty, in the person of Ferdinand VII, constitutional
government was made a mockery. A hundred thousand
soldiers overran Spain as far as Cadiz. The Cortez
passed out; the despots entered.

Then came the turn of the South American countries.
The American Revolution had been heard of there.
A popular document was the Declaration of Independence, translated into French and circulated at
the capitals. The thrilling liberty cries of the French
Revolution likewise found an echo in the great forests
and savannahs of the southern continent. Therefore,
when in Napoleon's time, a favorable opportunity
came, the Spanish subjects in South America were in
a mood to free themselves. Even some of the pro-
Spanish people preferred home republics to governments conducted by Napoleon's brother Joseph, in
Madrid. Others gave allegiance to the juntas in Spain.
The result was that the South Americans became practically self-governing during the later Napoleonic
period.[1] Portuguese royalty, retiring before the French,
fled from Lisbon to Rio de Janeiro; and, in 1815,
organized Brazil into a joint kingdom. In 1822, Pedro,
Prince Regent, declared Brazil independent of Portugal;
and assumed the title of Emperor, which was transmitted to Dom Pedro, the famous "friend of the United
States," who was lionized in this country during the
Centennial Exposition at Philadelphia. Such in brief
was the promising political condition of what are now
the republics of Brazil, Colombia, Ecuador, Bolivia,

---

[1] The leading liberators in South America were: Francisco de Miranda (1752-
1816); the great Simon Bolivar (1783-1830) and Jose de San Martin (1778-1850).

Peru and the great states in the region of the Rio de la
Plata — inchoate Latin American republics, with the
fires of liberty burning.[1]

It was the Holy Alliance that threatened to put out
these fires, and to destroy something else at the same
time. That something else was the trade established
with the non-Spanish world. The Bourbon king wished
to monopolize this trade as he had done of yore. Ferdinand was of the mind to have his dependencies back.
His reason for delaying the ratification of the sale of
Florida to the United States was based upon the fear
that Monroe might recognize South American independence as soon as the other matter should be clinched.
The American Minister to Spain was Hugh Nelson of
Virginia, who had succeeded John Forsyth, a Georgia
adherent of Monroe. But Forsyth had failed to reach
Berlin; Gallatin's successor, James Brown of Louisiana,
had not as yet arrived at Paris; and the only capable
American diplomat in that part of the world was
Richard Rush. This worthy and zealous minister
wrote many letters to Monroe, who profited greatly by
the correspondence.[2]

George Canning, British Foreign Secretary in the
Portland ministry, whose Orders in Council had done
so much to worry us into war, was again in power and
had made a *volte face* with respect to America. As we
have noted, Lord Castlereagh had gone out of his
head and made an end of himself. Canning assiduously
cultivated Rush. "His old taunting tone was gone,"
says Schouler. Rush sat near him at a diplomatic
dinner-party, and Canning asked him to take a glass
of wine.

---

[1] "The second period in the history of national development in Spanish America,
extending approximately from 1852 to 1876, may be characterized as 'the struggle
for stability. . .' Capital cities like Buenos Ayres, Montevideo and Lima, in which
the European population enjoyed some influence, had a considerable share in the
process."— Latin America, by W. R. Shepherd. In 1853 the Argentine Confederation became the Argentine Republic.

[2] Schouler, Hist., Vol. III; Monroe Mss.; Richard Rush's Residence at the
Court of London. Rush was subsequently Secretary of the Treasury in John
Quincy Adams's Cabinet.

"Our Minister proposed as a toast, 'Success to neutrals.' 'Good!' said Canning, and drank it off. This led Rush to thank Canning for a speech he had lately made in the House of Commons, which contained some flattering reference to the neutral doctrines of our government in 1793. 'Yes!' replied Canning, 'and I spoke sincerely'; and went on to say that he had lately read with the utmost interest the American State Papers of that epoch, and particularly Jefferson's letters. 'They are admirable,' he added, 'they form as far as they go a complete neutral code.' These words and Canning's fervent manner of expressing himself Rush felt the more, because the Russian Ambassador sat near them, and most probably overheard the whole conversation. Soon afterwards our minister received a revised copy of this speech, which in a private note, full of personal compliment, Canning begged him to forward to President Monroe."[1]

Canning watched the Holy Alliance and courted the friendship of the United States. By midsummer, 1823 he knew enough to conclude that the Powers meant to back the Bourbon of Spain in an attempt to regain and once more enfetter the South American countries. Canning's continental entanglements kept him from recognizing the republics, but he wished the United States to do so. In an interview with Rush, September 18, Canning brought matters to a head. He said he wanted an understanding with the United States in regard to South America. He proposed that the two countries should enter into a convention. Why not? Why not jointly oppose the Holy Alliance? Why should not the United States be represented in the proposed European Congress on South American colonial questions? Rush said: "My country has

[1] Schouler, Hist., Vol. III, pp. 283-284; Rush to Monroe, April 24, 1823, Monroe Mss.; Rush to Monroe, July 13, 1823.   Stratford Canning (Viscount Stratford de Redcliffe), a cousin of George Canning, was Sir Charles Bagot's successor as minister at Washington.   He remained twenty-two months.   Adams called him "overbearing"; he spoke of Adams as "domineering."   In Stratford Canning's life by S. Lane-Poole, 2 vols., vol. I, pp. 301-338, we find much about Monroe, Adams and social ways at Washington.

acknowledged the independence of these South American Republics and wishes to see them received into the
family of nations. . . . I must procure instructions from
home before entering into any joint understanding. . . .
Immediate recognition offers, however, the true basis
of our concert." He wanted Canning to recognize
the republics. But Canning drew back. Rush wrote
home. Again, on September 26, Canning saw Rush; but
the second interview was substantially a repetition
of the first.

Monroe, upon receipt of Rush's secret despatch,
replied: "You could not have met Canning's proposals
better if you had had the whole American Cabinet at
your right hand."

Monroe lost no time in consulting Jefferson and
Madison. What was back of Canning's eagerness?
asked the cautious Madison. But Jefferson was less
suspicious. Here is his reply:

"The question presented by the letters you have
sent me is the most momentous which has ever been
offered to my contemplation since that of independence. That made us a nation; this sets our compass
and points the course which we are to steer through the
ocean of time opening on us. And never could we
embark upon it under circumstances more auspicious.
Our first and fundamental maxim should be, never
to entangle ourselves in the broils of Europe; our second,
never to suffer Europe to meddle with cis-Atlantic
affairs. America, North and South, has a set of
interests distinct from those of Europe, and peculiarly
her own. She should therefore have a system of her
own, separate and apart from that of Europe."

With this endorsement of his own views, Monroe
prepared the most remarkable document with which
his name is associated. Of his advisers Schouler says:
"Wirt was timorous, Calhoun open to conviction,
Adams bold as a lion. But the President whose experience in European diplomacy we should remember was
greater than that of all his cabinet, felt confident of

his ground. He had determined neither on the one hand to provoke the Alliance by a tone of taunting defiance, nor on the other to give this country the appearance of taking a position subordinate to Great Britain. . . . The President's Message of December, 1823, toned down from the solemn exordium of the first draft, which Adams feared would alarm our people like a clap of thunder, put forward therefore, two distinct declarations." The first was a protest against future colonization by any European power. The second was a protest against any extension of the system of the Holy Alliance to this hemisphere.[1]

The Czar's arm was as long as that of the Holy Alliance. One reached from Spain across the Atlantic to South America, or tried to; the other, thrust out four thousand miles across the Pacific, actually menaced us in the Alaskan quarter of North America. With the Oregon dispute in abeyance, we owned no land on the Pacific coast, but had important interests there. The first American ship to sail around the world, the "Columbia," touched at Nootka Sound in 1788, for a cargo of furs, which she took to Canton, sailing thence with a cargo of tea to Boston — a complete circumnavigation.[2] In 1798, the Russian American Company, trading in furs, was organized. The Russians wished to monopolize the region, and were about to exclude all American traders in 1806, when they realized through an incident at Sitka that our ships were necessary.[3] Only by the arrival of the American ship "Juno" were the Sitka settlers saved from starvation. After this

[1] Schouler, History III, pp. 289-294. Also "The Monroe Doctrine," Chapter VII, in Gilman's Monroe. Both Gilman and Schouler disagree with the late Senator Sumner, in his "Prophetic Voices," when he says that Canning originated the Monroe Doctrine. See Charles Sumner's "Prophetic Voices," pp. 157-160. Canning said Dec. 16, 1826: "Contemplating Spain, such as our ancestors had known her, I resolved that if France had Spain, it should not be Spain *with the Indies*. I called the New World into existence to redress the balance of the Old." He was Spain's friend in Europe; her enemy in America." See Canning, by W. Alison Phillips, 1903.

[2] American Diplomacy, by Eugene Schuyler, 1886, pp. 292-305, "The North Pacific."

[3] Schuyler, Diplomacy, citing Robert Greenbow's History of Oregon and California.

striking proof the Russians ceased to threaten expulsion, but they were none the less aggressive and domineering. They claimed the coast as far south as the Columbia river. John Quincy Adams, who had represented the United States in St. Petersburg and who was especially fitted to deal with Russo-American problems, was fortunately in the State Department just at the time when he was most needed there.

Suddenly, on February 28, 1822, Adams was notified by M. Poletica, Russian Minister at Washington, that the Czar had issued an ukase in September, 1821, claiming the northwest coast of North America from Behring Strait to the fifty-first degree of north latitude. The Czar did not declare the North Pacific a closed sea, but warned all save Russians to keep one hundred Italian miles (three leagues) off shore. M. Poletica accompanied the ukase with a mass of matter in proof of Russian rights to overlordship. Adams knew better. He asserted American trading rights in the seas covered by the ukase, fixing the fifty-fifth parallel as the southern limit of Russian influence. Baron de Tuyl soon displaced Poletica as Russian representative at Washington; Minister Middleton was American representative at the Czar's Court. Adams wrote to Middleton that no Russian territorial right "could be admitted on this continent, as the Russians appear to have no settlement upon it except that in California." Middleton was to propose an arrangement with Russia whereby the whole coast would be open to navigation; or, if the Czar would not agree to that, Middleton was to arrange the matter so that the Russians would keep to the north of the fifty-fifth parallel. Adams went deeply into the whole subject. Finally he made up his mind. Speaking of an interview with Baron de Tuyl, he says:

"I told him specially that we should contest the right of Russia to any territorial establishment on this continent; and that we should *assume distinctly the principle that the American continents are no longer subjects for any new European Colonial establishments.*"[1]

---

[1] Adams, Memoirs, Vol. VI, p. 163.

Here we have a clear-cut statement as to the origin of the colonization clause in the Monroe doctrine.[1]

Adams won his point as to American rights in the North Pacific, for on April 17, 1824, a Russo-American convention was agreed to on his lines. Americans could thereafter sail the seas in the disputed region, and fish and trade with the natives at points unoccupied by Russian traders. As for the southern limit of Russian privilege, that was to be fixed at 54° 40′ north latitude.

Important as was the convention thus arranged, the principle enunciated was of infinitely greater value because it read a new truth into the fundamental American policy with respect to alien Powers. Madison wrote to Monroe, August 5, 1824, congratulating him on the convention with Russia. It was well that America had become "the leading power in arresting" Russia's "expansive ambition." The English as well as American papers had a great deal to say about the convention, rejoicing at the success of America in putting a curb on the autocrat. Having thus presented the *raison d'être* of the Monroe Doctrine, we now straightway append the paragraphs in the seventh annual message that embody and constitute it. Monroe wrote:

"The occasion has been judged proper for asserting, as a principle in which the rights and interests of the United States are involved, that the American continents, by the free and independent condition which they have assumed and maintain, are henceforth not to be considered as subjects for future colonization by any European powers. . . . In the wars of the European powers, in matters relating to themselves, we have never taken any part, nor does it comport with our policy to do so. It is only when our rights are invaded or seriously menaced, that we resent injuries

---

[1] "It is interesting to regard Article VI of the [Franco-American] Treaty of Alliance as a sort of forerunner of that phase of the Monroe Doctrine which declares that 'the American Continent is no longer subject to colonization. . . .' As we have seen, the alliance with France was soon discarded, but the motive back of the act was not sympathy for England but a real vision of national destiny which would be foiled and frustrated were the nation to be drawn into the 'European Vortex'. . . . Hence, of course, the American policy of isolation, the first and main pillar of the Monroe Doctrine"— French Policy and the American Alliance, by E. S. Corwin, 1916, pp. 201, 369.

or make preparation for our defence. With the movements in this hemisphere we are of necessity more immediately connected and by causes which must be obvious to all enlightened and impartial observers. . . . We owe it therefore to candor and to the amicable relations existing between the United States and those powers to declare that we should consider any attempt on their part to extend their system to any portion of this hemisphere as dangerous to our peace and safety. With the existing colonies or dependencies of any European power we have not interfered and shall not interfere. But with the governments who have declared their independence and maintained it, and whose independence we have, on great consideration and on just principles, acknowledged, we could not view any interposition for the purpose of oppressing them or controlling in any manner their destiny, by any European power, in any other light than as the manifestation of an unfriendly disposition toward the United States. In the war between those new governments and Spain we declared our neutrality at the time of their recognition, and to this we have adhered and shall continue to adhere, provided no change shall occur which, in the judgment of the competent authorities of this government, shall make a corresponding change on the part of the United States indispensable to their security. . . . It is impossible that the allied powers should extend their political system to any portion of either continent without endangering our peace and happiness; nor can anyone believe that our southern brethren, if left to themselves, would adopt it of their own accord It is equally impossible, therefore, that we should behold such interposition, in any form, with indifference."

Elihu Root said in his address on "The Real Monroe Doctrine"[1]:

"As the particular occasions which called it forth have slipped back into history, the declaration itself has grown continually a more vital and insistent rule of conduct for each succeeding generation of Americans. Never for a moment have the responsible and instructed statesmen in charge of the foreign affairs of the United States failed to consider themselves bound to insist upon its policy. Never once has the public opinion of the people of the United States failed to support every just application of it as new occasion has arisen. Almost every President and Secretary of State has restated the doctrine with vigor and emphasis in the discussion of the diplomatic affairs of his day. The governments of Europe have gradually come to realize that the existence of the

---

[1] Presidential Address at the Eighth Annual Meeting of the American Society of International Law, Washington, April 22, 1814. From addresses on International Law. Root, by R. Bacon and J. B. Scott, 1916.

policy which Monroe declared is a stubborn and continuing fact
to be recognized in their controversies with American countries.
We have seen Spain, France, England, Germany, with admirable
good sense and good temper, explaining beforehand to the United
States that they intended no permanent occupation of territory,
in the controversy with Mexico forty years after the declaration,
and in the controversy with Venezuela eighty years after. In
1903 the Duke of Devonshire declared 'Great Britain accepts the
Monroe Doctrine unreservedly.' Mr. Hay coupled the Monroe
Doctrine and the Golden Rule as cardinal guides of American
diplomacy. . . . No one ever pretended that Mr. Monroe was
declaring a rule of international law or that the doctrine which he
declared had become international law. It is a declaration of the
United States that certain acts would be injurious to the peace
and safety of the United States and that the United States would
regard them as unfriendly. The declaration does not say what
the course of the United States will be in case such acts are done.
That is left to be determined in each particular instance. . . . The
doctrine is not international law but it rests upon the right of
self-protection and that right is recognized by international law.
The right is a necessary corollary of independent sovereignty. . . .
The international right upon which the declaration expressly
rests is not sentiment or sympathy or a claim to dictate what kind
of government any other country shall have, but the safety of
the United States. . . . We frequently see statements that the
doctrine has been changed or enlarged; that there is a new or
different doctrine since Monroe's time. They are mistaken.
There has been no change. One apparent extension of the statement of Monroe was made by President Polk in his messages
of 1845 and 1848, when he included the acquisition of territory by
a European Power through cession as dangerous to the safety of
the United States. It was really but stating a corollary to the
doctrine of 1823 and asserting the same right of self-protection
against the other American States as well as against Europe. . . .
The fundamental principle of international law is the principle
of independent sovereignty. Upon that all other rules of international law rest. . . . The Monroe Doctrine does not infringe
upon that right; it asserts the right."

During the Yucatan Bill debate, in 1848, Calhoun
said that what should be done "must be determined
and decided on the merits of the question itself."
Buchanan said, in 1848, that "we should be compelled
to resist the acquisition of Cuba by any powerful
maritime State." Clayton said in 1849 that the news
of the cession of Cuba to any foreign power would be

in the United States the instant signal for war. Seward
said, when Napoleon III sent troops to Mexico, in 1865,
that the President wished France to be respectfully
informed on two points: (1) the United States desired
"to continue and cultivate sincere friendship with
France; (2) that this policy would be jeoparded unless
France should desist in Mexico."
   Cleveland said in 1895:

> "The doctrine upon which we stand[1] is strong and sound because
> its enforcement is important to our peace and safety as a nation,
> and is essential to the integrity of our free institutions, and the
> tranquil maintenance of our distinctive form of government. It
> was intended to apply to every stage of our national life and
> cannot become obsolete while our Republic endures."

   We are warned by Elihu Root that the Monroe
Doctrine is by no means a be-all or do-all. It is dangerous to harbor a false conception of what it demands
and what it justifies, of its scope and its limits. Since
the Monroe Doctrine is a declaration based upon this
nation's right of self-protection it cannot be trans-
muted into a joint or common declaration by American
States or any number of them. Let there be no gran-
diose scheme in connection with it. He concludes:

> "The intolerance which demands that control over the conduct
> and opinions of other peoples, which is the essence of tyranny,
> invokes the Monroe Doctrine. Thoughtless people who see no
> difference between lawful right and physical power assume that
> the Monroe Doctrine is a warrant for interference in the internal
> affairs of all weaker nations in the New World. Against this
> supposititious doctrine, many protests both in the United States
> and South America have been made, and justly made. To the
> real Monroe Doctrine these protests have no application."

   Many miss the point of the Monroe Doctrine. Con-
ceited patriots on each continent of the western hemi-

---

[1] That of non-intervention of European powers in matters relating to the
American continent. The Olney doctrine of 1895 was thus expressed: "No European Power has the right to intervene forcibly in the affairs of the New World;
that the United States, owing to its superior size and power, is the natural protector
and champion of all American nations; and that permanent political Union between
a European and an American State is unnatural and inexpedient."

sphere misconceive its purpose and misconstrue its meaning. Often it is because they themselves never have read the two simple clauses that constitute the Doctrine, but have accepted some erroneous hearsay interpretation originating in ignorance or perversity. In a vainglorious way, a North American may plume himself on his superior strength and virtue. Yes, he will look after those sister republics. Let them fear not. He condescends, he patronizes, with every breath he makes an enemy. He has his counterpart in South America, where, as Root indicates, there is all too frequently a "misunderstanding of the attitude and purposes of the United States." Bryce reminds us that the regard of the early South American republics for the United States and their "confidence in its purposes never quite recovered the blow given by the Mexican War of 1846 and the annexation of California." Moreover, Latin America is now strong. Apprehensions of aggression have vanished. Bryce repeats the words of one who said: "Since there are no longer rainclouds coming from the east, why should a friend, however well-intentioned, insist on holding an umbrella over us? We are quite able to do that for ourselves, if necessary." "Many a Chileno and Argentino," says another South American traveler,[13] "resents the idea of our Monroe Doctrine applying in any sense to his country and declares that we had better keep it at home. . . . Such republics as Mexico, Argentina and Brazil, Chile and Peru, no more need our Monroe Doctrine to keep them from being robbed of their territory by European nations than does Italy or Spain." Georges Clemenceau in "South America of Today," 1911, notes that at the Pan-American Congress in Buenos Ayres, where he met "only jurisconsults, historians, men of letters or of science," Henry White, representing the United States, needed all his gracious affability "to disarm the distrust aroused more espe-

---

[1] Hiram Bingham. Across South America, 1911. See also The South Americans. by Albert Hale, pp. 303-309.

cially by the proposal to place Southern America under
the banner of the Monroe Doctrine." Foolish indeed,
are those friends of the Doctrine who misread it, or
unwittingly drift away from its great central purpose.
They should read Root, who says: "The Monroe
Doctrine does not assert, or imply or involve any right
on the part of the United States to impair or control
the independent sovereignty of any American State."
If Russia had fastened despotism upon what is now
British Columbia, if imperial France had set an Austrian
upon the throne of Mexico, if other autocratic aliens
had seized the struggling Latin American countries
and established kingdoms there, the United States
would have been imperiled in every quarter. Wars or
rumors of war would have been unceasing. Self-
protection from such dire contingencies was at the
bottom of the Monroe Doctrine in its inception. That
is the fundamental idea now. However strong a nation,
some sinister Power, or combination of Powers, may
rise to overwhelm it. Hence the perpetual protective
use of the Monroe Doctrine.

What Louis Napoleon, who made bold to violate it,
thought of the Monroe Doctrine is given us by the
Earl of Malmesbury. This Emperor, having invited
Malmesbury to dine at the Tuileries, March 20, 1852,
talked to him about England and France:

"He said he was anxious to go *bras a bras* with England
on every question, not *pour les beaux yeux* of one another
but for our solid interest; that two great subjects
were now paramount — namely, the maintenance of
the Turkish Empire and the new International Code
broached by America called 'the Monroe Doctrine';
and that these two points comprehended the whole
policy of the world, the maintenance of peace, and the
advance of human civilization and improvement.
Russia was a barbarous Monarchy, and America a
barbarous Republic, but both young, vigorous, *et
pleines de sève.*"

The history of the Monroe Doctrine is so long as to force us to be content with a summary.

In Continental times, Congress handled our relations with other countries by means of (1) the Committee of Secret Correspondence, (2) the Committee of Foreign Affairs, and (3) the Secretary of Foreign Affairs.

Under the Constitution, the Secretary of State took up this work. Thus Jefferson, first Secretary of State, enunciated and established the fundamental doctrine of neutrality. This was the keynote of the Washington administration and to it all of Washington's utterances were attuned.

One of Jefferson's biographers, John T. Morse, Jr., calls attention (p. 235) to a letter to Gouverneur Morris in which Jefferson "faintly foreshadowed the Monroe Doctrine." England had threatened to seize the North American possessions of Spain. Jefferson wrote: "We wish you therefore to intimate to them (British Ministry) that we cannot be indifferent to enterprises of this kind. That we should contemplate an exchange of neighbors with extreme uneasiness. That a due balance on our borders is not less desirable to us than a balance of power in Europe has always appeared to them."

"When the war broke out between France and England," says John J. Conway, in "Footsteps of Famous Americans in Paris," Edmund Randolph, who had succeeded Jefferson, "drafted the Neustrelitz Proclamation, which said that the United States meant to hold aloof from European complications; subsequently this developed into the Monroe Doctrine."

Not long after the Copenhagen outrage, the British had it in mind to send Wellesley with nine thousand men to South America. In "The Great Duke" (page 165) W. H. Fitchett says: "A fleet of transports had assembled at Cork for the expedition. The force consisted of nine thousand men and Wellesley was to be in command. Had the expedition sailed Wellesley might, no doubt, have made his mark in South America as ineffaceably as he did in India, and today there might be a South American Canada under the British flag and no Monroe Doctrine."

"The policy of non-intervention, which prevailed in the United States," says John Bassett Moore, "was severely tested in the struggle of the Spanish colonies in America for independence; but under the guardian care of Monroe and John Quincy Adams, it was scrupulously adhered to." The Greek and Hungarian effort to shake off despotism found sympathizers in the United States; but Clay reminded Kossuth of America's "ancient policy of amity and non-intervention."

We have seen under what circumstances the Monroe Doctrine itself was formulated and declared. "The Latin-American countries have ever since understood that in case of aggression upon them by European powers the United States would help them out, not because Monroe thought that a good policy, but because it is to the manifest interest of the United States." So says Hart, adding that from 1823 to 1845 there was little to do in foreign affairs. Then came the second great annexation period. England's American interests were debated. There was a threat that Texas might become a colony of England. Would California be transferred to a European power? Questions arose as to Mexico, Yucatan, Cuba. Canning's regard for the Monroe Doctrine did not prevent British bristles from showing long before the Venezuela episode. But "in all the debatable territory England gave way." In the matter of the Panama Canal, England, under the Clayton-Bulwer treaty, obtained recognition as an American power. We have mentioned the French incursion into Mexico. With regard to Cuba in 1873, President Grant made "the novel proposition of joint intervention with European powers." We cannot extend this summary to cover questions of colonization, the "Open Door" in Asiatic regions or the aftermath of the World War. Nor can we go further into the various views of it to be found in Mexican, Central

American and South American . publications. The
so-called Drago Doctrine of Dr. Drago, in 1903,
Minister of Foreign Relations of the Argentine Republic, had to do with the coercive collection of debts.
The so-called Calvo Doctrine, which originated with
Carlos Calvos, also of Buenos Ayres, insists that
"internal public law does not admit of intervention of
any sort on the part of foreign peoples, whoever they
may be." Under this harsh laws against foreigners
have been enacted.[1]

Let us conclude with the words of Dr. Lyon G. Tyler:
"The most living State paper outside the Constitution
is the message of James Monroe announcing the Monroe
Doctrine."

In the family letters of Mrs. Samuel Harrison Smith
(Margaret Bayard)[2] we have many spirited little
flashes that light up the drawing-rooms of Washington,
and restore for us the social palpitations of Mrs.
Monroe's day. Mrs. Smith's father was a Federalist;
her husband a Republican; she herself was of the
Jeffersonian stripe, and made a hero of Jefferson.
Her novel: "A Winter in Washington, or Memoirs of
the Seymour Family," published in 1824, deals with
the period of which we tell. Writing to Mrs. Kirkpatrick, wife of Chief Justice Andrew Kirkpatrick, of
New Jersey, she contrasts Mrs. Madison and Mrs.
Monroe:

"Mrs. Madison was extremely attentive and polite, but looked
very ill. She had on a blue velvet, blue headdress and feathers

---

[1] The Calvo and Drago Doctrines are treated in "The Monroe Doctrine" by
T. B. Edington, 1904; and by H. W. Bowen, in *The Independent*, April 18, 1907.
For Clay, Cass, Polk, Fillmore, Clayton-Bulwer, Buchanan, Lincoln, Grant, Cleve-
land, McKinley, John Hay, Roosevelt and the Monroe Doctrine, see the Lives of those
statesmen and Poole's Index and Reader's Guide. There are eighty references in
Vol. III of this Guide. The Monroe Doctrine is treated in connection with Canada,
Cuba, San Domingo and other countries. It is well considered in John Bigelow's
Life of S. J. Tilden. There is no lack of scholarly studies of it by such specialists
and historians as Moore and Hart in North America, as well as notable writers in
the Southern Hemisphere. See also "A Century of the Monroe Doctrine," by
John A. Stewart, Review of Reviews, Vol. LXIII., No. 376.

[2] The First Forty Years of Washington Society, edited by Gaillard Hunt, 1906.
Smith was a noted editor; later a successful banker. Mrs. Smith, daughter of
Colonel John Bayard, was a story writer of some celebrity.

HOUSE IN WHICH MONROE DIED
No. 61 PRINCE STREET, NEW YORK CITY

with some old finery and her face looked like a flame. With
Mrs. Monroe I am really in love. . . . She is charming and very
beautiful."

Mrs. Dolly, it seems, used art to heighten her complexion. She was just going out; Mrs. Monroe, with
her stately manners, was just coming in. It was
bitterly cold that winter of 1817, yet the fine old beaux
could not be kept away from the concerts and dances.
Mrs. Smith tells us of lovely girls, with sparkling eyes,
and their love affairs. One of the most interesting of
the *diplomatiques* was Jose Correa da Serra, Portuguese
Minister, who first called Washington "the city of
magnificent distances." Mrs. Smith writes November
23, 1817:

"People seem to think we shall have great changes in social
intercourse and customs. Mr. and Mrs. Monroe's manners will
give a tone to all the rest. Few persons are admitted to the great
house, and not a single lady has yet seen Mrs. Monroe, Mrs.
(Richard) Cutts excepted. . . . She is always at home to Mrs. Cutts
and Mr. Monroe has given orders to his Porter to admit Mr. Clay
at all times, even when the Cabinet Council is sitting, and the
other day, when he called and declined the servant's invitation
into the Cabinet, Mr. M. came out and took him into the council.
Altho' they have lived 7 years in W., both Mr. and Mrs. Monroe
are perfect strangers not only to me but all the citizens."[1]

---

[1] "President Monroe was a stately Virginian. He was polished in manner and
was always carefully dressed in a dark blue coat, buff vest, small clothes and top-
boots. He wore a cocked hat of Revolutionary style and he has been called 'the
last of the cocked hats,' for he was the last of the Presidents to adhere to the
fashions of the past century. His face was mild and grave and although he was
very courteous, he was never familiar in his intercourse with men, and was given
to a liking for the strict observance of official ceremony. He had been in public
life from youth, and was highly esteemed for his true gentle nature, and it has been
recorded of him that he was 'one of the purest of public servants that ever lived.'

"His wife was a highly accomplished lady. She had a beautiful face, a tall
graceful person and elegant manners. She was familiar with fashionable life abroad
and introduced into the White House many English forms of etiquette. Her
receptions were numerous and were attended by the highest and most exclusive
classes of the city. She held them in the East Room, which was also used for State
dinners, and full dress was always required.

"It was customary for Representatives to wear their hats in the house during
the sessions, and it was not until 1828 that the practice was discontinued. Ladies
were excluded from the galleries for a time but at last, after some discussion, they
were admitted and even had seats reserved for them. As many Congressmen were
inveterate snufftakers, urns filled with 'old scotch' were placed in each House and
officials were charged with the duty of keeping them filled. Even to this day (1884)

The White House itself in Monroe's time interested the public, on account of its new French furniture as well as because it had just been reconstructed. Let us glance at the life there. The Monroes had bought for their own use a great deal of French furniture, and this they transferred to the Government.[2] But the chairs, tables, lamps and the like of the Monroe household would not go far; so, under Monroe's specific directions, a large order was sent to Russell and La Farge in Paris. In his message, February 12, 1818, Monroe said that every article chosen was selected with a view to its fitness for the President's house. The objects chosen were durable, in order that they might be "handed down through a long series of service." The bills were much heavier than had been counted upon; but so manifestly fit, substantial and artistic were all the objects purchased that not even the surliest watch-dog of the public purse had it in him to growl. Nevertheless, as Van Buren tells us in his "Autobiography," page 769, he was attacked on the stump years after by Colonel William C. Preston, Whig Senator from Virginia, because of the "gold spoons" of the Monroe period.

The Monroes were on their guard with respect to the punctilious diplomats and their watchful wives. They remembered Jefferson's troubles with the Merrys. "The Monroes," remarks Esther Singleton, "were people of . . . good breeding. They were used to Kings' Courts and the elegancies and luxuries of life." So was the Secretary of State; and to him Monroe turned

---

in the Senate Chamber there is a large box containing choice snuff which 'is freely used by the 'most potent, grave and reverend' senators.

"Previous to 1816 the compensation of members of Congress was six dollars per day, and when a bill was passed in that year to raise the pay to $1500 a session, a sum barely sufficient to defray the expenses of a decent living in Washington, it aroused great excitement throughout the country. In an ancient record it is stated that, 'the whole Nation, was shaken to its centre.' So great was the feeling that Congress at its next session repealed the obnoxious bill and made the compensation eight dollars a day."— Joseph West Moore —"Picturesque Washington."

[2] At Montpelier, "in the President's own chamber was the four-post bed with a crimson satin canopy brought by James Monroe from the Tuileries."—Colonial Manors of Virginia, by Edith Tunis Sale, 1909.

for advice as to how the foreign ministers should be received. It was decided to ask them to the White House on the opening day a half-hour before other mortals. Mrs. Monroe was less fortunate in her resolve not to pay first visits. Mrs. Madison had done so; or, as Adams puts it, "had subjected herself to this torture." "Mrs. Monroe," he adds, "neither pays nor returns any visits." Mrs. William Winston Seaton, the editor's wife, wrote, March, 1818:

"It is said that the dinner parties of Mrs. Monroe will be very select. Mrs. Hay, the daughter of Mrs. Monroe, returns the visits paid to her mother, making assurances in the most pointedly polite manner, that Mrs. Monroe will be happy to see her friends, morning or evening; but that her health is totally inadequate to visiting at present. Mrs. Hay is understood to be her proxy; and there this much agitated and important question ends."

But that it did not end so smoothly we have evidence enough, and to spare in Adams's diary. Adams seems to have been aggravated with the White House ladies, especially with Mrs. Hay, whose influence over her father was marked. The diarist declares that Mrs. Hay was "one of the principal causes of raising this senseless war of etiquette-visiting." Adams conveyed to Monroe Minister Hyde de Neuville's express wish that he and Mrs. Monroe should attend the de Neuville ball. Monroe demurred. Should they go to this one they might have to attend other balls. Upon invitation, Adams went to see Mrs. Monroe and Mrs. Hay; and the ball and etiquette questions were discussed. Adams hardly liked such matters. No wonder —he was a big and busy man. As for Mrs. Hay, she knew very well what she was about. She was trying hard to save her mother; and she did, in a measure save her, though the strain upon that lady was more than she should have been subjected to.

The pet of the White House was little Hortensia Hay, namesake of her mother's schoolmate, Hortense de Beauharnais, Queen of Holland and mother of Napoleon III. Hortensia became Mrs. Hortensia

Rogers, and was for many years mistress of Druid Hill Mansion,[1] Baltimore.

The New Year reception in 1819 was a large affair. Adams says that the White House was "more crowded than I ever saw it on a similar occasion." Though "the President with his wife and two daughters entertained his friends and political supporters at many elegant dinners and hospitable 'drawing rooms,' the ladies of Washington society," according to Esther Singleton, turned their backs upon the Monroes.[2] Mrs. Seaton writes, December 18, 1819: "The drawing-room of the President was opened last night to a beggarly row of empty chairs." The "etiquette-visiting

---

[1] This estate, now the beautiful Druid Hill Park, had but two private owners: the first was Lloyd Buchanan, son of Dr. George Buchanan, one of the founders of Baltimore. Lloyd Buchanan in 1760 obtained grants of two tracts from the Colony of Maryland—"Hab a Nab at a Venture" and "The Level." These he called "Auchentoroly." His daughter Eleanore ("Good without Pretense," her tombstone tells us), married her cousin Nicholas Rogers, aide-de-camp of General De Coudray and later aide to Baron de Kalb. La Fayette was his friend and a frequent guest at Druid Hill, inherited by Eleanore Buchanan Rogers. Her son and heir, Nicholas Lloyd Rogers, married, first Eliza Law, great-granddaughter of Mrs. George Washington and, second, Hortensia Hay. Nicholas Lloyd Rogers left descendants by both wives. The late Mrs. George B. Goldsborough of Maryland was the last to call Druid Hill Mansion "home." Mrs. Goldsborough owned the Rembrandt Peale and Lambdin portraits of Monroe and other Monroe, Hay and Custis family heirlooms. Hortensia Hay wore over her wedding gown a lace overdress that was worn at her mother's wedding, and her grandmother's wedding. Hortensia's daughter wore it, too, and so did her granddaughter, Hortensia Hardesty, when she married Congressman William Watson McIntire. Thus Mrs. Monroe's lace has been worn by five brides. Hortensia Hay died before her husband, who sold Druid Hill to Baltimore for $500,000. It was opened to the public October 19, 1860. When General J. E. B. Stuart raided Baltimore, in 1863, General R. E. Schenck in command ordered the noble trees cut down at Druid Hill, thus facilitating defence. Col. John M. Wilson begged to put a negro wood-chopper at the foot of each tree, ready to cut on definite alarm news. The trees were saved. The present writer is indebted to Mrs. Elizabeth K. Hardesty Richardson, descendant of President Monroe, for these facts.

[2] "Mrs. Monroe made up her mind to retrench some of those profuse civilities with which her predecessor had fatigued herself. Mrs. Madison had retired from office equally regretted by the poor of Washington and by its high life; but she had gained this popularity at severe cost. She had called on all conspicuous strangers; Mrs. Monroe intended to call on nobody. Mrs. Madison had been always ready for visitors when at home; her successor proposed to receive nobody save at her regular levees. The Ex-Presidentess had presided at her husband's dinner parties; and invited the wives of all the men who were to be guests; Mrs. Monroe staid away from the dinner parties; and so the wives were left at home. Add to this that her health was by no means strong, and it is plain that there was great ground for a spasm of unpopularity. She, however, outlived it, and re-established her social relations, gave fortnightly receptions, and won much admiration which she probably deserved."— Thomas Wentworth Higginson, in Harper's Magazine, Vol. LXVIII, p. 940.

affair" was considered at a cabinet meeting, December 29; and so it went. Under date of November 21, 1820, Adams wrote: "I dined at the President's with a company of about thirty-five persons, members of Congress principally, all men, the state of Mrs. Monroe's health not admitting of her attendance at numerous dinner parties." But Mrs. Monroe and other ladies were present at a White House dinner described by James Fenimore Cooper. The oldest Senator present led Mrs. Monroe to the table. The President took a lady and followed:

"The table was large and rather handsome. The service was china, as is uniformly the case, plate being exceedingly rare if used at all. There was, however, a rich plateau, and a great abundance of the smaller articles of table-plate. The cloth, napkins, etc., etc., were fine and beautiful. The dinner was served in the French style a little Americanized. The dishes were handed around, though some of the guests, appearing to prefer their own customs, coolly helped themselves to what they found at hand. Of attendants there were a good many. Mrs. Monroe arose at the end of the dessert, and withdrew, attended by two or three of the more gallant of the company. No sooner was his wife's back turned than the President reseated himself, inviting his guests to imitate the action. After allowing his guests sufficient time to renew, in a few glasses, the recollections of similar enjoyments of their own, he arose himself, giving the hint to his company that it was time to rejoin the ladies. In the drawing room, coffee was served, and every one left the house before nine."

Samuel F. B. Morse wrote to his mother, Washington, December 17, 1819:[1]

"I have been here nearly a fortnight. I commenced the President's portrait on Monday and shall finish it to-morrow. I have succeeded to my satisfaction, and, what is better, to the satisfaction of himself and family; so much so that one of his daughters wishes me to copy the head for her. They all say that mine is the best that has been taken of him. The daughter told me (she said as a secret) that her father was delighted with it and said it was the only one that in his opinion looked like him; and this, too, with Stuart's in the room. The President has been very kind and hospitable to me; I have dined with him three times and taken tea as often; he and his family have been very sociable and

---

[1] "Samuel F. B. Morse." His Letters and Journals edited by his son, Edward Lind Morse, 1914; 2 vols. Vol. I, pp. 226, 227.

unreserved. I have painted him at his house, next room to his cabinet, so that when he had a moment to spare he could come in to me. Wednesday evening, Mrs. Monroe held a drawing-room. I attended and made my bow. She was splendidly and tastily dressed. The drawing-room and suite of rooms at the President's are furnished and decorated in the most splendid manner; some think too much so, but I do not."[1]

On Thursday evening, March 9, 1820, there was a wedding in the White House. The ceremony was in the East Room.[2] The bride was Maria Hester Monroe, the President's younger daughter, who married her cousin, Samuel Lawrence Gouverneur. Mrs. Marian Gouverneur tells us:[3] "Only the relatives and personal friends attended; even the members of the Cabinet were not invited. The gallant General Thomas S. Jesup, one of the heroes of the War of 1812 and Subsistence Commissary General of the Army, acted as groomsman to Mr. Gouverneur. . . . After this quiet wedding, Mr. and Mrs. Gouverneur left Washington upon a bridal tour and about a week later returned to the White House, where at a reception, Mrs. Monroe gave up her place as hostess to mingle with her guests, while Mrs. Gouverneur received in her place. Commodore and Mrs. Stephen Decatur, who lived on La Fayette Square, gave the bride her first ball, and two mornings later, on the twenty-second of March, 1820, Decatur fought his fatal duel with Commodore James Barron, and was brought home a corpse." The death of Decatur gave the Monroes a profound shock. Invitations already out for an entertainment at Commodore David Porter's in honor of the bride and groom were recalled.[4] Not for a long while did Washington recover.

---

[1] The portrait thus painted was ordered by the Common Council of Charleston, S. C. It still hangs in the City Hall there.

[2] The officiating clergyman was the Rev. Dr. William Hawley, rector of old St. John's. He wore knee breeches and shoe buckles. During the War of 1812, he commanded a company of divinity students in New York. Because he would not march against the enemy when ordered, Decatur refused to attend St. John's.

[3] In "As I Remember," pp. 256-258.

[4] Mrs. Marian Gouverneur says in "As I Remember," p. 259: "I never had the pleasure of knowing my mother-in-law, Mrs. Maria Hester Monroe Gouverneur,

Samuel L. Gouverneur, Sr., was Monroe's private secretary. He entered the New York Legislature in 1825. From 1828 to 1836, he was Postmaster at New York. He was very much a man of the world — fond of race horses, owner of the celebrated "Post Boy." "Mr. Gouverneur," writes his daughter-in-law, "was a man of decidedly social tastes and at one period of his life owned and occupied the De Menou buildings on H. Street in Washington, where during the life of his first wife he gave some brilliant entertainments." According to Rear-Admiral John J. Almy, "sixteen baskets of champagne were frequently consumed by the guests during a single evening." The second wife of Samuel L. Gouverneur, Sr., was Mary Diggs Lee, of Needham, Frederick County, Maryland, granddaughter of Thomas Sim Lee, second Governor of that State. Eliah Kingman, the Washington newspaper man, said of S. L. Gouverneur, Sr., "he even possessed a seductive voice."

Mrs. Marian Gouverneur says in "As I Remember," page 177, that when William L. Marcy was taking leave of the clerks in the War Department, "he shook hands with an elderly colored employee named Datcher, who had formerly been a body servant to President

as she died some years before my marriage, but I learned to revere her through her son, whose tender regard for her was one of the absorbing affections of his life and changed the whole direction of his career. At an early age he was appointed a Lieutenant in the regular Army and served with distinction through the Mexican War in the Fourth Artillery. On one occasion subsequent to that conflict, while his mother was suffering from a protracted illness he applied to the War Department for leave of absence in order that he might visit her sick bed; and when it was not granted he resigned his commission and thus sacrificed an enviable position to his sense of filial duty." The father of Mrs. Samuel L. Gouverneur, Jr., was Judge James Campbell of New York, whose elder daughter married United States Minister Charles Eames. Until her death in 1890, Mrs. Eames was one of the most noted of Washington's hostesses. For many years Mr and Mrs. Samuel L. Gouverneur, Jr., bore an especially distinguished part in society — at New York and Newport, as well as Washington. They lived awhile in China, where S. L. Gouverneur, Jr., was U. S. Consul at Foo Chow. Upon their return, Gouverneur edited for publication "The People the Sovereigns," a posthumous work by James Monroe. They lived at Frederick, Md., quite a while; then in Washington, where they entertained. Mrs. Gouverneur's book of reminiscences touches upon some hundreds of celebrities — not the least interesting one being her friend "Tim," or Mrs. Septima Randolph Meikleham, a seventh daughter, the last surviving grandchild of Thomas Jefferson. Thus the Jefferson-Monroe friendship was kept up through several generations.

Monroe and said: 'Good-bye, Datcher; if I had had your manners, I should have left more friends behind me." Mrs. Gouverneur had passed down to her "Uncle James," a venerable colored man who had long served her husband's family. Marcy's brother-in-law, George Newell, once asked her: "Who is that man?" "An old family servant." "Well, he is the most polite man I ever saw."

Attorney-General Wirt was quite a favorite with the Monroes. It was about the time of the publication of Wirt's "Patrick Henry." Wirt was a most important person; and, what is more, a learned, witty and genial one — a good friend and hail-fellow well met. He and his family are well described in a Saratoga letter[1] written by Mrs. Anne Jean Lyman, wife of Judge Joseph Lyman, of Northampton, Mass.:

"The great Mr. Wirt, with an interesting family was there from Washington, which was a source of much enjoyment to me. Mrs. Wirt was not a lady of great mental attainments; but of much delicacy and refinement and good judgment, and of many showy accomplishments. Although the mother of twelve children, she looked young and handsome, and played elegantly on the piano; and played battledore with the agility of fifteen, for hours together. Her eldest daughter, who was with her, resembled her in character, except that she had more reserve. I should hardly dare to attempt a description of *him*, except in the most general terms. His appearance is magnificent in an unusual degree, and everything he does exhibits a moral grandeur, in perfect conformity to that appearance. There is something so imposing in this look, that you feel it a condescension, if he pays you any attention. At Ballstown we had the satisfaction of looking at Joseph Bonaparte, who calls himself Count Servillier; his appearance is that of a John Bull much more than that of a Frenchman — very fat, and easy with a most benevolent expression of face; his suite requires twelve rooms."

Wirt, writing to his daughter Laura, May 23, 1820[2] describes a visit to Squire Thomas Law "at Silver Hills," Anacostia Heights. Squire Law, "a grave sweet

---

[1] To Mrs. William Greene, August 4, 1821. Recollections of My Mother, by Susan I. Lesley, 1886, pp 139, 140.
[2] Greanleaf and Law, by Allen C. Clark, p. 299; also Kennedy's "Wirt".

old man" was "Washington's first rich man." He
lived on the Maryland table-land, two miles across the
eastern branch of the Potomac. He was entertaining
Monroe, his heads of departments and others. Wirt
exclaims:

"Such a splash as we had at Mr. Law's yesterday! Near a
hundred gentlemen; all the farmers of Prince George's County for
many miles around, and all the gentry from Washington. And no
more ceremony and quite as much festivity and playfulness as
among a flock of children just broke loose from school. . . . Such
a rattling of carriages and clattering of horses' hoofs! But, first,
such a dinner! But, before that, such fine punch down at the
spring, beyond the pavilion, on the hill, in the woods. Graff had
a Dutch parody on 'Jessie of Dumblane' which is admirable.
The President laughed till he cried; and I believe he would have
danced if the fiddle had struck up. The good man sat at the table,
beating time with his fork to the songs sung by Graff and others,
with all the kindness and amiability of his nature. . . . Mr. Law
delivered a great speech. It was a meeting of the Agricultural
Society, but the speech was over before I got there. On asking
Mr. Adams (John Quincy Adams) for an account of it, he said:
'It was a love song about murder; in other words an agricultural
speech about manufactures.' Quite in his style. . . . At this dinner
there was 'ease and no ceremony;' the hundred guests ate lamb,
ham, chicken and blackberry pie; and drank claret, brandy and
fifteen-year old whiskey."

George Ticknor, January 16, 1825, wrote to William
H. Prescott:[1]

"The first time we were in Washington we passed a little less
than a fortnight; the last time between three and four weeks. It
is altogether a very curious residence; very different from anything I have seen in any part of the World. The regular inhabitants
of the city from the President downwards lead a hard and troublesome life. It is their business to entertain strangers, and they do
it, each one according to his means, but all in a very laborious
way. . . . The President gives a dinner, once a week, to thirty or
forty people — no ladies present — in a vast, cold hall. He
invited me to one, but I did not go. I was, however, at a very
pleasant dinner of only a dozen that he gave to La Fayette, when
the old gentleman made himself very agreeable; but this was
quite out of the common course. . . . Mr. Adams gives a great
dinner once a week, and Mrs. Adams a great ball once a fortnight;

---

[1] Life of George Ticknor, 1877, 2 vols. Vol. I, 349.

it keeps her ill half the time, but she is a woman of great spirit, and carries it through with a high hand. . . . Calhoun's, however, was the pleasantest of the ministerial dinners, because he invited ladies, and is the most agreeable person in conversation at Washington;— I mean of the Cabinet — and Mrs. Calhoun is a very good little woman, who sometimes gives a pleasant ball. The Russian Minister is a strange retired fanatic, in feeble health, who gives splendid dinners once a week. Addington, the British *chargé*, is a very acute, well-informed man of letters, who gives very agreeable little dinners *en garcon*, twice a week. The Baron de Mareuil is a truly elegant gentleman. . . . The truth is that, at Washington, society is the business of life. . . . Every morning we went to return visits. . . . then to the House or Senate if there were any debate."

Monroe's message to the House, January 30, 1824, must have made strange reading for Jefferson. It advocated a peace establishment for the Navy. "The Navy," wrote Monroe, "is the arm from which our Government will always derive most aid and support of our neutral rights. Every power engaged in war will know the strength of our naval force, the number of our ships of each class, their condition and the promptitude with which we may bring them into service, and will pay due consideration to that argument." He added: "The great object in the event of war is to stop the enemy at the coast. If this is done our cities and whole interior will be secure." He instanced the mouth of the Chesapeake, near which stands Fortress Monroe, named in his honor.[1]

On May 21, Monroe sent to the Senate a slave trade convention, March 13, with Great Britain. Its idea was to make that nefarious calling piratical. Adams, in his Diary,[2] tells how deeply interested Monroe was in this treaty, which, however, failed of ratification.

That summer was a busy one with the President. He had "scarcely a moment" for his friends. In his letters to Jefferson and Madison, he apologizes for his inability to pay them as much attention as he would

---

[1] For this message, see Messages and Documents and Writings of Monroe, Vol. VII, pp. 3-11.
[2] Adams' Memoirs, Vol. VI, p. 344, *et seq.*

like. Late in July he went to Loudon, but was obliged to return to the Capitol to greet a party of Indians who had come from the Far West to see the Great Father. There were twenty chiefs. In writing to Madison, explaining why he could not present himself at Montpelier, he thus refers to Mrs. Monroe:

"Her health is much impaired by many causes, particularly by our long service and the heavy burdens and cares to which she has been subjected, and to which the strength of her constitution has not been equal."[1]

In the fall he wrote to Jefferson:[2] "I shall be heartily rejoiced when the term of my service expires, and I may return home in peace with my family, on whom, and especially on Mrs. Monroe, the burdens and cares of my long public service have borne too heavily." His references to his wife from this time on, indicate increasing solicitude in regard to that faithful and worthy mate for whom he had the tenderest affection.

In an Oak Hill letter to William Wirt, September 27, 1824, Monroe pronounced the affair known as "the A. B. Plot," "one of the most painful of my life." He was exceedingly anxious to preserve the honor and tone of his administration; hence this "A. B." scandal made him wince. In reality, it amounted to little. Some letter, signed "A. B." appeared in a Washington newspaper, accusing Secretary Crawford of malfeasance in office. Who was the writer? Monroe had appointed United States Senator Ninian Edwards, of Illinois, to be Minister to Mexico; and, having been confirmed, Edwards started for his post. But, on the way, he wrote to the Speaker of the House, avowing himself to be the author of the attack upon Crawford. The Sergeant-at-Arms, who was at once sent after him, overtook and brought him back to Washington, where he vainly attempted to prove the truth of what he had said. He resigned the Mexican mission and the affair was closed.

[1] Monroe to Madison, August 2, 1824.
[2] Monroe to Jefferson, October 31, 1824.

Some matters of moment of that autumn and winter were the signing of the Columbian Treaty, October 3, 1824; the proclamation of the Russian Treaty, January 12, 1825, and the signing of the Indian Spring Treaty[1], February 12. On March 3, the day before his retirement from the Presidency, Monroe approved of the act incorporating the Chesapeake and Ohio Canal Company.

Monroe adopted the example set by Washington and followed by Jefferson and Madison with respect to the two-term tenure. No third term for any one became the rule; or, as Buchanan expressed it, "this principle is now become as sacred as if it were written in the Constitution." A recurring question, therefore, was: Who should succeed Monroe? He would be a Republican. That was taken for granted. But would he represent the new nationalizing tendency, or would he be some strict constructionist of the older type? Here was Jefferson scolding about the tariff. He wrote to William Branch Giles: "The younger recruits, having nothing in them of the feelings or principles of '76, now look to a single and splendid government of an aristocracy, founded on banking institutions and moneyed corporations." [2] Madison, too, had doubts about the wisdom of a tariff that built up manufactures at the expense of agriculture. But he saw nothing in the Constitution against the tariff act of May 22, 1824.[3] Then there was the question of internal improvements. Monroe's veto had been less popular in the western counties of his own State than was agreeable to him.[4] Monroe was personally embarrassed by the number of presidential aspirants in his Cabinet. Crawford was

---

[1] This treaty provided for the cession by the Creeks of their Georgia land and several million acres in Alabama. The consideration was $400,000. Monroe's Message on the removal of the Georgia Indians appears in Messages and Documents, and Writings of Monroe, Vol. VII, pp. 14-17. He thought it would be better for them as well as for the whites if they should migrate to the West. Nevertheless it was a sad thing — the bodily transfer of the Cherokee nation from under their own blue sky to the Indian Territory.

[2] Jefferson's Writings (Ford), Vol. X, p. 365.

[3] Madison's Writings, Vol. III, pp. 483, 507.

[4] Sectionalism in Virginia, by Charles Henry Ambler, 1909, p. 122.

plotting for the presidency; and had been, right along.
He it was who put through the four-year tenure act.
Under this act the collecting and disbursing officers of
the Government were to serve for four years. Crawford
hoped to use the act to further his candidacy. Other
political devices had come into use: the gerrymander,
and the system of proscription whereby administrative
officers disagreeing with the factional policy of the
State leaders were removed.[1] Crawford was an
intriguer. He worried Monroe a great deal. Maria
Monroe was one day in her father's office during his
presidency, when William H. Crawford came in, urging
something on Mr. Monroe which he wanted time to
consider. Crawford insisted with vehemence on its
being done at once; saying at length: "I will not leave
this room till my request is granted." "You will not?"
exclaimed the President, starting up and seizing the
poker. "You will *now* leave the room or you will be
thrust out." Crawford was not long in making his
exit.[2] Monroe, usually so mild, so equable, could not
always control his much-harrassed nerves. He even
flared up against John Quincy Adams when they were
talking of the case of Jonathan Russell. Adams had
spoken of "my report" in the matter. "*Your* report?"
said the President in a sharp tone of anger, " 'tis *my*
report. It is no report at all until I have accepted it."[3]
Adams had back of him an excellent record of statesmanship and the support of New England manufacturers. Moreover, that section was entitled to the
presidency. He was nominated by the New England
Legislatures. Clay, also a tariff man, was the recognized
champion of internal improvements, and had a popular
following in Kentucky and the West. The Legislature
of his own State nominated him for the Presidency
and other Legislatures endorsed his candidacy. Crawford, nominee of the regular caucus, was identified with

---

[1] Hart, Formation of the Union, pp. 246, 277.
[2] Court Circles of the Republic, by Mrs. E. F. Ellet, 1869; p. 167.
[3] Diary of John Quincy Adams, Vol. V, p. 508.

the older order of things. And there was still another —
a hero to be shouted over till finally shouted into the
White House in 1828, in which year, "the pacific
Monroe and the respectable second Adams made way
for the violent Jackson."[1]

But though nominated by the Tennessee Legislature
in 1822, and the Pennsylvania Legislature in 1824, the
man whom Benton called "the candidate of the people
brought forward by the masses"[2] was to lose the prize
in his first contest. He had ninety-nine electoral votes;
Adams, eighty-four; Crawford, forty-one; and Clay,
thirty-seven. Clay's men went to Adams, by Clay's
own expressed wish, January 8, 1825; and Adams
became President-elect. Some of the Clay Congressmen
who thus voted lost their seats at the next election.
When Clay entered the Adams cabinet as Secretary
of State, John Randolph cried out that it was "a
coalition of Blifil and Black George — a combination
unheard of till now of the Puritan and the black-leg";
but no proof exists of a corrupt bargain between
Adams and Clay. As for Calhoun, he was of recognized
presidential calibre; but, when he saw that there would
be no chance for him, he quietly accepted the vice-
presidential nomination and was unanimously elected.

The great event of the summer of 1824 was La
Fayette's arrival on his farewell visit to the land he had
helped to free. Monroe sent him an invitation, February 4; and urged him to come in an American frigate,
but La Fayette preferred to make the voyage in a
merchantman — the "Cadmus," which landed him at
Vice-President Tompkins's house, Staten Island, August
15. La Fayette's fortune had been shattered, so that
he was obliged to borrow money to come over. Jefferson
and Monroe, who were both in financial straits, understood the predicament of the nation's guest. Jefferson
wrote to Monroe, February 5, expressing the hope that
Congress would do the handsome thing by La Fayette;

[1] Life of William Lloyd Garrison, by Lindsay Swift, 1911.
[2] "Really," corrects Hart (Formation, p. 250) "by his neighbor Major Lewis."

and it did, voting him lands and money — a township
and $200,000. As for the old hero, who was accom-
panied by his son George Washington La Fayette,
M. Levasseur and Bastien, the General's valet, he had
no idea when he landed of the extraordinary heartiness,
joy and glory awaiting him.[1] He asked some one on the
"Cadmus" if he could perhaps find a hack at the wharf
in New York to take him to his hotel. He was seized
upon and lionized from the moment he set foot ashore.
At New York, in New England, in the Middle States,
in the South, in the West — wherever he went — he
was saluted, fêted, embraced and shouted over to his
heart's content. He was the guest of the nation for
fourteen months. Not the least of his satisfactions was
found in his reunions with his comrades of the Revolution, of whom Monroe, at the White House, was one.
Monroe himself was overjoyed at the heartiness of the
nation's welcome, auguring well, he thought, for the
continuity of that regard which Americans felt for the
founders of the Union.

When La Fayette reached Washington the air was
surcharged with politics. Apropos, here is a paragraph
from Schouler:

"La Fayette's presence at Washington had its influence in
preventing all indecorous (political) scenes from first to last.
Jackson bore his defeat, to all outward appearances, with admirable
grace and composure, having during the whole canvass carried
himself with more of the presidential manner than any other
candidate. At Monroe's drawing-room on the evening which
followed the ballot, he came up to the President-elect, a lady on
his arm, and shook hands with him very cordially, his countenance
altogether placid and friendly. But at heart he was deeply angered;
he could now believe that all Monroe's Cabinet excepting Calhoun
had worked constantly to defeat him at all hazards; and in private
letters he denounced Clay as the 'Judas of the West' who had
closed the contract for thirty pieces of silver."[2]

---

[1] Chapter X in the writer's "True La Fayette," 1919, is devoted to General
La Fayette's tour of the United States in 1824-1825.
[2] Schouler's Hist., Vol. III, p. 329; Jackson's letter to Lewis, February 14, 1825.
Parton's Jackson.

As he neared the close of his last term, Monroe became anxious for an investigation of his accounts; and a month after he had sent in his Eighth Annual Message, he addressed Congress on the subject. "It is my wish," he said, "that all matters of account and claim between my country and myself be settled with that strict regard to justice which is observed in settlements between individuals in private life." According to Thurlow Weed,[1] there were good and sufficient reasons for Monroe's much-talked of Era of Good Feeling. He says: "During the administrations of James Monroe and John Quincy Adams, the welfare of our people and the strength of our government were promoted and augmented by an enlightened national policy. All our interests moved forward harmoniously. All the industries of the country thrived, farmers, mechanics, manufacturers, merchants, importers and capitalists found themselves working together with reciprocal interests and to mutual advantage. While all our domestic occupations proved abundantly remunerative, our canvas — the canvas of our own well-laden ships — whitened every ocean and sea. And amid all this individual prosperity and happiness, the nation was advancing by rapid strides to wealth and power."

"When Monroe retired from the presidency on March 4, 1825," says Hart,[2] "the internal authority of the national government had for ten years steadily increased, and the dignity and influence of the nation abroad showed that it had become one of the world's greatest powers."

Adams in Monroe's Cabinet and Adams in the presidency were noticeably different. "He praised in courteous terms his predecessor and his predecessor's policy and yet," says Schouler, "old Republicans saw this proselyte to their faith pushing principles beyond Monroe's experimental standard." He had no constitutional scruples as to internal improvements. On the

---

[1] Autobiography, Vol. II, p. 115.
[2] Hart, Formation of the Union, p. 244.

contrary, he thought the thing to do was to go ahead and spend money for roads and canals; and was willing that the government should build "a light-house of the skies," otherwise a national observatory. He wanted a national university, too. In a word, he was progressive; and not afraid to spend the people's money. A new Cumberland road bill was passed in 1827; and this time it was not vetoed. But with Clay in his Cabinet, Adams could not hope for political peace. And, in course of time, it became clear that like his father, he would be a one-term president. The Crawford men went to Jackson, who was the rising star.

Calhoun for his part was a changed man. He was breaking away from his nationalistic moorings, and was solidifying into a less liberal, less happy character, more Southern, more sectional, as if set apart to take on a Roman robe in a civic tragedy of blood and woe.

Calhoun was as fond of Monroe as Monroe was of him. They continued to correspond; but Monroe could no longer see as Calhoun saw. "Monroe in a kind and fatherly way, opposed Calhoun's theories,"[1] says Schouler. . . . "We should provoke no issue to shake the system. . . . A singular change truly was Calhoun's mind now undergoing, his new-born infatuation for Southern rights under the spur of an ambition still wavering in its upward endeavor to the chair which Washington and Monroe had occupied."[2]

Monroe did not belong to the school of disunionists then just developing. He was a true Union man; and must have been shocked and saddened when, in his retirement at Oak Hill, he bethought him of the likelihood of a great quarrel between North and South.

Though Monroe weakened physically, he seemed to grow stronger in his wish to see the country served with

[1] A summary of John C. Calhoun's correspondence appears in the Author's Final Note, by Schouler, Vol. III, pp. 547-549. The letters, lost during the Civil War, were recovered by J. F. Jameson and published in the Collections of the American Historical Association. See Report, 1899, Vol. 2.

[2] Quoting from the Monroe Mss., Schouler says that John McLean wrote to a friend in 1831: "Calhoun, I fear, has gone forever. For four years past he has been infatuated with his Southern doctrines. In him they originated."

a conscientious regard for the public welfare. He wrote to John McLean: "No person at the head of the government has, in my opinion, any claim to the active partisan exertions of those in office under him." Schouler[1] thinks that McLean was trying to keep Monroe in line with his avowed neutrality. More than once the Democratic managers "seriously feared an embroilment between Jackson and Monroe which would bring out the latter on Adams's side." Southard at a dinner party spoke of Monroe as the "real savior of New Orleans." Naturally this galled Jackson. Jackson's friends had slighted Monroe's claim in Congress; and this in turn annoyed Monroe.[2] Southard was working for Adams. Another Adams plan was to have Madison and Monroe placed on the Virginia electoral ticket in 1828; but the Ex-Presidents declined to serve. Adams's managers wanted Monroe to run for Vice-President on the Adams ticket in 1828; "and many an effort was made to draw him from his neutrality."

Just after Monroe left the White House, he was gratified to receive a complimentary copy of Chief Justice Marshall's latest volume, with a letter in which his old friend said:

"Believe me when I congratulate you on the circumstances under which your political course terminates, and that I feel sincere pleasure in the persuasion that your administration may be reviewed with real approbation by our wisest statesmen."

The Monroes left Washington for Oak Hill, where they welcomed the spring of 1825 with anticipatory joys — free at last from their onerous White House cares.

Monroe spent the remainder of 1825 and the years 1826, 1827, 1828, 1829 and the spring of 1830 at Oak Hill. Major R. W. N. Noland gave Gilman this account of the place:

[1] Monroe Mss. 1826, 1827, letters to and from McLean, as quoted in Schouler.
[2] Schouler's Hist. Vol. III, p. 433, *et seq.* McLean's letters in Monroe Mss.; Adams's Diary 1828; Madison's Writings.

"The Oak Hill house was planned by Mr. Monroe, but the building was superintended by Mr. William Benton, an Englishman, who occupied the mixed relation to Mr. Monroe of steward, counsellor and friend. The house is built of brick in a most substantial manner, and handsomely furnished; it is perhaps, about 90 x 50 feet, three stories (including basement) and has a wide portico, fronting south, with massive Doric columns thirty feet high, and is surrounded by a grove of magnificent oaks covering several acres. . . . The house in two directions commands an attractive and somewhat extensive view, but on the other sides it is hemmed in by mountains, for the local names of which 'Bull Run' and 'Nigger Mountain' it is to be hoped the late President is in no wise responsible, and indeed the same may be said of the river, or creek, which breaks through these ranges within a mile or two of Oak Hill. Tom Moore, in a poetic letter, as brilliant as it is ill-natured, satirizing Washington City, writes: 'And what was Goose Creek once is Tiber now'; but the fact is that no such stream is found in the neighborhood of the National Capitol. The little stream that washes the confines of the Oak Hill Estate once bore the Indian name of Gohongarestaw (the River of Swans) and is now called Goose Creek."[1]

In a Richmond, Virginia, letter to the writer, Mrs. Eugenia T. Fairfax (Mrs. Henry Fairfax) says:

"I have just recently sold Oak Hill. As you perhaps know, it was built by the President during his first presidential term on property left him by an uncle named Jones (Judge Joseph Jones). In 1850, my father-in-law, Col. John W. Fairfax, purchased it from Monroe's son-in-law, Sam'l. L. Gouverneur. In 1870, Col. Fairfax sold it to Dr. George Grimby, of New York, from whom my husband purchased it again in 1885.

"The house is very simple but very solidly and beautifully built. The bricks were all burned on the place and all the inside woodwork was cut out by hand. The walls are solid and very thick. The columns are beautifully proportioned, hollow brick and stuccoed.

"Here Monroe entertained La Fayette . . . and the marble mantels in drawing and dining rooms were ordered for him by La Fayette and sent over from Italy. I also have a lovely gaming table, French, given him by La Fayette."

President Adams had some unfinished business that came to him from the Monroe administration; such as that of Captain Porter, of the Navy, who had

---

[1] Gilman's Monroe, pp. 219, 220. See also Howe's Historical Collections of Virginia, p. 356.

given Monroe a great deal of trouble; but, in the main, one period merged with smoothness into that of the other. Adams was to have plenty of trouble, great quarrels were to arise — yet he was enabled to say that his four years in the White House "were the most pleasant, agreeable years of his life."[1] He was "the first man up in Washington;" "lighted his own fires;" swam in the Potomac; and when he wanted to go to Quincy, Mass., rode there and back on his horse. He tells how on June 13, he went swimming with his son John and his man Antoine at the Van Ness grounds, foot of Seventeenth Street West, west of the Washington Monument, where the Tiber entered the Potomac. The small leaky boat he was in sank and he barely escaped drowning. He hid, well-nigh naked, under the bank, while Antoine, who had lost all his clothes, made his way by hook or by crook after a carriage.[2]

Thurlow Weed says (Autobiography, Vol. I, p. 179) that being in Washington on a hot June morning, he saw "a gentleman in nankeen pantaloons and a blue pea-jacket walking rapidly from the White House towards the river. This was John Quincy Adams, the President of the United States. I moved off to a respectful distance. The President began to disrobe before he reached a tree on the brink of the river, where he deposited his clothes, and then plunged in, head first, and struck out fifteen or twenty rods, swimming rapidly and turning occasionally upon his back, seeming as much at his ease in that element as upon *terra firma*. Coming out he rubbed himself thoroughly with napkins, which he had brought for that purpose in his hand. The sun had not yet risen when he had dressed himself and was returning to the presidential mansion."

Adams notes, July 4, the return of Secretary Southard from a visit to Monroe at Oak Hill; and on July 13, the return of General Jacob Brown from the same point,

---

[1] This statement was made to Benjamin F. Perry, of South Carolina, in 1846, the year of Adams's first stroke and two years before his fatal stroke.
[2] Memoirs of John Quincy Adams, Vol. VII, p. 27, *et seq.*

President Monroe's Tomb in Hollywood Cemetery, Richmond

bringing an invitation for the President and General La Fayette to visit Oak Hill. Adams[1] gives a long account of this farewell visit by La Fayette to his old friend. Here is a summary:

At four P.M., Aug. 6, General La Fayette, his son, George Washington La Fayette, and Mr. (Tench) Ringgold left for Oak Hill. John Adams and M. Levasseur were with the party. Bastien, La Fayette's valet, and Antoine Michel Giusta, in a carryall with one horse, took the baggage. William, the groom, followed on horseback. They reached Fairfax Court-House at sunset. La Fayette was greeted by the Fairfax people. Up and off at five, they breakfasted at the private house of a lame veteran of the Revolution, with six miles further to go. An axle-tree broke; it was spliced; and La Fayette and Adams proceeded on wheels. Some others of the party were obliged to walk. By and by they met Monroe's son-in-law, Judge George Hay, on horseback. "We got to Mr. Monroe's house just before noon," says Adams; "and our fellow-travelers joined us there about an hour later. We found Mr. Monroe in good health and spirits. Mrs. Hay and her daughter Hortensia were there, but Mrs. Monroe is at New York with her daughter, Mrs. Gouverneur. We found there also Dr. Wallace, an eccentric personage, who spent a great part of last winter at Washington with Mr. Monroe and had just arrived here upon a visit. . . . There were several other visitors in the course of the day. . . . There was a heavy thunder shower about the dining hour, and the evening was fresh and cool. 8th.— The night was cool, and this morning fresh, but I was all this day unwell. The heat of the season returned in all its force, so that we were confined almost entirely to the house. Numerous visitors came in the course of the day." La Fayette was invited to Leesburg. "The day was spent in desultory conversation with Mr. Monroe, Mr. Hay, General La Fayette, Dr. Wallace, Mrs. Hay and the visitors at the house. Dr. Wallace engrossed much of the conversation and was much gratified by the appearance on the porch of the house of a small moccasin snake which he caught and descanted on for perhaps an hour, showing us all its beauties and especially the venom-bag under its forked tongue. He told me he was just recovering from a dropsy brought on by swallowing the whole contents of a rattlesnake's venom-bag.[2]

[1] Memoirs, Vol. VII, pp. 40-44.
[2] Like Dr. Wallace, Washington was a close observer. "On one occasion," writes Thomas Handasyd Perkins in his Memoirs, telling of a visit to Mount Vernon in the summer of 1796, "a toad passed near to where I was conversing with General Washington, which led him to ask me if I had ever observed this reptile swallow a firefly. Upon my answering in the negative he told me that he had; and, that from the thinness of the skin of the toad, he had seen the light of the firefly after it had been swallowed."

The Doctor is extremely solicitous to go out on the Brandywine as an extra surgeon."

The " Brandywine " was to take La Fayette back to France. Dr. Wallace seemed determined that some-body should be entertaining if the three great men then at Oak Hill were not.

One wonders why Jefferson did not ride up from Monticello and Madison from Montpelier. It would have made a memorable gathering. But, considering the August heat in Loudon, it was no doubt better that they remained at home, where La Fayette was to visit each a little later. The next day, August 9, was the hottest of the season. Two troops of horse arrived at Oak Hill and escorted La Fayette to Leesburg, where there was a grand muster and a public reception, with Ludwell Lee speaking for the county of Loudon. Under a canopy in the courthouse yard there was a dinner with toasting and speaking.

Thurlow Weed in his Autobiography (Vol. I, p. 180) tells us that the chief reason why John Quincy Adams failed to secure a second term was his "political imprac-ticability." Benton said: "This administration, even if it be as pure as the angels in Heaven, must be put down." Adams disregarded or overlooked what Monroe, Madi-son and Jefferson had deemed essential, namely political organization and personal popularity.

That Monroe was one of the company at Monticello when La Fayette was there, we learn from several sources. For instance, in Barrett's "Old Merchants of New York"[1] there is this passage concerning two brothers of that city — one "Nathaniel Wolfe, who became a noted lawyer of Louisville, Ky."; and the other Udolpho Wolfe, the rich New York and Hamburg merchant:

"Mr. Jefferson wished the children at the school to form a mili-tary company to receive La Fayette. It was done, and they were regularly drilled, Udolpho Wolfe being the Captain. A stand of

---

[1] The Old Merchants of New York City, by Walter Barrett, clerk, fourth series, 1860, p. 189.

colors was presented to them. At the grand dinner given to La Fayette in the rotunda, the 'soldiers' were invited to be present; and they sat directly facing General La Fayette, his son George, Thomas Jefferson, James Madison, James Monroe, Gov. Barbour, Rives, Gordon, Southall and all the chivalry of Virginia. Fancy such a sight! Three men who had been President of the United States in succession."

This certainly would have been a historical picture worth sketching and reproducing on canvas. Both Madison and Monroe were Justices of the Peace. "The ex-Presidents," says Judge Staples, "did not feel it beneath their dignity to hold such a minor office, till the day of their death."[1] In 1826 Monroe became a Regent of the University of Virginia. He was much honored when he visited Charlottesville. On what is called "Monroe Hill" had stood his house when he was Jefferson's near neighbor. But the time had now come when these three friends must part. Jefferson died on July 4, 1826 — about an hour after John Adams. As for Madison, he and Monroe were to come together before the public on one more great occasion.

In the fall of 1828 the voters of Virginia decided, 21,896 to 16,646, that a Constitutional Convention should be held. Monroe was among the many notables chosen as delegates. They assembled at Richmond, October 5, 1829. Madison named Monroe for the chair; no one else was suggested; and Marshall[2] led him to the seat of honor. Madison, in a faded brown surtout, sat on the left of the Speaker. "Mr. Monroe," says Campbell,[3] "was very wrinkled and weather-beaten, ungraceful in attitude and gesture, and his speeches only commonplace. Mr. Giles, who

---

[1] Memorials of Old Virginia Clerks, by Frederick Johnson of Roanoke, p. 280.

[2] Chester Harding, the artist, who "found great pleasure in painting the whole of such a man" as Chief Justice Marshall, was invited by the latter to the Quoit Club, a mile from Richmond. He reached the grounds ahead of his host. He says: "I watched for the coming of the old chief. He soon approached with his coat on his arm and his hat in his hand, which he was using as a fan. He walked directly up to a large bowl of mint-julep, which had been prepared, and drank off a tumbler full of the liquid, smacked his lips, and then turned to the company with a cheerful 'How are you, gentlemen?' He was the best quoit-pitcher there, and could throw heavier quoits."— A Sketch of Chester Harding, Artist; edited by his daughter, Margaret E. White, 1890.

[3] Charles Campbell, the Virginian historian, "Notes by an Itinerant," in Southern Literary Messenger, Vol. III, 1837.

wore a crutch, was then Governor of the State." Of
the ninety-six members, besides the two ex-Presidents
and the Chief Justice, there were such able men as
Upshur, Barbour, Doddridge, Benjamin Watkins,
Leigh, Chapman, Johnson, Drumgoole, Tyler, Powell,
Summers, Tazewell, Gordon and Alexander Campbell.[1]
As Ambler[2] analyzes it, "there were three clearly
defined classes of political thinkers in the convention,
viz.: the reformers and the old and new school of
conservatives." The men of the western section
favored the new nationalizing tendencies of the time;
the men of the old Tidewater counties opposed them.
The question was, should representation be upon the
"mixed basis," favored by the Tidewater people, or
upon the "white basis" favored in the western part of
the State. Monroe said: "I am satisfied, if no such
thing as slavery existed, that the people of the Atlantic
border would meet their brethren of the west upon
the basis of a majority of the free white population."
"James Madison's last political battle," says Ford,[3]
"was fought over this issue [freehold suffrage] when in
1830, with the aid of James Monroe and others of the
elder statesmen, he succeeded in retaining the freehold
qualifications in the Virginia Constitution, thus exclud-
ing from the franchise about 80,000 white male citizens
of his State." "As for throwing off the incubus of
slavery, which the philanthropist had prayed for,"
says Schouler, "Virginia was unequal to the sacrifice.[4]
La Fayette, who loved the Old Dominion for her
traditions, appreciated the influences which dragged
the State downward. 'Oh! how proud and elated I
should feel,' he wrote to Monroe,[5] 'if something could
be contrived in your Convention whereby Virginia,
who was the first to petition against the slave trade

---

[1] Life of Henry A. Wise, by his grandson, Barton H. Wise, who refers frequently
to Monroe.
[2] Sectionalism in Virginia, 1776-1801, by C. H. Ambler, 1910.
[3] Life of Hamilton, p. 362.
[4] Schouler, Hist., Vol. III, p. 470.
[5] La Fayette to Monroe, June 17, 1829, Monroe Mss., Niles's *Register*, Vol.
XXVIII.

and afterwards forbid it, who has published the first declaration of rights, would take an exalted station among the promoters of measures tending first to meliorate, then gradually to abolish the slave mode of labor."[1] But even Jefferson in his day seemed powerless to initiate any practical Virginia measure in this regard; and Madison and Monroe, after the Missouri Compromise, found the question altogether beyond them. Jefferson and La Fayette, anti-slavery enthusiasts, were of a different type from the less assertive statesmen who, in their old age, were called upon to attend the Convention of 1830. Their presence was largely honorary; their influence limited. "Madison and Monroe," says Ambler, "were strict constructionists, admirers of the works of the fathers and intensely fearful of the increasing power and prominence of the West." The smaller class of conservatives, opposed to nationalism, were "the political forerunners of such men as R. M. T. Hunter, H. A. Wise, James A. Seddon, John Y. Mason and Roger A. Pryor." Only a compromise could be obtained by those who tried to put Virginia upon a new and nationalistic plane. The vote at the Constitutional election in April was: For 26,055; against 15,556.[2]

Monroe had neglected private for public affairs. His claims before Congress largely related to his losses while in the diplomatic service under Washington and Jefferson. He had put in a statement of expenses while associated with Pinkney in England; for some reason Madison had suspended payment on it; and, then, when Monroe himself entered the State Department, his delicacy prevented him from referring to it. Now that he was about to leave the public service, he felt himself entitled to the money. This was but

---

[1] In the story of the Life of William Lloyd Garrison, told by his children, 4 vols. Vol. I, p. 154, Monroe's action in the Convention is classed as "pro slavery." S. L. Gouverneur is condemned for refusing, while Postmaster of New York, to forward papers of the American Anti-Slavery Society, p. 493.

[2] See Debates, Virginia Constitutional Convention, 1829-30. Monroe's Slavery reference is on p. 149.

one instance. How the entanglement of private with public affairs worked to his detriment was shown in the case of his nine hundred and fifty acre tract of land above Charlottesville. This tract was sold in his absence for neighborhood debts; had he been allowed an outfit on his mission to France, this would not have happened.[1] As to the charges made in Congress against Monroe with respect to the sale of lots in Washington city, Monroe wrote to Madison (December 13, 1824) of the malignity with which his enemies acted. There was no ground whatever for the charges. As James Buchanan said (in the House, May 18, 1824) Monroe "was the very last person against whom the charge of an avaricious love of money, and base collusion with a subordinate officer would ever be brought, or could ever be substantiated."[2] In fact, Monroe now paid the penalty for extreme attention to the public business and lax methods in handling his own. We read: "Mr. Monroe was so devoted to the public, and his own affairs were so neglected that two munificent grants, one at the last session of Congress of $30,000, will scarcely pay his debts."

Madison found it necessary to sell some of his land and part with some of his shares of stock. On his farms he was raising tobacco, horses and mules, but was by no means unembarrassed for funds. Hunt says that he "was repeating in a less degree the experience of Jefferson, who, if he lived much longer, would have been obliged to abandon Monticello, and of Monroe, who was finally obliged to give up Oak Hill."

In a letter congratulating Monroe upon his "honorable retirement," John Jacob Astor reminded him of a loan and says: "I would be glad if you would put it in a train of 'Sittlement.'" (Sic.) [3]Mrs. Marian Gouver-

---

[1] For Monroe's private losses while in the public service, see Writings of Monroe, Vol. VII, pp. 53, 54.

[2] Works of James Buchanan, edited by John Bassett Moore; 12 vols., Vol. I, p. 117.

[3] Wife of Samuel L. Gouverneur, Jr., Monroe's grandson. In 1911 she published "As I Remember, Recollections of American Society during the 19th Century."

neur, who owned the letter, assures us in her book that Astor was duly paid.

Quite a contrast with the letter from the business-like fur-trader was one from a certain unbusiness-like Frenchman. La Fayette, having heard of Monroe's money troubles, wrote to him in 1828, expressing the hope that Congress would come to his rescue. He added:

"In the meanwhile, my dear Monroe, permit your earliest, your best, and your most obliged friend to be plain with you. It is probable that, to give you time and facilities for your arrangements, a mortgage might be of some use. The sale of one-half of my Florida property is full enough to meet my family settlement and the wishes of my neighbors. . . . You remember that in similar embarrassment I have formerly accepted your intervention. It gives me right to reciprocity. Our friend Mr. Graham has my full powers (of attorney). Be pleased to peruse the enclosed letter, seal it and put it in the post office. I durst not send it before I have obtained your approbation."

Generous indeed was the old General, thus offering Monroe a portion of the land given him by Congress. But Monroe could not see his way to profit by the large-heartedness of one so like himself in sacrifices made to their mutual goddess, Liberty. He declined La Fayette's offer.

In his Diary, May, 1827, John Quincy Adams says that Monroe refers to his pecuniary embarrassments "and acknowledges himself to have been under some obligations to Ingersoll in reference to them."[1] According to Ambler, Monroe had to sell Oak Hill and become "dependent upon his friends and relatives in New York." He struggled hard against it. While at Oak Hill, despite the discouragement of Judge George Hay,

---

[1] Memoirs, Vol. VII, p. 267. Allowances to Monroe and J. Q. Adams, p. 471. In the Life of Charles Francis Adams, first, by Charles Francis Adams, Second, the author says with reference to his grandfather: "The fact was by reason of incorrigible carelessness in private monetary matters he escaped ruin and want — the fate of his predecessor, Monroe — only through the prudent management on the part of his son, who, in 1835-36, practically, though without that gentleman's consent, put the ex-President under financial guardianship." John Quincy Adams rarely lived within his income. His pay as a member of Congress, $1500 or $2000 a year, was a material part of this.

he composed a treatise on free government, possibly
with the hope that the sale of the book might help him
out of his difficulties. The work was entitled: "A Comparison of the American Republics with the Republics
of Greece and Rome." Judge Hay said to him: "A
history of your Life and Times written by yourself
would really be interesting and valuable." He was
right, of course. Judge E. R. Watson of Charlottesville,
whom Gilman[1] quotes, added: "The idea seemed
quite new to Mr. Monroe; such was his modesty and
self-depreciation that he had never thought of it before."
Judge Watson says:

"In person Mr. Monroe was about six feet high, perhaps rather
more; broad and square-shouldered and raw-boned. When I
knew him he was an old man (more than seventy years of age)
and he looked perhaps even older than he was, his face being
strongly marked with the lines of anxiety and care. His mouth
was rather large, his nose of medium size and well shaped, his
forehead broad, and his eyes blue, approaching gray. . . . In his
intercourse with his family he was not only unvaryingly kind
and affectionate, but as gentle as a woman or a child. He was
wholly unselfish. The wishes, the feelings, the interests, the
happiness of others were always consulted in preference to his
own. . . . He always used the plainest, simplest language, but
was not fluent. . . . He lacked the versatility, and I should say also
the general culture requisite for shining in the social circle, but
was always interesting and instructive; when with good listeners
he led in conversation, and talked of the scenes and events
through which he had passed, *et quorum magna pars fuit*. . . .
Love of country and devotion to duty appeared to me to be the
explanation of his success in life and the honors bestowed upon
him. . . .

"My impression is that during his whole presidential term he
appointed no relative or near connection to office. His two sons-
in-law were George Hay of Virginia and Samuel L. Gouverneur
of New York. The former was a lawyer of eminent ability and a
man of the very highest character, and was promptly appointed to a
Federal Judgeship . . . by John Quincy Adams but he received
nothing at the hands of Mr. Monroe. And so with Mr. Gouverneur;
he was a talented and popular young man, of one of the best
families of New York, but he received no Federal appointment
till Mr. Adams had succeeded Mr. Monroe. Then Adams made

---

[1] Gilman's Monroe, pp. 186-195. Monroe gave an outline of the work in a letter
to S. L. Gouverneur; Gouverneur Mss.

him Postmaster of New York. Judge Hay had a son (by his first marriage), Charles Hay, who was made chief clerk of the Navy Department under Mr. Adams, but held no office under Mr. Monroe. The latter, as I heard from his own lips, was not willing, in making appointments, to lay himself liable even to the suspicion of being influenced by any other consideration than the public good. . . . He wrote with no great facility, but with pains. His handwriting was very bad. Some time in 1829, possibly in 1830, by his horse falling with him, he sprained his right wrist very badly, and for some time could not write at all. I often acted as his amanuensis. His correspondence was immense and with the best and wisest men of his day. . . .

"Mrs. Monroe was Eliza Kortright of New York, the niece, I think, of General Knox of Revolutionary fame. Even in old age and feeble health she bore traces of having been very beautiful in early life. She survived Judge Hay but a short time. I was at Oak Hill, on a visit, when she died. She was not buried for several days, the delay being occasioned by the construction of a vault, designed not only for her remains but for those also of Mr. Monroe, as he himself told me. I shall never forget the touching grief manifested by the old man on the morning after Mrs. Monroe's death, when he sent for me to go to his room and with trembling frame and streaming eyes spoke of the long years they had spent happily together, and expressed in strong terms his conviction that he would soon follow her."

Prior to 1903, Mrs. Monroe's grave, in the garden at Oak Hill, was shaded by a towering pine. Her daughter Maria was buried beside her in 1850.

Of Mrs. Monroe, John Quincy Adams said: "This lady, of whose personal attractions and accomplishments it were impossible to speak in terms of exaggeration, was for a period little short of a half a century, the cherished and affectionate partner of his life and fortunes. She accompanied him in all of his journeyings through this world of care."

After the death of his wife, Monroe moved to New York that he might live with his daughter and her husband. Their house was a Dutch-roofed dwelling at Prince and Marion Streets, near the Bowery. New York at that time had a particular charm, found perhaps not so much in its beautiful old buildings, its packet ships, white-winged like sea birds, its steamboat life, its early touch of cosmopolitanism — not so much in these things, as in the spirit of its people, given fresh access by the opening of the Erie Canal.

John Watts De Peyster, in his reminiscences of 3 Broadway, where dwelt his grandfather, Hon. John Watts, then seventy-three, "straight as an arrow, the handsomest old gentleman I ever saw . . . with bright, dark blue eyes like sapphires — and the most exquisite, silky, silvery, curly or wavy hair"— paints a boyhood picture of Monroe also as he appeared in New York. De Peyster says: "Uncle Bob (Watts) was bosom friend of Sam Gouverneur, who married a daughter of President Monroe. The latter lived with Sam . . . and there La Fayette was a constant guest. I perfectly remember the aged President, in his satin knee-breeches, hovering over a grate in the dingy parlor — for dingy it was to me, accustomed to grand bright rooms[1] . . . . When I was about nine, he (Monroe) came to live permanently with his son-in-law, Sam Gouverneur. Sam was a real genial man — no saint. He resided in Prince Street, just east of Broadway. Mr. Monroe looked just like the usual pictures of him. He was very kind to me; I recall him in his black velvet or satin knee-breeches sitting close in by the side of the front parlor fireplace. He did not strike me as a man who should be or had been, President of these United States. My uncle, Robert Gilbert Livingston de Peyster, who helped Jacob Barker to save the picture of Washington when the English burnt the National Capital, twenty-fourth of August, 1814, knew him well. . . . He (Monroe) was exactly like all his likenesses, painted or engraved — a venerable gentleman of the old school. . . . Jackson looked like a man, but was a decidedly rough specimen. Van Buren, polished, but foxy, he looked his character. Harrison an invalid. Tyler, a sharp Virginian — that is, keener than the Yankee, with better manners. Taylor, another rough specimen with a benevolent hearty

[1] John Watts De Peyster, by Frank Allaben, 2 vols., Vol. I, p. 95.

expression, which Jackson lacked. . . . Of all the Presidents I have ever seen — Jackson, Van Buren, Harrison, Tyler, Taylor, Millard Fillmore, Franklin Pierce, Buchanan, Lincoln, Johnson, Grant — the noblest figure was Fillmore. He was a perfect type of what an American President should be, affable, yet dignified, with a very fine presence. . . . Fillmore belonged to the Washington type."

Monroe made himself useful in New York whenever an occasion arose requiring his services. There was a great meeting at Tammany Hall, November 26, 1830, to organize a celebration of the dethronement of Charles X of France. Monroe presided. November 25, Evacuation Day, was set for the affair. Samuel Swartwout was made grand marshal and Samuel L. Gouverneur orator. As it happened, the day was stormy; and the actual celebration was postponed until the twenty-sixth. Then New York outdid itself. The heroes of the occasion were such liberty men as Monroe himself: David Williams, who helped to capture Andre; Enoch Crosby, the original of "Harvey Birch" in Cooper's "Spy," and Alexander Whaley, who had taken part in the Boston Tea Party.[1] Anthony Glenn, who had raised the flag when the British had evacuated the city, and John Von Arsdale, the sailor who mounted the staff, rode with the other heroes in a barouche. Monroe in his carriage with Gallatin, Gouverneur and Duer had the post of honor. The route from Canal Street to Washington parade ground (Washington Square), two and a half miles, was lined with applauding thousands: Firemen; printers, printing an original ode on sheets which they showered upon the populace; butchers, with leg-o'-mutton sleeves; mounted cartmen, in white frocks; the Whitehall boat carried by watermen; French citizens and thousands of others constituted this memorable procession. A *feu de joie* closed the day. We enumerate

---

[1] Reminiscences of an Octogenarian of the City of New York (1816-1860), by Charles H. Haswell, 1896, p. 249.

these matters local to New York to indicate Monroe's standing in the city where he was to spend his few remaining months. Lombardy Street was renamed Monroe Street in his honor. In the Diary of Philip Hone,[1] under date of November 28, 1830, we find this reference: "I made a pleasant visit this morning to Colonel Monroe, ex-President of the United States, who is residing with his son-in-law, Mr. S. Gouverneur, in Prince Street, No. 66. Mr. Monroe is very feeble and appears in worse health than usual, the effect of a cold; but his mental faculties are unimpaired, and his manner and conversation are exceedingly interesting."

Monroe was not to die without one more political worry. As he himself in Washington's last illness, had unwittingly troubled the great General, who really loved him, so now the shadow of another fell across his own deathbed. The shadow was Jackson's. The story about it is by no means inconsequential. So significant has it all along appeared — this sequel of the Seminole War of 1817-1818 — that it has been a fascinating topic for historians. James Schouler wrote of it in the brilliant and important third volume of his American history; and, under the title "Monroe and the Rhea Letter,"[2] in the *Magazine of American History*. Edward N. Vallandigham, in magazine and newspaper articles, has made a thorough study of it, and William G. Sumner and John Spencer Bassett are among the biographers of Jackson who have treated it with due consideration.

We have already indicated the effect upon Monroe's Cabinet, the country and the world at large of Jackson's headlong and provocative campaign in Florida. We have also dwelt upon Monroe's disavowal of Jackson's course, and have said that all was well that ended well

---

[1] Edited by Bayard Tuckerman, 1889, 2 vols., Vol. I, pp. 24, 25, 32. Hone at forty had made a fortune. He went abroad in the "James Monroe," and on his return opened a big house at 225 Broadway and lent himself with great spirit to public betterment. Webster and Clay made his house their headquarters. He entertained Fanny Kemble, Captain Marryatt, Charles Dickens, and other celebrities.

[2] Vol. XII, pp. 3-8, *et seq.* Reprinted in Schouler's Historical Briefs, p. 97.

when at last Florida was secured for the sum of $5,000,-
000. Jackson's act had brought him into greater favor
than ever. A while ago it was New Orleans; now it was
a Floridian stroke *a la Jupiter Tonans.* "That's the
fellow for us!" said the men at the plow, in the mill,
on the schooner's deck, in the tavern and on the
Court House green. It is true, Crawford, Clay and
others set afoot a congressional investigation, hoping
thereby to show that Jackson had imperiled the country
as he might do again, being impulsive, precipitate
and unsafe — just the opposite of Monroe, just the
kind of man to use in war, if he could be used in the
right way, but to keep down in peace. Schouler says:
"Jackson was resolute, headstrong, self-reliant, dis-
inclined to obey orders from any one, strongly persistent
in his own views, and by no means considerate toward
those he fought or argued against. Monroe, on the
other hand, was at this epoch, as all accounts agree,
patient, tolerant, slow in reaching conclusions, but
magnanimous and considerate — an Executive who
both sought counsel and encouraged the confidence
of his counsellors; a Chief Magistrate who took just
and comprehensive views of public policy, who was
sensitive (on the point) that all his official acts should
be rightly performed, and as a man the soul of generous
honor."

Now Jackson had a neighbor and friend, Major
William B. Lewis, whom Professor Sumner calls "the
great father of wire-pullers." He it was who saw to it
that Jackson became the popular candidate for the
presidency in succession to Adams. Other men around
Jackson were Eaton, Livingston, Lee and Swartwout.
Jackson was no friend of Clay, nor of Crawford; but
clung to Calhoun. When Jackson was elected President
in 1828, Calhoun, re-elected Vice-President, looked for
Jackson's support for the higher place in 1832. But
there were to be comedies and tragi-comedies in the
Washington theatre of politico-social activity before
the arrival of that year of grace. Jackson had a

"Kitchen Cabinet," as well as official Cabinet. Major Lewis, the Tennessee wire-puller, was at the head of one, and Martin Van Buren, the most finished graduate of the New York school of genteel statecraft, at the head of the other. Associated with Van Buren in the official Cabinet, was Lewis' brother-in-law, John H. Eaton, Secretary of War, who had for wife Mrs. Timberlake, ex-purser's widow, born Peggy O'Neil at her father's tavern in Washington. Over Mrs. Eaton, *persona non grata* to Mrs. Calhoun, as to most of the other high-toned ladies of the Washington official circles, there was as bitter a war as there had been with the Seminoles.

But how did the Seminole cat get out of the old Monroe Cabinet bag? James A. Hamilton, son of Alexander Hamilton, was associated with Major Lewis in furthering Jackson's interests. He decided to sound Crawford in Jackson's behalf, but first saw Governor Forsyth, of Georgia. Forsyth said that it was not Crawford but Calhoun who had spoken against Jackson in Monroe's Cabinet. Forsyth wrote to Hamilton to that effect, and Hamilton showed the letter to Lewis. In November, 1829, President Jackson gave a dinner in honor of Monroe. One of the speakers, Tench Ringgold, said that Monroe had stood by Jackson in 1818; whereupon Lewis and Eaton buzzed each other so knowingly that Jackson's suspicious curiosity was aroused. Lewis and Eaton were plotting to supplant Calhoun with Van Buren, provided Jackson's lack of health should make it imperative upon him to retire from the White House at the end of his first term. They were not a Rozencranz and Guilderstern, these two, nor was Jackson a Hamlet; but they knew all his stops and could play upon him with less likelihood of rebuke than the would-be manipulators of the melancholy Dane.

And now for the crisis: Crawford betrayed Calhoun to Jackson. Cabinet secrets that should have gone to the grave with him were now revealed under Crawford's own

·hand. For the first time Jackson learned that Calhoun had condemned his Seminole proceedings, and had wished him to be court-martialed. The Tennessean was enraged. "Dazed" at first, it was said; but soon enraged. He wrote to Calhoun. Was it true? he asked. Calhoun replied as best he could. He tried to make it clear that what he felt as a man — warm regard — and what he thought as an official were different things. Jackson knew no such refined distinctions. Calhoun was either for him or against him. From that moment, he was Calhoun's enemy. Calhoun's chances for the presidency vanished. He could now devote himself to his southern idea. Nullification? Jackson would stop that business; but Calhoun would never be the same; he had been a good genius, what would he be now? he would live longer than Jackson; he would presently represent the dread idea of disunion and death on many a bloody battlefield. What a tragedy! How much was here involved! Such was the quarrel that arose between Jackson and Calhoun; and that, too, on account of the letter to which we referred in the preceding chapter. This letter, known as the "Rhea letter"[1] or "Jackson's January letter" because written by Jackson to Monroe, January 6, 1818, was received by Monroe when he was in bed too sick to read it. He handed it to Calhoun, who saw at a glance that it was confidential and said so. Crawford declared that it was read at a cabinet meeting when the Seminole matters were discussed; Calhoun said it was not read; Monroe was of the decided impression that it was "not brought into consideration in 1818 at all." But why the pother about it? Because Jackson found warrant and excuse in the letter for doing as he pleased in Florida. Monroe was to connive secretly at a smashingly aggressive campaign and pass his assent along through Jackson's confidential friend, Congressman Rhea, who would see that it traveled by the grapevine

---

[1] See Parton's Life of Jackson, Vol. II, p. 433, for the letter in full; also Schouler's Historical Briefs, p. 100.

route to the right person. "What impression," observes
Schouler, "would such a private letter from a commanding general have been likely to produce upon the mind
of such a President under circumstances like these?
Much the same, we imagine, as McClellan's famous
letter on the slavery question, written as he started
on his peninsular campaign, produced upon President
Lincoln's mind. The General, meantime, had received
his military orders and was bound to pursue them;
consequently personal advice as to delicate questions
of a political character, whose tendency was to compromise the Chief Executive, would be weighed but
not discussed by the latter at this juncture. In truth,
free advice from Jackson was nothing new to Monroe;
he had been receiving it ever since his election to the
Presidency, and, appreciating Jackson's friendship as
well as the originality and force of all he might say,
he had constantly encouraged him to speak his mind
freely, but at the same time pursuing the tenor of his
administration after his own deliberate convictions.
In point of fact, however, Monroe never read nor
reflected upon Jackson's January letter at all until
after Pensacola had fallen." Schouler cites John
Quincy Adams, who, in his scrupulous diary, reveals
the truth concerning the Seminole sensation as affecting
Monroe and his Cabinet. "The capture of Pensacola,"
says Schouler, "was an entire surprise to the Cabinet,
Calhoun included, and to the President, who had
summoned them for counsel. The question for consultation here was not (as Jackson, long years after, chose to
believe) whether to punish the General commanding for
disobedience, but whether to approve or disapprove of
his proceedings. Not only did Monroe state the capture
as a breach of orders; but the news of Pensacola's
surrender came at the very moment when, under favor
of the French Minister at Washington, negotiations
with Spain for the purchase of Florida had been taken
up anew, with fresh hopes of success. Dispatches
relating to the execution of Arbuthnot and Ambrister

had miscarried, and hence the full scope of Jackson's conduct did not yet appear; but, as to the Spanish posts, all the Cabinet finally concurred in the conclusion that their capture must be disavowed as having been made without authority. The President generously admitted that there might be justification for taking Pensacola under some circumstances, but that Jackson had not made out his case. Adams gives further incidental proof of the President's good faith. He says that while candid and good-humored as to all that the Secretary of State had suggested in Jackson's favor, Monroe was firm on the main conclusion."[1]

It stands out in Monroe's letters to Jackson that he sympathized personally with that officer, but realized his breach of official orders. Monroe wrote, December 21, 1818:

"On one circumstance, it seems proper that I should now give you an explanation. Your letter of January 6 was received when I was seriously indisposed. Observing that it was from you, I handed it to Mr. Calhoun to read, after reading one or two lines only myself. The order to you to take command in that quarter had before then been issued. He remarked, after perusing the letter, that it was a confidential one, relating to Florida, which I must answer. I asked him if he had forwarded to you the orders of Gen. Gaines on that subject. He replied that he had. Your letter to me, with many others from friends, was put aside in consequence of my indisposition and the great pressure on me at the time, and never recurred to until after my return from Loudon, on receipt of yours by Mr. Hambly[2] and then on the suggestion of Mr. Calhoun."

To this Jackson did not reply. Nor did he cease to "cultivate Monroe's friendship." But why did Monroe write an explanation? Adams says in his diary, December 17, 1818:

"At the President's I met Secretary Crawford who was reading to him a violent attack upon himself in a letter from Nashville published in the (Philadelphia) *Aurora*, of the day before yesterday.[3] The letter was signed 'B. B.' and charged the Govern-

---

[1] Diary of John Quincy Adams, 1818; Annual Message, November 17, 1818, Madison's Writings, 1819; Monroe Mss.

[2] William Hambly brought the Pensacola dispatches in 1818.

[3] The Aurora of December 15, 1818.

ment knew Jackson's views on the capture of the Spanish forts before he marched his army into Florida."

From this time on there was talk about the matter; and in his letters to Madison and Rush, Monroe was at pains to defend himself.[1] He wrote to Calhoun, January 28, 1827:

"I solemnly declare that I never read that letter until after the affair was concluded; nor did I ever think of it until you recalled it to my recollection by an intimation of its contents and a suggestion that it had also been read by Crawford, who had mentioned it to some person who might be disposed to turn it to some account.[2] . . . I asked Mr. Rhea in a conversation whether he had ever intimated to Gen. Jackson his opinion that the administration had no objection to his making an attack on Pensacola, and he declared that he never had. I did not know if the General had written him to the same effect as he had to me, as I had not read my letter, but that he might have led me innocently into a conversation in which, wishing to obtain Florida, I might have expressed a sentiment from which he might have drawn that inference. But he assured me that no such conversation ever passed between us."

Commenting on the Rhea letter, Professor Bassett[3] says:

"This letter was sound in its military ideas and unsound in its notion of foreign policy. . . . The suggestion that Florida be held as indemnity was impracticable. . . . Later Jackson asserted that while on his way to Fort Scott, in February, 1818, he received from Rhea the expected assurance and that it was in consequence of that information that he carried his army boldly into Florida. He also asserts that he preserved Rhea's letter till the Seminole controversy of the succeeding winter became warm, and that he then, April 12, 1819, burned the letter at Rhea's request, who said that he urged it at Monroe's solicitation. He also said that he wrote a note to this effect on the margin of his letter-book the day the communication from Rhea was destroyed, and that his friend, Judge Overton, saw the letter while it was extant. . . . Monroe's story differs totally from Jackson's. . . . The historian must choose between the statements of the two men. Both are persons of conceded honesty, and we cannot impugn the intentions

---

[1] Madison's Writings, 1819; Monroe Mss.
[2] Monroe Mss.
[3] The Life of Andrew Jackson, by John Spencer Bassett, 1911, 2 vols., Vol. I, p. 246, *et seq.* "It was not candid in Monroe," adds Bassett, "to allow Jackson to believe that Calhoun was his friend in the Seminole matter."

of either. But Monroe, as an educated man and a trained official, probably had a more reliable memory. Jackson's defense, which he prepared at the time but did not publish, shows that he was not judicially minded. There is more probability that his memory was poorer than Monroe's."

Professor Bassett enumerates certain other facts that weaken Jackson's story. The letter-book referred to would furnish corroborating evidence but it cannot be found. What harm would the Rhea letter have done commensurate with the commotion caused by its assumed destruction? The Florida cession treaty was signed seven weeks before the letter was said to have been destroyed. "When Rhea was called on later to corroborate Jackson he was so old that his faculties were weak. He wrote at least three letters to Jackson before he was able to recall all that Jackson desired and he did not succeed till he received some important promptings." Yet Professor Bassett cannot believe in Jackson's obliquity in the matter. He goes back to the time when Jackson protested against Secretary Crawford's direct orders, over his head, to Major Long. When Calhoun succeeded Crawford in the war office he conciliated Jackson. About that time Rhea had a conversation with Monroe "in which the latter said many complimentary things about Jackson." November 27, and again December 24, Rhea wrote to Jackson "expressing the President's high regard for the general." Bassett adds:

"All this shows that Rhea considered himself a mediator between his two friends in this matter. Now the bearing of this situation on the letter of Jan. 6th is this: It is possible that some approving expression of Monroe in a later conversation with Rhea was reported by the latter to Jackson in such a way as to convey a world of meaning to the expectant Jackson. We can hardly doubt that Jackson burned, as he alleged, a letter from Rhea containing some statement, which he took for permission; the statement so interpreted must, therefore, have referred to something else. This explanation seems more probable, since neither Jackson nor Overton gives any definite notion of how the permission in the burned letter was worded."

Here the whole Monroe-Calhoun-Jackson-Rhea affair might well rest; but your historical controversy, like Banquo's ghost, will not down — or, at least, it has a way of reasserting itself and will not stay down long whatever one may wish. So we have the Rhea letter up again, in Monroe's sick room, sixteen days before he died. Monroe's mail that spring was forwarded to 66 Prince Street. Samuel L. Gouverneur was empowered by Monroe to handle it. Among the letters that came was one from John Rhea, who wanted to know whether Monroe had "received a confidential letter from Andrew Jackson dated January 6, 1818." Rhea continued:

"I had many confidential conversations with you respecting General Jackson at that period. You communicated to me that confidential letter, or its substance, approved the opinion of Jackson therein expressed and did authorize me to write to him. I did accordingly write him. He says he received my letter on his way to Fort Scott, and acted accordingly. After that War a question was raised in your Cabinet as to General Jackson's authority, and that question was got over. I know that General Jackson was in Washington in January, 1819, and my confidential letter was probably in his possession. You requested me to request General Jackson to burn that letter, in consequence of which I asked General Jackson, and he promised to do so. He has since informed me that, April 12, 1819, he did burn it."

Compare this with Rhea's letter to Jackson in which he could hardly remember a thing; he had reinforced his memory now, and it is as clear as can be; he remembers everything. He is aggressively definite.

Gouverneur was troubled by this rather brutal letter. It was outrageous that Monroe should be obliged to take up such a matter at such a time. Gouverneur consulted William Wirt, in whom both he and Monroe had the greatest confidence. Wirt advised Gouverneur to take Monroe's statement. So, on June 19, 1831, Monroe made a deposition in the presence of witnesses, "signing his familiar name firmly and legibly at the close." It was "the last of his State papers." Here it is:

THE MONROE PEACE AND FRIENDSHIP MEDAL
(From Loubat's "Medallic History of the United States")

DENUNCIATION OF THE INSINUATIONS
of
JOHN RHEA

"A letter of John Rhea of Tennessee is shown to me this nineteenth day of June, 1831, for the first time, nor have I previously had any intimation of the receipt of such a letter or its contents. It was received by Mr. Gouverneur, as I am told by him, and after having been read, kept from me, for reasons which he will explain, until this time. Had it been communicated to me before, I should have made, as I do now, the following declaration and reply thereto, which I wish to be filed with the said letter as my reply to its contents.

1st. It is utterly unfounded and untrue that I ever authorized John Rhea to write any letter whatever to General Jackson, authorizing or encouraging him to disobey, or deviate from the orders which had been communicated to him from the Department of War.

2d. That it is utterly unfounded and untrue that I ever desired the said John Rhea to request Genl. Jackson to destroy any letter written by him, the said John Rhea, to Genl. Jackson, nor did I at any time wish or desire that any letter, document, or memorandum, in the possession of Genl. Jackson, or any other person, relating to my official conduct, in respect to the Seminole War, or any other public matter should be destroyed.

A note applicable to this subject will be found among my papers at Oak Hill, in Virginia, to which, as well as to my whole correspondence with General Jackson, as well as others, I refer for the truth of this statement.

JAMES MONROE.

This statement was signed by James Monroe and declared to be true in the presence of us on this 19th day of June, 1831.

M. Gelston
Edwd. M. Greenway. } [1]

John Quincy Adams is severe in his censure of Rhea and Jackson. He says:[2]

"There is a depth of depravity in this transaction at which the heart sickens. . . . Jackson's excessive anxiety to rest the justification of his invasion of Florida upon a secret, collusive and unconstitutional correspondence with Mr. Monroe can be explained only by an effort to quiet the stings of his conscience for the baseness of his ingratitude to me. Writhing under the consciousness of the return which he has made to me for saving him from public indignation and defending him triumphantly against the ven-

---

[1] Writings of Monroe, Vol. VII, pp. 234, 236.
[2] In his Diary, Vol. VIII, pp. 404, 405; under date of August 30, 1831.

geance of England and Spain, the impeachment of Congress, the disavowal of Mr. Monroe, and the Court-martial of Calhoun and Crawford, he struggles to bring his cause before the world and before posterity upon another basis. . . . It is that his conquest of Florida was undertaken and accomplished, not, as I had successfully contended for him, upon principles warranted by the law of nations and consistent with the Constitution of the United States, but by a secret fraudulent concert between him and Mr. Monroe. . . . He has been laboring not only to blast the good name of Mr. Monroe, but to cover with infamy his own. His moral conceptions are so confused and discomposed by his convulsive passions, that, in his eagerness to throw off his obligations to me and to ruin the reputation of Mr. Monroe, he blinds himself entirely to the inevitable recoil upon himself. It is fortunate that Mr. Monroe lived and retained his faculties to make a solemn and authentic declaration of the total falsehood of John Rhea's abominable statement."

Adams, being in an indignant and vituperative mood, used a number of abusive phrases better deleted, considering how close to a deathbed we now are.

For Monroe lost strength day by day. He retained his faculties to the last. During his last week on earth his mind went back to old Virginia and to his friends there. Madison learned in a letter from Alexander Hamilton, Jr., that Monroe was dying. On the day of the funeral, Tench Ringgold wrote to Madison that "in his last illness he had often spoken of Madison and "their friendship of forty years," expressing his regret "that he should leave the world without beholding you."[1]

From the contemporary newspaper accounts we glean these facts; "For several days his death had been momentarily expected"; "he expired without a struggle," at half past three o'clock in the afternoon of Monday, July 4. As John Adams and Thomas Jefferson had died on the fourth five years before, Monroe's death added to the wonder; as though a power aloft had taken cognizance of the peculiar patriotism of these mortal men and had translated them. In a more superstitious age, the coincidences might have constituted a marvel.

---

[1] State Department Mss.; Hunt's Madison.

The funeral was the largest that had been held in New York up to that time. It was an event of Thursday, July 7. Niles' *Register*, of July 23, has a three-page account of it, reprinting the official announcements, military and civil, including the tribute of the Society of the Cincinnati. The address of President Duer of Columbia College and the order of the funeral procession as they originally appeared in the New York *American* may be found in the Niles compilation. Here is a condensed contemporary account:

"The body was delivered into the charge of the Committee of the Corporation (of New York City) at three o'clock, who, under an escort of cavalry, removed it to a platform erected for the purpose in front of the City Hall, the muffled bells of the different churches tolling and the batteries firing minute guns. At the commencement of the funeral ceremonials, business throughout the city was generally suspended and shops and offices closed. When the coffin containing the remains reached the Hall, it was placed upon the platform, while W. A. Duer, Esq., President of Columbia College, pronounced, before the thousands assembled in the Park, a short and appropriate address. He spoke of the coincidence of the death of Adams and Jefferson on Independence Day; and now Monroe's. Even then the Monroe Doctrine stood out: 'His administration,' said Duer, 'was signalized by the firm attitude and enlightened principles which it assumed in regard to the South American Republics, and in support of the integrity and inviolability of the Western Continent.'

The military in the meantime had formed in line on the west side of Broadway and the societies and bodies of citizens had moved to the Park from their different places of assembling. When the address was concluded the body was carried through Broadway into St. Paul's Church, the Tompkins Blues acting as a guard of honor, followed by the relations and mourners, the clergy, the corporation, faculty and students of Columbia College and citizens. The funeral service was performed by Bishop Onderdonk and Dr. Wainwright. When it was concluded, the coffin was brought out and placed in the hearse, which waited at the north door of the front entrance of the church; and after a brief interval the procession commenced in the designated manner at about half past five o'clock. It was computed to extend two miles. The body was carried in a hearse covered with black cloth, fringed with gold. From the centre panels the national flag hung reversed and eight black feathers waved above the whole; the hearse was drawn by four black horses. On either side of the hearse, in open barouches, rode the pall-bearers, viz.: the Hon. Samuel L. Southard of New Jersey, the Hon. David Brooks, Colonel Richard Varick, Col. John Trumbull, John Watts, Esq., Gov. Aaron Ogden of New Jersey, John Ferguson, Esq., naval officer, Thomas Morris, Esq., U. S. Marshal."

S. L. Gouverneur owned a lot in New York City Marble Cemetery,[1] and Mrs. Gouverneur wished her father to be buried in the vault lately constructed there. Accordingly the procession moved to this point on Second Street, East Side, then well in the suburbs.[2]

Arrived there, the military took open order, and the body was deposited in the vault. Three volleys were fired over the grave.[3] The crowd was immense.

Due honors were paid to Monroe throughout the country. Flags on land and water went to half-mast; there was crepe on the colors and on the left sleeves of officers and officials; twenty-one minute guns were fired at the navy yards; and, on July 10, at the army posts thirteen guns at dawn and twenty-four at sunset.

News of Monroe's death reached Richmond on July 8. The General Court went into mourning. Bells were tolled from three o'clock in the afternoon till sunset. For an hour before sunset minute guns were fired. The Richmond *Enquirer* said: "No one has departed this life in the United States since Adams and Jefferson, who was more beloved by the people than James Monroe." One who examines the old newspaper files is rather stirred with the spontaneity of the tribute to a leader whose services in the field and in the cabinet had caused him to be loved by those who acclaimed him.

After twenty-seven years, Monroe's body was removed from New York to Richmond, Virginia. In "Olde New York," Charles Burr Todd says:

[1] There was a New York Marble Cemetery on Second Avenue, between Second and Third Streets. The New York City Marble Cemetery was on Second Street between Second and First Avenues. This latter was incorporated in 1832. One of the first vaults received the remains of President Monroe. The Kipps brought over from Kipps Bay were buried here.

[2] Life of John Ericsson, by William Conant Church; 2 vols. Vol. II, p. 324.

[3] "In Olde New York" by Charles Burr Todd, 1907, p. 32. There is a view, p. 34, of the spot where Monroe was first interred.

"A simple incident led Virginia to take this action. Early in 1857, a number of gentlemen, natives of that State, but resident in New York, conceived the plan of raising a monument over the unrecognized vault that held the dust. The project was hinted abroad and in course of time reached Virginia, where it seems to have touched State pride and jealousy to the quick. That it should be left to New York to commemorate a son of Virginia who had filled the chair of the Chief Magistrate was deemed a reflection on the Commonwealth and steps were at once taken to have the remains removed to the State Capital. To create public sentiment in favor of this, exaggerated reports as to the condition of the President's grave were spread broadcast through the State. He was reported as lying in an old unused burying-ground overgrown with weeds. Cattle roamed over the unmarked grave, said rumor."

While this story was altogether untrue, it had its effect; the result was a determination on the part of Virginia to reclaim the dust of her illustrious dead. It was in April, 1858, the centenary of Monroe's birth, that the Legislature voted the honor. As a first step, the surviving descendants of Monroe were consulted. These were the three children of Mrs. Gouverneur. In "The End of an Era," John S. Wise, son of Henry A. Wise, who, as Governor of Virginia, had much to do with the affair, says of the three descendants: "The eldest, bearing his name, deeply afflicted by Providence, and the second a daughter, spoke through their father, Samuel L. Gouverneur of Frederick County, Maryland; the third, Samuel L. Gouverneur, Jr., spoke for himself." They consented to the transfer, whereupon, in New York and Richmond, provision was made for the disinterment, carriage and reburial of the venerated bones.

A Virginia committee of two attended the New York ceremony. "At the yard," says Todd, "the exhumation was conducted with secrecy, the family being desirous of avoiding a crowd. At 4.30 o'clock on the second of July, 1858, a carriage drove up to the cemetery gate. It contained Alderman Adams, representing the Common Council, and was soon joined by carriages containing the Virginia delegates, Messrs. Mumford and O. Jennings Wise, Col. James Monroe and S. L. Gouverneur, representing the family, a delegation of resident Virginians, and the undertaker. At five o'clock the coffin of the Ex-President was placed in the hearse and amid the tolling of bells, with the flags of the shipping in the harbor at half-mast, was conveyed to the church of the Annunciation in Fourteenth Street. Here, and at the City Hall, it lay in state for several days, and was then conveyed to Richmond by the steamer Jamestown, its escort, the famous Seventh Regiment, proceeding by the "Ericsson." As a ceremonial, intra-State affair, with a patriotic appeal, the removal excited warm interest throughout the country. The great sectional quarrel then in progress was interrupted; and, for a while, Monroe dead, as well as Monroe when alive, helped to quiet the storms of menacing partisanship. Another event of 1858 had a similar effect. On the bleak twenty-second of February, Crawford's noble equestrian statue of General Washington was unveiled in the Capitol grounds at Richmond. Young John Wise, who saw the people assemble on that occasion, noted the passing of the old and the incoming of the new.[1] Few were the queues he saw — few survivors of the olden time of flint-locks and powderhorns. What impressed him was not so much the elders in stocks and shadbellied coats, not so much General Winfield Scott and the survivors of the War of 1812, but the presence of men like Col. Robert E. Lee and Major Jackson, with his cadets from the Virginia Military Institute. A new time had come — a new type.

As at the unveiling of the Washington statue, the military and civic organizations of Virginia assembled at Richmond on Monday, July 5, to do honor to Monroe. It was deemed less a mortuary event than a belated centennial celebration of his birth. The sky was clear and a good southerly breeze relieved the heat. All Richmond was at the Rocketts — the military commands drawn up at the landing-place, and the populace on the hillsides overlooking the river, up which now

[1] The End of an Era, by John S. Wise, 1899, pp. 104-112.

steamed the "Jamestown," the "Ericsson" and other craft. The body was under escort of the Seventh New York, Colonel Duryee's famous regiment. This officer it was who afterwards organized Duryee's Zouaves and led them against the very soldiers who now saluted him fraternally. Here is a contemporary account, giving in detail the story of the day:

"The Jamestown came in sight at ten minutes past eight o'clock, and slowly approached the wharf, with flags and signals at half halliards. As the ship came alongside her wharf the committee and guests from New York stood on the upper deck, and regarded with much interest the exciting scene on shore. The remains of President Monroe having been removed from the forward saloon to the upper deck and placed under an awning, the Governor and Mayor proceeded on board the Jamestown and received the guests, and an interchange of friendly greetings took place." A platoon of Richmond Grays relieved the New York guard. The steamer with the Seventh Regiment tied up at the Rocketts at 10.10. The Virginia troops presented arms as those from New York disembarked and passed on to the right of the line. "The hearse, drawn by six white horses, attended by six negro grooms dressed in white, now proceeded to the steamer, and, under direction of the pall-bearers, received the remains. The troops presented arms, flags were lowered, drums rolled, and trumpets sounded, after which the Armory Band played a dirge while the hearse proceeded to its place in the line. Minute guns were fired and bells tolled, continuing during the progress of the procession to the cemetery. The procession moved at half past eleven o'clock. The route lay directly up Main Street to Second, down Second to Cary, and thence out to Hollywood.

"All along the route of the procession. a distance of more than two miles, the sidewalks were lined with spectators; every balcony, porch, and window overlooking the street, every available spot on the line was crowded with ladies, children and men. The minute-guns continued firing. . . . The troops marched with reversed arms. . . . When the remains were lowered into the grave, the troops presented arms, the Seventh Regiment rested on arms and the band played a dirge." Then Governor Wise, with eloquence, spoke of the career of the son come home to his Mother State. As he ended, the artillery without fired three salvos.[1]

---

[1] Mrs. Marian Gouverneur notes in "As I Remember," p. 109, that John Cochrane of the New York bar, was the orator of the occasion at the time of the transfer of Monroe's body. Mrs. Gouverneur says: "Tragedy seemed to pursue the Hamilton family with unrelenting perseverance until the third generation. . . . After the ceremonies in Richmond were completed, but before the Seventh Regiment

Monroe's grave is on a rise of ground in the southwest corner of Hollywood, where also rest multitudes of the victims of the great war he would have given his all to prevent.

In 1903 it was decided by the Virginia Legislature that the wife should be at the husband's side. Accordingly, the body of Mrs. James Monroe and that of Mrs. Maria Hester Gouverneur were removed from under the pine in Oak Hill garden to the Monroe plot in Hollywood. They were reinterred, in the presence of the family, on opposite sides of James Monroe's grave.

---

had embarked upon its homeward voyage, one of its members, Laurens Hamilton, a grandson of Alexander Hamilton, and a son of John C. Hamilton, was drowned near Richmond. All the proceedings connected with the removal of Mr. Monroe's remains, both in New York and in Richmond, were published some years later by Udolpho Wolfe (son of Major Benjamin Wolfe who had first nominated Monroe for Governor of Virginia), a neighbor and admirer of the late President. I recall an amusing anecdote which Mr. Gouverneur told me upon his return from this visit to Richmond. While the great concourse of people was still assembled at Monroe's grave in Hollywood Cemetery, Governor Henry A. Wise, always proud of his State, remarked: 'Now we must have all the native Presidents of Virginia buried in this inclosure.' Immediately, a vigorous hand was placed on his shoulder by a New York Alderman, who had accompanied the funeral cortege, who exclaimed in characteristic Bowery vernacular: 'Go ahead, Governor, you'll fotch 'em.' "

INDEX

"A B Plot," the, 421.
Accolade fraternelle, to James Monroe, 182–185; to Joshua Barney, 191.
Accomac County, Va., 1.
Accounts of Monroe, as student, 26; as official, 426.
Acts of Congress, concerning Monroe papers vii; secret, 378.
Adair, John, Senator from Ky., 362n.
Adams, Abigail, Mrs., 214, 367.
Adams, Charles Francis, Sr., 310, 437n.
Adams, Charles Francis, Jr., 437n.
Adams, Henry, historian, 210, 219, 229n, 230, 231, 235, 237, 238, 242, 243, 244, 247, 248; on Jefferson's "Canons of Etiquette," 263; 267, 272n, 277n, 280, 282, 283, 284; criticizes Monroe, 285; criticizes Jefferson, 290; on Smith's non-importation resolutions, 294; on Randolph's assault upon Madison, 295; on Monroe as a centre of intrigue, 296; on diplomatic insults to Monroe, 297; his "Insults and Popularity" chapter, 298; 304n, 306, 308, 310, 311, 324, 331, 333, 335, 336, 340.
Adams, Herbert B, 73n.
Adams, John, President, 25, 86, 105, 136, 150, 153, 192, 203, 210, 211, 213, 214, 219, 222, 223, 224, 292n, 310, 367, 368, 374n; death of, 433; 452, 453, 454.
Adams, John, son of J. Q. A., 430.
Adams, John Quincy, President, 95, 103, 121, 122, 136, 156, 170, 184, 185, 198, 202n, 206, 294n, 295, 297, 308, 309, 310, 311, 330; at Ghent, 345, 346, 354n, 355, 356, 357, 358, 360, 371, 373, 377, 379n; treaty with Spain, 383; electoral vote cast for, in 1820, 383; 384, 385, 387n, 389, 390, 391; and Monroe Doctrine, 394, 397; and Russia in the North Pacific, 401, 402, 409; and White House Etiquette, 412, 413, 414, 415, 419, 420, 423, 424, 426, 427, 428; as President, 429, 430; visits Monroe at Oak Hill, 431, 432; and private money management, 427; and Monroe's friends, 428; 429, 437; on character of Mrs. Monroe, 439; and Monroe's good faith in the Florida entanglement, 447; his censure of Rhea and Jackson, 451, 452.
Adams, Mrs. John Quincy, 419, 420.

Adams, Hon. Thomas (married Betsy Fauntleroy), 7.
Adams, William, 345.
Adamses, the, books about, vii, 210.
Addington, Henry (Lord Sidmouth), 263.
Addington, British *chargé d'affaires* at Washington, 420.
Addison, William Dulaney, 303.
Adet, P. A. 167, 199, 202, 205.
Admiralty Courts, British, 280, 281.
Alabama, admission of, 391.
Albemarle Co., Va., 147, 151, 152, 153, 298, 299.
Alexander I, Czar of Russia, 345; and the Holy Alliance, 394, 401.
Alexander William (see Lord Stirling).
Alexandria, Va., 19, 204, 243.
Alger, J. G., 179, 180, 181, 182.
Alien and Sedition laws, 224.
Allaben, Frank, 440n.
Allertons, the, of Virginia, 13.
Allston, Mrs. (Theodosia Burr), 364.
Almy, Rear-Admiral John J., 417.
Alquier Citizen, 234.
Alsop, George, historian, 11.
Alsop, John, 142.
Ambler, C. H., quoted, 422, 434, 435, 437.
Ambler, Edward, 7n, 91.
Ambler, Jacquelin, 91.
Amblers, the, of Virginia, 8n, 91.
Ambrister, R. C., 380, 381, 446.
Amelia Island, 317.
Amendments to Constitution, first ten, 150; twelfth, 216.
American Anti-Slavery Society, 435n.
American Historical Association, 427n, 434, 435.
Ames, Fisher, 318.
Amphictyonic Council, 135.
Anderson, Capt. R. C., 56.
Anderson, Gen. Robert, 56.
Andrews, E. Benj., quoted, 97.
Annapolis, 22; Congress at, 100, 118; conference of Commissioners from 5 states at, 126, 127, 128; 165.
Anti-Federal party, 363.
Apollo Room, Raleigh Tavern, Williamsburg, Va., 25, 26.
Appalachicola River, 378; massacre on, 379, 380.
Aranjuez, 274, 278.
Arbuthnot, Alexander, 380, 381.

314; and war deputation, 315; and New England opposition, 316, 317; is re-elected President, 318; 323; offers Monroe general command, 324; 326; worried, 330n, and British attack on Washington, 332, 333; appoints Winder, 334; and Armstrong, 335, 342; at Bladensburg, 336, 337; and Mrs. Madison, 338; and Cockburn, 339; retires into Virginia, 340, 341; appoints Monroe Secretary of War, 342; and peace negotiations, 344-347; happiness of, 348; description of, 349; humiliations of, 350; successor of, 351; at Monroe's inauguration, 352; as "James the First," 353; 357, 363; and neutrality on Great Lakes, 373; and the Gordian Knot in West Florida, 376; 378, 379n, and slavery, 388; vetoes Cumberland Road bill, 392; 393; and Canning's eagerness, 399; congratulates Monroe on curbing Russia, 402; 412, 420, 421, 422, 432; as Justice of Peace, 433; in Virginia Constitutional Convention, 433-435; last political battle of, 434; and slavery, 435; decreasing income, 436; 447, 448; at the time of Monroe's death, 452.

Magruder, Allan B., cited, 30n.

Mahan, Capt. A. T., on Monroe, 319; 345, 346.

Maine, admission of, 391.

Malmesbury, Earl of, quoted, 407.

Marat, Jean Paul, 175, 176.

Marblehead regiment at Trenton, 51.

Marbury, William, 225.

Marbois, M. de (see Barbé-Marbois).

Marcy, William L., 417, 418.

Maret, H. B. (Duc de Bassano), 307.

Marion, Gen. Francis, 82.

Marie Antoinette, 176, 256.

Marieul, Baron de, 420.

Marryat, Capt., 442n.

Marshall, Mrs. John (Mary Willis Ambler), 91, 92.

Marshall, John (Chief Justice), 20, 21, 22, 23, 29, 30, 64, 65, 69, 70, 72, 77, 79; as friend of Monroe, 91; comments of, 89-94; courtship of, 92; letters of, and Jefferson's, 93; 101, 112, 116, 131, 133; in Virginia Convention, 134; 151; envoy to France, 203; made Chief Justice, 222; and Federalist principles of, 223; imposes his will, 224; case of Marbury vs. Madison, 224; Monroe's suggested impeachment of, 225; important constitutional rulings of, 225; and Monroe's friendship, 226;

227, 349, 351n; Monroe sworn in by, first inauguration, 353, 362; Monroe sworn in by, second inauguration, 386; 428; at Virginia Constitutional Convention, 433, 434.

Marshall, Col. Thomas, 20, 21, 30, 62, 92; moves to Kentucky, 93.

Martin Luther, 227.

Martineau, Harriet, visits Madison, 388.

Maryland, wild lands of, 105; 110; and Paine, 176, 177; and choice of Presidential electors, 217, 218; vote of, in Jefferson-Burr Contest, 221; Militia of, at Bladensburg and Baltimore, 334-344.

Mason, George, 100, 126, 129, 130, 131, 132, 133, 134, 137, 212.

Mason, Thomson, 100n.

Masons, the Va. family of, 4.

Mason, John Y., 435.

Massachusetts (New York) boundary, 121, 122, 124; Monroe's visit to, 366-368.

Masseys, the Va. family of, 5.

Massanutton mountain, Washington's proposed retreat to, 39.

Maurys, the Va. family of, 5.

Maxwell, James H., 145.

Mazzei, Philip, 120n.

Meade, Bishop, 16, 17, 18, 20n.

Melbourn, Julius, quoted, 290n.

Meigs, Return J., Postmaster-General, 356.

Meikleham, Mrs. S. R., 417n.

"Melampus," deserter from, 284.

Menara, Mlle. Hervas de, 256n.

Mercer, Gen. Hugh, 31, 32, 42n, 52.

Mercer, Col. Hugh (son of Gen. Hugh), 84n.

Mercer, the Va. family of, 5.

Mercer, Margaret ("Hannah More of America"), 69n.

Mercer, John, of Stafford, 69n.

Mercer, John Francis, Gov., 27, 69, 70, 73, 85, 100, 117.

Merlin, Antoine (de Thionville), 182.

Merlin, Antoine Phillipe (de Douai), 182

Merrick, Samuel, of Bucks Co., Penna., 45.

Merry, Anthony, British Minister, 263-266; 283, 294, 306, 346, 412.

Merry, Mrs. Anthony, 263-266; 412.

Merwin, H. C., quoted, 242, 252.

Messages, Monroe's, 372, 377, 412; on slave trade, 420, 422n; Monroe's 8th annual, 426, asking settlement of accounts, 426.

Mexican War, and Monroe Doctrine, 404.